DATE DUE

MAR 2 4 2000	
F 232 487 C76 1992	218743
Msgr. Wm. Barry Memorial Library	
Barry University	
Miami, FL 33161	
CROFTS	
OLD SOUTHAMPTON	

GAYLORD   PRINTED IN U.S.A.
                                    FG

OLD SOUTHAMPTON

*Politics and Society in a
Virginia County,
1834–1869*

OLD SOUTHAMPTON

Politics and Society in a
Virginia County,
1834–1869

DANIEL W. CROFTS

UNIVERSITY PRESS
OF VIRGINIA

Charlottesville and London

THE UNIVERSITY PRESS OF VIRGINIA
Copyright © 1992 by the Rector and Visitors
of the University of Virginia

First published 1992

Library of Congress Cataloging-in-Publication Data
Crofts, Daniel W.
   Old Southampton : politics and society in a Virginia county,
1834–1869 / Daniel W. Crofts.
      p.   cm.
   Includes bibliographical references (p.   ) and index.
   ISBN 0-8139-1385-3
   1. Southampton County (Va.)—Politics and government.
2. Southampton County (Va.)—Social conditions.   I. Title.
F232.S7C76   1992   92-6778
975.5′552—dc20   CIP

Printed in the United States of America

For Elizabeth Maxfield Crofts

CONTENTS

❧

ILLUSTRATIONS

MAPS

PREFACE

FROM SEVEN MILES IN THE SKY over Petersburg, Virginia, one may look out the window of an airplane on a clear day and see a green expanse stretching between the James River and Albemarle Sound. At the edge of the distant horizon, the Atlantic Ocean glistens in the sun. Southampton County, still a predominantly rural agricultural region in Virginia's tidewater, occupies the center of this panorama.

Aerial vistas, however captivating, minimize the human drama below. Even more obscure are the experiences of those who lived a century and a half ago, now far beyond the direct recollection of any living person. My task during the past few years has been to learn more about mid-nineteenth-century Southampton and the world of which it was a part.

The historian studying Southampton enjoys certain advantages. When asked "Why this county?" I answer, "sources." What originally whetted my interest in Southampton was its poll lists showing how individuals voted. In Virginia before 1867 each voter indicated his preferences orally, and clerks tallied the names of supporters for each candidate. A uniquely extensive run of Southampton poll lists survives.

One may therefore build files of information about persons living in antebellum Southampton, combining evidence from local poll lists and tax records and from federal census manuscripts for population and agriculture. Such data, when subjected to analysis through the marvel of modern computers, yields many insights. Here better than for any other locality in the country, one may trace the evolution of political behavior over time. We may discover who voted, who didn't vote, who voted for which party, who supported secession, and how variables such as residence, slaveholding, and religious affiliation influenced voter behavior.

If Southampton intrigued me for somewhat specialized reasons, I recognized, too, that the county already commanded interest. Anyone curious about the South learned during the late 1960s, if they had not known before, that Southampton had a troubled history. Here in 1831 Nat Turner led the bloodiest slave insurrection in American history. William Styron's 1967 novel, *The Confessions of Nat Turner*, put antebellum South-ampton on the map of popular consciousness. Although acknowledging that he had allowed himself "the utmost freedom of imagination in re-constructing events," Styron considered his portrayal of Turner not merely fiction but rather "a meditation on history."[1] The novel reached a wide audience. Turner remained, however, a controversial enigma. Some readers, including several prominent historians, found Styron's efforts convincing and moving; others, including a group of black writers, con-demned the novel. Plans for a filmed version of *The Confessions* fell through, denying Southampton its opportunity to provide the setting for a major movie.

Perhaps the most productive consequence to grow out of the contro-versy was the search for more authentic information about Nat Turner and the county where he lived. Three contributions were especially no-table. Henry Irving Tragle established that a great deal of historical ma-terial remained untapped. His book, *The Southampton Slave Revolt of 1831*, amassed an impressive variety of sources. Stephen B. Oates, avail-ing himself of Tragle's work and drawing upon his own additional re-search "to bring the historical Turner alive in the context of his time," sketched a believable biography, *The Fires of Jubilee: Nat Turner's Fierce Rebellion*. Thomas C. Parramore's *Southampton County, Virginia*, a fine history of the county, included three riveting chapters on the Turner up-rising.[2] Parramore did much to validate and elucidate the confession nar-rated by Turner shortly before his execution.

Additional unpublished sources about Southampton have become available in recent years. Within the past decade, two extensive South-ampton diaries have been deposited at the Virginia Historical Society. The diarists, Elliott L. Story and Daniel W. Cobb, revealed much about daily life in Southampton between the late 1830s and the 1870s. Because Story and Cobb had quite distinct personalities and political outlooks, the two diaries are marvelously complementary. In certain ways, this book is a biography of these two very different individuals.

Neither the diaries nor the poll lists provide new revelations about the Turner insurrection. It must be emphasized that this is not a book about Nat Turner. Recognizing that historians have carefully combed the rec-ords pertaining to the insurrection and have provided as plausible a life of the famed slave rebel as the evidence will support, I have directed my energies and attention to other matters.[3]

IMPRESSIVE EVIDENCE SUGGESTS THAT a broad consensus united the whites of the Old South. They valued the liberty of free white men, and they believed such liberty antithetical to freedom for blacks. Worried about growing northern power, they tenaciously resisted any erosion of "southern rights." Ultimately, the overwhelming majority of white male citizens in eleven states sided with the Confederacy and fought for the lost cause.

Yet how united really was the Old South? We know that no more than one-quarter of white southern families owned slaves in 1860. We know, too, that class resentments pervaded white society, most acutely during the disastrous failure of the war for southern independence. The dominance of the planter class required unending renegotiation, and it was never assured. The spread of universal white male suffrage gave less privileged white southerners far more leverage than subordinate classes at other times and places ever dreamed of obtaining. Southern elites had to avow an egalitarianism that their counterparts elsewhere would have scorned.

Furthermore, we know that spirited partisan rivalry flourished in the late antebellum South. Even if class resentments and partisanship only infrequently overlapped, one ought not simply wave aside the significance of a competitive two-party system on grounds that both parties supported the broad white southern consensus.[4] Politics, as historian Lacy K. Ford, Jr., has observed, both "engaged and divided whites." Reasoning that "something was clearly at stake in these contests," Ford contends that historians "pass too quickly over the rich public life of the Old South."[5]

My study, although confined to a single county, probes some of these paradoxes about the Old South. Southampton was in many ways planter dominated, and it cast not a single vote against secession six weeks after the war started. Its apparent unity was deceiving, however. The county had a long tradition of disagreement among whites, and it sustained a fiercely competitive two-party system from the mid–1830s until 1861. Two months before the war started, a majority of Southampton voters opposed secession. Embedded in the county's history are many clues about the larger society of which it formed only a small part. Southampton can tell us much about the Old South.

Like my first book, *Reluctant Confederates: Upper South Unionists in the Secession Crisis,*[6] this volume has been written both for the general reader and for the specialist. I hope both to entertain and to instruct. *Old Southampton* recreates the flavor of life in one fascinating microcosm of the Old South. It also provides a vantage point from which to view the traumatic decade of Civil War and Reconstruction. By focusing on a single locality, one meets particular individuals rather than southerners in general. History should, however, offer more than local color and a "good read." The specialist will discern that I have traced the rise of political parties and suggested how partisan allegiances tied Southampton to a wider world, while at the same time institutionalizing the means through which its citizens could disagree and compete for power. The combination of an increasingly democratic polity with an oligarchical social and economic structure created revealing strains in Southampton and across the Old South.

Why the title *Old Southampton?* Because that is what people called it. As early as the 1830s the Richmond *Enquirer* hailed the results from "Old Southampton" in a closely watched special election. The phrase remained in use throughout the Civil War era, so that an 1872 article in a Norfolk newspaper ran under the headline: "Old Southampton Aroused." Moreover, residents of the county themselves embraced the designation. James Maget entitled his account of a neighborhood get-together "The way things work down here in old Southampton." Elliott L. Story likewise had a sentimental fondness for "Old Southampton." Having grown "more and more attached" to friends and neighbors and to the "native hills and fields" of the county where he "first drew breath," he resisted the temptation to migrate elsewhere. During a century when the number of Americans increased exponentially and the West and the cities experienced incessant growth, long-settled parts of the southeastern tidewater, Southampton included, lost population. To outsiders the county appeared bypassed by the modern world, its residents stick-in-the-mud traditionalists, its courthouse village "somewhat antiquated," its significance located at some distant point in a largely forgotten past. An almost defiant sense of local pride attached those who remained behind to "Old Southampton."[7]

THE NARRATIVE EMPLOYS BOTH a topical and a chronological approach. Following the Prologue that briefly surveys the layout of the modern county, the first chapter introduces a number of antebellum

Southamptonites, both white and black. The unhappy tale of John Young Mason and his slaves illustrates the inadequacies of paternalism. Chapter 2 narrows the focus to the diarists Elliott L. Story and Daniel W. Cobb, the two residents of Old Southampton about whom we know the most. The third chapter examines the rhythms of agricultural life, around which everything else was organized in late antebellum Southampton. It also considers the institutions, particularly the churches, that brought people together.

Chapters 4, 5, and 6 examine local politics between the emergence of the second American party system in the 1830s and the outbreak of the Civil War in April 1861. Chapter 4 traces the emergence of political parties in Southampton. The upper part of Southampton, northeast of the Nottoway River, became a region of Whig strength, whereas lower Southampton, southwest of the river, became even more solidly Democratic. The fifth chapter considers the impact of Virginia's reform constitution of 1851, which established universal white male suffrage and provided for popular election of governors, other state officials, and the previously self-selecting county court which was the mainspring of local government. Chapter 6, on the presidential election of 1860 and the secession crisis, details Southampton's response at the Old South's great moment of decision. Polarization between the upper and lower county reached an all-time high in early 1861, as upper-county voters, especially those from nonslaveholding families, opposed secession, whereas lower-county voters monolithically favored separation from the Union. Readers with a specialized interest in political history will find numerous tables in the Appendix that supplement chapters 4–6.

The final chapters of the book depict Southampton during the Civil War and Reconstruction. Chapter 7 shows how wartime hardships fell with particular severity on less privileged whites, fueling resentment against the Confederate cause that most leading Southampton families eagerly supported. During the last year of the war, as fighting raged close to Southampton's borders, the county court bought and distributed food to alleviate starvation, growing numbers of slaves escaped to Union-controlled areas just across the Blackwater River (whereupon many joined the Union army), and Confederate morale withered.

The last two chapters and the Epilogue describe the collision of opposites in Southampton during Reconstruction. Resisting attempts by landowners to maintain a system of coercive labor, former slaves sought to live as free men and women. Chapter 8 examines the formidable advantages that whites enjoyed—and the dangers that they perceived—during the first two years after the end of the war. The startling emergence of blacks as a political force in 1867 provoked a bitter struggle, both in Southampton and across the South. Chapter 9 and the Epilogue focus on the interconnected political and economic aspects of the black awakening. Although the county included a number of whites who had long been out of step with the status quo, local political divisions quickly polarized along racial lines during 1867, as in most other rural parts of eastern Virginia. By fair means and foul, white Southamptonites joined hands to thwart Radical Reconstruction.

The dates 1834–69 reflect the political emphasis of the book. Two-party politics arrived suddenly in Southampton in 1834. The Whig and Democratic parties evolved for more than a generation within the framework that took shape during the 1830s. Partisan allegiances persisted to some extent through the war and the first years of Reconstruction. Between 1867 and 1869, however, Southampton whites joined the Conservative party, to counteract black support for the Republican party. Local politics thereafter differed greatly from earlier patterns.

ONE MATTER SHOULD BE addressed at the outset. I am a Yankee. My own ancestors, among them some with strong antislavery convictions, lived in Maine and Ohio. Although my spouse had a Virginia grandfather on one side, her other side (and it is the dominant side) traces back to Quaker Ridge in inland Maine. Southampton County is closer than Quaker Ridge to our home in Pennsylvania. Culturally, however, I feel rooted in Maine while I must remain an exotic outsider in Virginia. Nevertheless we sometimes choose to study what we know less well and what we wish better to understand.

Entirely by coincidence, I live in Southampton, Pennsylvania, once a country town and more recently a Philadelphia suburb, originally settled even before Southampton County, Virginia. In one matter of nomenclature, when I differentiate between the upper and lower regions of Southampton County, I have imposed terminology used in my home community. Although such usage may be unfamiliar to Virginians, the two contrasting halves of Southampton County, microcosms of the upper and lower South, make my terminology both convenient and appropriate.

SEVERAL INSTITUTIONS AND A larger number of individuals have done much to facilitate my research and writing. The Virginia Historical

Society has supported this undertaking in numerous ways, including several summer research fellowships, funded in part by a grant from the Andrew W. Mellon Foundation. Director Charles F. Bryan, Jr., and his capable staff—notably Nelson D. Lankford, Sara B. Bearss, Frances Pollard, and Janet Schwarz—have made my numerous visits to Richmond both productive and enjoyable. Special thanks to Howson W. Cole, Archivist Emeritus, for locating and acquiring several key collections used in this study.

The Virginia State Library and Archives, which holds Southampton's antebellum records, provided me with a second frequent destination when in Richmond. My particular thanks go to Lyndon H. Hart III, who has an extraordinary command of Southampton family relationships, John T. Kneebone, who alerted me to a trove of previously unused sources, and Brent Tarter, who extended himself above and beyond any reasonable call of duty to make that material available to me.

Members of the Southampton County Historical Society have been unfailingly courteous to this Yankee. I thank especially Lynda T. Updike, Gilbert W. Francis, Daniel T. Balfour, and Katherine K. Futrell.

Historians doing research in the Civil War era at the National Archives have an indispensable friend and adviser in Michael P. Musick. His ability to locate key sources in that labyrinth never ceases to amaze. Ira Berlin and his staff at the Freedmen and Southern Society Project, History Department, University of Maryland, allowed me free access to copies of documents from the National Archives in their collections.

A distinguished research grant and a timely subvention from Trenton State College gave me the time and resources to push ahead with this project. I thank the colleagues who recommended me for that grant and the faculty committee that awarded it. I also owe a particular word of appreciation to each of the following: Harold W. Eickhoff, president of Trenton State, Claire A. Hardgrove, acting academic vice-president, Richard Kamber, dean of the School of Arts and Sciences, John P. Karras, my department chair, Carol Y. Miklovis, who cheerfully located many items on interlibrary loan, and Anthony J. DiGiorgio, formerly academic vice-president at Trenton State, now the president of Winthrop College.

Essential assistance on computer-related aspects of my research was volunteered by John Baldwin and Angela C. Suchanic, both formerly of Trenton State, and Gary Youngberg of the WordPerfect Corporation. My father-in-law, William F. Maxfield, nobly prepared the maps, which were then put into final form through a computer graphics process.

For critical readings of the manuscript, I am indebted to Edward L. Ayers of the University of Virginia, Peter Wallenstein of Virginia Polytechnic Institute and State University, Richard Lowe of the University of North Texas, John McGuigan, formerly of the University Press of Virginia, Thomas C. Parramore of Meredith College, and Andrea J. Bataille and David B. O'Neill, two of my students from Trenton State. As editor and associate editor, Nelson Lankford and Sara Bearss improved my article, "Southampton County Diarists in the Civil War Era: Elliott L. Story and Daniel W. Cobb," *Virginia Magazine of History and Biography* 98 (1990): 537–612, from which, with their permission, I have extracted portions in revised form for chapter 2 and other parts of this book. Shearer Davis Bowman of the University of Texas and David F. Allmendinger, Jr., of the University of Delaware likewise offered useful suggestions for the article. My chapter on the wartime period benefited from Daniel T. Balfour's expert scrutiny. Bruce Eelman, a former student at Trenton State and now in the graduate program at the University of Maryland, commented ably on a draft of chapter 4. Even though I have not fully heeded all the advice offered by various readers, the book is much the stronger for their contributions.

One bright morning in early March 1989, John T. Crofts and I hiked out to a promontory overlooking Lake Superior. Because Pop confidently assumed he would outlive the century, it never crossed my mind that we were saying farewell to each other. That same visit, I happily recall, we also tended rabbits!

As this book has taken shape during the past several years, Anita Verna Crofts and Sarah B. Crofts have outgrown the family nest and ventured away to Haverford, Hidden Valley, Nanjing, and points beyond. Their rising generation of educated young women holds great promise. My dedication honors the lady who brought Anita and Sarah into the world, nurtured them on their upward trajectories, and gave them wings to soar. Betsy's unique mix of the practical and the prophetic is a gift to all who know her. I am the luckiest one.

OLD SOUTHAMPTON

Politics and Society in a
Virginia County,
1834–1869

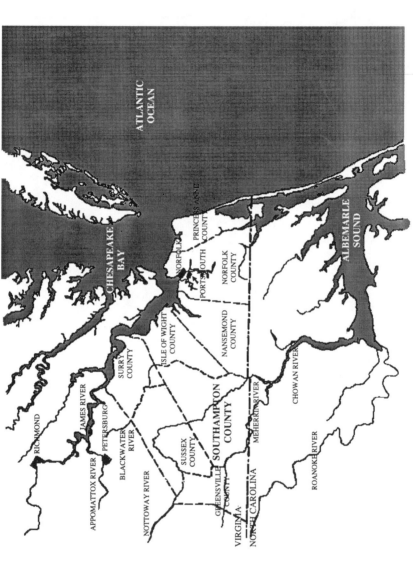

Map 1. Southampton region, 1860. *Map adapted from Stephen B. Oates, The Fires of Jubilee: Nat Turner's Fierce Rebellion (New York: Harper and Row, 1975), 72.*

PROLOGUE

Southampton Today

SOUTHAMPTON COUNTY IS ONLY an hour's drive from Richmond. After leaving Interstate 95 just south of Petersburg, one continues southeast on State Highway 35, the old Jerusalem Plank Road. The site of fighting during the last year of the Civil War, the road proceeds uneventfully past level fields and interspersed woodlands. At many points, the vista must closely resemble that of a century and a half ago. Only a few crossroads settlements vary the otherwise entirely rural appearance of Sussex County. Before long, signs mark the Southampton border, but the terrain remains much the same.

After passing Sebrell, earlier known as Barn Tavern, one skirts the productive bottomlands of the Nottoway River, where diarist Daniel W. Cobb and his father-in-law, Jesse Little, used slave labor to raise cotton. Characteristic cypress trees, with buttressed lower trunks standing in water, adjoin the road as it crosses Assamoosic Swamp. The home where Cobb lived no longer survives, but a nearby secondary road passes Little's early nineteenth-century residence, featuring paired brick chimneys at each end of the building.

The county seat, Courtland, a dozen miles beyond the Sussex line, was known until the late nineteenth century as Jerusalem. Local boosters, tired of gibes about the Arabs from Jerusalem, engineered the change of name. Southampton's courthouse, the most imposing building in Courtland, looms a few blocks beyond the center of town, snugly situated between the right side of the main road and the river. Photographs reveal that the original brick building, completed in 1834, lacked the current pillared portico, which was added early in the twentieth century. The original brick walls were whitened in even more recent times. During the

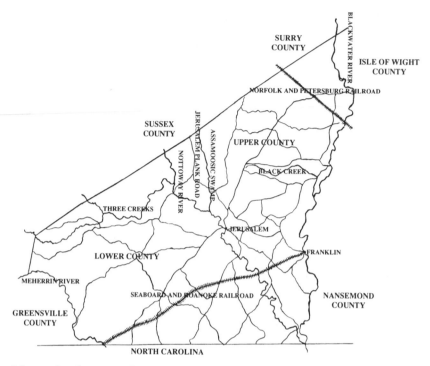

Map 2. Southampton County, 1860

Civil War, Yankee raiders torched many of Virginia's antebellum court-houses, such as the one in adjacent Sussex County. Had Southampton's suffered a similar fate, this book could not have been written; an unusually full array of antebellum records remained undisturbed in the old courthouse.

A Confederate monument, topped by the erect statue of a soldier facing north, sits close to the courthouse. It lists six companies drawn primarily from the county (four infantry, one artillery, and one cavalry). Bold lettering, carved in stone, proclaims:

> With shouts above the cannon's roar
> They joined the legions gone before
> They bravely fought, they bravely fell
> They wore the gray, and wore it well.

Several historic houses, dating from the late eighteenth and early nineteenth centuries, stand across the street from the courthouse. The South-

The Southampton courthouse as it appeared in the nineteenth century. (*Photo, ca. 1906, courtesy of the Walter Cecil Rawls Library and Museum, Courtland, Va., and the Franklin-Southampton Area Chamber of Commerce, Franklin, Va.*)

ampton County Historical Society is restoring the Rochelle-Prince house. A short distance ahead, the Episcopal and Methodist churches share with the courthouse the strip of land between the road and the river.

The Nottoway, a stream perhaps one hundred and fifty feet wide as it passes by Courtland, neatly bisects the county. Even though no striking differences impress the casual observer who ventures across it, the Nottoway in fact provided an important demarcation. The Anglican church divided the county into two parishes: Nottoway Parish, above the river, first occupied by whites after 1700, as the frontier of settlement extended beyond the James River Basin, and St. Lukes Parish, beyond the Nottoway, settled several decades later. Civil usage followed religious. Local tax records and U.S. Census lists in the mid-nineteenth century remained subdivided according to parish, even though the Episcopal church had by that time lost almost all its membership.

The distinction between the two halves of the county was especially pronounced during the late antebellum period. Demographic, economic,

The Southampton courthouse, 1989. (*Photo by author*)

social, cultural, and political differences separated Nottoway Parish, or upper Southampton (north and east of the Nottoway), from St. Lukes Parish, or lower Southampton (south and west of the Nottoway). In the upper county the white population approximately equaled that of the slave and free black populations combined. Few upper-county white families owned large amounts of property, but most owned some. Farmers owning small to middle-sized parcels of land and either no slaves or only a few were concentrated in far greater numbers and proportions in the upper county.

The lower county, by contrast, had a greater commitment to plantation slavery. Blacks far outnumbered whites in the lower county. Although it had many fewer white families of the middling type, the lower county had larger numbers of planters. With landholdings and slaveholdings concentrated into larger units, lower-county farms produced more for market. This was especially the case with cotton. In 1860 lower-county farm owners grew almost seven bales apiece of the white fiber; in the upper county, cotton output averaged less than one bale per farm. The largest plantations in the lower county produced more than fifty bales a year, whereas the overwhelming majority of farms in the upper county grew no cotton at all. The dominance of the plantation in the lower county restricted opportunities for ordinary folk. Larger numbers of white families there, compared with the upper county, owned neither land nor slaves.

Why did upper and lower Southampton differ? The soils of the lower county, consisting principally of Norfolk fine sandy loam, warmed more rapidly than the heavier clay soils of the upper county, thereby extending the growing season for cotton in lower Southampton by a crucial week or two. Because the county is situated at the northern limit of commercial cotton production, only the lower county was well suited for cotton.

At least as important as soil, however, in giving the two halves of the county differing economies and outlooks, was the impact of the evangelical movement in the late eighteenth and early nineteenth centuries. The local Quaker community, centered at the Black Creek meeting, initiated opposition to slavery in the latter eighteenth century and apparently made many Baptists and Methodists in the upper county receptive to antislavery evangelicalism. Even during the late antebellum era, when proslavery orthodoxies dominated the South, a number of white families in the Black Creek region still considered it wrong to own slaves.

When political parties took shape during the 1830s, upper and lower

[5]

Southampton developed contrasting party identities. The upper county became a Whig stronghold, while the lower county became even more monolithically Democratic. As a consequence, Southampton experienced far more political competition than most southern counties, which typically assumed a pronounced partisan identity. Southampton gave narrow margins to Whig presidential candidates in 1840, 1848, and 1852; Democrats achieved slender victories in 1836, 1844, 1856, and 1860. Party control of the county's seat in the state assembly likewise repeatedly changed hands.

At no point during the entire antebellum era did Southampton polarize so sharply as during the secession crisis. In February 1861, two months before the war started, over three-quarters of voters in the upper county opposed secession, whereas almost 95 percent of those from the lower county favored it. Moreover, secession also divided nonslaveholders and slaveholders, as almost 58 percent of the former opposed secession, while over 61 percent of the latter favored it. Even though upper Southampton did rally behind the war effort once the fighting started, large numbers of whites there regretted the division of the Union and feared that the South would reap the whirlwind.

Taking secondary roads northeast from Courtland, one soon arrives at sites associated with the upper county's distinctive history. The Black Creek Baptist Church remains vigorous, housed in a modern brick building that gives no immediate clue to the congregation's long and interesting presence in the county. There in the 1790s David Barrow preached against the injustice of slavery, as did his successor several decades later, Jonathan Lankford. Although the nearby Black Creek Friends Meeting was laid down in 1968, its two late nineteenth-century offshoots, Bethel and Corinth meetings, recently celebrated their centennials. The Corinth meetinghouse, an attractive example of rural vernacular church architecture dating from the 1880s, sits half a dozen miles north of Black Creek. In the early twentieth century before the establishment of public high schools, Corinth Quakers sponsored a boarding school that provided students from Southampton and the adjacent region with a college preparatory program.

One of the most historic sites in the Black Creek area is Beechwood, the well-preserved ancestral home of the Pretlow family. Dr. Thomas Jefferson Pretlow, who tried and failed to combine former slaves and anti-Confederate whites in the postwar Republican party, grew up at Beechwood. The oldest parts of the building date to 1720. The family graveyard includes members of the Denson and Scott families, who, along with the Pretlows, were pillars of the Quaker community. In more modern times Beechwood was owned by a Pretlow descendant, Colgate W. Darden (1897–1981), governor of Virginia and president of the University of Virginia.

Diarist Elliott L. Story, who taught school in the Black Creek neighborhood between 1838 and 1853, closely observed the rhythms of daily life. His notations introduce the modern reader to weddings and corn shuckings, to quiltings and protracted meetings. The gregarious young bachelor had a wide circle of acquaintances; his diary provides a unique record of what they said and did.

The eastern border of Southampton is the Blackwater River, which runs south toward Albemarle Sound. For several years during the Civil War, the Blackwater bristled with military activity because it divided regions of Union and Confederate control. As many as 10,000 often-hungry Confederates occupied the Southampton side, sufficient to warn away the bluecoats on the opposite shore but quite inadequate to stem the exodus of slaves who knew that only the narrow river separated them from freedom. Among the Southampton slaves and free blacks who crossed the Blackwater between 1861 and 1865, at least one hundred ultimately served in the Union army.

Downstream on the western side of the Blackwater lies Franklin. Although a small settlement developed before the Civil War where the Seaboard and Roanoke Railroad crossed the river, only with the postwar emergence of timber and later paper processing as the principal local industries did Franklin grow rapidly. It has since become an incorporated city, politically separated from the county.

Franklin grew because of the Union Camp Corporation. Although its extensive paper-manufacturing operations are located just across the narrow Blackwater in Isle of Wight County, Union Camp's plant dominates the eastern skyline of Franklin, where most of its labor force lives. The town includes a mix of neighborhoods, for the most part modest and unpretentious, with a more privileged section up the hill. A modern hospital and a community college make Franklin the metropolis of the region. Its suburban shopping centers, which have in recent decades eclipsed Franklin's downtown, draw customers from a wide area.

Driving southwest from Franklin one soon crosses the Nottoway into the lower county. The road leads to Thomaston, a fine antebellum residence with a huge oak tree in the front yard. Here is the boyhood home of Major General George H. Thomas, the "Rock of Chickamauga," one of the premier commanders in the Union army. Thomas has long stirred ambivalent reactions among local residents. Only recently has chagrin at his decision to fight against home and kin mellowed sufficiently to allow the local historical society to erect a plaque honoring one of the two most famous natives of Southampton.

Continuing south and west on secondary roads leading toward the North Carolina line past the small town of Newsoms, one encounters the Barnes Methodist Church, set back from a rural intersection. The current building has stood for almost a century, but the congregation's history extends twice that long. According to tradition, the most famous Southamptonite, Nat Turner, preached in the Barnes churchyard to fellow slaves the week before the 1831 insurrection. What message was delivered there by the charismatic bondsman, whose audacious acts soon shocked the entire South?

The ghost of Nat Turner stalks lower Southampton. A number of buildings visited by the rebels still stand. Bloodstains may still be seen on the floor of the Catherine Whitehead house. Gilbert Francis, an attorney and former president of the local historical society, lives just a few miles from where his ancestor Nathaniel Francis fought the attackers. Driving along the Barrow Road on a hot summer afternoon, past fields of ripening cotton, corn, and peanuts, one follows the destructive path of the rebels as they marched toward Jerusalem.[1] Even if Southampton has finally reconciled itself to honoring General Thomas, the legacy of Nat Turner is still too painful and divisive for easy commemoration.

Whites and blacks inevitably have differing perspectives on this most angry scar in the county's history. The most extensive study of the insurrection by a white Southamptonite, William S. Drewry, concluded that only a "warped and perverted" mind would lead a well-treated slave to rebel. Some blacks, on the other hand, have found in Turner a symbol of resistance to oppression. One summer day in August 1867, just at the time when former slaves were for the first time registering to vote, Joseph Gregory, Southampton's leading black politician of the Reconstruction era and the minister at the Cool Spring Baptist Church, led others from his congregation to a state convention of black Baptists. The arrival of delegates from a church located near "where Nat Turner first struck for freedom" thirty-six years earlier prompted enthusiastic handshaking and "general felicitation."[2]

The fertile Three Creeks region lies just north and west of the areas in the lower county attacked by Turner. Drewrysville (now Drewryville) is a small country town with a grocery store, a post office, and a number of attractive frame homes dating from the nineteenth century. Near here the Drewry family built a mill that gave the settlement its name. In the vicinity members of the Drewry, Pope, Claud, Ridley, Goodwyn, and Mason families built up the largest plantations in the county. Its concentrated landholdings, substantial cotton outputs, and heavy reliance on slave labor gave the Three Creeks area a Deep South ambiance. Some members of the Drewrysville elite did migrate to the Deep South. Others thought about doing so. Still others straddled, attempting to maintain a comfortable Virginia existence with the earnings of slave laborers sent to the Old Southwest.

When Virginia voters indicated in February 1861 whether they preferred to secede or to support further efforts to reconcile the crisis, those in the Drewrysville area unanimously supported secession. Across the Nottoway at the Black Creek Church voting district, all but two among more than a hundred voters opposed secession, starkly illuminating the differences separating upper and lower Southampton.

The modern traveler, unconcerned by history and eager to keep moving, uses the Southampton Parkway, U.S. Highway 58. This four-lane expressway, circumventing both Franklin and Courtland, knifes through the county from east to west, connecting Norfolk with the Southside and Danville. Trucks and automobiles thunder along the modern highway, which replaces an infamous two-lane "suicide strip." At almost any point, however, a turn to the left or right will place one on a secondary road with a far longer history.

The timber and wood products industries have not been kind to Southampton's native forests. Second-growth pine and recent cutovers intersperse with cropland. Occasionally, however, the older roads cross lowlying streambeds where canopies of tall hardwoods provide a dark, cool sanctuary. The few big trees that have escaped the ax and chain saw are living witnesses to the history recounted here. An enormous white oak shades the Hebron Baptist Church, founded in 1786. The tree may well predate the church. Were the oak not mute, it could reveal whether Thomas J. Pretlow convinced any of his 1860 audience that secession would destroy slavery and revolutionize the Old South. Just up the road, one comes to Persons Methodist Church. In the woods behind the church is Persons Millpond, where Nat Turner baptized a white man, Etheldred Brantley. The old trees there, too, assuming that a few inaccessible veterans have survived, would have a fascinating story to tell.

The familiar world of the late twentieth century lies just across Southampton's western border. There, near Emporia where U.S. 58 meets Interstate 95, the predictable array of motels and amenities awaits the modern traveler. One moves suddenly from somewhere in particular to the interchangeable America of our own era.

Let us retrace our steps. By sticking to the back roads, by admiring the historic churches, homes, and trees, and—above all—by sifting through the documentary record, we can learn a great deal about the very different world of Old Southampton and the people who lived there.

ONE

꙳

The Peoples of Old Southampton

SLAVERY AND RACE LARGELY predetermined the future of a child born in antebellum Southampton. Close to half the population was enslaved, and the lives of slaves differed in myriad ways from the lives of most who were free. Unusual for the Old South, approximately one-quarter of Southampton's nonwhites were not enslaved. Free blacks, however, suffered restrictions on their freedom that too often reduced them to semislavery. Together free blacks and slaves outnumbered whites (see appendix table 1.1).

A far wider range of possibilities characterized Southampton's white society. Fewer than one white family in ten owned enough slaves to qualify as members of the planter class. Notwithstanding that the political rhetoric of the times tended to downplay class gradations, white society in the antebellum South was sharply differeniated. On the other hand, a majority of white families did own either land or slaves. The stereotype of a few rich planters and an abject mass of poor whites ignores the broad middle. One may distinguish between privileged whites, smallholding whites, and nonpropertied whites (see app. table 1.2). These categories, even if somewhat arbitrary, correspond with contemporary perceptions of social reality.

The most conspicuous members of the privileged segment were the elite. Antebellum Virginia's elite formed a cosmopolitan upper class, typically with family linkages and networks of friendship and association that reached out to other counties and beyond the state boundaries. Elite children attended private academies; elite sons continued to the University of Virginia, the Virginia Military Institute, or the College of William and Mary, and occasionally to the University of North Carolina, Princeton University, or to the medical school at the University of Pennsylvania. Marriages to similar families in Virginia and across the South reinforced the wider horizons of the elite; they were the only families in the Old South who frequently married spouses from beyond the borders of their home counties. Able to renew and extend contacts during summer vacations at seaside and mountain resorts and having more incentive and opportunity to travel, elite families tended to develop stronger ties with each other than with their less privileged neighbors.

Only a small number of Southampton families, who typically combined wealth and political attainments, could be counted among the elite. Several branches of Ridleys and Urquharts, the two wealthiest families in the county, deserve first mention. These two families owned more slaves and land than any others in the county. Several Ridleys and Urquharts sat in the state legislature and at state constitutional conventions. The two families intermarried to some extent and were among the few in the county to maintain ties to the Episcopal church. The Urquharts also had connections by marriage to several elite North Carolina families. Other members of the Southampton elite included John Young Mason, a politician and diplomat who was better known outside the county than any of the other local gentry; Dr. Thomas J. Pretlow, physician, member of the county court, and state legislator, who studied at the University of Virginia and married Clarissa Ashton Garrett from a prominent Albemarle County family; William B. Shands, state senator and longtime Democratic party activist, whose mother was from the prominent Rives family and who married a granddaughter of President John Tyler; and Dr. Albridgton Samuel Hardy Burges, the scholarly son and grandson of the county's eighteenth-century Anglican ministers, who promoted education and who with Robert Ridley and John Young Mason was one of Southampton's three delegates at the 1850–51 Constitutional Convention.[1]

If some privileged families were elite, others were merely prosperous. The line between elite and prosperous families had more to do with outlook and attitude than with measurable accumulation of wealth. Most elite families were indisputably rich. Some with comfortably large accumulations of wealth were, however, too provincial to fit the elite category. The differences apparently resulted from the varying experiences of particular individuals. Those with less distinguished backgrounds or more limited education and aspirations had narrower outlooks and orbits of association.

Harrison P. Pope and Jesse Little were among the largest planters in Southampton, but neither stood among the elite. In 1860 Pope owned forty-three slaves, farmed 2,800 improved acres, and produced seventy bales of cotton, more than anyone else in the county. Pope also was a member of the county court and of Whiteheads Methodist Church. A youthful indiscretion may, however, have tarnished his reputation: in 1839, at the age of twenty-two, Pope was convicted of fathering a bastard child and ordered by the county court to pay $17.50 per year for seven years. The experience appears to have chastened him: in 1862 Pope admonished his younger brother-in-law in the Confederate army to avoid being "carried astray by the influences so naturally thrown around one engaged in a soldiers life."[2] Jesse Little, the father-in-law of diarist Daniel W. Cobb, was wealthy: in 1860 he owned seventy-two slaves, had 1,129 improved acres, and produced thirty-two bales of cotton. Little did not, however, assume a significant public role. He never served on the county court, and unlike most members of his class, he voted only intermittently.

Elite and prosperous whites together constituted only a small fraction of the white population. If defined by the conventional measurement of the planter class, the ownership of twenty slaves, the top rung of Southampton society included only 68 of the 1,219 white families in the county in 1850, less than 6 percent. Southampton's actual upper class was probably larger. A. S. H. Burges, for example, owned fifteen slaves; Thomas J. Pretlow, whose Quaker antecedents led him to make significant use of free black labor, owned only ten slaves. By lowering the prerequisite for membership in the privileged category to include all white families that owned ten or more slaves, one may create a more useful category of social analysis. So defined, 187 white families, about 15 percent of the total in 1850, qualified as privileged.

Smallholders, defined to include any family owning between one and nine slaves, as well as those nonslaveholding families who owned land, were the largest of the three groupings in Southampton's antebellum white society. Slightly more than half the white families in the county (640 of 1,219) met such criteria. Smallholders included quite a wide range, from nonslaveholders owning tiny plots of land to aspiring planters who lacked sufficient slaves to qualify as privileged. More typically, smallholding families owned tracts of land large enough to support subsistence agriculture. About half the smallholders also owned slaves. The social order in Southampton corroborates the findings of historian Frank L. Owsley, who argued that the largest number of white persons in the

Old South were neither rich nor poor. Smallholding families are precisely those he identified, in his pioneering volume with the same title, as the "plain folk of the Old South." [3]

About one-third of Southampton's white families (392 of 1,219 in 1850) owned neither land nor slaves. Nonpropertied family heads included tenants, farm laborers, poorer artisans, overseers, and others without independent means. More than twice as many white Southampton families were nonpropertied as were privileged. Nevertheless, smallholding white families constituted more than half the total number in the county, outnumbering the nonpropertied and the privileged combined.

Privileged whites, smallholding whites, and nonpropertied whites clustered somewhat unevenly in Old Southampton (see app. table 1.2). In the lower part of the county, between the Nottoway River and the North Carolina border, almost 19 percent of the white families qualified as elite or prosperous. In the upper county, between the Nottoway and Blackwater rivers, the comparable figure was under 13 percent. Even though upper-county white families outnumbered those in the lower county, 668 to 551, the wealthiest families were more concentrated in the lower county, 103 to 84.

Smallholders, conversely, clustered in upper Southampton, where landholdings were more widely dispersed. Almost three of every five white families in the upper county were smallholders, 395 of 668. In the lower county, which had larger numbers of privileged families, smallholders constituted less than 45 percent of the white families, 245 of 551.

Among white families in the upper county, 189 (or 28 percent) owned no property. Greater absolute numbers of nonpropertied white families lived in the lower county, 203, and there they constituted well over one-third of the total (about 37 percent).

In the upper county, therefore, smallholders far outnumbered the combined total of privileged families and those without independent means. In the lower county, by contrast, privileged and nonpropertied families together outnumbered the smallholders. Its larger middle segment gave upper Southampton a different social and political order than lower Southampton. The latter, with larger concentrations of both privileged and nonpropertied families, provided a setting more conducive to elite domination. Politics in the lower county, once the patterns of the second party system took shape, differed in many ways from politics in the upper county.

As was generally the case in tidewater and piedmont Virginia, most

Southampton whites had English antecedents. The most notable exception to this pattern was a nucleus of five Huguenot families (Sebrell,
Maget, Trezvant, Rochelle, and Denegre), all of which achieved prominence.[4] The Lenow and Luter families, of Germanic origin, were among
the early settlers in the upper-county village of Berlin, probably the oldest
town in Southampton.[5] A number of humble families of Irish descent,
with names such as Shelvy and O'Donolee, resided in the county during the nineteenth century. Also of Irish descent was a cosmopolitan
Southamptonite, Dr. Robert Murray.[6] A Corsican, Napoleon Bonaparte
Razierre, oversaw the rebuilding of the Seaboard and Roanoke Railroad
in the late 1840s. He married a woman from Isle of Wight County and
remained in Southampton until his death in 1860. His name most often
appears as it was apparently pronounced, "Razor."[7]

Even an occasional Yankee lived in antebellum Southampton. Dr.
Isaac Cox, from New York State, became a member of Nottoway Chapel,
a small Methodist church in the upper county. Though not averse to defending himself (in 1856 he employed fists and sticks in an altercation
with a neighbor), Cox feared "mob-law" after the outbreak of hostilities
in April 1861 and fled the area.[8] Joseph Ezra Gillette, the son of Connecticut migrant Ezra Gillet, also belonged to Nottoway Chapel. Unlike Dr.
Cox, however, Gillette was an ardent Democrat and secessionist. The
captain of Southampton's elite cavalry company and before long the major of a regiment, Gillette became the county's foremost Confederate
martyr.[9]

Slightly more than half the residents of the county were women. However much circumstances of race and class shaped the experiences of both
men and women, gender conventions prescribed separate and in most
ways subordinate roles for women.

When information about the property holdings of the white families is
broken down to separate households headed by men from those headed
by women, several significant differences come to light (see app. table
1.3). Nearly one-quarter of the white families had a female head. Most
were widows. Even though death by childbirth exacted a heavy toll
among Southampton's white women, those who survived their childbear-
ing years had an excellent chance to outlive their husbands, because
women typically married at a younger age than men.

Lavinia Hart Francis, born in 1813 and the mother of nine children,
was widowed before the age of forty by the death of her husband, Nathaniel, eight years her senior. They had married in 1830, when she was

seventeen and he was twenty-five. Lavinia Francis lived until 1885. Prosperous but certainly not elite, she managed competently her share of the family property. A photograph taken when Lavinia Francis was "an aging country lady" has been evocatively described by historian Nash Boney: "Neat, composed, proper, and a little stiff, she wears a dark, plain 'Sunday' dress trimmed in bits of lace. Her dark hair is parted firmly in the middle, and her strong hands—more accustomed to a pan than a fan—rest a little awkwardly in her lap." [10]

Jane Watson Denson Pretlow, the mother of thirteen children and the widow of magistrate Thomas Pretlow, probably lived in somewhat more refined circumstances. Her husband, born in 1786, died in 1843. The widow, only four years his junior, lived another thirty years, surviving to the advanced age of eighty-four. She managed the ancestral home, Beechwood, living with several unmarried daughters, three of whom survived her. Several of her sons, notably Dr. Thomas J. Pretlow, had distinguished careers. [11]

The households of Lavinia Francis and Jane Pretlow were hardly typical. On the whole, women were significantly less likely than men to own landed property or slaves (see app. table 1.3). Only a little more than one-quarter of households headed by white men were unpropertied, but nearly one-half of those headed by white women were in the bottom category.

The economic disparities between households headed by white men and those headed by white women did not begin to match the disparities between those headed by whites and those headed by blacks (see app. table 1.4). Of the 348 households in Southampton headed by free blacks, only 23, less than 7 percent, could be classified as smallholding. The great majority of free blacks lived in economic dependency, as hired farm laborers who owned no land of their own. Some free black men practiced trades—as carpenters, blacksmiths, coopers, or shoemakers. Others felled trees and sawed lumber. Few, however, owned land.

Seven out of eight free black male household heads in the upper county with listed occupations were categorized as farmers. Most of these were, of course, farm laborers. In the upper county white males apparently filled some artisan positions that were held by free blacks in the lower county, where only about two-thirds of free black male household heads were listed as farmers. Most free black male household heads with non-farm occupations lived in the lower county.

Almost half of free black households (170 of 348) were headed by women, twice the proportion for white households. Economic restrictions on free blacks apparently diminished the proportion of male household heads. So too, many free black households were only half-free, with one of the partners in the marriage still enslaved.

Virginia handicapped free blacks in numerous ways. Unable to vote, to serve on juries, to receive trial by jury, or to testify against whites in court, free blacks were required to register periodically with the county court and to keep free papers in their possession. Because whites regarded free blacks as a menace, manumitted slaves could not legally reside in the state without special permission of the legislature. An 1850 law placed a special $1 annual tax on adult free black men, ostensibly to establish a fund to colonize free blacks out of the state.[12]

Southampton's free blacks had a particularly troubled history. Brutally victimized in the aftermath of the Nat Turner insurrection, many fled the county. As many as three hundred, perhaps one-fifth the free black population at that time, accepted transportation to Liberia offered by the American Colonization Society. The emigrants included "the ablest and most talented of Southampton's free Negroes." The departure of George Liberty, emancipated as a young man more than forty years earlier by a slaveholder who concluded that slavery was inconsistent with his religious and political values, symbolized the retrogressive experience of Southampton's free blacks.[13]

Nevertheless, one finds instances of free black families that managed to overcome all the obstacles. Two neighbors of diarist Daniel W. Cobb were free black landholders. In 1850 Jordan Steward, age thirty-five, owned thirty acres valued at $72 on which he raised subsistence amounts of corn, peas, and hogs. During the wheat harvest in 1850, Cobb hired Steward at the attractive rate of $1 per day. An older man, James Taylor, age fifty-seven, owned almost one hundred acres, valued at $332 by the tax assessor. Taylor's farm included $201 worth of livestock, including a horse, three milch cows, two oxen, three other cattle, eleven sheep, and $65 worth of farm implements and machinery. Both Steward and Taylor had standing in the community. When Cobb and local landowners decided to underwrite the costs of a bridge across Assamoosic Swamp "for the benefit of the neighbourhood," Steward pledged $5, as much as any of the white contributors, and Taylor contributed $2, more than many whites.[14]

Lemuel Whitehead, a forty-nine-year-old free black carpenter, apparently leased a 160-acre farm. Aided by a horse and an ox, he and his eight-member family produced four bales of cotton, 250 bushels of corn, and 50 bushels of peas. The 1850 agricultural census also reports that they tended twenty-one hogs, two milch cows, and two other cattle. Ten years later, Colegate Whitehead, perhaps the son of Lemuel Whitehead, leased an even more productive farm. Its output included six bales of cotton, 750 bushels of corn, eighty hogs, and 90 bushels of peas. By farming on such a scale, historian Luther Porter Jackson has observed, Colegate Whitehead "ranked in a class with many white farmers of Southampton." [15]

Any assessment of opportunity and privilege in Old Southampton's social order must recognize that over 40 percent of the population was enslaved. Southampton slaves, like those elsewhere in the Old South, lived as families. [16] The federal census, however, lists slaves by owners, divided by sex and age but without names or indication of family connection. In the absence of any systematic listing of slave families or slave households, one must extrapolate. Assuming arbitrarily that the number of persons per slave household approximated that for Southampton's free blacks, one may venture some comparisons of all Southampton households (see app. table 1.4).

Several aspects of the social order deserve emphasis (see app. tables 1.5, 1.6, 1.7). Although only 7 percent of all Southampton households qualified as privileged, they enjoyed striking economic advantages. Privileged households—those including ten or more slaves—controlled more than three-quarters of the slave labor in the county. They also commanded more than half of the improved acreage and more than two-thirds of the assessed land value, suggesting that privileged families owned the best land. They likewise produced large shares of the county's agricultural output, ranging from more than half of the corn and swine to approximately two-thirds of the cotton and peas. Privileged households undoubtedly produced the overwhelming majority of agricultural products destined for market rather than for subsistence. In every category of agricultural output, privileged households averaged at least four times as great an amount as that for smallholding households. The disparities in property valuation were even greater: assessments of privileged households averaged almost eight times those of smallholding households.

One must, however, look at all households, white and black, in order to assess the position of the smallholding plain folk. Because only a handful of free black families qualified as smallholders and the overwhelming majority of blacks, whether free or enslaved, owned no property, the smallholding class enjoyed tangible advantages. Only one-quarter of the total households were smallholders; they and the privileged together included fewer than one-third the total number of households. Over two-thirds of all Southampton households owned neither land nor slaves. Compared with all Southamptonites, white smallholders constituted an upper middle class that had a substantial stake in the status quo. Moreover, the advantages enjoyed by whites were not merely economic. In the realm of social, legal, and political rights, all blacks were brutally stigmatized, while ordinary whites increasingly enjoyed the same rights as privileged whites.

During the great crisis of 1860–61 more than ever before, disagreements over secession tended to divide slaveholders from smallholding white nonslaveholders. A majority of slaveholders favored secession, while majorities of nonslaveholders, both those who owned land and those who did not, initially opposed secession. Once the war started, however, most smallholding Southamptonites joined hands with the privileged to support the Confederate cause. However much they disagreed about the wisdom of secession, white property holders both large and small had common interests after mid-April 1861. If the Federal effort to conquer the South was an attack on the very underpinnings of the social and economic order, as most whites saw it, then smallholders had ample reason to fight.

In short, class advantages in Old Southampton had a dual quality. The small privileged class certainly did control a disproportionately large share of resources, and it could capitalize on its advantages in many ways. White smallholders controlled a far more modest share of resources, especially when measured per household. One must keep in mind, however, that white smallholders produced close to half the county's output of corn and swine. Particularly after 1851 when all white men in Virginia gained equal access to the franchise, the plain folk occupied an enviable position in the larger scheme of things.

Most Southampton slaves had privileged owners (see app. table 1.5). Although small slaveholders outnumbered large slaveholders, 315 to 187, the great preponderance of slaves were owned by privileged whites (4,159) rather than smallholders (1,183). Close to half the slaves were owned by planters who held at least twenty slaves; more than a quarter were owned by household heads who held between ten and nineteen slaves; less than a quarter were owned by smallholders who held fewer than ten slaves.

A considerable amount of slave hiring took place in Southampton. Extra slaves and those whose situation was tied up in litigation over estates often were hired out on an annual basis. This practice to some extent redistributed slave labor from larger units to smaller ones, because those hiring slaves typically lacked the capital to buy as many slaves as they needed. Some hired slaves were owned, however, by smallholders. The actual residential situation for Southampton slaves did not, therefore, diverge markedly from the patterns of slave ownership. Slave hiring placed an additional increment of slaves in smallholding households. Over one-quarter of the slaves resided with white smallholders in any given year, but the figure could never have reached as high as one-third.

Who were the slaves in Old Southampton? And how did they perceive their situation? Two extensive interviews with former Southampton slaves were recorded by Works Progress Administration researchers in the 1930s. Allen Crawford and Marriah Hines were both born in 1835 and interviewed in 1937. The recollections of these two 102-year-olds provide an important window on the lives of almost half the population of the county a century earlier.

Allen Crawford grew up in lower Southampton on the Peter Edwards farm, located three miles from the Travis house where the Nat Turner insurrection began. Crawford's Uncle Henry, one of Turner's recruits, was hanged for his role in the affair. Crawford recalled hearing that Turner had hidden near the Edwards farm, where he finally was captured. Crawford said his grandmother struck the captured slave rebel in the mouth, asking, "Why did you take my son away?" Turner allegedly replied, "Your son was as willing to go as I was." [17]

Crawford also reported on torture tactics used by white soldiers at Cross Keys the day after the insurrection to extract information and confessions from captured slaves. The soldiers lit large log fires, "and every one dat was Nat's man was taken bodily by two men who catch you and hold yer bare feet to dis blazing fire 'til you tole all you know'd 'bout dis killing." When one of the blacks refused to talk, the "white devil" in charge ordered: "Well, stick him closer!" "Dam you I'll make you tell."

Crawford recalled that his first owner, Peter Edwards, was too old and paralyzed to dominate his slaves physically, although once when Crawford was still a boy, Edwards did whip him for playing in the woods when he was supposed to have returned with some firewood. Ben Pope, his second owner, was "fairly good but awful strict." As a young person, Crawford lived with his mother. His father, owned by John Briggs, lived nearby and visited on weekends.

Slaves traveling in the neighborhood risked encounters with slave patrols. Briggs promised to protect another of his slaves, Austin Sykes, from the patrollers, but Crawford recalled that Sykes was once beaten by a patrol anyway. Apparently Briggs "went back on 'im," and Pope, who witnessed the incident, chose not to intervene. Crawford reported that he had complained about the patrollers "giving Austin hell down dar," whereupon Pope's mother spoke up, saying they "ought to kill dat nigger!"

Allen Crawford must have been a field hand. He retained vivid memories of "dem old slave-time hoes," which were "hammered out of pig iron" and "broad like a shovel." Deliberately made heavy so they would "fall hard," the hoes had handles made of hickory limbs. The slave who wanted to keep any skin on his or her hands would have to "shave de knots off smooth an' scrape 'em wid glass."

Mrs. Marriah Hines was a tiny woman "with a pretty head of white hair covering her round brown face," who stood barely five feet tall and who weighed no more than one hundred pounds. She provided interviewer David Hoggard with a detailed account of her young life as a slave woman in antebellum Southampton.[18]

Hines belonged to "James Pressman" (probably John A. Persons),[19] a pious and unusually benevolent slaveowner who was condemned as a "nigger lover" by other whites in the neighborhood. Unlike many masters, Persons fed and clothed his slaves adequately. They never went hungry or felt the need to steal, and their clothing though not fancy was sufficient "to keep us comfortable." Persons would buy cloth "by the loads and heaps" and shoes "by the big box full."

Hines depicted her owner as someone who held his slaves to far less arduous work routines than the norm. The Persons slaves usually ate breakfast without the usual "hurry-scurry" before they went to the fields. By the time they arrived, slaves from other plantations had already been working "a long time." Only if the work had been held up by rainy weather did the Persons slaves have "to git to it early." They worked without any white overseer or black driver "watching over us." Persons himself would strut down the field "like a big turkey gobbler to see how the work was going on." He "always had a smile and a joke wid you" and would compliment the work even when it wasn't as well done as it should have been. Persons's slaves generally worked well because they did not want to disappoint their master. At midday they had two hours off for dinner when they could go home to eat, afterwards returning to the fields to work until sundown. During bad weather, Persons made no effort to work his slaves other than "little odd jobs." There was no "all day work in the cold"; the men simply needed "to git in fire wood."

Persons was a strict Sabbatarian. All food to be eaten on Sunday had to be cooked on Saturday. When inviting the preacher to visit after church, Persons would warn: "You plenty welcome to go home with me for dinner, but you'll have to eat cold vittals 'cause there ain't no cooking on Sundays at my house." The slaves thus had no Sunday obligations but would voluntarily "take turns helping 'em serve Sunday meals just 'couse we loved them so much." Persons would "sometimes give us a little money for it too."

Most slaves in the household, Hines recalled, "had 'fessed religion." Every evening they could join the white family in prayers, or they could pray by themselves. Although not required to do so, most went to church on Sundays and "stayed the biggest portion of the day." Persons's slaves also held a "general prayer meeting every Wednesday night," at which they had "a good time shouting, singing, and praying just like we pleased." The master presided over a ceremony in which Hines married her husband, Benjamin F. Hines.

At the end of the war, Persons explained to his slaves that "we could go where we pleased and come when we pleased—that we didn't have to work for him 'less we wanted to." Most stayed and raised their own crops, aided by Persons who gave some of his former slaves "a cow or a mule or anything he could spare to help us." Some eventually bought land and cabins from their former owner.

Yet another Southampton-born slave, John Brown, wrote an autobiography. His experiences, both in Southampton and in his later life at other places farther south, suggest that Marriah Hines's master was far from typical. Although Brown recognized that some slaves considered their masters humane, his certainly were not. "I suppose I had the misfortune to get a run of bad masters," he drily observed.[20]

His original owner, the widow Betty Moore, was "an old, big woman, about seventy, who wore spectacles and took snuff." Moore always carried a cowhide whip at her side; "it was painted blue, and we used to call it the 'blue lizard.'" She used it frequently because she liked to see her slaves "constantly employed." John Brown vividly recalled the "great trouble" that fell upon the Moore slaves when they were divided between Moore and her three married daughters. Brown and his mother ended up in the hands of James Davis in North Carolina. Brown's brother Silas and sister Lucy remained with Moore in Southampton, and Brown feared his mother would "die of grief" at having to leave two of her children behind.[21]

Worse would follow: Davis soon sold Brown to a slave trader, and the youngster never again saw his mother or the rest of his family. He fell into the hands of a series of Deep South tyrants who not only abused their slaves but failed to provide them even with adequate nourishment. Brown typically worked all morning before getting his first meal, around noon-time. The only other meal of the day did not take place until late in the evening. Brown and his fellow slaves ate little or no meat.[22]

Brown's autobiography, originally published in England in 1855, also recounts his escape from slavery and his experiences as a free man. He worked for more than two years in Michigan, including time as a copper miner in the Upper Peninsula. From there he resettled briefly with the community of free slaves in Dawn, West Canada. In 1850 he sailed to England, where he became an abolitionist lecturer and wrote his autobiography.[23]

THE EXPERIENCES OF THE MASON family illuminate the interaction between Southampton's privileged families and Southampton's slaves. A rich panorama unfolds in the family's surviving papers, as the scene shifted from the family estate, Fortsville, to Richmond, Washington, Paris, and a cotton plantation in the Mississippi Delta. Not surprisingly, men and women accustomed to privilege dominate the correspondence, but it also includes many letters from overseers, managers, and other less wealthy whites. The Mason papers also provide many glimpses of slave society, for throughout the antebellum era enslaved blacks on the Mason estates far outnumbered their white owners.

John Young Mason achieved far greater political prominence than any other antebellum Southamptonite. Elected to the House of Delegates in 1823 and the state Senate in 1827, he served three terms in Congress between 1831 and 1837, where he became chairman of the House Committee on Foreign Affairs. Although a dependable Jackson supporter on most issues, Mason, like most other Virginia Democrats, considered the President's stern challenge to South Carolina during the Nullification Crisis needlessly provocative. Mason held state and federal judgeships for seven years after 1837 and then returned to Washington as secretary of the navy and attorney general in the cabinets of Tyler and Polk between 1844 and 1849. An expansionist, Mason nevertheless favored accepting the controversial treaty that Nicholas Trist negotiated to end the Mexican War. Mason spent his final six years from 1853 until his death in 1859 as ambassador to France. He also sat in the state constitutional conventions of 1829–30 and 1850–51, presiding over the latter, and he served for several years as president of the James River and Kanawha Canal Company.[24]

Both Mason and his wife, Mary Ann Fort Mason, were born to privilege. Mason grew up on a plantation in neighboring Greensville County. After graduating at the age of seventeen from the University of North Carolina, where he became friends with James K. Polk, Mason proceeded to Judge Tapping Reeve's law school in Litchfield, Connecticut, considered by many the best in the country at the time (John C. Calhoun had earlier studied there; during Mason's sojourn in Connecticut, the Lyman Beecher family also lived in orthodox Litchfield, maintaining close ties to Reeve and other local luminaries). Mason's marriage to Mary Ann Fort in 1821 made him the proprietor of her father's plantation, Fortsville, an estate of over two thousand acres. Fortsville also established Mason's residence in Southampton, even though some of the property extended across the Greensville and Sussex county lines. Apparently freed of financial worries, Mason plunged directly into politics.

Mason's success gradually eroded his ties to Southampton. During the last two decades of his life, he rarely set foot in the county. His actual residence was an expensive home in Richmond, where his wife preferred living "to any other place." Overseers and his son Lewis did their best to manage Mason's farming operations. Although family members maintained a sentimental affection for "dear old Fortsville," visitors there during the late antebellum period remarked on the lonely countenance of the once bustling plantation residence.[25]

A combination of expensive living, financial reverses, and liability for debts incurred by relatives depleted Mason's once-substantial estate. The losing struggle to maintain his financial well-being constantly tormented Mason during his years of greatest national prominence. That struggle exposed the tawdry underside to the paternalistic values espoused by Mason and others of his class. In order to increase the profitability of his slave labor force, Mason sent at least sixty of them to a raw plantation in

Mississippi, where cotton yields were high and life expectancy was low. Eventually, pressure from Mason's creditors forced him to sell the Mississippi plantation and most of the surviving slaves there. By the time of his death, Mason's debts exceeded his assets.

The disappearing patrimony fractured the prospects for Mason's children. The eldest son, Lewis, who worked harder than any of the others to preserve the estate, lived in poverty after the war at Fortsville, his mother's ancestral home. Hosting other kin and misfits who were down on their luck, Lewis Mason brought a Faulknerian sequel to the Mason family saga. The troubles that confronted the Masons reveal much about the dynamics of late antebellum Southampton society. Their fall was more resounding than the norm; they were hardly typical. And yet their experiences had significant parallels.

In Southampton and throughout Virginia and the Southeast, people looked enviously at great fortunes being made in the southwestern cotton boom. The tendency was particularly pronounced among Democrats, whose ideological orientation predisposed them toward exploiting new lands rather than applying more intensive agricultural techniques or promoting industrial diversification. James Trezvant, prominent Southampton politician and Mason's immediate predecessor in Congress, suddenly uprooted to Tennessee in 1831, expecting to develop a plantation. The prosperous Maget family maintained residence in Southampton while transferring some of their slaves to a new cotton plantation in Arkansas, across the river from Memphis. Francis T. Ridley, one of the largest local slaveholders, reported in 1858 that he had "almost determined to buy land in Texas" and send "a portion of my hands there, as I am making nothing here." Ridley, like James Maget, hoped to manage at a distance, not wishing to uproot to the Southwest.[26]

John Young Mason's correspondence details the unhappy consequences of westward migration on black Southamptonites. Had more abundant evidence survived regarding the dealings of other families, the historian would have corroborating information. The Masons, however, left the most substantial paper trail. As early as 1844, at the time of his initial cabinet appointment, Mason began to consider buying land in the Southwest or sending his slaves there to hire at advantageous rates. These inquiries proceeded inconclusively for several years.[27] Eventually his search narrowed to a tract of almost eight hundred acres in Coahoma County, Mississippi, a premier cotton region about fifty miles south of Memphis on the river. Encouraged by reports that yields of one bale or more per acre could be expected there (one-third of a bale was the norm in Virginia) and that Mississippi planters normally expected to harvest between six and eight bales of cotton per full-time hand (at a time when the comparable figure in Virginia was around two), Mason decided in 1847 to buy the Mississippi property and stock it with surplus slaves from his estates in Southampton and adjacent Isle of Wight County.[28]

Mason always had taken pains to avoid separating slave families, to require that overseers make sure his slaves were properly clothed and fed, and to encourage slaves to earn money by cultivating their own garden plots. His paternalistic principles proved incompatible, however, with the realities of absentee ownership in the Mississippi Delta. Although he tried to keep nuclear families together, larger kinship networks inevitably were sundered.[29] Moreover, it became increasingly obvious that slaves in Mississippi were poorly treated.

Mason's son Lewis led the first contingent of slaves on an overland trek in late 1847, using wagons and tents. After two months en route, they reached Memphis and sailed downriver by steamboat for the last leg of the trip. He enticed two skilled artisans, Bob and Tim, by promising to buy their families and send them out next fall.[30] Upon arrival, Lewis Mason found that only 125 acres of the property were cleared for cultivation. He immediately set the men to felling trees, the wood from which could be sold to passing steamboats. On some land that had to be cleared, trees stood one hundred feet tall and five feet thick at the base. Needing to buy hay, fodder, plows, hoes, mules, cows, pots, ovens, and furniture but wishing to maintain the appearance of "a large planter and a *solvent* man," Lewis quietly arranged loans from prominent friends of his father.[31]

Lewis Mason hired an overseer, Pinkney C. Sims, and went back to Virginia. Next winter young Mason returned, probably with more slaves. By the summer of 1849, the overseer reported a slave force of thirteen men, ten women, nine girls and boys, and ten infants. Good cotton crops in 1848 and 1849 coincided, unfortunately, with low prices, forcing the Masons to keep renegotiating their indebtedness.[32]

Bad spring weather in 1850 appeared to have shrunk the crop dramatically. Lewis Mason tried to take the hopeful view that a smaller crop would be easier to harvest and that prices would rise because crop losses were widespread. In fact, however, the astonishing fertility of the delta generated a crop of almost 130 bales, about one bale per acre and five per hand (and the hands were also raising corn beyond their own needs and cutting a thousand cords of wood). The prospects for the Masons appeared more cheerful until late summer. Suddenly in September a cholera epidemic struck, killing seven of the forty-two slaves. John Young Mason "never witnessed a more touching scene" than the grieving Virginia mother of one of the victims. "Her face literally quivered, and the only words she spoke, were, 'Master, my poor boy is gone.'" The Mason slaves remaining in Virginia reacted predictably to the tragedy: "None of the negroes," their owner reported, were willing to go west.[33]

The cholera epidemic also persuaded the overseer, Sims, to leave for Texas. John Young Mason, believing that Sims had acted with "kindness to the negroes," readily accepted the overseer's suggestion that George S. Bradford succeed him. Sims represented Bradford as "perfectly honest, attentive to his business, never drinks and will treat his negroes well in sickness and in health." Mason's confidence was misplaced, at least on the issue of slave treatment. An indication of the real situation surfaced when two slaves, Sam and Tom Scott, ran off and were caught and punished. Nevertheless, they continued to abscond, as did slaves Edwin and Bill. Lewis Mason, who stayed in Mississippi for several months in early 1851 at his father's behest, informed John Young Mason that "the negroes have not been treated as you or myself desired. Sims was very harsh and often abused them. Sometimes he struck them with sticks and kicked them. I fear we will never get any man who will treat them properly." Not surprisingly, the new overseer whom Sims had recommended shared the same approach. Bradford, "like all the rest of the Mississippi overseers," Lewis Mason explained to his father, "is more severe than I would have him. I am old maidish about the treatment of negroes[.] I can[']t bear to see them very severely punished."[34]

News about Mississippi's diseases and overseers, which readily circulated back to the remaining Mason slaves in Virginia, made them all the more resistant to relocating. The Mason family finances continued, however, to deteriorate. John Young Mason considered it imperative to "pitch as large a crop of cotton as the hands can cultivate." Lewis Mason, increasingly his father's business and financial manager, determined that more slaves must go to Mississippi. "One thing is certain, I am going to carry them to the plantation as soon and as cheap as I can," he explained to John Young Mason. "They are not willing to go: but there is no reason why you should not send them." Lewis Mason and eighteen slaves, traveling by water to New Orleans and then upriver to the plantation, arrived in Mississippi in December 1851, just in time to aid the slaves already there, who were struggling to harvest a prodigious 200-bale crop.[35]

Lewis Mason, aware of discontent among the slaves, first thought them malingering. "They are very well off and have no right to be dissatisfied," he reported to his father. To his mother, however, he confessed that the slaves "have had a very rough time" and were "dejected and perfectly indifferent about every thing." Mary Anne Fort Mason provided Lewis Mason with a more sympathetic audience than her husband. The son had a closer emotional and temperamental bond to his mother, a far from surprising consequence of living in a household with a typically absent politician father. The mother praised her son's "noble efforts" to repair the family finances and to make sure that the slaves were treated humanely.[36]

The slaves had grounds for complaint. Lewis Mason soon reported glaring abuses to his father. The obsession to pick cotton had led to neglect of nine slave children under the age of two, who were "at great risk of being burned to death, and suffer for attention." Mason assigned one woman to supervise them. He also recognized that the slave cabins were "very bad indeed," especially in cold weather. He resolved to construct close, warm, framed houses. During a measles epidemic soon after his arrival, Mason treated as many as eight afflicted slaves at once in his own somewhat better quarters. Yet another danger threatened the health of the slaves: during midsummer dry spells, groundwater supplies failed, leaving only river and bayou water to drink. Construction of cisterns was needed to alleviate the problem.[37]

Cotton, however, remained king. When Mason returned to Mississippi in October 1852 after a summer in Virginia, the situation remained deplorable. Many slave children were ill, for lack of supervision and decent housing. "You know we put up houses here in a hurry, when we settled, and they are very common and very open—The negroes are very much exposed," Mason explained to his father. The log houses, lacking weatherboards, could not have provided much protection from the elements. "I intend to make the houses good," he resolved, "or we will lose all."[38]

How might he improve matters at the Mississippi plantation? Lewis Mason mused in 1852 about taking personal charge there. "Why should I not leave Virginia," Mason inquired of his parents, "and take to overseeing it out here?" Intrigued by the prospects for gaining a large fortune and making himself "independent of the country and the rest of mankind," Mason also was attracted by the warmth of nearby planters, notably the prominent Jacob Thompson. One evening, Mason reported to his father, he joined the Thompson family in singing cheerfully around the piano.[39]

Lewis Mason's distress at the treatment of the family slaves had much to do with his thought of relocating. "I am always unhappy about our negroes," Mason explained to his mother, "and feel always a desire to take control of each plantation when I am on it." Mississippi was "the finest farming country in the world and if the negroes had good houses, a kind overseer, and the liberty to work now and then for themselves," it would be "the best place in the world for them." Wishing "for them to have all three" but aware from hard experience that they had none, Mason surmised that he must act. The "*mono-mania*" gnawed at him. "All of my letter is about the negroes," he exclaimed to his mother. "My mind is full of them."[40]

Mason, of course, was no egalitarian. He thought blacks "strange," and he shared his mother's view that they were "week and dependant on their master." His disdain for "western barbarians" translated, however, into a concern for the well-being of the laborers. Convinced that responsible owners could benefit both themselves and their slaves, he rejected standard Mississippi slave management practices. To stimulate picking, he devised a system of cash incentives, with slaves classed in several categories and a fifty-cent daily bonus given to the best picker in each. The incentives boosted production while rewarding slaves for their extra efforts. His concern about housing had a similar rationale: healthy slaves made better workers. Mason likewise specified to suppliers that fabrics from which slaves would make their clothing ought to be "good and strong articles" and of "good quality."[41]

To establish himself in proper style, Mason first needed to build a better residence. During the summer of 1852, overseer George S. Bradford directed slaves to haul lumber and start making bricks. The project became more expensive than Mason expected, primarily because hired white workmen, whom he criticized as "lazy" and "worthless," nevertheless commanded high wages. The house, not completed until early 1853, cost $1,250 instead of the $450 Mason hoped to pay.[42]

Bradford's sudden death in August 1852 afforded Lewis Mason an opportunity to put the Mississippi plantation under more trusted supervision. Fed up with Mississippians who were unaccustomed to having a privileged Virginian complain about their methods, Mason rejected a bid by John F. Bradford to replace his deceased brother as overseer. Mason instead gave the job to Charles W. Barham, overseer at Fortsville, the Masons' Southampton estate. Mason insisted that Barham "govern as I want him to govern." He expected him to be "economical, attentive, and humane to negroes, and horses." He had "borne with overseers too much already," Mason explained to his father. "Be exacting of them, as well as of negros, is a good rule, I think." [43]

Barham's numerous letters to Lewis Mason provide the most direct evidence available about the mental world of one of the elusive non-propertied whites from Old Southampton. The overseer, a member of Whiteheads Methodist Church who owned neither land nor slaves, insisted on taking all his "numerous" family to Mississippi, including his mother-in-law, notwithstanding Mason's fear they would "keep him bothered by sickness." Barham expressed himself in idiomatic prose. He boasted to Lewis Mason about "a Shot that I made with a wriffle" that felled both a goose and a swan. With breezy informality, Barham sent greetings from himself and his wife ("the old hen") to John Young Mason. Barham also readily questioned decisions made by Lewis Mason. He was "seprised" when the latter hired Sam Rawlings to oversee the Fortsville property. Although "he may be a better man than I think he is," Barham doubted whether sufficient "reffermation" of Rawlings's character had taken place. [44]

The transplanted Virginia overseer also proved able to manage the plantation more to Lewis Mason's satisfaction. Reports about runaways ended, and Barham found time to construct better cabins. He built up enough corn production to raise plenty of hogs and pigs: both the work animals and the slaves had adequate food. Although slaves at the Mason plantation continued to suffer frequent illnessess and occasional deaths, under Barham's supervision they apparently enjoyed better health than others in the neighborhood. [45]

Barham marveled at the productivity of cotton plants in the Mississippi Delta. He had "never seen cotton so butyfully branched in all my life." Some plants stood shoulder high and "so full of boals that the lims are weighted to the ground." Inevitably, the picking season extended into the next calendar year, so that the slaves finished harvesting one crop not long before the time they had to start planting another. The last shipment of cotton in March 1853 brought the total crop for 1852 to 173 bales. For 1853, they planned to plant fully 260 acres, hoping for one bale per acre. Severe rainstorms in late summer and an early frost shortened the 1853 crop to 147 bales, but the next two years yielded, respectively, 233 and 240 bales, each of which commanded around $10,000 at prevailing prices.[46]

As it became apparent that Barham could manage the plantation successfully, Lewis Mason reconsidered his idea of moving there. Mississippi whites were "ignorant" and "entirely selfish," he decided. The Democratic victory in the 1852 presidential election led him to muse about other possibilities entirely: a $1,200 office in Washington "sucking Treasury pap" might appeal. If Lewis Mason did not want to relocate to Mississippi himself, however, he remained confident that the family slaves would earn a better return there. He urged his father to sell more Virginia property and keep sending slaves to the Delta plantation.[47]

Circumstances intersected to undercut the Masons' Mississippi venture. Lewis Mason did not receive a federal office (and it is not apparent whether he actively sought it), but his father, John Young Mason, received one of the Pierce administration's premier appointments, ambassador to France. Although he did not speak the language, Mason welcomed the prestigious assignment. Financially, however, it proved ruinous. American ambassadors to France have always needed ample means, because expenses often surpass salary. Mason appeared to be a wealthy planter, but he was mired in debt and the move to Paris threatened to make a bad situation worse. Mason's style of living, his still substantial brood of younger dependents, and his belief that the American ambassador should entertain liberally all combined to make the family finances ever more precarious.[48]

Back in the United States, Mason's older sons, Lewis and John Young, Jr., made an inventory of their father's debts. They found, to their surprise and distress, that his obligations totaled $125,000, fully $20,000 more than any previous reckoning. They sent their father the bad news, warning that "you ought by all means to sell property which does not nett you more than 4 per c[ent]." Mason gave reluctant permission to start selling assets, including slaves, in order to scale down his debts. By so doing, however, he increased the pressure from his many creditors. "When people see property sold," his sons cautioned, "they may suppose there is danger and may come in for their part."[49]

First to go was the expensive home in Richmond. Even though their wealth came from plantation agriculture, the senior Masons had lost their attachment to rural life and preferred to live in town. Mary Ann

Mason especially regretted having to sacrifice her city home but sadly agreed to do so. Also liquidated in 1854 was Day's Neck, a corn and wheat plantation on the James River in Isle of Wight County, long managed by overseers. John Young Mason's prosperous son-in-law James Watkins Cook agreed to buy Day's Neck and most of the its slaves, thereby keeping the property in the family. Some Day's Neck slaves were hired or moved to other Mason properties.[50]

Although the Mississippi property represented the largest single family asset and potentially the most reliable generator of disposable income, the financial squeeze forced the Masons to consider putting it on the market. A distressed John Young Mason, in Paris, authorized his sons to sell his Mississippi plantation and all the slaves there (except Harriet and her family) if they could get the right price.[51]

Lewis Mason raised both practical and ethical questions about his father's decision. Under Barham's supervision, the Mississippi investment had proven profitable, generating large cotton outputs, to say nothing of the increasing value of the slaves there. Lewis Mason also had concerns about the welfare of slaves. Having struggled to impose his paternalistic values at the plantation, the younger Mason feared that sale of the property would inevitably compromise his obligation to faithful family retainers.

In early 1855, after first traveling to Mississippi to inspect operations there, Lewis Mason sailed to France to consult with his parents. John Young Mason must have persuaded his son that the family could not hold the Mississippi property. That fall, Lewis Mason placed an advertisement for it in a Memphis newspaper. Other members of the family suspected, however, that his commitment to selling the plantation was less than wholehearted. Roscoe Briggs Heath, another of Lewis Mason's brothers-in-law and a prominent Richmond attorney, cautioned against wrong-headed "tenderness for the negroes." Even if selling slaves was "disagreeable" because Lewis Mason necessarily held "some attachment for them," the "indulgence of that feeling" would do them no good. "If you keep any of them *now*," Heath admonished Mason, "they will very soon be sold for *debt*. And if you sell them at an undervalue to get good homes, you have no security that they will not be *resold* immediately. Get the best price." [52]

Although numerous potential buyers indicated an interest in buying the Mason slaves and plantation during the winter of 1855–56, Lewis Mason discovered that he lacked sufficient power of attorney to dispose of his father's property. The technicality delayed the sale for a year, much to the dismay of Mason creditors. However, a booming market for slaves enabled the Masons to benefit from the delay. They were able to insist on $1,350 to $1,400 for prime men and $1,100 to $1,150 for prime women. The land itself also appreciated: bought for $17 per acre in 1847, it sold nine years later for $35 per acre. Approximately two-thirds of the value of the property consisted of slaves.[53]

Jacob Thompson, a prominent Democrat soon thereafter appointed secretary of the interior in James Buchanan's cabinet, bought the Masons' Mississippi property in late 1856. Thompson, who already held a substantial adjoining plantation, grumbled that Lewis Mason demanded "the outside prices on every thing." By so doing, the Masons raised about $80,000 and reduced their debts to $17,000. The sale caused distress on two distinct counts, however. The only remaining Mason property, Fortsville, though relatively grand by Southampton standards, could not generate revenue on anything approaching the scale of the Mississippi Delta. So the family's income fell sharply. These professedly paternalistic and humane slaveowners must also have experienced some distress at having to sell so many of their slaves. However reassuring it may have been to entrust them to a supposedly like-minded person such as Thompson, Lewis Mason had enough firsthand experience with Mississippi overseers and the way they treated slaves to know that he had failed to live up to the standards that elite planters professed to honor.[54]

It fell to Lewis Mason to stabilize the family finances after the sale of the Mississippi property. He set about trying to pare costs while squeezing maximum revenue from Fortsville. Its annual production of cotton, brandy, corn, and wheat was worth around $3,000 in the late 1850s, with cotton alone providing more than half the value. The blacksmith shop earned another $1,000. To raise additional money, Mason hired out many of the adult slaves, relying as much as possible on child labor. Over twenty slaves hired out in 1858 and 1859 earned another $1,400 annually.[55]

His efforts were frustrated, however, by the continuing hemorrhage of family money in Paris. John Young Mason and his wife and daughters had become enamoured with Parisian life, and they entertained in high style. In 1856, for example, the "American Ball" in honor of George Washington's birthday attracted 800 guests to the Grand Hôtel du Louvre on the rue de Rivoli. In a letter describing the "magnificent affair," Mary Anne ("Mollie") Mason admonished her older brother Lewis against sending "dreary accounts" of the family's financial problems. His sons in the United States helplessly deplored the senior Mason's inability to economize. To make matters worse, John Young Mason in 1857 secured reappointment to the ambassadorship from his old friend James Buchanan. Longtime political cronies, Mason and Buchanan had worked closely together during the Pierce administration, when Buchanan represented the United States in Great Britain.[56]

The pain that the spendthrift ambassador inflicted on himself became an increasing source of concern and sorrow within the family. Public life had neither been "profitable" nor "a source of happiness," Mason glumly concluded. One of his daughters, who found her father "weeping like a child," feared that his "noble heart" would "burst." Mason's wife pleaded with a son-in-law to perform a financial rescue. "Poor old man," John Young Mason, Jr., observed: "His life has been one of excitement and triumph in what he desired most, an honest and well earned fame, but I fear in securing it he wrecked[?] his own happiness and much doubt whether the wreath that encircled his venerable brow, recompenses him for the many thorns that have harrassed and pierced him on the way." [57]

By 1859 Lewis Mason implored his father to trim expenses and save some of the money from his handsome salary. Send home the four younger children, Lewis Mason urged: future financial independence would be worth more to them than all "the glitter of courts, or the prattle of society." They were becoming "too fond of the excitement of Paris" and would have trouble adjusting to life in the United States if they stayed abroad any longer.[58]

John Young Mason's prodigality led to the ultimate humiliation in June 1859. Still needing to pay off the family's remaining debts and unable to persuade his father to save money, Lewis Mason had to sell Fortsville. He arranged terms with his obliging brother-in-law James W. Cook, who allowed the family to remain so long as it paid rent, with an option to redeem the property whenever it could raise the money. Once again, Mason beseeched his father to conserve the dwindling family estate. John Young Mason, engrossed in preparations for a Paris wedding between his daughter Mollie and Archer Anderson, son of the owner of the Tredegar Iron Works in Richmond, was not yet ready to reform his spendthrift ways. Only weeks later, on October 3, 1859, he suddenly died.[59]

One of Mason's Southampton admirers mourned the passing of "the gratest publick man of the day." [60] That hyperbolic judgment should be understood as an expression of local pride. Mason's most memorable contribution to public life was the notorious Ostend Manifesto of October 1854. In it Mason, Buchanan, and Pierre Soulé, the American ambassadors to France, Great Britain, and Spain, respectively, raised the issue of Cuban annexation in such a ham-handed and belligerent way as to reinforce northern fears about a slave power conspiracy. Passage of the Kansas-Nebraska Act earlier in 1854 had spawned the first stirrings of the Republican party. The authors of the Ostend Manifesto added fuel to the fire of North-South estrangement. They unwittingly contributed to the sectional impasse that ended the familiar way of life in Mason's Old Southampton.[61]

The spectacular liquidation of the Mason family fortune, soon followed by the upheaval of civil war, affected some of the children far more severely than the others. Mollie Anderson, married to one of the most prosperous businessmen in the state, remained in more than comfortable circumstances. Her husband found jobs at Tredegar after the war for two of her younger brothers, Simon Fraser Blunt Mason and St. George Tucker Mason. The Anderson family also enabled the Masons to maintain residence at Fortsville.[62]

The relationship between the Andersons and their kin grew difficult, however, when the less fortunate members of the Mason family became needy. Susan Harriet Barksdale Mason (usually called Harriet or Sadie), the widow of John Young Mason, Jr., who died during the war, experienced hard times, as did an unmarried Mason sister, Sarah Olivia Mason. By the mid–1870s the impoverished wing of the family was begging their better-off urban relatives for cash advances to pay off creditors, to buy a horse or a ton of guano, and so on.[63]

Lewis E. Mason, who worked harder than any other member of the family to stave off financial disaster, suffered crushing reversals. He and his sister Sarah lived in abject poverty at Fortsville during the postwar era. Once a member of the state legislature in the late 1850s, Mason eked out a precarious subsistence after the war by teaching school, attempting to farm, and receiving occasional small handouts from relatives. His tribulations more than fulfilled his mother's fears that his "dear Father's ruin" would also drag Lewis down. His sister Sarah, his sister-in-law Harriet, and a shadowy "Miss Philly" Jackson apparently judged Lewis Mason incompetent and tried to keep him under close supervision.[64]

By far the most bizarre sequel to the Mason drama centered around St. George Tucker Mason, the youngest of the brood, born in 1844, twenty-two years after the oldest, Lewis. St. George, a high-spirited young man who spent his formative years in Paris, joined the Confederate infantry at the start of war, soon after running away from boarding school. He transferred to the cavalry, where he ran up expenses that made the financial plight of the family that much more acute. His return to postwar civilian life proved no more successful than his earlier efforts to submit to the discipline of schooling. Whereas his brother Blunt worked at Tredegar for a decade and moved on to other comfortable white-collar jobs, George promptly soured on "business drudgery." [65]

Although determined to rebuild "the power and wealth of our family," St. George Tucker Mason decided first to satisfy his taste for adventure. He returned to France, joined the French Foreign Legion, and soon was assigned to a battalion in Algeria. George explained to Lewis, whose relationship to him was more that of a father than a brother, that this venture would cool his ardor and enable him to "return to you all a wiser and more experienced man," who would devote all of his energies to repairing the family fortune. Predictably, however, the move incurred additional indebtedness. [66]

The expatriate American found military service a welcome change from the vexations of civilian life. He commanded one company of an "excellent fighting regiment," among them many other restless souls from different parts of the world. The soldiers in his company were a "hard set" of "real adventurers." They committed more mayhem on each other and on civilians than on Arab raiders, who proved impossible to catch. Mason judged the indigenous Arabs unfit for civilization, and his opinion of the Algerian colonists was scarcely better: they were "a lazy set of insolent scoundrels, the scum of Spain and France." [67]

In 1874 Mason became a French citizen, explaining to his brother that he had "no desire to live in America," dominated as it was by Yankees who allowed "coloured men" to be "elected senators, representatives &c." He likewise mourned that free-labor agriculture at "poor old Fortsville" required contracting with "numberless nigger gentlemen" as tenants. Mason concluded that "the former fine, noble life of a southern gentlemen is really dead & buried; they are no longer free and independent as formerly, but now Southerners are simply voters and nothing else, they are forced to vote in order not to be crushed by yankee and negroe preponderance." The one thing that would bring him back to the United States, Mason insisted, would be a resumption of "our Confederate war." As soon as hostilities were declared, Mason vowed, he would leave

France "and hasten to our good old southern states where I hope our manly courage is not yet dead. May God Grant it!" [68]

Although still ready to fight for southern independence, Mason tired of service on the Algerian frontier. He sought a change of command and reassignment to France, recognizing that his company of cutthroats could never be posted at an "agreeable garrison" ("in ten days the town would be burnt and the inhabitants butchered"). Instead, Mason hoped to become the captain of a regiment in Paris composed of "good, little french soldiers who are obedient and behave well." He would then be able to find a suitable wife ("a good American or French girl") and would enjoy the pleasures of home, children, "comfortable slippers and hot tea." [69]

Mason suffered disappointment in hoping for transfer to a more congenial Parisian regiment. Nevertheless, his search for a suitable spouse was consummated in 1879, by which time he was thirty-five years old and displaying "many white hairs" on his head and mustache. Reporting to his impoverished brother Lewis, still "the head of the family," St. George Tucker Mason triumphantly announced his impending marriage to Emmeline de Fay, an eighteen-year-old "child" blessed with a "charming disposition" and "personal beauty" who would make "a good wife & a good mother." Moreover, Mason had determined that his bride-to-be, the daughter of a French "geometrician" who had lived twenty-eight years in Algeria as a land surveyor for the government, came from a family "as honorable as ours." Mason's "family pride" required that he check carefully the pedigree and references of his intended spouse: "I would have crushed my own heart sooner than to make love to a girl unworthy of my sisters." The couple had a son, St. George Lucien Mason, born in 1882. Two years later, the young mother was widowed when St. George Tucker Mason died on active duty in Hanoi, Vietnam, during the French conquest of Indochina. He may be considered the first American to die in Vietnam. [70]

FORTSVILLE, PARTS OF WHICH date to 1792, occupies a slight rise, perhaps three hundred yards back from a lonely road. A massive brick foundation, high enough to require five brick steps at the front entrance, undergirds the entire building. The wide symmetrical front includes two single story wings on either side of the two-story center. Because the center extends out at the rear, Fortsville would have the shape of a T if viewed from the air. Several more modest but similarly shaped antebel-

Fortsville, home of the Mason family. (*Courtesy of the Archives, Virginia Department of Historic Resources, Richmond*)

lum homes elsewhere in the county suggest that its harmonious architecture may have inspired imitation. No longer the seat of wealth or power, Fortsville hints only dimly of the vanished civilization it once nurtured.

John Young Mason's descendants have scattered, a process that began even before his death. A grandson bearing the same name did return to Southampton, serving as a school principal in one of the outlying county towns for several decades earlier in the twentieth century. Little is known about the fate of the many Mason slaves in the postslavery era. Negative evidence, however, speaks powerfully. The census of 1870 recorded few blacks in Southampton or in Coahoma County, Mississippi, who had taken Mason as a last name.

Perhaps justice was served in October 1867 when an ex-slave whose wife and children had been sent to Mississippi before the war was elected to represent Southampton in the Virginia Convention of 1867–68. Although that sequel did not involve the Mason family, it will occupy a prominent place in the subsequent narrative.

TWO

*The Diarists: Elliott L. Story
and Daniel W. Cobb*

Two Southampton residents, Daniel W. Cobb and Elliott L. Story, kept extensive diaries during the late antebellum period, the Civil War years, and Reconstruction.[1] Neither diary is complete, but most of the original volumes do survive. The complementary quality of the two diaries makes them uniquely valuable. Both diarists grew to maturity in smallholding families. Each diary therefore reflects a nonelite perspective. Though Cobb married a planter's daughter and Story had prominent friends, neither diarist thought of himself as part of the upper crust. The diaries, unlike most surviving manuscripts from the era, thus illuminate the experiences of the plain folk. Historians striving to recapture the "ever-elusive" *mentalité* of the Old South can find much to ponder in the two Southampton diaries, and all readers can appreciate the rich detail about the lives of two individuals.[2] At the same time, the two diaries illustrate vividly that antebellum southerners were not all of one mind. Cobb and Story had dissimilar temperaments and personalities. They viewed the same events through two quite different sets of eyes.

Daniel W. Cobb may have been the more typical Virginian of his era. Farming provided the focus for his life; his diary emphasizes agriculture and the weather. Cobb gradually expanded his holdings, building up a comfortable homestead and becoming a person of some stature in his neighborhood. His horizons, however, were limited. A pious Methodist, Cobb rarely read anything except the Bible and the sermons of Wesley. He never subscribed to a newspaper and only paid intermittent attention to politics and public affairs. His sources of information were oral.

Elliott L. Story, a teacher, farmed only for subsistence. Less tied to the

Old South's status quo than Cobb, Story welcomed innovation and new technologies. Though lacking any formal education beyond what was supplied by local schools, he read omnivorously. Newspapers enabled him to follow national and world affairs. Religious commitment, increasingly important in Story's later life, played a less central role for him at first than it did for Cobb. Conversely, Story was more active in local politics and served for a time as one of the elected magistrates on the county court. Story appears more modern than the provincial traditionalist Cobb.

The partisan identities that the two diarists formed in the late 1830s and early 1840s matched their distinctive mental outlooks. Cobb, a dour fatalist who was convinced that an avenging God had every justification for punishing sinful men, found the ideology of Andrew Jackson's Democratic party congenial. Cobb apparently agreed with its warnings that corruption and change endangered the pure republic. He shared Jacksonian doubts about the emergence of more complex economic relationships and institutions.

Story celebrated human achievement and identified with the progressive stirrings of his time. An optimist, he displayed greater confidence than Cobb in human rationality. Story therefore supported the party that promised to accept change and order it in ways that might provide benefits for all. In so doing, he embraced the Whig proclivities of influential patrons who sponsored his school.

As issues dividing North and South became politically more potent in the late 1840s and 1850s, Story and Cobb reacted differently. Here, partisan identity reinforced personal temperament. Southern Whigs placed a higher value on sectional accommodation than did southern Democrats. Story and his Whig friends viewed North-South polarization with far more alarm than did Cobb. They regarded secession as a tragic mistake for Virginia and the South. A very reluctant Confederate, Story thought the war an exercise in folly and madness. Had more southerners shared his views, it is difficult to imagine how the combination of southern resentment and fear could have reached sufficient proportions to trigger the disunion movement.

Unlike Story, Cobb did resent the North. He feared abolitionists and made no distinction between them and the Republican party. Also unlike Story, Cobb worried about potential dangers to the slave system. He entertained deep pathological suspicions about the black men and women who composed over half the population of the county and provided the

backbone and muscle that enabled him and other privileged Southamptonites to live in relative comfort. Although Story never expressed any of
the apprehensions that one might expect to find in a county which had
during his formative years witnessed the bloodiest slave insurrection in
American history, Cobb never exorcised the ghost of Nat Turner.

Predisposed to favor a militant defense of southern rights, the Democrat Cobb was exactly the sort of southerner who stood ready to march
toward the precipice so long as trusted party leaders took the lead and
trusted party loyalists marched with him. Cobb, in short, demonstrated
how the secessionist appeal took hold. Many others, especially in the
lower South, reacted similarly. To understand the upper South's initial
reluctance to leave the Union, however, one must recognize that many
did not share Cobb's readiness for confrontation. Only the outbreak of
war compelled southern Whigs such as Story to embrace the Confederate
cause.

The Civil War impinged more directly on Cobb than on Story. Because
his eldest son immediately enlisted in the Confederate cavalry and participated in many of the major Virginia campaigns, Cobb necessarily found
the war an engrossing spectacle. In the end, he lost both his son and his
slaves.

Cobb continued to farm for a living after the war, unlike Story, who
supported himself with a variety of official jobs. Cobb therefore experienced firsthand the wrenching transition to a free-labor economy. His
diary illustrates vividly how black strivings for economic autonomy and
political rights challenged the prerogatives of white landowners. Far
more regularly and faithfully recorded during the 1860s than Story's, the
Cobb diary reveals much about civilian life during wartime and Reconstruction.

ELLIOTT STORY, BORN IN 1821, began keeping a diary in January
1838, before his seventeenth birthday.[3] An alert observer, Story conveyed
a sense for the rhythms of everyday life. His diary includes a wealth of
information about farming, slavery, courtship, marriage, illness, death,
and religious experience. Because Story was gregarious, his diary men-
tions many different people. It shows how broader economic and political
developments affecting the mid-nineteenth-century United States resonated in Southampton.

Story knew that he lacked the advantages of wealth or inherited distinction. He aspired, however, to enlarge his horizons and improve his

Elliott L. Story. (*Courtesy of Daniel T. Balfour*)

status. Though raised in a farm family at a time when most young southern men followed their fathers into farming, Story had other ambitions.
Characterizing himself as "Independent," he sought opportunities that
his father had never enjoyed.[4]

Story would have rejected the idea that the Old South stood fundamentally outside the modern world. He combined a broad faith in liberal
rationalism and self-improvement. Advances in human knowledge promised a future in which men would act on the basis of reason rather than

passion. He admired scientific study because it revealed "the regular, systematick and harmonious machinery of the universe." To broaden his own grasp of the field, Story tried to discipline himself to read five pages of scientific texts each morning and evening. Technological innovations also impressed him. He was delighted to find that a railroad could whisk him thirty miles to Portsmouth in only two hours, and he commended a new rotary steam press in Norfolk as "one of the greatest improvements of the age."[5]

Story filled his diary with homilies that echoed Benjamin Franklin and anticipated Horatio Alger. He thought it irresponsible to spend a day idly. He prized "regularity and industry." Repeatedly he resolved to use his time well and to employ amusements "only as intermission." He considered it essential "to restrain every indulgence and inclination, from exceeding its proper bounds and from running out into extravagant desire."[6]

Story's outlook on life attracted him to the cause of temperance, the most widely supported instrument for self-improvement and national uplift in antebellum America. Though not as popular in the South as in the North, temperance apparently attracted the same constituency in both sections: upwardly mobile young artisans, tradesmen, and professionals who were receptive to schemes for self-improvement. Adolescent experimentations with alcohol may have left Story with a bad taste: "Intemperance the parent of wickedness to you I say FAREWELL," noted Story's friend Sam Willeford in 1839 after the two young chums had spent a weekend together, "loitering around." In 1843 Story attended several temperance meetings held at local churches and reported that "the temperance cause seems to be gaining ground in this community." Unwilling to join a temperance society or take a temperance pledge, possibly because he could see no problem with moderate consumption of alcohol and tobacco and because he feared the zeal of prohibitionists who would employ other than "gentle means," Story nevertheless remained sympathetic to the cause. He once argued before his debating society that ardent spirits caused more devastation than warfare.[7]

Story grew up in a far more oral culture than our own. Visiting and conversation occupied a substantial part of his time. He preferred to talk about matters of consequence, so that sociability could reinforce self-improvement. Discussions about "things relating to the cultivation of the mind" pleased him much more than the normal discourse among young Southamptonites, whose "sole and whole conversation" too frequently consisted of "so much useless jabbering about Belles and Beaux, about this ones fascinating manners, and that ones genteel person, dress and equipage[,] about this ones wedding and that ones courtship." [8]

Story was not, however, a humorless prig. He took real pleasure in "the animating story, the pleasant joke, the cheerful anecdote." Swapping yarns with a "good fellow" such as Lewis W. Bishop stirred Story's "natural propensity for fun and jollity" and kept him from being too serious. One of the most animated scenes in the diary describes a "long-to-be-remembered journey" to Petersburg by wagon in December 1842, during which Story and Sam Willeford amused each other with "merry jokes and cheerful tales," defying a howling storm with "peals of laughter." Story also enjoyed the company of several older men. He found Patrick Rowe "humane, liberal, candid and honest." The "jovial" Rowe's "only fault" was an addiction to "ardent spirits," which he struggled to overcome. Elderly John Moore, a neighbor and father of his good friends George and Orris Moore, captivated Story by recounting his experiences as a youngster in Philadelphia at the time of the Revolution. Moore could "tell about the doings of those days with the accuracy of a historian," Story marveled. [9]

Education provided Story with a window to a wider world and a career that enabled him to escape from farming. Between the ages of eight and eleven, he attended local schools and studied under several different male teachers. Story judged Brookes R. Trezvant an excellent instructor until he became too preoccupied with courtship. Joseph Pretlow, "too indulgent with his schollars," succeeded only "tolerably well." Obliged to help his father with farm work, Story attended school only irregularly between his twelfth and fourteenth years. The family included a younger brother and four younger sisters, and his father had no other source of help at the time. [10]

At the age of fifteen, in 1836, Story took a job in a store at the county seat, Jerusalem, assisting Theodore Trezvant, a relative of his former teacher. As a fringe benefit Story could read the newspapers and thereby acquire "a great deal of useful information." Story pursued his new career despite his father's disapproval. The elder Story doubtless regretted losing his son's labor. Young Story's mercantile career proved brief. A dangerous fever in August 1837 put him under the care of a doctor. The illness coincided with a decline in the store's business, in part because the owner treated his customers indifferently but primarily because construction of the Portsmouth and Roanoke Railroad through the southern part of the county curtailed Jerusalem's trade, shifting it to a new settlement, the future city of Franklin, where the railroad crossed the Blackwater River.[11]

In 1838 several prominent men in the Black Creek area northeast of Jerusalem, among them James Holmes, Joseph Pretlow, and Dr. Carr Bowers, the local school commissioner, solicited Story to open a school. One year later, in February 1839, Bowers and Holmes agreed to build a schoolhouse. Public funds covered only 40 percent of the cost; the two patrons contributed the remainder. By the end of March 1839, young Story and his pupils occupied the new building. For the next fourteen years, until 1853, Story presided over the Black Water Free School.[12]

Story earned $100 per year from the state Literary Fund, earmarked to support the education of poor children, so long as he could raise an equal amount from parents able to pay. Toward the end of each year, Story visited parents in the neighborhood, knowing that his job would continue only if a nucleus of paying students attended his school. Bowers worked to maintain the $100 subsidy and to persuade the sometimes discouraged Story to keep teaching. Without Story, Bowers insisted, the school would probably close.[13]

Story and his students put in a longer school day that averaged eight hours, less in winter but more in summer. The typical day lasted from 8 A.M. to 5 P.M., with an hour for lunch and "playtime." The only significant vacations, each several weeks long, occurred in August and December. Student attendance regularly fell during the busiest agricultural seasons in spring and fall and also on rainy days. Story's brother Frank and sister Martha were among the students at the school during Story's early years of teaching. The three of them walked an hour each way along a path through the woods, because the school was located over three miles from the Story home.[14]

As Story gained teaching experience, he displayed increasing confidence. Once "almost a purgatory" to him, school became by 1846 the place where he felt most at home. He characterized his students as "attentive, industrious and cheerful" and "advancing rapidly in their studies." By laying down and enforcing a set of well-understood rules, Story minimized discipline problems. He required his pupils to write compositions, something that had never been demanded of him. Although some students found writing irksome, Story considered their efforts "remarkably good considering their ages and opportunities."[15]

He became good friends with Matthew Harris, a progressive Quaker farmer who sent several children to the school and visited it "oftener than any one of my patrons." Story and Harris shared an enthusiasm for public education and pride that it had become well supported in the Black Creek neighborhood. "Some may boast of more fertile farms of larger purses and of larger possessions," Story noted, yet if they lacked wisdom and knowledge, they would remain "incapable of properly enjoying their many blessings." Story and Harris agreed that no nation or people could be "truely prosperous and happy" without good schools.[16]

Story gained perspective from the cosmopolitan patrons of his school, notably Dr. Carr Bowers. Wealthy and widely read, Bowers represented the county in the legislature on a number of occasions between 1814 and 1843. A prominent Baptist layman, he also enjoyed a reputation for philanthropy. Bowers, however, did not fully share the young Story's confidence about human reason and progress. The "plain peaceable hardworking" Bowers had "no great faith in men." He thought the rod indispensable in handling lazy students; Story preferred verbal appeals and considered the rod a last resort.[17]

Story often borrowed books from his patron's well-stocked library. He admired Alexander Pope's *Essay on Man* and Laurence Sterne's *Tristram Shandy*, he discovered Shakespeare, he devoured political biographies, and he attempted to fathom a geological text. Story observed in 1848 that there were few other persons "whose opportunities for reading are no better than mine, who have read more than I have during the last ten years."[18]

Story most enjoyed reading and teaching about history, especially the period of the American Revolution. He repeatedly reread Mason Weems's "interesting and delightful" life of George Washington until he knew the book almost by heart. Story found William Wirt's life of Patrick Henry similarly engrossing. His historical curiosities were not, however, narrowly national. He studied William Grimshaw's English history and a translation of Julius Caesar's *Commentaries*. He tackled Washington Irving's *Life and Voyages of Christopher Columbus*, an 800-page volume, and he read a translation of Adolphe Thiers's four-volume history of the French Revolution. After systematically working through Charles Rollin's four-volume ancient history, he pronounced the work "very entertaining."[19]

Story found history a source of instruction as well as pleasure. Alexander the Great's astonishing early triumphs resulted in part from his original "temperance, moderation, and simplicity." As these traits gave way to "voluptuousness, cruelty and extravagance," he became a less capable leader. Story's study of Greek and Roman history led him to doubt the wisdom of choosing military men for civil office. Faced with the presidential nominations of General Zachary Taylor and former general Lewis Cass by the two major parties in 1848, Story thought "we ought to look back at other nations and see what this great love of military fame has brought them to, and profit by their examples." [20]

Story's abilities gained him the confidence of several prominent men, but he originally felt barred from polite society. He did not receive an invitation to Emily Joyner's wedding in 1840. When a "large and pompous collection" of mourners attended the funeral of a local dignitary, Story observed that class inequalities operated in death as in life: "How different from many an humble soul, whose passage to the tomb is scarcely enough noticed to cause them to say 'He's dead.'" Although resentful of gentry snobbishness, Story recognized that wealth and social position could not satisfy his own system of values. Were he to win a lottery and no longer need to remain in an "obscure schoolhouse, unable to clear hardly a hundred dollars a year," Story fantasized, he would continue to live simply, put most of the money to draw interest in a savings institution, and devote his time to the acquisition of knowledge. "I enjoy more real happiness in my present state in life," Story judged, "than if I had money enough to make a fool of me." [21]

By his mid-twenties, Story developed a circle of friends from comfortable and privileged households. In 1847 he and the other bachelors founded a debating society that met twice each month on Saturday evenings. These occasions pleased Story, who always welcomed opportunities for self-improvement. Equally satisfying was the way debating brought together "good companions," making them "easy in each others company." An audience of young ladies stimulated the debaters to make good impressions; debating lost "half its interest" when the ladies failed to appear. [22]

Several times during the late 1840s Story participated as a "waiter" at a wedding. These ceremonies, typically held during the slack agricultural seasons of late summer or early winter, involved a carefully orchestrated series of events that extended from Thursday evening through the weekend. In mid-August 1846, for example, Mary M. Joyner married Thomas Boykin. The marriage took place at the Joyner home at 8 P.M. Six young women and six young men performed as waiters, accompanying the bride and groom in the parlor on the main floor as they said their vows in the presence of a minister. The waiters then helped to serve supper to one hundred guests in the Joyner basement, which had been arranged in a "very pleasant and commodious" manner. The meal continued until around 11 P.M., after which the waiters played parlor games and engaged in "the usual talk for such occasions." The ritual continued the next day, with the Joyners providing a dinner for the wedding party in the early afternoon. A procession of buggies thereupon conveyed the waiters and the young couple to the Boykin home in the upper county. There another elegant supper awaited the celebrants.[23]

Story found the protracted wedding festivities an ordeal. The combination of too little sleep, too much to eat, the dusty buggy ride, and the hot August weather left him and the other waiters "languid and dull." When he finally returned home on Sunday evening, Story described himself as "almost completely broken down and sick." He also complained about the stiff formality of the wedding party, which inhibited conversation and caused time to pass slowly. Recognizing that events of this type were designed to give eligible unmarried women the chance "to make impressions," Story remained unimpressed. Their "distant reserve" prevented any "general ease and enjoyment."[24]

During Story's first years as a diarist, Americans wrestled with economic uncertainties and seized upon political parties as a means to establish more effective popular control over public life. The two developments were related. The perplexing combination of economic opportunity and dislocation, intensified by cycles of boom and bust, left many men receptive to new political appeals.

Through the decade of the 1830s, Southampton enjoyed good prices for its principal cash crops, pork and cotton. In February 1839, for example, Story's father received fourteen cents a pound for the cotton he shipped to Norfolk and eleven cents a pound for his bacon. Soon thereafter, however, cotton prices tumbled. From late 1839 through 1848, the white fiber often sold for less than half its early 1839 price. Virginia's cotton production, never large, decreased by half between 1839 and 1849. Pork prices suffered similarly. By early 1842 the prices of hogs had fallen below $5 per hundred pounds, and bacon sold for seven and a half cents. An influx of western animals drove prices even lower in 1846, when bacon prices slumped to six and a quarter cents. As prices for its cash crops skidded and the national economy moved from bad to worse, Southampton became mired in debt. "I do not suppose there has scarcely if ever been so universal a failure, of men in every line of business as at present," Story observed in January 1843. "Those who a few short months ago were considered safe for almost any amount, now have creditors, groaning over their losses, without a shadow of hope for the future." [25]

Story's diary shows how traditionally localized and small-scale economic activities were beginning to face competition from more distant large-scale enterprises. He had shoes made by a local craftsman, Uriah Bracey, using leather purchased from his neighbors, the Moores. The clothes Story wore, however, included a mixture of hand-tailored and "ready made" garments, with the former apparently cut from manufactured cloth. He enlisted two of his sisters and a tailor in Jerusalem to cut, fit, and sew coats and "pantaloons." To get ready-made clothing, he visited Norfolk. Once he encountered a proprietor who insisted "that every piece I put on was the most perfect fit he ever saw, when some I could hardly get into, and others hung like a cloak around me." With proper caution, Story apparently could find suitable standardized sizes. [26]

Story likewise had farm implements made and repaired by his blacksmith friends, William Lankford and George Moore, and Story himself replaced the wooden handles. He also contracted with a local artisan to build a cart. However, umbrellas, which came in handy during Southampton's frequently rainy weather, must have come from a distant manufacturer. When Story had a house built several years later, he purchased nails, doors, and window sashes. [27]

As local patterns of exchange and reciprocity gave way to a more complex national economy in which people increasingly bought and sold goods at a distance rather than face-to-face, disagreements about economic issues helped to sharpen political rivalries. President Andrew Jackson and his managers, playing upon public anxieties about economic change, built the Democratic party into a formidable national political organization. Opponents of Jackson and his chosen successor, Martin Van Buren, coalesced into an opposition political party, the Whigs. By the late 1830s, two mass-based national parties competed for support. Democrats, warning that banks and promoters of paper money posed an insidious threat to popular liberty and economic opportunity, maintained a hard-money antibank stance. Whigs insisted that Democrats had thrown the country into an economic trough by pandering to popular fears and creating financial uncertainty. Convinced that all would benefit from economic development, Whigs promised that they could better enlarge the sphere of opportunity. [28]

Story's diary records the emergence of competitive two-party politics in Southampton. The key moment occurred in 1839, when Southampton's Whigs and Democrats grappled furiously to control the county's seat in the House of Delegates. The rival candidates circulated public letters to explain their stands on public issues, visiting dignitaries made speeches in their behalf, and local promoters entertained voters with such events as fish fries. With four outlying polling places established for the first time, voters no longer had to travel to the courthouse, and turnout soared. Democrats emerged with a sixty-vote margin out of more than seven hundred votes cast. Their success spurred the Whigs to work even harder. Southampton remained a hotly contested partisan battleground throughout the antebellum era.[29]

An avid newspaper reader and gregarious conversationalist, Story developed political awareness long before he could vote. By 1840 "politicks were running very high" in Southampton as Whigs and Democrats across the country squared off for the first truly partisan presidential election. Story decided to study more about politics, "not with the view of becoming a politician, but in order to enable myself to judge correctly in these matters." The famous log cabin and hard cider campaign gave Southampton's Whigs cause to celebrate: they carried the county by six votes for successful presidential candidate William Henry Harrison, as 750 voters trooped to the polls.[30]

It appears that Story's patron, Carr Bowers, tried to remain politically independent. In 1839 Bowers showed Story a "dramatic production" he had written satirizing both Whigs and Democrats. Four years later, Bowers startled local politicians in both parties by announcing his candidacy for the legislature less than a week before the election. The Whigs decided to allow Bowers an unobstructed race against the incumbent Democrat, William A. Spark, whom Bowers then upset by a nineteen-vote margin. "If I had a vote I should give it to Bowers because I believe him honest and capable," Story noted.[31]

Bowers, well known and widely respected, could still win a local election in the early 1840s primarily on the strength of his own reputation, rather than a party endorsement. His 1843 victory was, however, the exception that proved the rule. Parties had acquired a near monopoly power to choose candidates for office. Most voters (and many adult white males who were not yet eligible) identified with one party or the other. For Story, the optimistic rationalist who welcomed progress and change, party identity was foreordained. From the first vote he cast in an 1846 legislative race, Story invariably supported Whig candidates.[32]

Story's party affiliation had communal as well as individual dimensions. Voters in Virginia before the Civil War specified their preferences orally, and neighborhoods often voted with near unanimity. Whigs generally ran strongly in the upper part of Southampton County where Story lived, including the Black Creek neighborhood where he taught school. Even if Story's patron Bowers thought of himself as organizationally independent, he was ideologically Whiggish and regularly voted for Whig candidates, as did most others in Black Creek. Bowers's wide-ranging intellect and his commitment to education and philanthropy predisposed him toward Whig values, even if he was far more skeptical about human nature than the young Story.

Story's attachment to his county of origin offers additional insight into his political outlook. Whigs generally sought to develop already-settled regions through education, new technology, improved transportation, and better use of natural resources. Democrats, on the other hand, favored expansive rather than intensive development, by widening the frontiers of settlement and adding to the pressures for "the further enlargement of national boundaries." Story's satisfaction with teaching and "the pleasant associations with the neighbours about my old schoolhouse" strengthened his commitment to Old Southampton. Aware that some people could "never rest satisfied with their situation in life" and were "ever eager for a change," while others kept moving "from a love of novelty" or an expectation of bettering their condition, Story regretted that so many suffered the "haunt and torment" of believing that other locations and occupations would "answer their purposes better."[33]

Story knew perfectly well why so many natives of eastern Virginia had abandoned the land of their birth. The struggle "to dig a scanty support out of our barren soil in this poor region of the country" had discouraged many farmers. In Story's neighborhood they had to "toil and strive the year round" to gain a bare subsistence. The "close and stiff land" in much of upper Southampton held average yields well below the more favored plantation regions in the lower county. Story certainly recognized the attractions of better land. His readings about the Southwest and conversations with people who had visited there made him keenly aware that "our industrious farmers" had to settle for far less than what others elsewhere got "from the same labour." He found it surprising that emigration from

Virginia "is not greater than it is." Story himself had "often longed to go and seek my fortune" in the West, suspecting that he could live comfortably on "two hundred acres of the rich soil of Tennessee." Story, however, placed more value on the ties that bound him to "old Southampton" and to "old Virginia." He would not abandon the soil upon which he "first drew breath." For Story, relationships to family, friends, and neighbors took precedence. His system of values was broadly corporate rather than individualistic: life was best lived when "brethren" could "dwell together in unity" and neighbors could "live social and friendly." [34]

His father's death in 1845 left Story the male head of the household, responsible for his widowed mother, a younger brother, and two younger sisters. Story's teaching salary provided the family's principal source of income, but he also supervised a limited amount of farm work performed by his brother Frank and one or two hired free blacks and slaves. Story himself, even though giving lip service to Jeffersonian notions that farming was "the occupation for which man seems to have been chiefly designed by his creator" and "in which our health and constitutions are most likely to be preserved sound and vigorous," recognized that he would find it too arduous a way to earn a living. "Unless I was toughened a great deal from what I am now," Story wrote in 1847, "it would soon wear me out." [35]

A series of major transitions made the years between Story's mid-twenties and the age of thirty an eventful period in his life. He confronted his father's death and a sister's fatal illness, he suffered rebuffs from two young women he tried to court, and he experienced religious conversion. It appears probable that the stresses created by Story's growing awareness of personal mortality and his inability to attract a spouse became catalysts for his religious awakening.

Story's diary for the year his father died is no longer available, but his demise at the height of the sickly season, on September 3, 1845, suggests that Benjamin Story was one of the many Southampton residents fatally afflicted by the chronic fevers of late summer and early fall. The diary does, however, provide a sad record of the far more protracted decline of Story's sister Mary, who lived for over four years as a bedridden invalid. The wife of Elijah Williams and mother of a young son, Jimmy, Mary Williams fell ill in early 1847. She became "low-spirited," and Story found it depressing to visit her. "Sickness and all its attendant evils" were the only topics in which she took an interest. Shortly before she died, in June 1851, she told Story that she was confident of going to Heaven.

"Oh!" the diarist exclaimed, "how valuable is religion at such times as these." [36]

Buffeted by illness and death within his family, Story also had to deal with romantic heartaches. He was attracted by Mary Hare Pretlow, five years his junior, who had earlier been a student at his school. Mary, the daughter of a Quaker family, apparently rejected his suit. When James Massenburg, the son of a local doctor, successfully wooed her, Story remarked ruefully in his diary about "having attempted what Jim had successfully accomplished." Not long afterwards Story tried again. The new object of his affections, Catherine Joyner, also had attended Story's school. A frequent visitor at the Joyner house, located near his school, Story had a "particular respect" for the family. Unfortunately for Story, Catherine did not prove receptive to his overtures. A cryptic diary entry records the receipt of a letter from her "which looked very pretty and sounded very well, except the conclusion. Its last dolorous notes fell on my ear like a death knell." Neither "time or doctors," Story mourned, could cure the "withering chilling effects" of her letter. [37]

Raised in a Baptist family, Story had attended Joyners Baptist Church. He found the minister there an "honest and good man" but "one of the most fatiguing speakers I ever listened to." Story enjoyed seeing "the same old familiar faces" but found the sermons tedious. This circumstance apparently prompted him to shop around on Sundays. Finding that the minister at Black Creek Baptist Church spoke more effectively and attracted a larger audience, Story often attended there, as did many of his friends. [38]

Church services provided more than religious edification. No other institution in local society served so effectively to bring people together. The social function of churches was never more visibly displayed than during the "protracted meetings" or revivals that sometimes stretched as long as a week in late summer or early fall. Denominational lines, not sharply drawn by most Southamptonites, blurred even further during these meetings, when Baptist and Methodist ministers collaborated to hold the attention of large audiences drawn from miles around.

It was at such a meeting, held in October 1847 at Nottoway Chapel, a Methodist church near his home, that Story experienced conversion. Influenced by friends he described as irreligious or deists, Story had once been "deeply tinctured with deism myself" and had looked upon religious conversion "as a superstitious excitement of weak minds." A severe attack of bilious fever (typhoid) in 1843, however, made him realize that he was "far from being ready" to die and left him with "a great desire for religion." With his anxiety about the subject steadily increasing, he resolved before attending the Nottoway gathering to yield to "those heavenly impressions" if they touched him. They did, and he did. Nothing "can be such a solace and a comfort in times of discouragement and adversity as religion," Story concluded.[39]

Curiosity about his conversion experience found Story needing to explain what had happened. Both James Holmes and Jesse Lankford, prominent residents of Black Creek and patrons of Story's school, engaged him in lengthy discussions about religion. A defensive tone crept into Story's notations on the subject. Some, including those of undoubted piety, ridiculed "the meetings where these great excitements prevail," Story observed. He continued to justify protracted meetings, however, on the grounds that people had "a great diversity of temperaments." Many "enjoy their religion best in this way, by giving vent to their feelings." Story's more active interest in religion prompted him to read the Bible straight through, which he had never done before, and sent him to search out scriptural references about baptism, a much-discussed issue in Southampton, where many of the faithful including Story tried to weigh the competing interpretations offered by Methodists and Baptists.[40]

Story's horizons began to shrink during the 1850s. He devoted less time to reading, and his intellectual curiosity tended to focus on conventional religious topics, especially the question of whether early Christians practiced baptism by immersion.[41] A series of misfortunes and reversals diminished his earlier gregariousness and inquisitiveness. The last two surviving volumes of his diary, which begin in 1851, record Story's passage from optimistic young adulthood to a narrowed, more provincial middle age. Before long, calamities on a national scale reinforced his personal tribulations.

As late as July 1851, Story wrote enthusiastically about teaching, thinking that no other employment could give him "so much delight." Even though his students performed less capably than a few years before and refused to write proper compositions or to "exert themselves much," Story remained dedicated. That attitude changed during the long unpleasant winter months in early 1852, when Story frequently found himself "gloomy and depressed," suffering through "one of the most lonely seasons of my life."[42]

By late 1852 Story had almost decided to enter the mercantile business, but he backed off at the last minute and decided to teach another year of school. Soon, however, he received an offer to join Robert G. Edwards in an already established business at Franklin, the emerging metropolis of the county. Rejecting the counsel of his patron Carr Bowers, Story plunged ahead. In order to acquire his share of the firm's inventory, Story borrowed money from at least one prosperous neighbor, Dr. Robert Murray. Within months the press of business was such that Story had closed his school and stopped making entries in his diary.[43]

The store's transactions were conducted more by barter and credit than by cash. Story and his partner ordered wholesale quantities of products that local farmers might wish to buy—dry goods, flour, salt, salted fish, sugar, coffee, and fertilizer. In exchange, the store owners bought all kinds of goods produced in the county—especially cotton, pork, peas, corn, and lumber. Story confessed in retrospect that his inexperience made it "quite an awkward business to me at first." The store earned small profits even though sales during the busy spring and fall seasons proved brisk. Analysts for R. G. Dun and Company credited Edwards with "good character and standing" but doubted his abilities as a businessman.[44]

Then disaster struck. In August 1854 congestive fever felled Edwards. Fearing that he lacked the necessary experience or capital to run the business himself, Story searched unsuccessfully for a partner. A month after Edwards's death, Story sold the firm's goods at 5 percent below wholesale cost. He netted $6,000 in cash but found that $5,000 was still owed him by customers scattered throughout the county. During the next year Story continued the troublesome task of collecting money. Otherwise unemployed, he finally settled about 80 percent of the accounts.[45]

At this low ebb in his life, in July 1856, Story, the seemingly confirmed thirty-five-year-old bachelor, married Mary Eliza Judkins, the daughter of James H. Judkins, a successful farmer who owned eleven slaves and lived in the neighborhood. No details of the courtship survive because Story had abandoned his diary at the time. It is apparent that Story never had reconciled himself to a single existence; he acknowledged being "not quite satisfied" and having "an aching void." The behavior of married men made Story ambivalent about matrimony, however. Only infrequently did he see much of former companions such as George Moore, James Devany, and Robert Pretlow. "I hate for old friends and associates to get married most on this account," Story confided to his diary. "They scarcely ever feel the same to me afterwards." He likewise complained that married men too often conversed only about pedestrian details of farming.[46]

When Story resumed regular diary entries in January 1857, he and his wife were living at the Story homestead, recently purchased from his widowed mother. Story also bought most of her personal property along with the interest in the house owned by his brother and a sister. Circumstantial evidence suggests that Story's father-in-law provided the newlyweds with financial assistance. Story thus "settled down to farming" to support his new wife.[47]

Story's farm produced only modestly. He ran short of corn in 1857, after a bad crop the year before, but he thought the seventy barrels harvested in 1857 would carry him through 1858. Story also raised peanuts, first grown commercially in the area during the 1850s. He tried to boost peanut output by enriching the soil with a mixture of leaf compost and lime, and he battled to fend off the crows, who were more eager for peanuts "than any thing I ever saw planted." Story also sowed peas, both Irish and sweet potatoes, and two and a half acres of oats fertilized by guano. He and his wife peeled and dried apples from their orchard, because Story had "scruples of conscience" against making brandy. His biggest cash crop was probably pork. By penning up hogs and fattening them on peas in the late fall, he rendered the creatures "much improved" before the annual winter killing season.[48]

For Story to live in reasonable comfort, he needed to supplement the income from his farm. Involvement in local government enabled him to do just that. Elected in 1856 to the county court, a position that combined administrative and judicial duties, Story presided each month over a local court in Vicksville, north of Jerusalem, or in Franklin. Though he found it disagreeable to deal with characters who had run afoul of the law ("a very ungovernable and not a very sober crowd"), Story did earn money for his troubles. He also received pay for serving as clerk of the board of overseers of the poor, helping his friend Billy Murfee keep county tax records up to date, and presiding over elections and keeping voter lists. In 1860 Story won reelection as a magistrate. He and three other Whigs from his voting district easily defeated a slate of Democrats, including the other diarist, Daniel W. Cobb.[49]

Curiously, Story became involved in local politics despite growing doubts about partisan competition. Apparently sharing a point of view widespread in both North and South by the early 1850s, Story had lost his "relish for politicks." The Virginia constitution of 1851, which allowed voters to choose county officers for the first time, introduced "too much Partyism," Story thought, "for the best interest of our community." Observing in 1857 that politics was "nearly worn out" in his neighborhood, Story welcomed the lull. He feared, however, that politicians would find "some new issue" to stir voters "into a fury again." [50]

Story felt sufficiently prosperous to have a new home built. The project, begun in June 1857, continued for over a year, with most of the work done by a carpenter named Lyttleton and Story's old chum and brother-in-law George Moore. They promptly framed and raised the timbers, aided by two hired hands; balloon frame construction evidently had not yet reached Southampton. It was late autumn before they attached weatherboards, made shingles, and laid the brickwork (doubtless for a chimney). Interior carpentry continued until the next summer. Story reported the house complete except for lathing in June, and he was able to occupy it at the end of July 1858. His sentimental nature made him regret abandoning the old house where he had lived since birth, parts of which were cannibalized to provide a porch for the new house. The new structure must have pleased his wife's genteel tastes. It included a staircase similar to that in the home owned by the eminent Carr Bowers. [51]

Story's plans for the future were, however, entirely at the mercy of dangers beyond his control or understanding. Outbreaks of feverish diseases routinely occurred in the late summer and early fall in low-lying Southampton, which was dotted with swamps and lacked good drainage. Heavy summer rains in 1857 and 1858 made a bad situation catastrophic. Outbreaks of dysentery and typhoid fever ravaged the populace and struck deadly blows at Story's immediate family. Within a two-week period in August 1857, the scourge carried away his mother and his younger sister Martha. Doctors could do nothing to avert the calamity. Another of his younger sisters, Elizabeth, soon lay dangerously ill, and typhoid killed Giles Whitney, one of his best friends. Story himself experienced a severe attack of rheumatic fever that left his knees so swollen and painful that for several months he could walk only with the aid of crutches. The condition persisted: almost two years later he received electric shock treatments to improve his knees. Weakened and depressed, Story found himself unable to do anything more strenuous than light hoeing in his garden. When an opportunity presented itself in November 1858 to open a school in Jerusalem, he turned back from farming to teaching. [52]

The cruelest blow soon followed. Mary Judkins Story had survived childbirth in June 1857, even though her baby daughter died within hours and the mother suffered from a high fever afterward and a case of typhoid fever later in the summer. One year later, in June 1858, she experienced a miscarriage following a severe attack of measles and dysentery. A third pregnancy terminated normally in September 1859 with the birth of a boy, but an attack of puerperal fever killed Mary Story two days later. Her grieving husband mourned the loss of "the tenderest tie that ever bound me to earth." His sister Nancy, the wife of George Moore, volunteered to raise the motherless infant.[53]

The conjunction of personal affliction and national disintegration sapped Story's spirits. A month after Mary Story's death, John Brown attacked Harpers Ferry, throwing Virginia into an uproar and casting a long shadow over the upcoming presidential election.

DANIEL W. COBB, Southampton's other diarist, had a personality and world view that differed markedly from Story's. Cobb, who had already reached his thirtieth birthday and had recently married, started to keep a diary in 1842.[54] Whereas the largest part of Story's diary features the musings and enthusiasms of a young single person, all the voluminous Cobb journals reflect the perspective of an older man who faced more immediate responsibilities. Solitary and lacking close friends, Cobb had a greater need than Story to record his innermost thoughts. Cobb's diary bares the soul of an introverted, humorless personality. He hardly ever let a day go by without making an entry. Story, more gregarious than Cobb, only made intermittent diary entries after his early thirties.

Cobb's diary recounts a long struggle to build a one-horse farm into a plantation. His sense of self-worth required that he provide his growing family with the comforts of gentry life. By doing so, he achieved greater material success than Story. Success, however, exacted a high price. An unhappy marriage blighted Cobb's spirit. He did not share the drive, especially apparent in Story's young adulthood, to supplement a scanty formal education. Cobb, even though regarded as a person of stature in his neighborhood, remained narrow, while the more literate Story won appointment and election to significant county offices.

Cobb's diary functioned primarily to allow the author to get complaints off his chest and to preserve his equilibrium. His wish to communicate with a future audience was, at best, subsidiary. He warned that "the reader mus punctuate as he reads" and "look over bad spelling and incorrect writing." Readily acknowledging that "mi[s]takes is n[u]merous with me," Cobb contended that his diary could be "undestud by those who wishes to read." Why did someone who had taught school for over a decade make so little effort to express himself correctly? In part he pleaded haste: "I make many errors in writing owing to hurry." Cobb confessed, too, that "I wright with bad penns[.] I cant buy to throw a way after the 1st point is worn." He also blamed his wife: "I would rite more Correct," he noted, "but it is seldom I ever take my seat to rite but they be a tongue clash in the house which throws me out of harnes." Unlike Story, an omnivorous reader who visualized words and therefore spelled correctly, Cobb lived a world of spoken rather than written language. Vernacular prose and seat-of-the-pants spelling showed that his cultural horizons were primarily oral. His orthographic imprecision had one durable legacy: attempting to honor Major Joseph E. Gillette, who commanded his oldest son's cavalry regiment, Cobb named his youngest son "Mager." Born in 1862, Mager Cobb lived until 1936, always spelling his name just as his father had.[55]

Cobb's diary offers only hints about his early life. Born "poore" with "non of this world['s] good[s]," Cobb spent most of his youth working on his father's modest lower-county farm. He did, however, manage to attend school for parts of five or six years, enough to qualify him for "school keeping." From his late teens until the age of thirty, Cobb supported himself as a teacher. In his own subsequent view, he had spent these years foolishly. Instead of saving money, he traveled across the Southwest, leaving himself few assets with which to start married life. Cobb wished he had lived more purposefully but recognized that "milk spilt on dry ground cant be gathered up."[56]

One event in Cobb's young adulthood stood out. Mordecai Yell, a Methodist evangelist, converted Cobb in 1835 and shortly afterward baptized him in the icy waters of Brush Creek in Robertson County, Tennessee. Since boyhood, Cobb had regularly prayed, sometimes even "prostrated on my face upon the coald ground," but he did not know "the nature and the substance of the converting power of God." Misled by those who said it took "from 10 to 12 years to get Religion," Cobb expected that God would communicate with him in a "tremendious grate voice as loud as the peals of thunder" to proclaim that his sins were forgiven. "I might have waited until dooms day & would not have heard any such voice," Cobb noted ruefully. Yell persuaded Cobb that the repentant sinner must actively seek God's forgiveness rather than wait pas-

Daniel W. Cobb. (*Courtesy of the Franklin-Southampton Area Chamber of Commerce, Franklin, Va.*)

sively for God to act. Cobb's diary includes many vigorous defenses of religious revivals. They showed "the mark of an Almighty God the great judge." Some of Cobb's happiest dreams involved listening to "greate and able speakers," who inspired him to overcome his inhibitions and shout aloud.[57]

The Story and Cobb diaries show that fundamental differences separated the two men. Story, who welcomed progress and innovation, had a comparatively modern outlook. Even though Story probably never set foot outside Virginia, while young Cobb traveled extensively, Story was more cosmopolitan. Cobb, who often calculated prices in shillings and pence and who recalled the "oald stile count" of the pre–1752 Julian calendar, remained rooted in a more remote era.[58] Nevertheless, Cobb was a more typical man of his time than Story. Cobb's ideas about folklore, religion, economic change, politics, and slavery reveal much about traditional thought in the rural antebellum South.

Cobb held a number of folk beliefs about the weather. By observing conditions during the first twelve days of January, for example, he thought one could predict the weather for the next twelve months. A pleasant day on January 4 would ensure good weather for the spring planting in April, the fourth month; but a violent storm on January 9 would portend trouble for the September harvest. Cobb also believed that the moon influenced the weather, indeed, "that most of things is governed by the moon entirely." It might be better, he speculated, to "count time as the Indians did," with a lunar calendar having thirteen moons in a year. Each lunar month would have as many cloudy weeks as there had been cloudy days during the "four first days of the [new] moon." If the lunar calendar exerted such an influence, could one still trust an annual weather forecast based on the first twelve days of nonlunar January? Cobb did not confront the dilemma.[59]

Cobb's folk wisdom about weather prediction and the occult powers of the moon could not easily be reconciled with his belief in an all-powerful God. "I'm not like sum [who] believe the God of heaven has nothing to do with the weather—for he rules all things," Cobb avowed. Surely a God who could "destroy the whole world in the twinkling of an eye" had the power to control weather and to make rain fall in South-ampton County. Indeed, during an alarming summer drought in 1851, when it appeared that a storm had passed through with "much Thunder and pearceing lightning" but only a few rain sprinkles, God intervened. With quaintly mixed metaphors, Cobb celebrated the skill of a "Captain that was able to stear the ship and to command the clouds and rains to be steady and to throw a plenty of water on our thursty lands." But why should God empower sinful man with the capacity to discern future weather patterns and thereby penetrate his inscrutable will? Logically, such knowledge would remain a divine prerogative. For this reason, or perhaps also because moon-based weather prediction failed to live up to Cobb's expectations once he had begun to farm for a living, there is infre-quent mention of the subject after the first few years of his diary. Cobb, however, never entirely abandoned the folk beliefs.[60]

Repeatedly, Cobb acknowledged that God alone could determine whether Southampton's crops would reach successful fruition. Although always hoping that he and his neighbors might receive divine favor, Cobb knew that undeserving sinners could never earn or deserve such a blessing. Furthermore, a conundrum was involved. Whenever "plenty is around us," men would become disobedient. Wealth, "the rival of God in the heart," was thus "so dangerous a possession." People would never humble themselves before God until scarcity "stare[d] us in our faces."[61]

Yet it had once been different. In 1776, Cobb believed, people had subordinated all self-seeking rivalry and had gathered "as one Band compleately." God had favored America, but with what result? "We are scattered and broken as if allmost in the darkest of Hethanism," Cobb regretted, with "every man for himself." He believed that God temporarily suspended normal human proclivities in 1776. Retrogression was therefore fated, and the founding fathers wisely recognized as much. Only the "blessed laws of the land" could keep man's "beastly" nature in check. Story also regarded the American Revolution as a centrally important event. No books pleased him more than biographies of George Washington and Patrick Henry, written in the heroic mold. But Story, who celebrated the achievements of his own age, did not share Cobb's retrogressive assumptions.[62]

Cobb did not consider new technologies essential or even desirable. When he learned in 1855 that some people had broken down telegraph poles and wires, suspecting that telegraphy had caused a drought, Cobb responded sympathetically. "If it be so," he reasoned, "I am for putting a stop [to] telegraphing news and go[ing] back to the oald slow way[,] the mail that prevents not the rain." Was spinning cloth by hand a "slow way to get a coat now a days"? Cobb acknowledged as much, but when winter weather kept his slave women indoors, he put them to work hand spinning, because "half a loaf is better than no loaf at all." To treat the diseases that frequently wreaked havoc in low-lying Southampton, Cobb favored traditional home remedies. He administered alarming concoctions—mixtures of vinegar, brandy, salt, black pepper, oil, and paregoric "well stirred and drank"—persuading himself that the medicine had "not yet failed."[63]

By the time he started keeping a diary, Cobb had already developed a firm partisan identity, one that dovetailed conveniently with his other views. Ambivalence about economic change and a preference for the "oald slow way[s]" usually translated into Democratic loyalties in Jacksonian-era politics. Cobb offers a case study that contrasts directly with Story, the Whig who admired innovation and new technology.

Even as Cobb worked diligently to advance the fortunes of his family and to allow them to live with greater gentility than he had known as a young man, he clung stubbornly to the hope that traditional arrangements could be preserved and a virtuous society restored. Banks? Paper money? Cobb viewed the economic miseries of the early 1840s from the perspective of an uncompromising Jacksonian Democrat. He hoped banks could be "intirely dun away" with and that business could be conducted with "nothing but a hard currency." Some said that there was "not a nuff of that brite evill," but Cobb thought otherwise. Its value could be arbitrarily doubled; "I know we can live as people did in times of old."[64]

Cobb filled the first diary he kept with partisan barbs. "This day a Whig has been on the seat 12 months [in the] presidency," Cobb noted in March 1842, "and Oh! that the four years was at an end." He blamed the Whig administration in Washington for hard times, in which rich and poor suffered together and bankruptcies had become epidemic. The prosperity that people had enjoyed under Democratic presidents between 1834 and 1838 had been buried by low prices, higher taxes, and severe indebtedness. Never did Cobb deviate from his Democratic attachments. Rather than follow politics in close detail, however, he relied on the Democratic party to uphold his interests.[65]

Maintaining absolute authority over Southampton's slaves and free blacks probably headed Cobb's list of vital interests. Abolitionists infuriated Cobb, who believed that slaves would never rebel without insidious external influences. All insurrections were "headed by white persons," he insisted. Turncoat whites were "the meanest thing" in the world, "wors than a rattle snake in the grass." They must have played a role, he assumed, in the suspected plot to blow up a theater in Petersburg during a Fourth of July celebration. Cobb also pointed an accusing finger at a favorite antiabolitionist target, "oald Britain." In 1842 he thought the United States should declare war because of the *Creole* case. Britain had "treated us a miss," Cobb complained, by providing safe harbor in the Bahamas for a shipful of slaves who mutinied while being transported from Virginia to New Orleans. Throughout the antebellum era Cobb faithfully noted any rumor about slave discontent. Anxieties most often developed during the late-summer slack season, when farm work lightened and protracted religious meetings took place. Then, Cobb never needed to be reminded, Nat Turner and his accomplices had struck.[66]

Story and Cobb differed unmistakably in self-image and outlook on life. Story certainly had unhappy intervals, especially after his first wife died in 1859. Throughout his life, however, and particularly during his

[63]

younger years, he recognized that he was one of the most well-informed persons in the county. He also considered himself a good teacher and took pride in the achievements of his students.

Cobb, on the other hand, periodically exhibited serious depression throughout the thirty years he kept his diary. In June 1842 he pronounced himself "miserable," with "no inducement to live in this life." He thought he had enjoyed himself "less than any other human Male or female that has lived 30 years." Musing suicidally, Cobb wrote that he might "put a stop" to his existence if there were no hereafter and if he were no more than a beast. He knew, however, that as an "accountable being," he must await God's call. In his worst moments, Cobb seemed to invite the divine summons: "If it was the will of God to take me a way I am almost per-swaded in my mind that it would be best [for] my hearte seameth almost to shuder with-in me." Rather than remaining on earth, Cobb later in-sisted, he would rather live with his children and Christ in paradise. Cobb felt better when his "religious feelings" were "roused," but more often than not he remained vulnerable to depression. Even then, religion helped: "All that consoles me when in my dark and gloomy hours is to look in to eternity," believing that "when I die I shall be happy for ever more." [67]

It takes no unusual psychological insight to identify the reason for Cobb's distress. His marriage was not "pleasing and satisfying." He and his wife were "unequal[ly] yoked" and "in opposition" to each other. "If one ox of a yoak fails to do his duty," Cobb noted, "the faithfull one has a hard urquesome task to perform." Rather than giving Cobb the love and support he craved, Mary Jane Cobb constantly fretted and scolded. "The one [on] who[m] all happiness should depend is the one who causes all uneas[i]ness[,] discontent and lowlyness of spirit," Cobb mourned. "My feelings is always pressed and my sole greaved at my disappoint-ment in life." Cobb thought marriage would bring him "much happiness and content," but it proved to be "as different from the way I expected as White from Black." [68]

All the evidence about the relationship comes, of course, from the hus-band's hand. Cobb, however, wrote compulsively about the troubles af-flicting his marriage, so that his wife's complaints and sometimes her ac-tual language are recorded in his diary. From the beginning, the two Cobbs were mismatched. Mary Jane Little, not yet seventeen at the time she married the almost thirty-year-old Cobb in June 1841, probably had been a student in the local school he taught. Her father, Jesse Little, a wealthy planter, disapproved of his oldest daughter's choice and refused to have more than a minimal ceremony. The wedding included no waiters or supper, as was expected in Southampton's polite society, only the minister and no guests except members of the family. Cobb recalled that Little did "not so much as give my wife a new dress to be married in," telling her that "if she wanted any thing for me to get it." "Our marriage was nothing more than two of his servants," Cobb complained.[69]

Not surprisingly, Cobb nursed a continuing grudge against the Littles. "Her family do not treet me with no respect only what they is oblige," he once wrote. Cobb's resentment boiled over in October 1851 when his wife's younger sister, Rebecca, married a prosperous physician, John W. Gurley. Cobb refused to attend the lavish wedding ceremony the Littles provided for the couple. His diary continued to echo with complaints that the Littles were treating the Gurleys far more favorably than they ever had the Cobbs. His feelings about Jesse Little smouldered until the father-in-law's death in 1863. Little's other three children "swam in his urnings for 20 years passed," Cobb charged in 1861, whereas he and his wife got "the least of his estate" and "lived hard."[70]

Perceived snubs from his in-laws reinforced Cobb's self-image as a poor man. Throughout his life he identified himself as one of God's poor, who had to "indure the fatigs & burdens o[f] the day," the cold of winter and the heat of summer. He and other poor farmers had a "hard loansome time" and had to "bare it ruff." By contrast, "the rich enjoys sleep untill brekefast with a servent to fan him[,] the best of drink & finest of diet[,] the best quality waring apparel and in fact every thing pleasant." Moreover, the rich had the poor "in their clutches . . . they bare on them heavy and hard." Cobb remained confident, however, that "the Lord is with the pore as well as the rich." Indeed, Cobb eagerly interpreted New Testament strictures against the rich as evidence that God stood closer to him and the other exploited poor. "The Rich has there good things on earth in this life," Cobb wrote, but the poor would have "their Comforts in the world to come." Because Cobb was building up to a level of slaveholding and farm production that placed him above 90 percent of southern white families, his poor-mouthing may seem suspect. His frame of reference, however, was the Little family, who refused to respect him and did not believe him fit company—"and the reason is because I am poor." His "unkind and unthankful wife" and her father expected more from Cobb than he could provide.[71]

To make matters worse, Mary Jane Cobb did not share her husband's piety, particularly his strict Sabbatarianism. He considered Sundays best devoted to churchgoing and quiet contemplation, on grounds that God had commanded men "to do nothing on the Sabbeth that might be don on [a] weak day." Cobb therefore always shaved on Saturday night. Sunday emergencies, for example when he had to retrieve a destructive runaway hog at a neighbor's, bothered his conscience. He suffered similar qualms after buying some freshly caught fish on a Sunday. Though he loved a fish dinner ("now if that wa[s]n[']t nice tell me what is"), Cobb confessed that he would rather never eat another fish than "miss heaven . . . and being with Christ." [72]

Sabbatarianism became a source of friction between Cobb and his wife. He disliked the widespread practice of Sunday visiting, thinking it improper to spend the Sabbath "stralling over the neighbour hood to here unnecessary news [or] to here tattling tales." He acknowledged, however, that "when company comes in we must attend to it for the politeness of the land requires it." Cobb and his wife apparently disagreed about whether one should invite Sunday guests ahead of time and whether it was proper to cook fresh meals for them. Mary Jane Cobb also grated on her husband's religious sensibilities by interrupting his prayers. Cobb complained bitterly in his diary about instances when he was "in the act of praying on my knees," but she, "instead of being on her knees her self," would be raising a fuss or causing confusion. Once while he attempted to pray, she was "quarling with the servants and whipping them . . . [and] it appered to me she dun it to disturb me." Cobb resentfully concluded that "my wifes ways[,] acts and tongue" were "a grate Cross to my religious views." [73]

Cobb's marriage became especially unhappy during the 1850s. He and his wife had a ghastly argument in June 1851, and she blurted out that home was a "hell" to her and the sight of Cobb a "torment." If she were a man and "could keep her rights," Cobb quoted her as saying, "she would go a way never to come back again." She then accused Cobb of "running after every negrow & woman that will let me have any thing to do with them." The accusation, for which there is no corroboration in the diary, left Cobb's mind "almost destroyd." [74]

Blowups of this type occurred with depressing frequency. Though Cobb considered his wife's behavior entirely unreasonable, his diary makes it apparent that she wanted desperately to escape the treadmill of repeated childbirth. Mary Jane Cobb's fourth child was born in February

1851, when she was still only twenty-six. Soon thereafter, her sister died in childbirth. Married to a man for whom any ardor she may once have felt had long since cooled, Mary Jane Cobb attempted to curtail his sexual access. Cobb's "pleasures," always "fiew," became fewer.[75]

Their relationship reached a miserable impasse in the late 1850s. Mary Jane Cobb bore one more child in 1853 but then managed to avoid becoming pregnant for several years. Following the birth of her sixth child, Junius, in July 1858, she decided to resist all Cobb's sexual overtures. She renewed accusations about his infidelity, denouncing her flustered husband as a "hog" with no principles who came from "one of the meanest trifflingest no count" families. In the weeks and months that followed, Cobb "almost despaired of life." For over a year Mary Jane Cobb remained unwilling for her husband "to cooperate with her at any time," leaving him "to take a bed a lone and to have nothing to do with her in that respect." The unhappy wife kept up a drumfire of insults, declaring that Cobb's presence was disagreeable to her, that he was mean and degraded, and that she cared no more for him than for any "Tom, Dick or Hary."[76]

The norms of polite society required, however, that private woe be concealed from public view. In private, Cobb thought his family "more devided than any family I'v ever known," and he feared that "a family divided Cant stand," using the same scriptural reference that Abraham Lincoln employed in a different context. "To the eyes of the people at large," however, he needed to appear "well satisfied." Cobb and his wife continued to live in the same house, and he had to support her so long as they did. Mary Jane Cobb was constrained as well by the need to preserve appearances. During one of her frequent visits to her father's family, Cobb noted that "she says she would rather be with them than at home with me . . . and if it was not for shames and the worlds talk I doant believe she would stay with me at all."[77]

Cobb complained bitterly about being "opposed in all of my undertakings" and allowed no "enjoyment," while still being required to provide his ungrateful wife with "all to ware and to eat." Moreover, she insisted on having three house servants, thus depriving Cobb of laborers he wanted for farm work. To see other families living happily together "gives me pain and sorrow," Cobb wrote enviously; "it greaves me to the verry sole." His own "help mate," by contrast, did nothing to maintain a harmonious household. Cobb never wondered whether other apparently happy marriages, trapped on the same treadmill of relentless pregnancy but required to maintain correct appearances, suffered from afflictions similar to his own.[78]

Cobb's domestic troubles coincided with physical ones. During the 1850s, when his marriage hit rock bottom, Cobb suffered an assortment of maladies. Chronic constipation and bloody piles plagued him. More debilitating was a kidney or urinary problem, which Cobb blamed, perhaps correctly, on "the gravel." When he tried to "make water," he experienced a burning sensation "like pepper water passing threw me up in my belly." The problem flared suddenly in 1854 and continued for several years, leaving him in constant pain and greatly reducing his physical strength.[79]

Cobb's religious sensibilities obliged him to disdain the common faults of white southern men, drinking and fighting. He certainly did so during his early years as a diarist. Thereafter, however, he retreated from the unequivocal positions he had once occupied. Young Cobb considered "ardent spirits" to be "poison," he condemned "the awful affects of intoxicating liquors," and he hailed the rapid spread of temperance societies. Nondrinkers enjoyed better health, he believed, "and above all they provided well for their household and their family." Cobb frequently cited alcohol as a cause of death: intemperance, liquor, or a "brandy fit" destroyed many Southampton men. He deplored the drunken rowdiness that frequently broke out at Southampton's court day.[80]

His temperance stance did not, however, prevent Cobb from becoming a brandy distiller. His apple and peach trees, planted during the 1840s, began to yield ample harvests a decade later. Cobb first hoped to make vinegar and medicine with his apples so as to "lay good examples for the rising generation." He soon changed his mind. Drunkards killed by drink, he decided, would be "not much missed." Furthermore, he rationalized that they would kill themselves with "Whiskey Rum & Jin" if brandy was unavailable.[81]

To maximize the profitability of his orchards, Cobb purchased the requisite mill, press, and still. First operated in 1856, the distilling equipment ran on a daily basis during August and September. In 1859 he produced eight or more forty-gallon barrels of brandy and an unspecified amount of cider. Each barrel of peach brandy that year commanded a premium price of $48, almost twice the $25 for apple brandy. Cobb's still earned at least $280 in 1859, three-quarters or more of what he received for his cotton crop. Cobb himself apparently did not drink, but unlike Elliott

Story, whose temperance principles remained firm and who peeled and dried apples rather than converting them to brandy, Cobb supplied alcohol to his slaves and his guests, and he obviously made large quantities available on the market.[82]

Cobb and Story both criticized violent behavior, but Cobb's response became more ambivalent. His reaction to an incident in 1850 suggests that his professed opposition contained elements of hidden fascination. That summer two neighbors, George Clemmons and Joseph H. Barham, attacked each other at close range with loaded shotguns. The exchange mangled Clemmons's left arm, whose shot at Barham therefore missed. Shouting that he had been wounded, Clemmons ran to locate a doctor. "He lost a greate deal of blud as he made off," Cobb recounted. It was a "bad business," Cobb insisted, "dangerous and sinfull." The vivid diary entries suggest, however, that he was intrigued as well as repelled.[83]

Cobb entered a similarly animated account of the 1856 clash between Calhoun Barrett and George A. W. Newsom. A prominent merchant and hotelkeeper who earlier had represented the county in the state legislature, Newsom "spoke in a slanderous manner" to a lady who refused to dance with him at a party. Barrett, a relative of the insulted woman, chastised the intoxicated Newsom. Later that night Newsom accosted Barrett, who retaliated by wounding Newsom slightly with a six-shooter. The latter vowed to kill Barrett or die trying. The next morning, both men armed themselves with double-barreled shotguns. When they encountered each other, Newsom was riding in his carriage. Barrett wounded Newsom with his first shot and "blowd off his head" with the second. Newsom "fell dead from his buggy" without ever getting off a round. A month later, the grand jury cleared Barrett, concluding that he had acted in self-defense.[84]

Cobb must have gained vicarious satisfaction from writing detailed accounts about violent altercations. Although living a life of private torment and resentment, he held himself under rigid control, ignoring slights from the haughty Littles and refusing to respond to his wife's taunts. He appears to have kept his grievances to himself and his diary. However unhappy the marriage, there is no evidence that Cobb and his wife ever came to blows. He probably never consciously recognized why he found violence appealing as well as abhorrent.

Cobb often made note in his diary when he experienced nightmares. He dreamed vividly about occupational hazards, such as being chased by large oxen, and he found crowds in Petersburg disorienting. Far larger than any town in the Southampton area, Petersburg was a thriving regional commercial center. Not long after one of his visits there, Cobb dreamed that he had lost his horse and cart amid the throngs and that he had searched four or five days to locate them. Combining his anxieties about blacks and about cities, Cobb dreamed that he and his wife were staying at a Petersburg hotel. "I saw 2 large black rusty negrow men on the same bed with my-self and family," whereupon he called for aid from his "boys" and the landlord. The imagined intruders nevertheless escaped. The dream about menacing black men in bed reflected, of course, the ultimate white male racist bugaboo.[85]

Cobb once experienced a terrifying glimpse of the apocalypse, as depicted in the Book of Revelation, with the earth "splitting open in every direction so as to swalow up houses." The dream, Cobb reported, "alarmed me much" and made his night "much interrupted," because he felt powerless to escape. Yet he recognized Halcum Davy, one of Jesse Little's slaves, who seemed "not to be alarmed at all." Why did Cobb dream that God, his "friend out of site," had allowed him to remain paralyzed with fright while a slave stood unafraid? Cobb never experienced conscious guilt about exploiting slaves. Could the vision have hinted at some unconscious qualms? Whatever its significance, Cobb found it impossible to interpret: "The sign of it I know not."[86]

Did Cobb feel the same ambivalence as Story about staying in the East while others made handsome fortunes in the West? Apparently so. He dreamed that he had packed a two-horse wagon to go to Texas, but a friend persuaded him not to go. Perhaps the friend did him a favor. Later that same year, Cobb "wrested bad" because of "disagreeable dreams of travling & being in unpleasant places and in not agreeable company."[87]

Cobb's marital problems also affected his dreams. At one of the most troubled moments in the marriage, Cobb experienced a nightmare about two prominent dead Southamptonites, William Sebrell and Captain Edward Butts. The two, he dreamed, were doing bizarre things such as cutting out children's clothes and filling barrels with dirt. Alarmed to have dreamed about the dead, Cobb blamed his "dissatisfied mind," made so because his wife was "a fuss all ways at table."[88]

Between 1843 and 1859 Cobb transformed himself from a marginal smallholder to a prosperous agriculturalist.[89] He and his slaves worked unremittingly. He craved both economic security and recognition as a gentleman. His quest reminds the modern reader of the fictional Thomas Sutpen, whose strivings were so unforgettably depicted by William

Faulkner. Both Cobb and Sutpen appeared successful on the eve of the Civil War, but for each, success proved illusory. Each would sacrifice his eldest son and much of his fortune in the doomed effort to preserve the southern way of life.[90]

When he started farming in 1843, Cobb and his wife lived in a "lonely smoky cabin," aided at first only by one horse and three slaves: a man, a woman, and a boy. His wealthy father-in-law, Jesse Little, provided the land and probably the slaves; Cobb had to supply the planning and management. Lacking the animal power or manpower to generate large harvests, Cobb was further handicapped by low crop prices. The year 1848 was an especially bad one. Still in debt, Cobb feared that he might have to "brake up house keeping."[91]

Cobb's fortunes improved rapidly around midcentury, stimulated by rising prices for farm products. Cotton, which had fallen to a ruinous six cents per pound in 1848, rebounded to better than ten cents during the next several years. The value of his peas and pork also appreciated. Cobb took full advantage of the opportunity by buying better horses and increasing his slave labor force. Between 1846 and 1851 he appears to have owned only five slaves, but he hired five others by 1850. Cobb, who already controlled an abundance of land, thus secured sufficient labor to start producing in quantity and earning regular profits. Able to plant only six acres in cotton as late as 1849, he steadily expanded his cotton acreage to around thirty by the mid–1850s. Soon he paid off what he owed for his new house and other improvements. Cobb must have felt a mixture of pride and relief as he settled in full his obligations to the haughty Jesse Little.[92]

By the end of the 1850s, Cobb moved close to the planter class. Consistent profits enabled him to buy more slaves, horses, and agricultural implements. Growing surpluses of corn, cotton, peas, pork, and brandy coincided with an era of favorable prices. By 1859 his net worth approached $20,000. Rising slave prices provided the backbone of his wealth: he valued the eleven slaves he owned in 1859 at $12,000. Cobb's increasingly comfortable home and its furnishings, his animals, implements, and outbuildings, plus 700 acres of land (most still owned by Jesse Little but willed to Cobb and his wife), together had a value of only $5,400. Obviously Cobb was more a "labor lord" than a landlord.[93]

Cobb estimated his annual crop production at $2,000. This figure included 250 barrels of corn, worth $3 each, or $750; between seven and ten bales of cotton, worth on average $375; 8 or more barrels of brandy, worth at least $280; 20,000 pounds of corn fodder (blades and tops), worth $200; 150 bushels of peas, worth $150; and 4,000 pounds of slaughtered hogs, worth $300. A substantial portion of the food products and fodder was for home use. The brandy and cotton were, however, cash crops. Cobb also sold his surpluses of other products, especially peas and pork. Cobb probably sold about half ($1,000 worth) of his annual farm production.

Economic success began to gain for Cobb the respect he craved. Though he still resented Jesse Little and considered him the "hardest man to pleas" that he ever had known, Cobb deliberately made friendly overtures that Little could hardly spurn. For example, when Cobb butchered a steer, he sent a quarter to Little. (Without refrigeration, beef would soon spoil; by dividing it for prompt use, several households could enjoy a welcome variation from the dietary routine of salted pork.) Cobb's neighborly gesture required reciprocation, and reciprocation inevitably conveyed a recognition of Cobb's status in the community. Once Cobb sent the Littles three quarters of freshly killed beef (Little had enough slaves so that the meat would not have gone to waste). Within a week, Mrs. Little invited the Cobb family to visit for the first time in years.[94]

In other ways, too, Cobb gained stature. He helped to underwrite the repair of a nearby bridge that carried the Jerusalem Plank Road over Assamoosic Creek. He joined with several prosperous men in the neighborhood to build a schoolhouse for Barn Tavern Academy (Cobb contributed $40 of the requisite $100). He served as a trustee for the academy, where his eldest son, Asbury, attended, and he took in several of Asbury's classmates as boarders. Cobb also sponsored dinners for Barn Tavern students on the Fourth of July and at "sendoff" time in late November. Starting in 1855, he became a poll keeper in Jerusalem on election days. Local Democrats in 1860 honored him with the party nomination for one of his voting district's four seats on the county court, although the political allegiances of the district ensured that Elliott Story and three other Whigs would win the election.[95]

Cobb's educational interests brought him directly in contact with Story in 1857, when Cobb hired Story's sister Elizabeth "to take charge of a small school at my house." Cobb's younger children doubtless would have been among the pupils, and Elizabeth Story planned to board in Cobb's home. Story took his sister there by buggy over muddy roads on Sunday, February 1. Apparently he stayed for an hour or more. A week later, however, Elizabeth Story quit. Story noted that she "had been sick all the while she had been there and seemed to fear she should not have her health if she continued." Cobb's diary suggests that she had already "beg[ged] off" by Tuesday, February 3, though she waited until the weekend to return home. It appears that Elizabeth Story quickly decided against staying at Cobb's. Her professed health fears may have provided a face-saving excuse. Given what his diary reveals about the tensions in Cobb's household, her decision is hardly surprising.[96]

ALTHOUGH MANY DIFFERENCES SEPARATED the two diarists, Cobb and Story had several similarities. Not only did they live in the same county at the same time; they also occupied broadly similar positions in society. Neither would have been counted among the county elite, but both stood well above the common folk of Southampton. In the heavily stratified and relatively static social order of tidewater Virginia, both Cobb and Story achieved more prominence and stature than their fathers.

Cobb and Story also had similar religious commitments. Both experienced conversion in their mid-twenties and remained pious Methodists for the rest of their lives. Initially, the two diarists displayed differing religious temperaments: Cobb repeatedly insisted on God's overwhelming power and man's depravity, whereas Story, more optimistic about human capabilities, embraced religion in order to confront mortality and death with more assurance. As the two men aged, however, their religious sensibilities converged. Story, severely buffeted by the deaths of all his close kinfolk, became more devout. Cobb, increasingly comfortable but deriving no real satisfaction from his comfort, lost some religious zeal.

Nevertheless, the differences separating the two men command attention. It has often been argued that southern Whigs and Democrats disagreed only about inconsequential matters and that a shared commitment to the slave system ultimately overrode partisan rivalries, ensuring that the great majority of white southerners became good Confederates.[97] The examples of Cobb and Story require that these important generalizations be examined with more subtlety.

Both Story and Cobb owned slaves, both identified themselves as southerners, both supported the Confederacy, and both opposed Radical Reconstruction. What ultimately stands out, however, is Cobb's far greater commitment to the old order. Story deliberately sought ways to make a living without relying on slave-labor agriculture; Cobb eagerly pursued the traditional ladder to wealth and eminence. Story appeared confident—perhaps overconfident—that progress and change could be

reconciled with his southern loyalties; Cobb had an emotional investment in every aspect of the Old South's status quo.

Story's and Cobb's diaries, which offer rich detail about the texture of
life in the antebellum era, also offer many insights about secession, war,
and Reconstruction, when Old Southampton and the Old South found
themselves engulfed in an irreversible torrent of upheaval and change.
The trauma of war and Reconstruction saddened Story, but he remained
hopeful that the new order might bring "blessings in disguise." [98] Cobb,
who believed that the very foundations of society had been swept away
by Yankee cruelty and Radical fanaticism, remained entirely unreconciled.

THREE

Life, Labor, and Leisure

THE AGRICULTURAL CYCLE SHAPED life in Old Southampton. Most whites and almost all blacks labored on farms. Year in and year out, the agricultural routine maintained its seasonal rhythms. Winter tasks, although frequently interrupted by adverse weather, included cutting timber for firewood or mauling it into rails, grubbing out overgrown fields, and butchering hogs. For five months from early March through early August, an unrelenting sequence of plowing, planting, and cultivation proceeded until the crops could be laid by. The late-summer slack season afforded whites (and to a lesser extent, blacks) a breather before the labor-intensive fall harvest that stretched from latter August into November. Vicissitudes of weather and the almost equally unpredictable movement of prices made each new year a fresh gamble. No matter how conscientious, the farmer only exercised partial control over his fate.[1]

People worked hard in Old Southampton, but they did not work all the time. Nobody, white or black, performed regular labor on Sunday, which was given over instead to churchgoing, visiting, and relaxation. If religious activities provided the principal opportunities for sociability, they were not without competition. Court day, muster, and the annual general parade also brought people together. So did corn shuckings, weddings, debating clubs, and the occasional visiting circus. Politics, too, functioned as a form of popular entertainment.

SOUTHAMPTON'S AGRICULTURAL ECONOMY, although having its own distinctive features, was a variant of the "mixed farming" or "general farming" pattern that prevailed across much of the antebellum upper

[75]

South. Diversified agriculture in Virginia dated from the late eighteenth and early nineteenth centuries. Wheat supplanted tobacco as the state's principal cash crop, and almost all farms produced a variety of grains, vegetables, and livestock.

An influential study of two upper piedmont counties by historian John Schlotterbeck suggests that between 1800 and 1850 a "dense network of social and economic exchanges between local residents" superseded the drive to produce for external markets. A "social economy," emphasizing stability and self-sufficiency, provided the "cement" that held the community together. Only in the last antebellum decade, as railroads penetrated the interior and wheat and tobacco prices surged, did agriculture in that area once again move decisively toward production for external markets.[2]

Other parts of the state remained tied to market agriculture. The Shenandoah Valley became a major wheat-exporting region during the antebellum years. Tidewater locations with good access to river transport likewise generated commercial outputs of corn and wheat. With the Erie Canal closed several months each winter and railroad links to midwestern wheat-growing regions not completed until after 1850, Virginia wheat producers enjoyed favorable transportation access to customers in the urban Northeast. Spurred by reformers, notably Edmund Ruffin, some tidewater farmers applied scientific agricultural techniques to increase yields. During the late antebellum period Virginia ranked fourth in the nation in wheat production as it raised more wheat and corn than any other state east of the Appalachians. Farmers in eastern tidewater counties immediately adjacent to Norfolk likewise discovered the advantages of an expanding northeastern market for fresh fruits and vegetables, which could be shipped by water to Baltimore or New York. Between 1840 and 1860 truck and garden farming emerged as major enterprises in the Norfolk region.[3]

Southampton's small farmers attempted primarily to meet their own needs. Diarist Elliott Story, atypical in that he had a teaching salary, nevertheless reflected an outlook that was widely shared. Hired laborers and his younger brother raised modest outputs of corn, wheat, potatoes, cotton, peas, pork, and garden crops on the Story farm. They sought to supply the household for the next year, "without buying." Story took a dim view of market agriculture. He thought the "close stiff land" in his neighborhood could not sustain large outputs. Even though it had become "customary . . . to raise a few hundred weight of bacon for market," Story suspected that fattening hogs ate enough corn to undercut any profit. The small farmers of upper Southampton helped each other through neighborly corn-shucking gatherings in October and November and hog-killings in December and January. They paid the owners of local gristmills in kind rather than with cash.[4]

In Southampton, however, many farmers sought more than self-sufficiency, even before the last prosperous antebellum decade. To a greater extent than in the upper piedmont region studied by Schlotterbeck, those Southampton farmers with larger landholdings and labor forces appear to have had a strong market orientation. Daniel Cobb's diary, the most extensive available record of an antebellum Southampton agriculturalist, shows that he made frequent notations about prices and adjusted his mix of crops to maximize his cash return. He produced $2,000 worth of farm products annually by the late 1850s, with at least half destined for market. Many similar examples could be cited. For example, Story's prosperous father-in-law, James Judkins, finished the 1857 season with 200 barrels of corn, 150 good hogs, and 400 bushels of peanuts to sell.[5]

Southampton farmers enjoyed increasingly good rail access to commercial centers. The Portsmouth and Roanoke (subsequently the Seaboard and Roanoke) cut through lower Southampton in the mid–1830s, just as the Petersburg and Weldon skirted the southwestern corner of the county. Farmers in the upper county, however, continued sending crops to Petersburg and Smithfield by wagon. The Jerusalem Plank Road, completed in the mid–1850s, facilitated the trip to Petersburg. At the very end of the antebellum era, the Norfolk and Petersburg Railroad linked the upper county to those two cities and points beyond.

Broad price swings during the three decades between 1830 and 1860 had a pervasive impact on commercial agriculture. Good prices generally prevailed until the end of the 1830s. Hard times became increasingly acute in the early 1840s, and prices remained low through 1848. The agricultural economy then improved, with sustained high prices from the mid–1850s onward. Prices for Virginia corn offer a convenient measurement of the broad pattern. Selling for over sixty cents a bushel in every year except one between 1830 and 1838, and at one point reaching eighty-eight cents, corn fell below fifty cents a bushel in every year except two between 1839 and 1848. Corn prices rebounded somewhat between

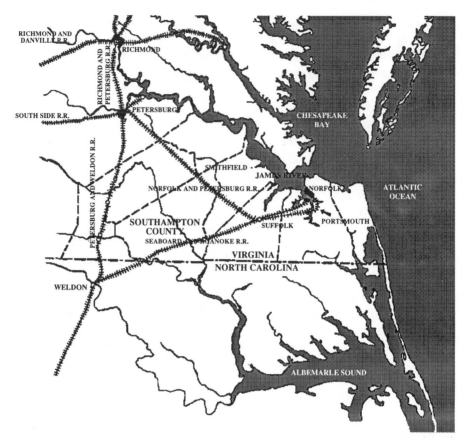

Map 3. Transportation in the tidewater, 1860. *Map adapted from Stephen B. Oates, The Fires of Jubilee: Nat Turner's Fierce Rebellion (New York: Harper and Row, 1975), 72, and William Glenn Robertson, Back Door to Richmond: The Bermuda Hundred Campaign, April–June 1864 (Newark, Del.: Univ. of Delaware Press, 1987), 15.*

1849 and 1852 and then stayed high between 1853 and 1860, a period featuring five years with prices over seventy cents and one year above eighty cents.[6]

Old Southampton fashioned a distinctive pattern of mixed farming, one that excluded almost entirely the state's traditional staple crops, tobacco and wheat. In both 1850 and 1860, its output of swine, peas, and cotton exceeded that of any other Virginia county. It ranked first in sweet potatoes in 1850 and third among Virginia's 148 counties in 1860. The county also produced large surpluses of corn and brandy. After the Civil

War it emerged as one of the major peanut-growing counties in the nation. The postwar era also witnessed the growth of the timber industry, symbolized especially by the rise of the Union Camp Corporation.[7]

The county's agricultural reputation was based on quality even more than quantity. Southampton, "where the hog grows to the pink of perfection," produced the "choicest hams," acclaimed as "equal if not superior" to English Westphalia ham. One of "Urquhart's celebrated Southampton hams," an appreciative newspaper editor proclaimed, was "made from corn-fed hogs," was "juicy, tender and finely flavored," and was "so delicate that an invalid is tempted by it when nothing else is palatable." Another enthusiastic observer insisted that the county produced "the finest sweet potatoes, and the best apple brandy to be found in the world." Southampton brandy, or "Apple Jack," was considered a local specialty, "proverbially peculiar to this county."[8]

The staple crop called "king" in the Deep South, though poorly suited for most parts of Virginia, played a significant role in Southampton. Virginia's involvement in the cotton economy dated from the period of high prices following the War of 1812, which encouraged local production of the fiber previously grown in states to the south. Between 1815 and 1825 cotton prices rarely fell below fifteen cents per pound, and they occasionally approached the astronomical level of twenty-five to thirty cents. By the mid–1820s, especially after the disastrous loss of the wheat crop in eastern Virginia in 1825, cotton farming extended as far north as Richmond. Several Virginia cotton crops during the mid–1830s were, however, "almost entire failures," because early autumn frosts nipped the plants before many of the pods had matured sufficiently to open. One disgusted Surry County farmer called in 1837 for "total abandonment" of cotton.[9]

That call was widely heeded. The opening of fresh cotton lands in the Southwest increased overall output so rapidly that cotton prices fell, especially during the economic doldrums of the 1840s. High outputs per acre in the Southwest allowed planters there to profit even with lower prices, but cotton producers in the Southeast experienced hard times. Amid growing evidence that Virginia lay too far north to grow cotton, most Virginia cotton planters either shifted to other crops or joined the southwestern migration. The cultivation of cotton in adjacent Nansemond County, for example, was reported in 1838 as "almost abandoned" because of "the low price and the unsuitableness of our climate to its production."[10]

Increasing demand for alternative crops hastened the retreat from cotton in most parts of southern and southeastern Virginia. In the southern piedmont, just west of Southampton, tobacco solidified its position as the paramount cash crop. That region had a slightly shorter growing season than the tidewater, plus a type of soil that proved splendidly well suited for the production of flue-cured bright tobacco, production of which soared in the 1850s. Brunswick and the Southside counties west and northwest of there in the Roanoke valley, became the most productive tobacco region in the nation during the late antebellum period.[11]

As other crops expanded, Virginia's cotton production declined. Only in the tidewater near the North Carolina border did a sufficiently long growing season make cotton a reasonable choice. Low prices, however, shrank production from the 8,736 bales the state recorded in 1839. By the late 1840s cotton remained significant only in the three-county region of lower Southampton, lower Sussex, and eastern Greensville. In the census year of 1849, which followed one of the two worst years for cotton prices before the Civil War, Southampton produced 857 bales, Greensville 715, and Sussex 780, for a total of 2,352 bales. Small amounts of cotton grown elsewhere in the Southside and tidewater brought the Virginia total to a scant 3,388 bales, 70 percent of which came from the three-county area.[12]

During the 1850s, however, cotton enjoyed a significant revival in the three-county area, even as it effectively disappeared from all other parts of Virginia. In Southampton, the banner cotton county in the state, production tripled. The county's 2,560 bales in 1859 amounted to half the cotton grown in the state.[13] Gradually rising prices stimulated the recovery. Farmers who had earned as little as six cents for their cotton in the early 1840s and in 1848 received more than twice that figure in 1856 and 1858. Despite price fluctuations from year to year, the crop usually brought around ten cents between 1849 and 1855, and it moved significantly above that figure between 1856 and 1860.[14]

Based on a figure of one-third of a bale per acre as a probable average output, Southampton would have required 7,680 acres planted in cotton to achieve its 1859 output. A full-time agricultural laborer could manage 6 acres. In reality, however, the laborers who tended cotton—mostly slaves, of course—typically spent an equal amount of time working in corn and other crops. A realistic estimate would credit each Southampton laborer who tended cotton with responsibility for no more than 3 acres, so that each therefore contributed perhaps a single bale of cotton. With

5,407 slaves in the county and certainly never more than two-thirds of the total ever available for work in the fields, it appears likely that a majority of Southampton's adult slaves played some role in the planting, cultivation, or picking of cotton to achieve an output of 2,560 bales.[15]

The light sandy soils of the tidewater, deposited in quite recent geological times, were well suited for cotton. The best of these soils, known as Norfolk fine sandy loam, occurred in broad contiguous areas, including much of the lower Southampton below the Nottoway River. All but 401 of the 2,560 bales of cotton produced in 1859 came from there; 325 lower-county farms produced 2,159 bales, an average of 6.6 bales per farm. Most farms there produced at least one bale, and the largest exceeded 50 bales. By contrast, upper Southampton produced very little cotton except in several farms favorably located near the river, including Cobb's and that of his father-in-law, Jesse Little. The 468 farms in the upper county grew only 401 bales of cotton, an average of less than one bale per farm. A large majority of farms in upper Southampton grew none whatsoever. Cotton production in lower Southampton was, however, sufficiently extensive that the entire county averaged over three bales per farm in 1860.[16]

FOR SOUTHAMPTON FARMERS, the agricultural year divided into four seasons, corresponding to months of the year. Winter began in December and continued through February; the three spring months followed, starting on the first day of March; summer encompassed the three months of June, July, and August; the fall harvest season began in September and ended in November. The cycle of the seasons defined life in Old Southampton.[17]

In the yearly cycle, the winter months of December, January, and February were something of a slack season. So long as temperatures stayed above freezing and the ground was not saturated, fields could be plowed and new ground broken up. Outdoor work, however, remained vulnerable to weather-related disruptions. A sustained hard freeze in January 1852 reduced normal farm work to a minimum. "To feed and attend to the stock, cut and haul wood[,] make fires and go to the mill is about all that we have been able to do about home for some time passed," Story noted. The repair or extension of fencing became a major cold-weather activity, as logs were mauled into "riders" and hauled to sites where needed.[18]

A cold snap in December or January was also the right moment to kill

and salt pork. Not only did the annual hog-killing allow Southamptonites to achieve self-sufficiency in the staple meat of the southern diet, it
also provided many with their principal cash crop. A hog-killing required
a day or two of intense effort, often with the assistance of neighbors and
their slaves. The carcasses had to be cleaned, cut, and salted immediately.[19]

A month or six weeks after its initial butchering and salting, Southampton ham needed to be hung up and smoked. "We have always since I
could remember here been smoking with green red oak and pine sap,
using mostly the red oak," Story recorded. Others in the neighborhood
used sap "almost entirely." Story acknowledged that smoked sap gave the
meat "a beautiful color," but he suspected that ham treated in that fashion would not keep so well.[20]

The animals that provided Old Southampton's celebrated hams probably lived in enclosures, sustained by the county's bountiful corn output.
Story, for example, remarked that his hogs would "squeal and cluster
around" at feeding time, eating corn with "eager delight." Once after a
lean year for corn, Story's supply of food for his hogs ran short and he
had to buy more. With the bare bottom of the corncrib staring at him in
late April, Story observed that one ought not own more hogs "than he
can feed well."[21]

Many Southampton hogs, however, roamed in the woods, searching
for acorns and other sustenance. Squeezed by inadequate corn supplies
and low hog prices, Story in 1847 waited until late fall to enclose his
hogs. A diet of peas then rendered the creatures "much improved" before
the winter killing season. Cobb also allowed hogs to roam free for most
of the year, even though harsh winter weather could exact a severe toll,
especially on immature piglets. After the fall harvest, however, he tried to
enclose hogs in potato fields. Foraging there protected the animals from
poisonous mushrooms in the woods and fattened them for winter slaugh-
ter. The semiwild creatures sometimes eluded capture. In September 1859
Cobb reported some of his hogs enclosed, but "for want of a paster where
all hogs ou[gh]t to be kept," others were "out in the woods."[22]

Spring weather in some years reached Southampton by late February
or early March. In other years farmers had to contend with repeated
chills through March and April and even into May. Weather notwithstanding, farmers tried to maintain a scheduled pattern of springtime activity. By mid-March, they expected to plant garden crops—collard
greens, Irish potatoes, peppers, onions, garden peas, and others—most

of which were for home consumption, enabling farm families to minimize their dependence on outside suppliers of foodstuffs. March also was the time to plant oats for animals.[23]

Peanuts, more often called "ground peas" and eaten as a snack, had scant commercial significance before the 1850s. Planted in late April, they blossomed in June and were dug up in the fall. By the early 1850s Story started sending ground peas to market, and by 1857 he reported larger producers growing them in volume. The 1858 peanut crop came in so short, however, that some farmers soured on the crop. Not until shortly after the Civil War did peanuts emerge as the paramount cash crop in the county.[24]

The plowing for Old Southampton's principal antebellum crops— corn, sweet potatoes, and cotton—needed to be well advanced in March so that planting could start by late March or early April. Cobb started planting corn as soon as he judged the threat of heavy frost had passed. Story, fearful that cold wet weather would rot freshly planted corn, waited longer than many other farmers. Both Cobb and Story plowed cornfields in the traditional lattice pattern of intersecting rows about four feet apart in each direction, creating a "hill" at the point where the plowed ridges intersected. Several corn kernels were planted in each hill, and farmers would calculate the number of hills in a field. In 1857, for example, Cobb planted 250,000 hills of corn. Subsequent plowing threw up additional soil around the rapidly growing corn plants in each hill. Where kernels failed to sprout, the corn needed to be replanted.[25]

As soon as they had planted the corn, Southampton farmers immediately turned to sweet potatoes. White or Irish potatoes, started the month before, were mostly for home consumption. Sweet potatoes, planted in much larger volume, doubled as an important source of food and a significant cash crop. Farmers saved some of the previous year's harvest as "plantains." In 1847, for example, Story used fourteen bushels of his own seed potatoes but needed to buy six more. Often seed potatoes were composted in advance to develop sprouts, or "slips," which could then be transplanted. Depending on weather and the progress of corn planting, farmers got seed potatoes and slips into the ground between mid-April and early May. Slips, or "draws," were cut from growing vines late June or early July, allowing additional potato vines to propagate. Sweet potatoes needed plenty of manure. As with corn, sweet potatoes grew in ridges of soil thrown up by plowing. Additional plowing, or "hilling," during the cultivating season added soil to potato ridges.[26]

Cotton planting usually occurred in late April and early May, immediately after sweet potatoes. By this point, the corn needed cultivating. The multiple pressures of three crops made the pace of labor intense for the next three months and more, until the crops were laid by.

Cobb, who grew increasing amounts of cotton during the 1850s, tried various ways to increase output. He always had slaves spread manure on the cotton fields. In 1856 he supplemented the manure with thirty barrels of lime, deliberately varying the amounts of lime and manure to see what combination might best stimulate the cotton. Lime did not impress Cobb. One year later, he tried mixtures of guano, manure, and ashes, apparently with greater success. In 1858 he consulted a book on agricultural chemistry, attempting to discover how to gain maximum benefit from his investment in guano. The prescribed formula specified using 100 to 120 pounds of guano per acre, mixed with five to six times its weight in charcoal, ashes, and fine soil, all to be plowed in and rained on before planting cotton seed. The 1858 venture was the closest Cobb ever came to applying scientific agricultural techniques. All his other agricultural experiments were more primitive. He never indicated that he read an agricultural journal. His example suggests why agricultural reformers such as Edmund Ruffin faced an uphill struggle in antebellum Virginia.[27]

The recent oceanic origin of tidewater soils meant that deposits of marl, composed of fossil shells, were scattered throughout the region, often quite near the surface. Ruffin urged Virginia farmers to marl their fields in order to reduce acidity and increase yields. He thought marl especially well suited for Virginia cotton, because it allowed plants to mature more rapidly and ripen before frost stunted the pods. Rather than dig for marl, however, tidewater cotton farmers such as Cobb more often bought lime or guano in bulk once they became readily available in the 1850s. Ruffin, discouraged that so few eastern Virginia farms used marl, considered Southampton particularly retrograde.[28]

When he first began to plant cotton, Cobb used seed from his father-in-law, who owned the local gin. By 1851, however, Cobb invested in "pedagulf" (Petit Gulf) seed and was pleased to see that it substantially increased his yields over "oald Virginia cotton." Petit Gulf cotton, often called "petty gulf," was developed by Louisiana planters from a Mexican strain; the seeds deteriorated in quality after several seasons, obliging cotton planters to buy more from Louisiana. Cobb also experimented successfully with "prolific" cotton, an exceptionally productive variant of Petit Gulf developed in Mississippi. In 1852 Cobb found that "prolific" seed surpassed "pedagulf," and he resolved to use "prolific" thereafter. In 1853, however, he reluctantly used seed from Jesse Little after being unable to purchase the type he wanted. Despite hopes of growing twelve to fifteen bales that year, he produced less than ten (a total of 13,000 pounds of seed cotton). Enough other southeastern cotton planters may well have discovered the advantages of southwestern seed, temporarily depleting supplies in the Virginia periphery of the cotton kingdom.[29]

Cotton seed, like corn and sweet potatoes, was planted in plowed ridges. Unlike corn, however, the rows of a cotton field went only in a single direction, and cotton therefore grew in rows rather than hills. Cobb decided in 1858 to reduce the width of his cotton rows to 3¼ feet, rather than the 3½ to 4 feet he earlier used. A seed drill, loaded with manure as well as seed, facilitated cotton planting. By the end of April, Cobb usually had his cotton in the ground.[30]

Throughout the growing season the corn, potato, and cotton crops proceeded in sequence. Corn, planted earliest, received first attention. As soon as they had planted the cotton, farmers and their slaves began the first of four laborious corn plowings and weed choppings. A second round, in which six to eight sweeps of the plow through each row built a mound of soil around the young corn plants, needed to be completed by late May. Third and fourth corn plowings and weed choppings took place between early June and mid-July, by which time corn became the first of the principal crops to be laid by. Sweet potatoes and cotton required much the same regimen as corn, as plows threw mounds of soil around the young plants, and each required repeated hoeing and chopping. Cotton plants also needed to be thinned by hand, typically after the second plowing. Cultivation of the three crops required careful timing and coordination. As the days became long and warm in June and July, young corn, potato, and cotton plants sprinted ahead, closely pursued by weeds that the farmer and his laborers struggled to subdue.[31]

Farmers in Old Southampton planted peas in their cornfields in early to mid-June, after the second plowing, when cornstalks had "gotten the start of them enough" to support pea vines. If one waited until late June, the corn might grow so tall as to prevent the peas from making proper headway. The custom of combining corn and peas originated long before European settlement. Indians routinely planted the two crops together, along with squash and pumpkins. It is now known that peas, a leguminous plant, fix nitrogen in the soil, thereby improving corn output and making the field more productive if subsequently planted in cotton. Several different types—white peas, black-eyed peas, red peas, and coffee peas—grew well enough in the area to provide a dependable cash crop. Peas and pea plants also provided animal nutrients. Farmers fattened hogs on peas before the winter killing season. Horses, mules, and cows also foraged among the cornstalks and pea vines.[32]

The long days of early summer confronted farmers with many responsibilities. In late May they needed to shear sheep, a task that left Story worn-out in 1847 after working with dull shears. Small wheat fields, planted in the fall, ripened by mid or late June and required prompt harvesting. Either then or later in the summer, wheat needed to be thrashed or fanned, taken to a local mill, and ground for flour. The modest local outputs of wool and wheat were for home use. Oats, which ripened during July and provided supplementary feed for horses, also competed for attention.[33]

Chilly weather or frosts during the early growing season worried Virginia cotton farmers. Cobb feared a "large frost" that clung to his young plants for an hour after sunrise one still morning in late May had wrecked his crop, but the plants proved resilient and five days later stood ankle to half-thigh high. Although cotton could withstand a prolonged dry spell, Cobb understandably fretted when rains did not fall. Too much moisture rather than too little also could pose a problem. Rainy weather left the crop "grassy," a condition that required repeated chopping with a hoe around individual cotton plants, after the "middles," or furrows, had been plowed.[34]

Insufficient cultivation allowed weeds to compete for rainfall and sunlight, but the farmer who plowed his crops too closely risked damaging their roots and diminishing their productivity. Scientific farmers warned that cotton roots radiated widely; indeed, during the wet years that brought greatest competition from weeds, cotton rooted nearer the surface, having no impetus to seek moisture in the subsoil. Cobb did not record how he attempted to protect his plants. By shrinking the distance between his cotton rows during the late 1850s, he increased the likelihood that the "siding" process in late June and July would exact a price.[35]

Cotton plants in Virginia began to show buds, or cotton squares, in mid-June, and the first flowers followed in late June or early July. New flowers continued to appear, making cotton a crop that required repeated pickings over a period of time in the fall. To persuade the plant to concentrate its energies on enlarging existing bolls rather than trying to develop new bolls late in the season, farmers routinely "topped" the plant at a height of about three feet in late July or early August, just after the last round of plowing and cultivation.[36]

With mature corn and cotton laid by in early August, the tempo of ultural labor slowed perceptibly. Visits among family and friends sed. Cobb marked the end of the cultivating season by giving his several days of holiday and a feast or "dining," featuring such del-.ies as fresh meats and fish. Although usually compulsive about keep-ing his hands at work, Cobb chose to emulate the prominent planters in the neighborhood with this festivity.[37]

In August, and sometimes also in September and October, religious revivals, or "protracted meetings," ran as long as a week or more and drew substantial audiences. Blacks also attended protracted meetings, suggesting that they, too, had more time for themselves in August. Cobb's slaves, however, worked steadily except during the holiday weekend. They could not take time off on any day other than Sunday. Cobb and like-minded white Southamptonites knew that Nat Turner launched his bloody insurrection during the August slack season.

The respite from labor, such as it was, did not last long. Around the beginning of August, fruit growers in Southampton started to transform ripe apples and peaches into cider and brandy. To make brandy, the coun-ty's acclaimed beverage, fruit was ground up in a mill. The resultant liq-uid, after being squeezed out with a press, needed to be distilled. The still at Cobb's, typically fired up early in August, often continued operating into September.[38]

Soon after the middle of August, corn fodder needed harvesting. La-borers first stripped the blades and then cut the tops. Gathering fodder as it ripened, rather than allowing it stand in the fields, was thought to as-sure a more nutritious diet for horses and cattle. The fodder harvest usu-ally continued at least through the first week of September. In 1845, for example, Cobb and his hands began to pull blade fodder on August 20 and had most of the plants finished by September 5, when they started to cut tops. Eventually they piled nine stacks of blade fodder and a fifty-foot stack of tops. The corn itself waited for harvest until later in October or November.[39]

Peas matured by early September. Cobb maintained sufficient pea pro-duction during the 1840s and 1850s to sell between forty and fifty bush-els annually. Story also raised and sold peas. Cobb regularly carried wagonloads of peas to Smithfield in the fall. Both in 1846 and 1850 he twice made the trip in October with twenty-bushel loads. Frustrated to learn that he could have sold his peas locally for only five cents less than he received in Smithfield, Cobb wondered whether he gained anything by making the two-day trip and sleeping out en route.[40]

The first cotton bolls opened by mid-September. As soon as they collected corn fodder and harvested peas, Cobb's hands shifted immediately to his cotton fields. Cotton picking was a prolonged activity, involving men, women, and children and extending from late September into November or even early December. In 1854, for example, Cobb had seven slaves at work picking in early October. Their ages ranged from seven to seventy-five. The best picked over 100 pounds per day each, but the smallest and weakest only around 30 pounds. Overall the group averaged 500 pounds per day. In other years, cotton may have been more abundant. Cobb calculated in 1852 that his best male hands were picking between 100 and 125 pounds per day, the women between 80 and 90, and the boys 40 to 50. To spur his slaves to extra effort, Cobb sometimes offered cash incentives to those who could pick over 100 pounds per day. Cobb expected cotton pickers to do best in the first month of the season, when bolls were large and daylight longer. By November, diminishing daylight and smaller bolls caused the yield to fall to around 50 pounds per picker per day.[41]

Although planters in the Mississippi Delta expected slaves to harvest over 200 pounds of cotton daily by the 1850s, the average Virginia slave gathered less than half that amount, perhaps 70 to 80 pounds per day of seed cotton during the picking season, or around 20 pounds of ginned cotton per person per day. Thus a single 400-pound bale of Virginia cotton required at least sixteen "person days" of picking and an even larger investment of time during the growing season. Plainly, cheap labor made the cotton economy possible. With slaves, one could turn a modest profit farming cotton in Southampton during the 1850s. Many local planters, however, removed their slaves to the Southwest, expecting that each slave there could produce twice or three times as much cotton.[42]

During the 1850s Cobb's cotton crop increased enough to justify several trips to town with the baled product. He became especially restless to finish the first cotton picking because wholesalers in Petersburg usually paid higher prices at the beginning of the harvest season. As soon as his hands made their first sweep through the cotton patch, Cobb hauled the raw cotton to his father-in-law's gin and soon afterward set out to Petersburg by wagon. Meanwhile, the hands commenced a second picking in mid-October and a third in early November, each of which typically yielded about as much cotton as the first. After each picking, Cobb repeated his journey to the gin and then on to town.[43]

Festive corn-shucking parties punctuated the waning weeks of the long agricultural season. All the hands, joined by volunteers and slaves from nearby farms, turned out for these occasions. Reciprocity and neighborliness characterized corn shucking. The "good social fellows of the neighborhood" enabled the Story family to shuck their corn in November 1843. On farms large enough to require a crowd, the host and beneficiary offered his guests better than usual fare. In 1854, for example, Cobb provided corn shuckers with a turkey, a sheep, part of a yearling, and two gallons of liquor.[44]

Why did corn shucking become a memorable spectacle? No purely functional explanation seems convincing. Shucking was only one of several phases in the corn-harvesting process. A farmer and his hands had to pick the ears of corn and bring them in from the field in October and November. They also had to move the shucked corn into the crib. No time imperative, such as at the wheat harvest, required massed labor. Tradition nevertheless made autumn corn shuckings a highlight of the season. Through song, dance, and revelry, all celebrated the end of the agricultural cycle.[45]

Corn, still attached to the cob, was stored in a corncrib. That destined for human use would be shelled from the cob shortly before being ground. Story and Cobb periodically took modest quantities of shelled corn to local gristmills. Cornmeal did not keep well, and Southamptonites ground fresh supplies as needed. The disadvantage in this arrangement occurred during times of drought, when water flows from millponds became so depleted that gristmills could not operate.[46]

Seasonal festivities culminated during the week between Christmas and New Year, several days of which were set aside as holidays. The imperatives of production and labor suffered only brief interruption, however. If the weather turned suitably cold during Christmas week, Cobb and Story organized their annual hog-killing.[47]

Slave hirings for the coming year also took place during Christmas week. Some slaves available for hire were gathered at Vicksville, where both Cobb and Story secured laborers. A similar slave hiring took place at Drewrysville, in the lower county. Owners and renters often made direct arrangements. In other instances the slave's services for the next year were auctioned to the highest bidder. The general prosperity of the 1850s drove the price for a grown hand to over $100 per year, more than twice what it had been during the depressed 1840s. Cobb, who considered the "oald price" of $40 the "propper value" for a year of hired slave labor, blamed "lazy white people" for driving up prices. He attempted to make do instead with hired slave boys, whose labor could be had at prices significantly below the going rate. When one young hired slave started going blind, Cobb felt resentful and cheated.[48]

WHAT ACTIVITIES REGULARLY VARIED the agricultural routine? Religion and religious observance require first mention. Old Southampton's churches played a unique role in the social life of the community. By the mid-nineteenth century the once-established Anglican Church had all but disappeared. A few superelite families such as the Ridleys and the Urquharts maintained traditional Episcopal affiliations. Descendants of the eighteenth-century Anglican ministers Henry John Burges and his son Thomas Burges also remained prominent in the county. In some ways the most enduring Anglican legacy was the division of the county into two parishes divided by the Nottoway River. Nottoway Parish and St. Lukes Parish (upper and lower Southampton, respectively) had official status both in the federal census and in local property and tax records.[49]

Four denominations supplanted Anglicanism in Southampton. Quakers persisted from the colonial era, and three new evangelical denominations—Baptists, Methodists, and a Methodist offshoot that designated itself as "Christian"—attracted broad followings. All in the late eighteenth century challenged the morality of slaveholding. After 1800, however, the antislavery impulse atrophied, persisting only among Quakers and a diminishing minority of evangelicals. By the mid-nineteenth century Baptists and Methodists far outnumbered other denominations in Southampton.

Substantial numbers of Quakers lived in earlier-settled Isle of Wight and Nansemond counties. A 1702 record from Isle of Wight lists family names such as Denson, Scott, and Ricks, all subsequently prominent among Southampton Quakers. In 1758, shortly after Southampton split off from Isle of Wight as a separate county, Black Creek Friends Meeting first gathered. Before the Revolution, its members renounced slaveholding. When Virginia first legalized manumission in 1782, a number of Southampton Quakers formally emancipated slaves who had lived as free

Map 4. Churches, ca. 1850

men and women for almost a decade. Thomas Pretlow, Sr., for example, upon manumitting eighteen slaves in 1782, explained that he had for nine years "acted as guardian to them to keep them from being sold at publick sale which the law required." [50]

However unconventional their beliefs, Quakers appear to have been accepted and respected during the late antebellum years in Old Southampton. The "half year meeting," held on a Sunday in May, regularly attracted a large turnout of Quakers and non-Quakers, causing attendance at other churches in the neighborhood to decline. Elliott Story described the occasion in 1848, when two of the "ablest" Quakers spoke. He commended the "good sound doctrine" espoused by one gentleman.

Story was unable, however, to hear the other speaker, a lady, because he could not find a seat inside and "she did not speak sufficiently loud for it to be heard out of the house."[51]

Southampton Baptists, led by David Barrow, one of the most outspoken antislavery ministers in Virginia, challenged existing social and economic arrangements in the 1780s and 1790s at least as forthrightly as the local Friends. Barrow emancipated his own slaves in 1784. Soon afterwards his Black Creek Baptist Church initiated a wrenching debate about whether it was "a ritious thing for a Christian to hold, or cause any of the Humane race to be held in Slavery." Although a majority of the church membership in 1786 officially judged slaveholding "unrighteous," a minority disagreed. In 1791 several in the congregation, including Barrow's wife, absented themselves from communion to protest continued slaveholding and slave hiring by other church members. Dissension continued to plague the Black Creek church.[52]

In 1798 Barrow migrated to Kentucky, delivering as he parted a ringing affirmation of religious egalitarianism and political republicanism. Anticipating "the downfall of all despots and despotism," he prayed that "the *great trump of Jubilee may be shortly sounded from pole to pole*" and that all who were oppressed might be "delivered from the iron talons of their *task-masters*" to enjoy "the sweets of liberty." Barrow suspected that some might be offended by his condemnation of slavery, "especially those who are inclined to be merciful, and somewhat tender to their slaves." The nature of the situation was such, however, that slaves "were daily liable to fall into worse hands," so that "if we view the subject with all the horrors attending it, it is impossible for language to dress it in colours too dark."[53]

Controversy about slavery at Black Creek Baptist Church erupted once again, a quarter century later. Jonathan Lankford, the minister since 1816, startled his congregation in December 1825 by announcing that "in justice to his conscience," he could no longer "administer the ordinances of the Gospel of this Church." Lankford explained that he acted because of "his opposition to the subject of Negro Slavery, a part of the Church being slave holders." His unexpected declaration occasioned "much surprise as well as difficulty."[54]

The challenge posed by their heretofore respected minister plunged the congregation into "lengthy but brotherly and affectionate discussion." Lankford, unwilling to abandon the pulpit, continued to preach through the spring and summer of 1826, even though unwilling to perform the sacraments. In September 1826, however, a majority of church members voted to remove his name from the church roster, thereby terminating not only his ministry but also his church membership. Prominent Black Creek laymen, led by Carr Bowers, undertook to hire a new minister and to prepare a report justifying Lankford's ouster.[55]

Making no overt effort to defend slaveholding, the laymen stated that the issue of slavery was properly left to the conscience of each member, "as he might think proper." Lankford had been "at perfect liberty to enjoy his own opinion." The minister's critics charged, however, that he had acted from "self interested and improper motives" in trying to impose his own point of view on the congregation. He had tried "to split the Church asunder," believing that a majority of church members probably would "sustain him" because they did not own slaves. In so doing, the minister betrayed the church that had raised him from poverty and had given him land and a horse and saddle. The report concluded by congratulating church members for rejecting Lankford's insidious leadership.[56]

Lankford's excommunication and apparent isolation would seem to have made him a likely candidate to follow the example of his predecessor, David Barrow, by emigrating to a more congenial locale. In fact, however, Lankford stayed. Not prominent but by no means a pariah, Lankford lived on a small farm near the church at which he had once ministered and not far from Elliott Story's school. The young teacher and others addressed the old gentleman as "Rev. Lankford."[57]

By the mid-nineteenth century Southampton Baptists had congregations at Black Creek, South Quay, Joyners, Tucker Swamp, Millfield, and Jerusalem, all in the upper county, and at Hebron in the lower county. A majority of church members in the upper county affiliated with one or another of the Baptist churches there.[58]

Methodists constituted the most numerous denomination in the county, especially in the lower county where eight of Southampton's Methodist congregations were located. Clarksbury, Applewhites, Persons, Mt. Horeb, Whiteheads, Barnes, and Peetes stretched across the lower county in such a way that no family need travel more than a moderate distance to reach a Methodist church. A former Episcopal church, Vicks, also was used by Methodists during the antebellum era. Several Southampton families also attended New Hope Methodist Church, just across the North Carolina line. Among the three or four small Methodist congregations located in the upper county were Cobb's Indian Spring church and Story's Nottoway Chapel.[59]

Disagreements about slaveholding also troubled Southampton Methodists during the late eighteenth century. A Methodist offshoot, the Republican Methodist Church or Christian Church, led by the antislavery leader James O'Kelly, attracted a following in upper Southampton. One of the early leaders in the denomination, Burwell Barrett, ministered there for decades. Two congregations, Barretts and Union, remained vigorous throughout the antebellum era and beyond. The line separating the Methodist and Christian denominations did not remain strict. During the 1840s and 1850s, Union Christian Church was also considered a Methodist congregation.[60]

Qualms about slaveholding cut too deeply in Southampton during the 1780s and 1790s to have disappeared entirely. More than would have been possible in most parts of the South, antislavery Baptists and Methodists there gained reinforcement from the example set by local Quakers. So too, growing numbers of free black men and women as well as slaves responded to the evangelical message by joining local Methodist and Baptist churches. An outspoken heretic such as Jonathan Lankford lost his pulpit, but he would not likely have spoken out in the first place—nor would he have continued to live in the same community—had not some members of the congregation and others in the neighborhood agreed with him. If nineteenth-century southern evangelicalism remained haunted by "moral anxiety" about slavery, as historian Donald Mathews has persuasively argued, Southampton must have been a telling case in point.[61]

Religious commitment in the antebellum South should be understood as a partial repudiation of traditional social values and a buffer against disorder. The evangelical community refused to countenance many manifestations of white masculinity and conviviality, repudiating drinking, fighting, and general hell-raising. Churches required that members control their aggressiveness and practice self-discipline.[62]

Unique among the public institutions of the antebellum South, evangelical churches offered roles to subordinate members of society. "Without claiming too much or failing to recognize the multitude of ways slaves were not accorded genuine equality in these biracial churches," historian John Boles has noted, "it is still fair to say that nowhere else in southern society were they treated so nearly as equals." According to Donald Mathews, blacks found much to admire in a value system that affirmed the spiritual superiority of the oppressed poor, passed "cosmic judgment upon whites," and promised black believers something far better than "the world which the slaveholders had made." Blacks became, in their own eyes, "more Christian" than whites. An apocalyptic undercurrent in black Christianity, which usually took the form of an expectation that God would, in his own time and way, smite the wicked and allow the oppressed to go free, emerged more spectacularly in Southampton in August 1831 than at any other place or time in the antebellum South, when Nat Turner took it upon himself to execute the judgments of a wrathful God.[63]

While politics, court day, and muster excluded all except white males, churches enabled white women to develop networks of association with each other, thereby creating "the sense of breathing space between them and the people who lorded it over them." In Southampton and across the Old South, white women substantially outnumbered white men in evangelical churches, with black members further reducing the proportions of white males. In Story's Nottoway Chapel, for example, fewer than one-third of the white members (fifteen of forty-eight) were men. The church also included ten black members. Only six of thirty-three members at Cobb's Indian Spring church were white males; the congregation included seventeen white women and ten blacks. The relatively small numbers of white men doubtless exercised influence out of proportion to their numbers. Nevertheless, churches held white male members to standards that "continued to be at odds" with a value system that celebrated virility, honor, strength, pride, and worldly acclaim.[64]

Evangelicalism, originally a defiant challenge to the dominant gentry culture when it first burst on the scene in the eighteenth century, became a central expression of southern culture by the latter decades of the antebellum era. No longer a religion of plain folk who chose to stand outside the mainstream of society, evangelicalism increasingly became the mainstream. Even if evangelical values differed from the norms by which many white men lived, the dominant values of the late antebellum South reflected growing evangelical influence. "To a remarkable degree," John Boles has written, "evangelical religion shaped the mentalité of antebellum southerners, rich and poor, slaveholder and nonslaveholder."[65]

Southampton's two diarists, Story and Cobb, both committed themselves to evangelical values. Each nicely fit the paradigm developed by Donald Mathews, who noted that southern evangelicalism had less appeal to "the elites of a relatively stratified society" than to the "honest, hardworking folk, who aspired to become more esteemed by their fellows than they had been, but who had neither the family connections nor the wealth to enable them to do so."[66]

Temperament and circumstances gave Story many advantages in seeking to live by evangelical values. A reader who prized education and rationality, he had no use for traditional masculine assertiveness. He likewise avoided much of the inevitable brutality of plantation life by defining a career that enabled him to avoid primary dependence on slave-labor agriculture. Cobb, far more than Story, found it difficult to escape the contradictions between evangelicalism and the plantation, although he certainly tried to do so. Cobb rarely quarreled or fought, although he once used force "to protect my mate." It appears probable, furthermore, that he rarely beat his slaves. An 1854 diary entry reported that he arrived home to find that his "plougher" had not done his assigned work, whereupon Cobb decided "to chastise [him] for it and that I dun severly." Other planter diarists routinely made such entries, but there are few, if any, comparable passages in Cobb's extensive diary. It may be that Cobb usually chose not to mention something that he found distasteful, but the stream-of-consciousness quality of the diary rather strongly suggests that the 1854 incident was exceptional. Cobb nevertheless remained inherently suspicious and fearful of blacks. A system of religious values that in some respect affirmed the equality of all persons, white or black, free or slave, must have confronted Cobb with contradictions that he could not resolve.[67]

The tempo of life in Old Southampton slowed dramatically on Sundays. "Spent this morning in reading, talking and doing nothing till preaching time, when I went to preaching at Nottoway Chapel," Story noted in his diary. "From preaching I returned home & took dinner and a nap and went over to Mr. Moore's and spent the chief part of the evening, in conversation—about farming &c. &c. &c." Because churches were the principal institution that brought people together, one cannot disentangle religious commitment from sociability. For many churchgoers, both motives interacted. One winter Sunday, for example, Story attended Black Creek Baptist Church, where he "heard a wholesome lecture, saw a great many old acquaintances, several handsome young ladies, collected the news that was in circulation and returned home."[68]

Protracted meetings stretched over several days or as long as a week in late summer and early fall. Even more than regular Sunday services, the protracted meeting provided an opportunity for "beaux and belles" to admire each other and for those "without any proper design" to enjoy the spectacle. Nevertheless, these gatherings played a powerful role in the religious life of the community, functioning as "significant bonding and purgative occasions." Members of the evangelical community could reenact their own conversions while at the same time offering moral support to "mourners," who were wrestling to redefine their own spiritual condition. Protracted meetings "became the means through which Evangelicals could recapture the emotional vitality of the movement's early career, when spontaneity and ecstasy had not yet given way to the routine and order of successful institutions." [69]

During the 1840s and 1850s the region repeatedly witnessed flurries of protracted meetings. In 1842 Cobb recorded simultaneous meetings in early August at his own church, Indian Spring, and at Mt. Horeb. These followed meetings at Barnes and two churches just across the North Carolina line, which together enabled over 150 souls to experience conversion. A "great meeting" in Sussex County also occurred. During early September protracted meetings took place at Clarksbury and at Old South Quay; later in the month Cobb noted that "many of the most violent sinners" had made "their escape of hell" during meetings at Joyners and Nottoway Chapel. The often-dour Cobb took heart, confident that "Almighty God the great judge" had stimulated a powerful revival of religion. [70]

Three summers later, a similar story unfolded. Meetings at Mt. Horeb, Clarksbury, and Vicksville in August generated converts, some of them "wicked oald men." A Methodist circuit rider named Scott apparently played the principal role in organizing the gatherings. Toward the end of the month Cobb, pressed by the need to pull ripe corn fodder, reported missing a protracted meeting at Whiteheads but vowed to support it with his prayers. In early September, Scott moved his base of operations to Nottoway Swamp, where an outbreak of bilious fever held down the crowd and limited the numbers of white converts. At the end of the month, however, Scott and two others preached "fine sermonds" at Cobb's home church, Indian Spring. There, several men "of good standing and respectability" and several ladies "of high renown" made "a profession of religion." Cobb was "much greaved" that other obligations limited his attendance to the two weekend days. [71]

Elliott Story, himself a convert in 1847, reported in late August 1848 that a protracted meeting at Union had attracted large crowds, with gentlemen politely giving up their seats to ladies. Several weeks later, in September, a gathering at Mt. Horeb in the lower county generated twenty-six white converts and a larger number of black ones. Concurrently a well-attended meeting with multiple preachers began at Joyners.

Story, obliged to teach school, denied himself the pleasure of attending the church where he had grown up as meetings continued into the week. Two weeks later, however, he dismissed school one afternoon to attend a protracted meeting at nearby Black Creek Baptist Church. That gathering led to hard feelings, as one of the converts proved to be a member of Story's Nottoway Chapel, a Methodist church. "Many severe remarks" at Nottoway followed the decision by the nominal Methodist to switch his membership to Black Creek and to undergo a Baptist immersion ceremony. But the denominational scars healed quickly. Baptists at Millfield held a protracted meeting in early October that prompted forty persons to profess conversion. "It is a most glorious time for the Christian religion round about here at present," Story exulted. "The cause seems to be gaining ground rapidly in almost every direction." [72]

A decade later the cause appeared triumphant. Protracted meetings took place across the upper county—at Barretts, Union, Millfield, Joyners, and Nottoway Chapel—in September and October 1858. The meeting at Union, which started with little excitement, continued for nine days amid a growing outpouring of religious fervor. By the time it ended, forty whites and more than a dozen blacks had experienced conversion. The next year Methodist circuit rider Benjamin Franklin Woodward, a "forceful pulpit orator," arrived in Southampton. His efforts in late August and early September 1859 at New Hope, just across the North Carolina line, stirred as many as forty-five converts in a single day. The excitement swept into Southampton during the next month, with week-long meetings at Whiteheads, Union, and Applewhites. In each church one or two local ministers alternated with the celebrated Woodward. The crowds at Whiteheads grew so large that gentlemen surrendered all the seats in the church to ladies and a "dense mass occupied all the available standing room in every direction." Cobb and his family attended some of the meetings. "I never has seen Miniters labour with such zeal," he rejoiced. [73]

What does the protracted meeting reveal about the social order from which it sprang? Although some persons in Southampton disdained "the meetings where these great excitements prevail," seeing only a "scam and no reality" or attributing them to such phenomena as a bad crop year, the audiences included a broad cross section of the local population. Historian Mary P. Ryan's assessment of the evangelical impulse in upstate New York, which emphasizes the key roles played by "young men and women from farm, artisan, and shopkeeping families who were struggling to find a comfortable place for themselves within a changing social and economic structure" and who sought to achieve "self-control," appears applicable to the South. Both Cobb and Story fit Ryan's paradigm. Much that was happening in the North, however, had little analogue in the South: the increasing numbers of families who lived as urban consumers rather than rural producers, the prominence of women in moral reform associations, and the replacement of patriarchal authority by evangelical values in family life.[74]

Southampton's social order, especially when compared to the North, was rigid and static. Its market economy, stimulated by new rail lines and higher price levels during the 1850s, did expand, but economic activity took place within the old familiar grooves. Only about 20 percent of white male adults held nonfarm occupations, and large numbers of young men had to leave the county to find a livelihood. Compared with their counterparts in the North, Southampton's white women had less opportunity to build separate spheres. Patriarchal values in the South remained, as yet, substantially unchallenged.[75]

Nevertheless, religious devotion, especially as fueled by the protracted meeting, played an unmistakably functional role in Southampton's social order. No other voluntary activity stirred a comparable level of interest; nothing else reached so widely across lines of race, class, sex, and age. Sabbatarian values, promoted by churches and at protracted meetings, became deeply entrenched by the late antebellum era.[76] The traditional white male recreations of drinking and fighting, even if still widely practiced, elicited increasing disapproval.

Evangelicalism appealed to young white men such as Cobb and Story, who lacked inherited wealth or distinction and who sought greater self-discipline and enhanced self-esteem. Yet its appeal also reached larger numbers of white women and a substantial (if hard to measure) complement of blacks. Each group had their own reasons for embracing evangelical values, each derived differing types of support and fulfillment from church membership, and each interpreted the Christian message to suit their own needs. The legacy of antebellum southern evangelicalism necessarily became complex and contradictory.

ALTHOUGH CHURCHES AND RELIGIOUS activities provided the paramount type of voluntary association in Old Southampton, people had additional ways to vary the agricultural routine and interact with each other. The civic and political arena offered white men a range of opportunities, at which others could only spectate. Each month on the third Monday, court day transformed the sleepy village of Jerusalem. The county court, which administered local government, met monthly. Court days always attracted a big turnout. "It seems generally understood that any citizen of the county who wants to see any other citizen can find him here on that day," one observer reported. "Almost every profession or calling is represented in that mixed mass of human beings. Grave farmers discussing whatever questions may have reference to the soil; merchants busily seeking purchasers for their goods, each furnishing the gratifying assurance that he is selling at a lower price than the other; doctors with bundles of 'medical bills,' which now hardly pay for the carrying; keen-eyed disciples of Blackstone . . . ready to split hairs or transform mole-hills into mountains, or mountains into molehills, as may suit the cases of their clients—all stand forth prominently in this great picture of life." [77]

If most Southamptonites attended court day to see friends, to shop, to settle accounts, or simply to enjoy the spectacle, some used the occasion to stir up trouble. Cobb deplored the drunken rowdiness that frequently marred the occasion: "Plenty of brandy drank & quarling & broiling & some fiting & jailing," he reported after attending court day in August 1845. "I bin in 13 states & I believe as much fitting takes place at Jerusalem as any other place I have ever seen in the U. Nited states." The excesses of court day could dismay sober citizens. Story found that "court days always fatigue me in mind and body. . . . it seems to twist my head about and confuse my ideas so that it takes me a day or two to get straight again." [78]

The local militia held exercises on the first Saturday of the month between April and October. For Cobb, these responsibilities seem to have brought a sense of satisfaction. He joined the militia in 1830 and thereafter won promotion to the rifle company and then to the cavalry. His rifle company uniform cost him $12 in 1834. Nine years later in 1843, with local agriculture depressed and cash scarce, Cobb nevertheless invested $21.50 for proper cavalry attire ($8 for a coat, $2.50 for spurs, $4 for boots, and $7 for "panterloons," with the latter two useful for other wear). For Story, on the other hand, militia obligations appear to have been a chore. The experience of marching and countermarching typically drained his energy. In April 1848 he commended an "indulgent" captain for diminishing the usual routine and discipline. Story, however, did enjoy the sociable aspects of muster, and he was elected a second lieutenant in 1848.[79]

The general parade of the local militia at a field near Jerusalem, usually on the second Saturday in May, provided a festive occasion and special amusements. Although "unlikely weather" held down attendance at the May 1845 parade, Cobb expected a "wild frolick" that evening in Jerusalem. Following the parade one year later, Story listened to "an elegant band of musick at Jerusalem which seemed to delight many as well as me." In 1847 he invested twenty-five cents to view a "concert-negro-dance performance" at the courthouse, pronouncing himself "very much amused" by the "negrolike songs & odd manoevers." That evening Story found the town "echoing with the songs and speeches and hubbubs of those who had practiced too much at the bar."[80]

Some people in Old Southampton celebrated holidays, for example, by firing cannons on George Washington's birthday or by sponsoring get-togethers on Independence Day. Although he carefully noted many of these occasions, diarist Elliott Story had doubts about excessive "high living, merry making and holy-day," and he only rarely participated himself. He passed up a patriotic Fourth of July fish fry at Massenburg's Millpond, suspecting it would degenerate into "a drunken spree." Instead, he conducted school, just as on any other weekday. His students also missed the chance to see a "wild animals circus" in Jerusalem in March 1846 because their earnest teacher doubted whether circuses improved "the mind or the morals of a community." Court day had obliged him to lose a day of teaching earlier in the week, and he considered it improper to cancel school again.[81]

Sociable gatherings of young men and women proved more congenial to Story's taste. Such events, held on an evening or a weekend, and especially during Christmas week, brought together fifteen or twenty people for activities such as quilting, singing, pulling molasses, playing "the usual games of amusement," or exchanging "the common chit-chat of the day." A "very jovial" group spent the evenings of Christmas week in 1848 going from house to house in a continuous whirl of decorous parties. The weddings at which Story officiated as a waiter provided more structured and conventional opportunities for eligible young single persons to meet.[82]

National two-party politics and its local manifestations added new variations from the routine in Old Southampton during the 1840s and

1850s. It had long been customary for aspiring candidates to make speeches on court day or after muster. Partisan competition often transformed these events into overt debates. Rivals for the county's seat in the legislature or for the district's seat in Congress would appear together, allowing voters to make comparisons. Once in a while, prominent outsiders would visit. At the height of the 1848 presidential campaign, U.S. senator Stephen A. Douglas, an Illinois Democrat, made a joint appearance on court day with the former Mississippi Whig congressman Sergeant S. Prentiss. Three years later, General Winfield Scott, an aspiring presidential candidate, stopped briefly at Franklin. In 1859 the two candidates for governor, barnstorming together across the state, debated each other at Franklin.[83]

From Elliott Story's rational perspective, political debates served no useful function. A doctrinaire Whig, his responses were predetermined. He allowed that William S. Goodwyn, the Democratic candidate for the legislature, "made a pretty good speech considering every thing" after muster one Saturday in April 1846. Story judged, however, that the Whig candidate, Dr. Robert G. Griffin, "suited my notions much better and I think he gave Mr. Goodwyn some pretty sharp shot." For Story, who "seldom ever knew a publick speech to alter a man's mind on political questions," all such efforts were "labour lost." After the eminent Douglas and Prentiss spoke, Story had "no doubt but that every man who heard them thinks and will vote as he intended before."[84]

Story, alarmed by violence, disorder, irrationality, and sudden death, was ambivalent about the rough and tumble of politics. He admired Henry Clay's "brilliant intellect and gigantick mind," and he hoped that "Harry of the West" would become president. Political hullabaloo and partisan divisiveness impressed Story, however, as ominous. He observed that "politicks was running very high" in Jerusalem on court day in July 1848, "too much so I fear for the best." He likewise complained when rival newspaper editors in a neighboring county printed severe personal attacks on each other. Their "brutal and depraved" behavior was "uncontrolled by prudence and moderation."[85]

Looking toward a future in which men would control destructive impulses that modern society, for all its achievements, had only imperfectly contained, Story could not decide whether politics was part of the solution or part of the problem. Even today, the relationship between national two-party politics and the late antebellum social order remains a puzzle. Did partisan politics ameliorate social friction and sectional strains? Or did partisan rivalries fan the embers that burst into flame in 1861? One way to learn more about the subject is to observe closely developments at the local level. The following three chapters examine in detail Southampton politics, from the origins of two-party politics in the 1830s through the secession crisis and the firing on Fort Sumter, when political disagreements erupted into war.

FOUR

The Formation of Political Parties

SOUTHAMPTON COUNTY'S EXPERIENCE reveals, in microcosm, a great deal about the rise of popular partisanship. Mass two-party politics originated in the United States during the 1830s, sooner than anywhere else in the world. To fully comprehend the process, one must look beyond Washington, D.C., and the state capitals, heeding the old adage that all politics are local. Between 1833 to 1840 Southampton completed a major partisan metamorphosis, establishing patterns that persisted through the last eventful quarter century of the antebellum era. A county that supported Andrew Jackson by a decisive three-to-one margin in 1828 and with near unanimity in 1832 became a political battleground. New Whig and Democratic parties, each claiming about half the Southampton electorate by the mid–1830s, hotly contested the county's seat in the House of Delegates. By the end of the decade, popular interest in presidential politics surged. Seventy percent of eligible voters flocked to the polls in 1840, giving William Henry Harrison, the Whig victor, a thin edge over the incumbent Democrat, Martin Van Buren.

Southampton allows a unique perspective on the process of party formation. No other locality in the country offers such complete records about the votes that individuals actually cast as the party system formed. The evidence is voluminous—not just a single list or the breakdown of votes for a single election. Instead, Southampton has records of individual voter choices for most elections held between 1833 and 1840.[1] On the other hand, Southampton offers little evidence of the sort that political historians traditionally have used. The county had no local newspapers, and its politics received infrequent mention in the urban press. Only a few scraps of manuscript evidence survive.[2] To a great extent, therefore, the county's political history must be teased from computer analysis of data files, framed by information about the larger environment of state and national politics.

The story that unfolds extends beyond the obvious growth of voter interest, as manifest in larger turnouts. Loyalties to the two emerging political parties became ubiquitous during the 1830s. By the end of the decade, almost all voters had partisan identities. Whenever they voted—and most did so regularly—they supported only the candidates of a single party, whether for a seat in the state legislature or for the presidency of the United States. In the era of mass partisanship, voters had to choose sides.

Broader economic changes and social tensions shaped partisan controversy in Southampton during the 1830s. At both the state and national levels, disagreements about banking and money sharply divided Whigs and Democrats. Banks symbolized new wealth. Their creation and oversight necessarily expanded the role of government. And they promised to accelerate the forces of change. Throughout the United States, particularly in the Southeast, such tendencies caused alarm. New wealth created by banks appeared to result from a sleight of hand, rather than honest labor. More government—for whatever purpose—appeared equally ominous. Americans of the Revolutionary and post-Revolutionary generations suspected that concentrations of power would subvert republican liberty. Many likewise considered it axiomatic that an enlarged government would distribute its favors unequally, creating a network of parasitic clients who might corruptly perpetuate their undeserved advantages. A distrust of all change was implicit in much of this concern. John Randolph of Roanoke coined the classic formulation, denouncing the "*maggot* of innovation" and concluding that "*change* is not *reform*." [3]

Andrew Jackson demonstrated that banks and paper money could become lightning rods for widely diffused anxieties. Even if he could do little to arrest the momentum of change, his campaign against the "Monster Bank" and other carefully selected targets, such as the proposal for the federally subsidized Maysville Road, proved politically astute. Those who hoped to restore or preserve the virtuous republic embraced Jackson. His appeal to southeastern traditionalists waned, however, after his expansive assertion of federal power during the struggle with South Carolina over nullification. Many thereafter considered Jackson a dangerous centralizer.

For southeasterners, the momentum of change in the United States ap-

peared especially threatening. Northern manufacturers obt⸱
that some in the Southeast saw as a tax borne by cotton exp
portation improvements demanded by the North and We
promised to tax the South so that others might benefit. The ra
of the Southwest drained population from the Southeast and ⸱
the prices of cotton and other staple crops. Once dominant in
government, the Southeast viewed with dismay the erosion of
power.[4]

Nagging amid these concerns, and contributing to the tensiᴏ⸱⸱ ⸱⸱⸱
evoked, was the insoluble riddle and paradox of slavery. The bedrock of
the southeastern social and economic order, slavery nevertheless af-
fronted values that Americans—including white southerners—all
claimed to hold dear. Slave discontent, manifest most spectacularly in
Nat Turner's bloody Southampton insurrection of August 1831, added to
southern uneasiness about the peculiar institution. Grasping, in Thomas
Jefferson's phrase, a wolf by the ears that they could neither hold nor
safely let go, white southerners dithered. They agreed that they must
manage the matter for themselves, without officious nudging or interference. Increasing British and northern antislavery pressures aroused a hostile, defensive southern response.[5]

DEVELOPMENTS IN THE LATE 1820s provided the backdrop for the
emergence of parties in Southampton during the 1830s (see app. table
4.1, which summarizes Southampton election returns for 1828–42). In
1828 Andrew Jackson defeated President John Quincy Adams, 341–115.
The margin left no doubt that Adams's controversial call for broad-
construction use of federal power had, as in most of the South, proven a
political albatross. But unlike adjacent counties such as Sussex and
Greensville, in which Adams received hardly any support, Southampton
did have a nucleus of voters who resisted the dominant political current.
An "Anti-Jackson Corresponding Committee," which met in Southampton in April 1828, optimistically listed 130 names, slightly more than the
total number of votes polled against Jackson in November.[6]

Who were the 1828 Anti-Jacksonians? Of those still residing in the
county a decade later, approximately equal numbers lived north and
south of the Nottoway River. The absence of any geographical concentration contrasts rather surprisingly with the future Whig party, which enjoyed far greater support in neighborhoods north of the river. A surpris-

ingly large percentage of the Anti-Jacksonians owned no slaves or very few slaves. Few political lists from the era included such a large proportion of ordinary folk.[7]

State constitutional reform, which broke along regional rather than party lines and pitted the west against the east, dominated Virginia politics between 1828 and 1830. Southampton, voting even more monolithically than other parts of the tidewater and piedmont, opposed calling a convention, 495 to 18. Western voters prevailed, however, and a convention did meet in Richmond from October 1829 to January 1830. Three of its ninety-six delegates—John Young Mason, James Trezvant, and John B. Urquhart—lived in Southampton. Resisting all changes, they voted with a hard core of like-minded easterners, led by Benjamin Watkins Leigh. Trezvant, who represented the district in Congress, protested against any liberalization of suffrage requirements, fearing disruption of "the old and established order of things" and the "long-established habits of the community." He and his Southampton colleages likewise opposed any change in the formula for representation in the legislature, which favored the older-settled region east of the Blue Ridge.[8]

Although unable to prevent all change, traditionalists preserved the basic structure of eastern advantage. They defeated western efforts to base legislative apportionment on the white population but did allow some increase in western representation. Easterners also defeated unrestricted white manhood suffrage, while compromising to enfranchise a limited segment of nonlandowning renters and taxpaying household heads. Southampton and the east thereupon embraced the new Virginia constitution. The Southampton vote for ratification, held in April 1830, totaled 347 to 8.[9]

Anxieties about slavery haunted the Virginia Convention of 1829–30. Had "no such thing as slavery existed," former president James Monroe observed, the east would have yielded to the west on legislative apportionment. In fact, however, the irrepressible John Randolph of Roanoke characterized apportionment based only on the white population as "a declaration to all the world, that we are ready to surrender the question to the first Peter the Hermit, who shall cross the mountains with 'Universal Emancipation' on his flag." Suspecting that western critics of the slave system had allies in the east ("I would as soon trust the Quakers of Pennsylvania as the Quakers of any county in Virginia"), Randolph deplored the existence of a "fanatical spirit on this subject of negro slavery" both without and within the state. He grimly predicted that slaveholders might require armed force to protect themselves from the "monstrous tyranny" of "King numbers." [10]

The new constitution sharpened political competition in Southampton. In April 1830, at the last election under the old ground rules, future Democrat William B. Goodwyn and future Whig Benjamin Griffin won reelection to the House of Delegates without opposition. Under the new constitution, Southampton's representation dropped from two seats to one as the overall size of the lower house was shrunk by more than one-third. In October 1830, at the first election under the new system, incumbents Goodwyn and Griffin squared off against each other, with Goodwyn winning narrowly, 227 to 214. Less than a year later, in August 1831, just days before the Nat Turner insurrection, another close election took place, and turnout soared. With the polls kept open for three days, future Democrat Jeremiah Cobb narrowly defeated Griffin, 365 to 356. [11] But Griffin decisively won a rematch in April 1832, at another three-day election.

The new constitution, however much an eastern victory, plainly rocked the political status quo in Southampton. Because the county no longer held two seats in the House of Delegates, exciting rivalries ensued for the one remaining seat. This stimulus to voter turnout coincided with an expansion of the eligible electorate. A canvass of the 1832 returns showed that many who remained disfranchised would have liked to vote and that some indeed had tried to do so. [12]

Southampton's lively elections in 1831 and 1832 had little connection, however, to broader patterns of partisanship. Other 1831 contests on the local ballot revealed no party cohesion or discipline: three candidates divided the vote for state senator, while Democrat John Young Mason carried 556 of 708 votes for Congress against an out-of-county opponent. The presidential election in November 1832 attracted fewer than half as many Southampton voters as the state election earlier that year, and only 25 of 285 opposed Andrew Jackson's reelection. The president commanded such a great advantage in Southampton and statewide that his victory was effectively uncontested.

NAT TURNER'S SHOCKING RAMPAGE stirred an unprecedented internal debate about slavery in Virginia. In late 1831 and early 1832, the legislature addressed the touchy question of whether the Old Dominion should remain a slave state. Majorities voted to declare slavery an evil and to examine ways by which the state might get rid of it.[13] Few in Virginia during the early 1830s defended slavery or insisted that it remain permanently. Antislavery sentiment, strongest in the western part of the state, still commanded some support in the east. Alexander W. Jones, one of the most outspoken critics of slavery in the legislature, represented Warwick and Elizabeth City counties, a tidewater district on the James River. He articulated ideas that some whites in Southampton—though not a majority—probably shared.

Jones characterized the debate about slavery in 1831–32 as the "most momentous" that had taken place within Virginia since June 1776. He castigated the slave system for exercising a "baleful and disastrous influence" over the state's economy. It deprived free labor of opportunity, forced many to emigrate, and left Virginia increasingly behind the pace of agricultural and industrial development in the northern states. Not only was slavery "injurious to our interests," Jones charged, it was also "dangerous to our tranquillity." Making deliberate reference to Southampton, he painted a bleak picture of a society gripped by fear, forced to remain on armed alert. Even though any slave revolt would be "promptly crushed," that would afford "no consolation" to the family unfortunate enough to suffer the first attack.[14]

The impetus for slave revolt could never be extinguished, Jones asserted. The hope of "recovering lost liberty" was instinctive. In a country where political discourse routinely celebrated "the sacred rights of man," slaves had ample impetus to feel resentful. "The very nature of our institutions and the customs of our people" proclaimed that "man was never destined by his creator to be a slave." Moreover, a free press, which had in Europe prostrated "thrones and hierarchies" as well as "error, ignorance, and superstition," made it impossible to "retain any class of your population in gross and utter ignorance." Wherever a free press existed, Jones warned, "slavery perishes."

Unlike most tidewater and piedmont representatives, Jones endorsed a plan offered by Thomas Jefferson Randolph, the grandson of Thomas Jefferson. Randolph proposed that slaves born after July 3, 1840, who remained within Virginia after reaching adulthood be shipped to Africa. Jones ridiculed conservative demands that slaveholders receive compensation for slaves they thereby lost. The Randolph plan would not have secured freedom for most blacks, nor would it have confiscated any significant amount of slave property, because it allowed—indeed encouraged—owners to sell slaves outside the state. Ending slavery in Virginia meant, in effect, moving slaves farther south.[15]

Jones's speech was nevertheless significant. It showed that as late as the early 1830s, proslavery ideology in eastern Virginia had not yet become strong enough to preclude debate. Jones defined a public interest that conflicted with the unlimited rights of slaveholders. He recognized that his candor entailed political risks, acknowledging that his constituents might wish to return him to private life. That did not happen, however. Instead, the editor of the most influential newspaper in the district commended Jones for speaking "ably" and "fearlessly." Shortly thereafter, voters decisively reelected him.[16]

Just as a new legislature convened in December 1832 to continue wrestling with the possibilities for gradually eliminating slavery, an epic showdown developed between South Carolina and President Andrew Jackson. In late November 1832 the South Carolina convention adopted an ordinance forbidding collection of federal tariff revenues within the state after February 1, 1833. Jackson countered with a proclamation, dated December 10, 1832, denying that any state had the power to annul federal law and threatening to use armed force to prevent the "disunion" of South Carolina. The Nullification Crisis during the winter of 1832–33 stirred an especially intense response in Virginia. Convinced that both protagonists had dangerously overplayed their hands, many Virginians became absorbed in a searching discussion about slavery, states rights, secession, and the power of the federal government.[17]

Jackson's apparent determination to quash nullification militarily created widespread alarm. Although few Virginians originally approved of South Carolina's confrontationist stance, the president's threat to use armed force raised the specter of "military despotism" and "consolidated government." Many who had applauded Jackson's course before the proclamation began to fear executive usurpation. Some began to see nullification as a brave challenge to a would-be tyrant. If South Carolina had to "submit," would any slave state control its own destiny?[18]

The Nullification Crisis created an unpleasant dilemma for Jackson's many nominal supporters. Congressman Mason, to take the most important local example, tried to maintain loyalty to the president while still retaining support from constituents who opposed the proclamation. Mason faced a difficult task. One of his constituents, George Blow, considered Jackson's "Marplot Proclamation" a mixture of "error" and "folly." Trying to coerce South Carolina "whilst the passions of the people are inflamed" could trigger civil war. If forced to choose sides in a war between those favoring, on the one hand, "protective Duties, and a Consolidated National Government" and, on the other hand, a "southern State contending for her Sovereignty, Equal Taxation, and a Federal Government," the other slaveholding states would, Blow predicted, fight to defend South Carolina.[19] That did not happen in 1833. Congress instead arranged a face-saving compromise that resolved the crisis.

Nullification coincided with intensified abolitionist efforts, as "immediatists" gained the upper hand in the North over "gradualists" who coupled abolition with colonization. The growing chorus of external condemnation stunted the recently flourishing debate about slavery within the South. Stung by forthright criticism from northern immediatists, who attempted to mail pamphlets to the South and who flooded Congress with antislavery petitions, the South closed ranks. Virginia's antislavery initiative fizzled amid a conservative counterattack, which deplored the direct use of state power to tamper with the property rights of slaveholders and condemned the impropriety of public debate about slavery. The legislature contented itself with token annual appropriations for the American Colonization Society, which transported a trickle of black emigrants (primarily free rather than slave) to Liberia.[20]

The previously outspoken legislator Alexander W. Jones abruptly changed course. Claiming that he had "hazarded as much in the cause of Abolition as any man in this State," Jones denounced the "misguided philanthropy and hypocritical fanaticism" of northern abolitionists. Their efforts, he predicted, would encourage an "unprincipled majority in Congress" to assault slavery. Hopeful that Virginians would resist any effort "to interfere with a subject of such exceeding delicacy, magnitude and importance," Jones insisted that "the fate of South Carolina *to-day*, will be that of Virginia *to-morrow*." Virginia should, he reasoned, "sustain and uphold her sister" by supporting South Carolina's "noble" and "manly" challenge against arbitrary power. Only a readiness to use armed force could preserve liberty and prevent the rise of tyranny and despotism.[21]

Despite widespread opposition to Jackson's proclamation in eastern Virginia, the legislature ended up adopting an ineffectual middle course, explaining that it agreed neither with the president nor with South Carolina and offering to mediate their differences. The unchallenged dominance that supporters of Jackson enjoyed before December 1832 rapidly disintegrated, however. In congressional elections held in April 1833, only six of twenty-one victorious candidates, among them five westerners, unequivocally supported the president and his proclamation. In much of the tidewater and piedmont, opponents of the proclamation "went into permanent opposition to Jackson and his successor Van Buren." [22]

The chrysalid opposition party in Virginia embraced not only those disaffected by the proclamation but also the original anti-Jackson nucleus that dated from the 1820s. Most of the latter had no quarrel with the proclamation, but they and many heretofore loyal Jacksonians took strong exception to Jackson's removal of federal deposits from the Bank of the United States in October 1833. Because the Bank had few friends in the Old Dominion, the president's 1832 veto of its recharter proved popular. But Jackson's unilateral decision to withdraw deposits had an entirely different impact. It offended a broad cross section of Virginians, including many who approved the Bank veto. Although Jackson's renewed assault on the Bank led to economic jitters, its political impact had more to do with ideology than economics. Jackson's behavior appeared high-handed and arbitrary, fulfilling his critics' warnings. Widely condemned as an unwarranted exercise of presidential power, Jackson's removal of the deposits "destroyed Democratic supremacy" in the Old Dominion and thereby "revolutionized Virginia politics." By early 1834, barely a year after he was easily reelected, a formidable anti-Jackson coalition calling itself the Whig party emerged in Virginia and most other parts of the United States. [23]

The Virginia Whig party scored impressive victories during 1834. Littleton Waller Tazewell, a states rights traditionalist who broke with Jackson after the proclamation, was selected as governor in January. A month later, U.S. Senator William Cabell Rives decided to resign, rather than heed the state legislature's instructions to censure Jackson. The legislature thereupon replaced Rives with Benjamin Watkins Leigh, a prominent anti-Jacksonian whose outlook closely resembled that of Governor Tazewell and the state's other U.S. senator, John Tyler. The annual state elections in April 1834 gave Whigs an impressive majority in the legislature, sufficient to extend Leigh's Senate term. [24]

Wounded Virginia Democrats fought back tenaciously, recapturing the legislature in April 1835. They then attempted to instruct the two anti-Jackson U.S. senators, igniting a divisive partisan struggle. Tyler resigned rather than follow the instructions, and the legislature then selected

Rives, the loyal Jacksonian, to succeed him. Preliminary maneuvering for the 1836 presidential contest, in which Whigs tried to tarnish Jackson's designated successor, Martin Van Buren, added intensity to Virginia partisan rivalries.[25]

CONCURRENT WITH DEVELOPMENTS ELSEWHERE in Virginia, Southampton experienced a partisan awakening in 1833 and 1834. The 1833 legislative elections took place shortly after resolution of the Nullification Crisis. Drawing support from friends and neighbors rather than from coherent party organizations, the rival candidates each ran well within several miles of their homes, although turnout elsewhere in the county was low. The incumbent, Benjamin Griffin, enjoying a somewhat larger base north and east of Jerusalem, easily defeated Dr. James C. Harrison, 227–128, with Harrison's support confined primarily to the lower Nottoway River near his home. National politics did have some connection to the April 1833 race in Southampton, however: Harrison was a Nullifier.[26]

The voting of church members contributed a notable element to Griffin's victory. The candidate's home church, Black Creek Baptist, gave Griffin a 23–0 advantage. Voters from Barretts Christian Church and the Quaker meeting, plus members of two other upper-county Baptist churches for which only skeletal records exist, together added to Griffin's margin by at least 15–0. Griffin's strength in his home base therefore had significant religious roots.[27]

By 1834, much had changed in Southampton. Jackson's opponents took the initiative. Whigs pulled together a coalition described contemptuously by Jackson loyalist John Denegre as having three principal strands: "1st . . . some rank South Carolina nullifyers—2d Bank men 3d some aristocrats of the old stamp."[28] For Denegre as for the editors of the state's Democratic newspapers, the Whig alliance of Calhoun, Clay, and Adams supporters appeared unprincipled and opportunistic.

Although one candidate remained the same, the April 1834 election in Southampton differed markedly from that held just a year before. James C. Harrison, the avowed Nullifier who had lost in 1833, ran as a Whig. He soundly defeated a Jacksonian Democrat, Solomon Parker, 276–218. Almost two-thirds of the votes cast in 1834 came from voters who had not participated in 1833. And unlike 1833, the votes cast in 1834 showed definite relationships to national party allegiances.[29]

Slaveholders and nonslaveholders voted almost identically in 1833. By

1834, however, Democrats gained a stronger base among the largest slaveholders, a pattern that would persist for more than a generation (see app. table 4.2). Solid support for Parker in the wealthy Drewrysville region, in the western part of the lower county, meant that he collected over 40 percent of his vote from privileged citizens owning ten or more slaves. Fully 20 percent of Democrat Parker's votes came from planters owning at least twenty slaves. Harrison, even though supported by the most self-consciously Deep South element in the county, netted fewer slaveholder votes. Only 19 percent of Harrison's support came from those owning ten or more slaves; planters contributed only 8 percent of his total. Voters who did not own slaves decisively favored Harrison, the Whig, providing almost half of his vote but only a quarter of Parker's vote.

Consistent with the tendency for Harrison to do better among non-slaveholders, a striking reversal took place between 1833 and 1834 in the relationship between residence and candidate support. In 1833 voters known to have lived in the upper county solidly supported Griffin, almost five to one. Known lower-county voters favored Harrison, more than two to one. In 1834, however, Harrison became the favorite of upper-county voters, defeating Parker, 131 to 63. Whigs thereafter continued to collect two-to-one majorities in the upper county, where many white families owned no slaves and few had large slaveholdings. Harrison, with a base in his home neighborhood, increased his total vote in the lower county from fifty-eight in 1833 to sixty-eight in 1834. But Parker drew enough votes elsewhere in the lower county, which had substantially larger slave-holdings than the upper county, to defeat Harrison there, 93 to 68. In the future, Democrats amassed even more lopsided margins in the lower county, suggesting that the Nullifier element gradually returned to the Democratic party. This happened elsewhere in Virginia and across the South, as many of John C. Calhoun's admirers followed his lead.[30]

Patterns of religious affiliation, obviously salient in 1833, experienced substantial modification in 1834. Benjamin Griffin, Harrison's successful rival in 1833, voted for the Whig Nullifier in 1834. His action helps to explain why the Black Creek Baptist congregation, Griffin's home base, produced a 12–7 margin for Harrison in 1834. Overall, Harrison greatly improved his vote among known church members, defeating Parker, 39–30. One year earlier, he had lost to Griffin, 50–15.[31]

Voting patterns in 1834 did not, however, entirely supersede those of 1833. Harrison retained his base of local support, a neighborhood where people "for several miles round" had fallen victim to the "distemper" of

Calhoun doctrines, according to one dismayed Democrat.[32] Although Harrison also ran well in some future Whig strongholds east of Jerusalem, neither he nor Parker stirred much support in regions north and northeast of the county seat that became essential to Whig success in the future. Parker, considered by some Democrats a weak candidate, did show strength in wealthy lower county enclaves west and northwest of Jerusalem that Democrats would continue to dominate. But he failed to poll many votes in neighborhoods south and southwest of the county seat that Democrats in the future carried by large margins.

James C. Harrison's untimely death in late 1834 threatened to deprive Southampton of representation when the legislature convened in December. At a special election to fill the vacancy, held in January 1835, Whigs supported Captain Edward Butts, the sheriff of Southampton for a decade and a half. Democrats countered with Dr. William B. Goodwyn, who had several times before sat in the House of Delegates. Observers agreed that both nominees had stature. Democrats acknowledged that Butts was a "perfect gentleman" with "pleasing manners," who, as sheriff, had acted "with the greatest integrity and indulgence towards the people." A Whig likewise considered it fortunate that "gentlemen of such respectability and worth, and standing so high in the confidence of the people," had consented to run.[33]

The contest between Butts and Goodwyn pitted two of the wealthiest men in Southampton against each other. Butts owned fifty slaves; Goodwyn, sixty-four. Both were prosperous doctor-planters. The medical profession, which involved an unending round of home visits, often provided the basis for a political career in Old Southampton. James C. Harrison, who died before he could take office, was a doctor. Democrats William A. Spark and Nicholas M. Sebrell, who would represent the county in the legislature in the early and middle 1840s, also practiced medicine, as did Thomas J. Pretlow, a Whig who won the seat in 1851.

The January 1835 election attracted far more out-of-county interest than usual, because the closely divided legislature soon would select a U.S. senator. Some thought the "single vote of Southampton" might decide whether Benjamin Watkins Leigh would hold the seat he had won the year before. Whigs reminded potential voters that Leigh, the leading opponent of constitutional reform, made "great and arduous exertions for our benefit in the Convention of the State, by which our property was rescued from excessive and burthensome taxation." They derided Goodwyn as a supporter of the Force Bill, "who voted to invest the President with the authority to lead mercenary bayonets against the bosom of a sister Southern State." Democrats, sneering that Whigs had assembled "as piebald a Coalition as ever existed—the Nullifiers, the Nationals, and what not," hoped that Southampton would "not have any hand" in repudiating Andrew Jackson, the president who was "on the side of the people." Both parties tried to tar their opponents with the onus of Federalism.[34]

Southampton Whigs accused local Democrats of attempting to subvert "the will of the people." In late 1834 a committee of Democrats started collecting signatures to instruct Harrison. Whigs charged that the committee imposed on many citizens who later regretted signing the deceptively worded petition. Complaining that an "oligarchy" had acted as if it "actually possessed a deed of sale" for the "freemen of Southampton," one Whig commentator predicted that "yeomanry of the county" would resist being "transferred from one side to another—in fact, . . . bought and sold."[35]

An "unusually large" turnout of 665 voters appeared at the courthouse in Jerusalem, producing "a very full election for any season of the year, and particularly so for the month of January." Goodwyn, the Democrat, narrowly edged Butts, the Whig, 342 to 323. Democrats rejoiced at having defeated a candidate "stronger by fifty votes than their next best man." Whigs, complaining that "family influence decided it," promised that the regular April elections would better test "the politics of the county."[36]

The April 1835 contest featured a hard-fought rematch between Goodwyn and Butts. The polls remained open for three days, and both parties exerted themselves to the utmost. Butts displaced the incumbent, 397 to 354. Southampton Whigs thereby overcame the trend that saw their new party lose control of the state legislature. The turnout of 751 votes, which exceeded by one that in the presidential election of 1840, was among the largest turnouts in the county before extension of the franchise to all adult white males in 1851.[37]

Partisan feelings ran high enough by April 1835 to generate significant local opposition to Southampton's powerful congressman, John Young Mason, considered an aspirant for Speaker of the U.S. House. One Whig wrote a public letter complaining about Mason's "electioneering." Alleging that Mason had smeared Leigh as "*a Bank man*," had insinuated that Butts was guilty "of the odious crime of Federalism," and had expressed support for Van Buren rather than Senator Hugh Lawson White of Tennessee as Jackson's successor, the angry Whig accused Mason of putting his own ambitions for "the Speaker's Chair" ahead of "the wishes of a respectable portion of his *immediate* constituents." Southampton Whigs, although outnumbered in a Democratic congressional district, made the gesture of running a candidate against Mason.[38]

The third matchup between Butts and Goodwyn, in April 1836, gave the incumbent Butts a decisive advantage, 299–236. Although the 1836 election did not draw as large a turnout as the two in 1835, the survival of individual voting returns for 1836 allows a close look at the developing patterns of partisanship among the electorate.

Butts, the Whig incumbent, ran especially well in upper Southampton. Among voters known to have lived in the upper county, Butts gained a decisive advantage, 190 to 102. Goodwyn lost because he failed to amass a comparable margin in the proto-Democratic neighborhoods of the lower county. His margin among identifiable lower-county voters amounted to only thirty-one votes, 92 to 61. From 1834 until the Civil War, Whig candidates ran strongly in the upper county, not only in local elections but also in congressional and presidential ones. Democrats likewise dominated the lower county. Whigs in 1836 did a better job than Democrats in energizing potential supporters. An estimated 56 percent of eligible voters in the upper county did vote, compared to 43 percent in the lower county. Overall voter turnout in 1836 stood at exactly 50 percent of those eligible.[39]

The constituencies supporting the candidates in April 1836 continued to show a slightly larger proportion of nonslaveholders among Whig voters, although the pattern was less conspicuous than in 1834.[40] Despite Butts's impressive overall total, he did not run well among religious voters. Overall, Goodwyn defeated Butts 46 to 37 among known church members.[41]

Voting behavior in April 1836 displayed continuities from the first obviously partisan election in 1834. Harrison's 1834 supporters who voted in 1836 demonstrated strong Whig preferences, 126 to 23, although several former Harrison neighborhoods southeast and south of Jerusalem showed a definite movement toward the Democrats, led by notables such as Thomas W. Vaughan. Parker's 1834 supporters reappearing in 1836 voted Democratic by almost as large a margin, 94 to 25.[42]

AN ANTIABOLITIONIST FUROR, with repercussions both North and South, erupted in the summer of 1835. Southern whites who had earlier voiced misgivings about slavery fell silent. In Virginia and across the South, Whigs and Democrats sought ways to depict the other as unsound on slavery and tainted with abolitionism. Did public opinion in Virginia shift as dramatically as political discourse? The question cannot easily be answered, but the disappearance of debate in the public arena surely had an effect.[43]

Surviving sources shed no light on the antiabolitionist panic in Southampton. At Norfolk, the nearest major city, however, an uproar followed the arrival from New York in late July 1835 of abolitionist fliers entitled *Human Rights*. The Norfolk and Portsmouth *Herald*, denouncing the document as a "treasonable" and "incendiary" effort "to excite sedition among the colored population of the South," urged "the Southern people" to "speak out with one voice, and in a tone that shall not be misunderstood." Such "assaults upon Southern rights," unless promptly stopped, could scatter the Union "to the four winds of Heaven."[44]

Soon thereafter, on August 13 and 17, public meetings gave voice to popular indignation. Alexander W. Jones, the erstwhile antislavery spokesman, presided over the second meeting. Presenting a fiery preamble and resolutions soon unanimously adopted, Jones condemned the abolitionists who sent pamphlets to Norfolk as an "atrocious gang of lawless fanatics," who were attempting "to desolate the land with all the horrors of a servile war." Rather than tolerate continued insult and intrusion, he urged resistance. Southerners should fight, he insisted, if the non-slaveholding states or the federal government ever challenged their right to own slaves. "Three millions of freemen, with arms in their hands, may perish amidst the smouldering and bloody ruins of their habitations, and the devastation of the land, by fire and sword, but they never will tamely and voluntarily surrender," Jones proclaimed.[45]

The Norfolk resolutions, notable for their implied rhetorical threat of civil war, soon became a partisan football. The New York *Evening Post*, complaining that "more seditious and inflammatory sentiments never were expressed in this country," denounced the proceedings of the Norfolk meeting as "bellicose, inflated, and insulting towards the north." Whig newspapers in Virginia quickly pounced on the *Evening Post*, a prominent Democratic newspaper, insisting that southerners could not trust northern Democrats.[46]

A metamorphosis from theoretical antislavery to outraged antiabolitionism also marked the Richmond *Whig*, edited by John Hampden Pleasants. In 1832 Pleasants promoted the Randolph plan to rid the state of slavery. Three years later in July 1835, at the height of the hysteria, he took aim at northern "demons and fiends" who had insulted southerners and undertaken "to stir up their slaves to rebellion." Warning that "the *superstitious* love of the Union" was fast disappearing in the South, Pleasants remarked that "the Tariff was a light and trivial matter compared to this interference with slavery." From his perspective:

The Southampton insurrection in the summer of 1831, gave a great impulse to men's thoughts on the subject of emancipation, emboldened great numbers to avow their sentiments in favor of it, and organized its friends into a party so powerful, that they at least divided the State, and actually commanded a majority in the popular branch of the Legislature—a majority too, containing in its ranks a great proportion of the youthful and rising talent of the country. We belonged to that party, and were proud to belong to it. . . . The friends of prospective emancipation had the weight of numbers, the youth of the country, and as they thought, all the demands of patriotism on their side. Where is that gallant party now? Overslaughed, disbanded, annihilated, by the *wise and benevolent* interference of Garrison and Co.[47]

Under the circumstances, the 1836 presidential contest in Virginia generated partisan acrimony regarding slavery. Whigs insisted that Vice-President Martin Van Buren, the Democratic candidate, would not protect slaveholders from abolitionist attack. Governor Tazewell used his annual message of December 1835 to blame Democrats for the abolition menace. Affirming its southern loyalties, the Democratic majority in the legislature condemned "incendiary publications" and warned against any attempt by Congress to prohibit slavery in the District of Columbia or the federal territories. Van Buren repeatedly pledged to uphold the rights of slaveholders. Jackson aided Van Buren's cause by appointing three southerners to the U.S. Supreme Court, including Virginia traditionalist Philip P. Barbour, and by calling for removal of abolitionist literature from the mails. Virginia Democrats, led by Thomas Ritchie, editor of the Richmond *Enquirer*, insisted that northern Whigs had an abolition taint.[48]

THE INTERCONNECTION BETWEEN NATIONAL and local politics took shape over a period of several years. National developments in 1833 created the context for Southampton partisanship. Yet the annual contests to fill the county's seat in the House of Delegates initially stirred principal voter interest. Not until 1840 did turnout in a presidential election reach levels achieved in local races during the 1830s.

In the presidential election of 1836, many who had voted in the three hard-fought assembly races in 1835 and 1836 chose to stay home. At first glance, the phenomenon of decreased turnout at a presidential election appears paradoxical. Virginia newspapers during the mid- 1830s contained an incessant barrage of national partisanship, focused, of course, around the polarizing personality and policies of Andrew Jackson. By 1835 and 1836 the question of the presidential succession appeared absorbing. Pro- and anti-Van Buren forces marshaled for political combat long before the election. If national political struggles gave shape to emerging state and local partisanship, why didn't the presidential contest in 1836 stir more spirited interest and competition in Southampton?

That question may be answered, in part, by recognizing that the presidential contest in Virginia in 1836 failed to take shape in such a way as to maximize partisan energies. Although they ran a common slate of electors, Virginia Whigs could not agree on a candidate. States rights Whigs, principally in the east, favored Hugh Lawson White, whereas national Whigs, especially in the west, preferred William Henry Harrison. Under the circumstances, Martin Van Buren breezed to a relatively easy statewide victory, 30,845 to 23,412.[49]

Nevertheless, Southampton voting behavior in 1835 and 1836 diverged from broader Virginia patterns. Statewide voter turnout in November 1836 significantly exceeded that in the local contests the previous spring. Fewer than 44,000 Virginians voted in the spring, but more than 54,000 did so in the fall.[50] In Southampton, by contrast, voter turnout fell from 535 in April, itself a lower figure than the two local elections in 1835, to only 377 for the presidential contest.

Several vigorously contested local elections apparently energized Southampton politics at a faster pace than in most other parts of the state. One party dominated approximately three-quarters of Virginia counties, depriving local elections of the intensity frequently exhibited in Southampton.[51] Party organizers in counties where one party enjoyed a lopsided advantage probably found it harder to mobilize voters. Only when local votes contributed to a larger collective—that is, for congressional and state Senate candidates and in the quadrennial struggle for the presidency—did voters have incentive to turn out.

Comparisons between Southampton's two 1836 elections show that those who participated both times voted the same way in nearly every instance. Persistent Goodwyn voters supported Van Buren, 137 to 1, and persistent Butts voters favored the Whig slate, 148 to 3. Among those voting in April but not in November, Whigs suffered larger losses than Democrats, 148 to 98. Democrats, slightly more successful than Whigs at recruiting new voters, narrowly carried Southampton for Van Buren, 192 to 185.[52]

The November election was not, however, merely a shrunken repetition of the earlier legislative contest. The presidential race attracted a more privileged cross section of voters. Many ordinary folk stayed home, especially nonslaveholders living in the upper county. The Whig campaign against Van Buren, stuck in a tiresome groove of accusations that the New Yorker could not be trusted to defend slavery, failed to stir smallholding Southampton Whigs.[53]

BEFORE LONG, HOWEVER, national political developments stimulated Southampton's partisan awakening. Martin Van Buren's presidency, beset almost immediately by economic uncertainties, became enmeshed in fiscal and monetary controversies. Committed to a hard-money antibank policy, Van Buren clung to Andrew Jackson's 1836 Specie Circular, a deflationary measure that required buyers of public land to use hard money. Van Buren also insisted that Congress establish an Independent Treasury, to take federal deposits away from state banks that had earlier been able to use them to finance commercial activity. The Independent Treasury, not enacted until 1840, obliged the federal government to receive and hold its own revenues, which could be paid only in specie and specie-backed notes. The bruising political battle over the Independent Treasury sharpened partisan divisions, as the country fell into increasingly severe economic doldrums. Its opponents considered the Independent Treasury economically misguided, insisting that it would deprive state banks of needed capital.[54]

One cannot, however, understand the political impact of the Independent Treasury struggle in narrow economic terms. Fears of "an unnecessary enlargement of executive power and patronage" gave the issue ideological intensity. The Whig party coalesced in 1834 because of Jackson's domineering behavior. Although the military despotism that Whigs warned against never materialized, popular anxieties about a too-powerful president remained salient. Ideological concerns, shared not only by Whigs but also by many Democrats, probably loomed largest in Virginia.[55]

Van Buren's policies created a crosscutting reshuffle of southern political allegiances. On the one hand, some states rights strict-construction traditionalists, earlier alienated by Jackson's aggressive treatment of South Carolina and his vigorous assertion of federal supremacy, moved back toward the Democratic party. Led by John C. Calhoun, Van Buren's new southern supporters included such notable Virginians as former governor Littleton W. Tazewell and the Speaker of the U.S. House, Robert M. T. Hunter. They considered the Independent Treasury less menacing than the active-government wing of the Whig party. On the other hand, Van Buren's banking policies dismayed a faction of southern Democrats who favored a regulated system of federal deposits in state banks. So-called Conservatives, the most visible of whom was Virginia's U.S. Senator William Cabell Rives, moved gradually toward alliance with the Whig party. Virginia Conservatives held the balance of power in the legislature between 1838 and 1840.[56]

The 1837 legislative contest, held just before Van Buren's presidency became fractious, attracted little interest, either in Southampton or statewide. Upper-county Democrat James Clayton defeated lower-county Whig James W. Parker, 176–111. This result corresponded to patterns elsewhere, as Democrats won large legislative majorities. In 1838, however, James B. Urquhart, an elite upper-county Whig from one of the two wealthiest families in the county, won the seat back, soundly defeating Clayton, 262–179. In so doing, Urquhart mobilized a far better Whig turnout. Allegedly promising "that he was opposed to a United States Bank and opposed to the election of Henry Clay for his protective tariff principles," Urquhart held the support of the states rights element that had affiliated with the Whigs since the Nullification Crisis. Democrats throughout Virginia had difficulty in 1838, as Whigs and Conservatives together gained a majority of seats in the legislature.[57]

By 1839 some traditionalists who had supported Urquhart in 1838 considered themselves betrayed. Efforts to reelect U.S. Senator Rives provided a partisan litmus test. Abandoned by Democrats, Rives sought Whig and Conservative support. Although unable to garner enough votes to win the seat, Rives did have sufficient strength to block the Democratic nominee, Southampton's John Young Mason, and thereby to prevent the legislature from filling the vacancy. Urquhart's support for "the apostate

Rives" and his votes for other Whig programs such as the distribution of revenues gained from public lands sales set the stage for a fierce fight in the annual elections held in May 1839.[58]

To oppose Urquhart, Democrats countered with Robert Ridley. His family was the lower-county counterpart to the elite Urquharts. Ridley, a brother, and a cousin together owned 262 slaves, of which 107 were Ridley's alone, making him one of the two largest slaveholders in the county. James B. Urquhart owned 67 slaves; five Urquhart kinsmen owned 238 others. The Ridley-Urquhart matchup, repeated in both 1840 and 1841, had a major impact on Southampton politics. Election turnouts stabilized at a high level. And for the most part, voters maintained for many years to come the party allegiances forged between 1839 and 1841.

The 1839 campaign was a novel spectacle. Urquhart and probably Ridley issued printed circulars. Urquhart's friends sponsored a fish fry at Atkinson's Mill. On court day, the Monday just before the election, crowds in Jerusalem heard speeches from the rival candidates for Congress, Democratic incumbent Francis E. Rives and his Whig challenger, James W. Pegram. Young Elliott Story, still in his teens, sensed the excitement. "There is more electioneering in this county than I have ever known," he reported in his diary. "The cause I suppose is, that the approaching election is one of more importance than any one that has been for many years." [59] On election day over seven hundred voters went to the polls. Ridley decisively bested Urquhart, 387–331. Almost every voter adhered strictly to party lines, as the Democratic candidate for Congress won Southampton's vote by a nearly identical margin, 389–329.

The 1839 contest plainly roused strong feelings, which came close to instigating an affair of honor. The defeated incumbent, Urquhart, took offense upon hearing that former congressman John Young Mason, the disappointed U.S. Senate aspirant, considered Urquhart's public circular ghostwritten. Urquhart demanded that Mason repudiate his "gross calumny." Mason defused the situation, saying that he had been "misunderstood" and advising Urquhart to retract his "harsh epithets." [60]

Southampton's 1839 election contained elements of both continuity and change. Those who voted in both 1836 and 1839 held tenaciously to their earlier party preferences.[61] Older predilections could also be discerned: of the fifty persons voting in 1839 who opposed Andrew Jackson in 1828, thirty-eight voted for Urquhart. The 1839 election departed in significant ways, however, from earlier procedures and patterns. One change was structural: for the first time, voting took place not only at the

Map 5. Polling places, 1839–51

courthouse but also at four outlying points, two in the upper county and two in the lower county. Turnout inevitably rose once potential voters who lived at a distance could avoid the all-day trip to and from Jerusalem (the most remote parts of the county were more than twenty miles from the courthouse, and many voters lived ten or more miles away). Lower-county petitioners who requested "precinct elections" complained that they lived long distances from the courthouse and that their access to it had also been disrupted by "sudden and frequent freshets" in the Nottoway River.[62]

New voters played a decisive role in the 1839 legislative elections, especially for Democrats, who earlier enjoyed less success than Whigs in mobilizing large turnouts. More than half the 1839 Democrats had not voted in April 1836, and fully two-thirds had not voted in the presidential election that November. Fewer 1839 Whigs were new voters. Proportionately smaller Whig gains go far to explain the outcome of the 1839 race.[63] The Democratic surge centered in the lower county, which continued for more than two decades to provide the base of Democratic strength. Compared to the 1836 legislative election, turnout percentages increased in all areas. The lower county, however, showed the greatest gains, exhibiting for the first time turnout levels as high as those in the upper county. Turnout in both regions stood at 67 percent in 1839, compared to 56 percent in the upper county in April 1836 and 43 percent in the lower county.[64]

Data about religious affiliation pinpoints one major source of increased Democratic strength—among Methodists. Heretofore only minimally engaged by electoral politics, lower-county Methodists suddenly turned out in force, delivering a decisive margin for Ridley, 37 to 9. Urquhart enjoyed no similarly lopsided denominational advantage. The strong preference for Ridley among Methodists gave him a formidable margin over Urquhart, 74 to 50, among voters with known religious affiliations. Neither candidate had any direct claim to denominational support. The superelite Ridleys and Urquharts were among the few families in Southampton who maintained ties to the otherwise moribund Episcopal church.[65]

Democrats also demonstrated a stronger appeal to slaveholders.[66] The relationship between slaveholding and Democratic support was especially evident in the party's lower-county base, which Democrats carried, 238 to 55. One of the new voting districts, James Tavern, situated near Drewrysville in the fertile Three Creeks region of the lower county, had proportionately more large landholders and large slaveholders than any other part of Southampton. At James Tavern, Ridley defeated Urquhart, 69 to 13. Of the fifty Democratic voters there for whom records about slaveholdings may be found, fully 90 percent owned slaves, 64 percent owned ten or more, and 34 percent owned twenty or more. Southampton Democrats also depended on strong support from lower-county non-slaveholders, especially those at Cross Keys.[67] Elite preferences plainly influenced the rank and file. The new politics of partisanship and broad participation thereby retained some of the privileged flavor that characterized traditional Virginia politics during the prepartisan era.[68]

A different pattern emerged in the upper county, where voters registered a two-to-one Whig preference, 260 to 132. Upper-county Whig voters were less likely than lower-county Democrats to own slaves, and those with slaves had conspicuously smaller holdings.[69] Even though a few upper-county Whigs were very large slaveholders—a principal case in point being the 1839 candidate himself, James B. Urquhart—lower-county Democrats included a much larger proportion of the planter and near planter class. Only 19 percent of upper-county Whigs owned ten or more slaves, and only 9 percent owned twenty or more—half the comparable proportions among lower-county Democrats (40 percent and 17 percent).[70]

THE STRONG RELATIONSHIP BETWEEN party and neighborhood deserves emphasis. Partisan allegiances in the antebellum South had a more collective than individual quality, and the collectivity often had roots in geographical proximity. Neighbors and kinsmen, typically following the lead of a local notable or activist, usually voted the same way. In Virginia, where oral voting prevailed until after the Civil War, the voting process itself encouraged expressions of group affirmation. Oral voting was not, however, a prerequisite for collective rather than individual politics. Throughout antebellum America, voter mobilization was an intensely public spectacle, and voter loyalties tended to be exhibited rather than concealed. Party, in short, involved persons in groups rather than individuals in private.

Local land tax records specify the distance and direction of each piece of property from the courthouse, making it convenient to trace the relationship between voting patterns and residence for property owners and their households. One typically finds a cluster of voters living in proximity to someone of stature and position, with most or all of the neighborhood voting the same way. If no more than circumstantial, the evidence suggests strongly that local leaders exerted influence. "Knowing the nature of antebellum society," historian William G. Shade has observed in a study of partisan loyalties at a nearby Virginia locality, "one might assume that elite patterns of behavior helped structure the responses of the common people."[71] Overt campaigning must, in some instances, have produced the observed result. More subtle influences probably played a role, too. When the most prominent or wealthy person in a neighborhood acquired a partisan identity, his example doubtless had an impact, even if he made no effort to proselytize.

Throughout the upper county, Whiggish neighborhoods surrounded the homes of known party leaders. James B. Urquhart, the Whig legislator and aspirant during the late 1830s, lived sixteen miles north of the courthouse in the Light Water neighborhood at Warrique, a fortress with

Map 6.   Neighborhoods and residences, ca. 1850

massive brick walls nearly two feet thick dating from the late eighteenth century. Voters living within two miles of the Urquhart estate voted for their eminent neighbor, 31 to 4, in 1839. One year later, Whig presidential candidate William Henry Harrison carried the same neighborhood, 32–6. The Round Hill neighborhood, nine to twelve miles north of the courthouse and home to Anselm B. Urquhart, the brother of James B. Urquhart, voted Whig, 16–4 in 1839 and 21–3 in 1840. Other notable Whigs in the Round Hill area doubtless contributed to the pattern. Dr. A. S. H. Burges and Shugars Lain both lived within two miles of Anselm B. Urquhart.[72]

Between six and eleven miles east and northeast of the courthouse lay the Nottoway Swamp and Black Creek neighborhood, where Elliott L. Story taught school and where many members of the Black Creek Baptist

Church and the Quaker meeting lived. People such as Story's patrons Carr Bowers and James Holmes established a Whiggish tone in the area. Thomas Pretlow, longtime member of the county court and patriarch of the most prominent Quaker family in the county, also lived here. Voters in the vicinity supported James B. Urquhart's 1839 bid for the state assembly, 42 to 10. In the presidential race the next year, fifty Whig voters convincingly outpolled thirteen Democrats.

Although the upper county typically voted Whig by a two-to-one margin, it included several Democratic strongholds. Fourteen miles northeast of the courthouse, in the Seacock neighborhood, lived James Clayton, the owner of fifty-two slaves, who won the legislative seat in 1837 and then lost it in 1838. Residing within two miles of his plantation were twenty-one men who voted Democratic in 1839, versus only ten Whigs. Four nonslaveholding Raifords living just a mile from Clayton became loyal Democrats. In the 1840 presidential race, twenty-one voters from the neighborhood again turned out to support Democrat Martin Van Buren's unsuccessful try for a second term; the vigorous Whig campaign that year roused thirteen voters. Clayton's influence had limits, however. Four miles farther northeast from the courthouse lived another cluster of Whigs, who delivered a 9–2 party majority in 1839 and a 10–2 majority in 1840.

Southeast of the courthouse in the Nottoway River valley lay the neighborhood where James C. Harrison and like-minded Nullifiers raised the standard of revolt against the Jacksonians in 1833–34. Although influential leaders such as Clements Rochelle and Jesse Parker guided some former Harrison supporters toward the Whig party, the region became strongly Democratic by the late 1830s. Notables such as Thomas W. Vaughan, James Maget, and Davis Bryant enjoyed obvious success in recruiting Democrats. The region between six and seventeen miles southeast from the courthouse included the South Quay Baptist Church and future town of Franklin, where the newly constructed railroad crossed into the county at the Blackwater River. In 1839 Democrats carried the area 51 to 23, winning the upper side of the river 33 to 14 and the lower side by a comparable margin, 18 to 9. In 1840 Whigs did a little better, but the Democratic margin remained a robust 56 to 32. On the upper side Democrats won 34 to 21. Voters living across the Nottoway, which divided the upper and lower counties, voted 22 to 11 Democratic in 1840. Almost all the Whig votes cast on the south side of the lower Nottoway in 1839 and 1840 came from a neighborhood fifteen to seventeen miles southeast of the courthouse, home to the deceased James C. Harrison's two brothers, Edwin Harrison and William H. Harrison, and to the influential Henning T. Smith, a member of the county court who ran unsuccessfully for the legislature in 1845.

For the most part, regions below the Nottoway River became Democratic. Ten miles south and southwest of the courthouse lay the Cross Keys neighborhood. Here lived Thomas Newsom, whose 107 slaves made him one of the two largest slaveholders in the county. Newsom's name soon marked the depot on the railroad, which had recently intersected the area. Also nearby lived Westa Pope, Henry Kindred, and Richard J. Darden; each were men of substance from families that remained prominent in Democratic party politics for decades to come. Cross Keys, an area of poor turnout through most of the 1830s, became a banner Democratic area after an outlying polling place opened there in 1839. Voters living within a close radius polled a 29–2 Democratic margin in 1839 and 27–3 in 1840. A little farther southwest along the rail line in the Flat Swamp neighborhood, fourteen to eighteen miles from the courthouse, a similar pattern developed. Planters such as James Jackson, Peter Edwards, and Nathaniel Francis set the tone. Some voted at Cross Keys and others at James Tavern, but nearly all voted Democratic. In 1839 Democrats carried the area 20–3. In 1840 the margin increased to 24–3.

The most revealing concentration of Democrats occurred in the Three Creeks region. Southampton's planter class, if scattered to some extent across the county, clustered visibly around Three Creeks. Six miles west of the courthouse on the Barrow Road stood Bonnie Doon, the estate of Thomas Ridley, who owned 104 slaves. The brother of the Democratic standard-bearer in the important legislative contests between 1839 and 1841, Ridley no doubt helped to secure a 10–0 Democratic margin in the immediate neighborhood in the elections of 1839 and 1840.[73]

Four miles to the west of Bonnie Doon, Robert Ridley himself lived at the Rock Spring plantation, and two miles beyond stood Rotherwood, the plantation owned by his cousin, Francis T. Ridley.[74] The prominent doctor-planter-politician William B. Goodwyn, who sat several times in the legislature during the 1820s and 1830s, lived just beyond, as did Samuel Drewry, whose nearby mill attached his name to the settlement of Drewrysville at the center of the fertile Three Creeks district. Several miles to the west, where Southampton bordered Greensville and Sussex counties, stood the Fortsville estate, home to John Young Mason, the former Democratic congressman, U.S. Senate aspirant, and future cabinet officer and diplomat. Of this group, Drewry owned thirty-seven slaves in 1840, a fraction of the number he would eventually command; the others each owned at least fifty-one. Dozens of other planters owning more than twenty slaves lived in the Drewrysville vicinity. A very few were Whigs, but the great majority voted Democratic, especially in 1839 and 1840 after the region was politically mobilized and a polling place was established at James Tavern. In 1839 voters in the Drewrysville area supported their neighbor, Robert Ridley, 56 to 4. The 1840 presidential election demonstrated that local politics had done much to determine national party allegiances. Martin Van Buren crushed William Henry Harrison in the area, 57 to 7. Partisanship, substantially rooted in local ties and affinities, controlled the preferences of voters in national contests just as much as in local ones.

Nothing guaranteed that the big man of the neighborhood would control its political destinies. The influence of one prominent individual could be negated if other men of stature in the area had differing political loyalties. John A. Persons, a large and reputedly benevolent slaveholder, lived in political isolation, the only Whig for miles around in the intensely Democratic far southwest of the lower county. Joseph T. Claud, a member of the county court and the owner of sixty slaves, may have nudged two or three other lesser folk in a Whiggish way, but the proliferation of high-status Democrats in Drewrysville circumscribed Claud's influence. Prosperous William D. Hood, the owner of twenty-two slaves and soon a member of the county court, might have had influence elsewhere, but because he lived in the Round Hill neighborhood north of the courthouse near several notable Whigs, Hood's Democratic proclivities appear to have had little impact beyond three members of the slaveless Spivey family.

Neighborhoods containing both Whigs and Democrats sometimes resulted from the residential proximity of influential men with rival partisan allegiances. For example, Jeremiah Cobb, longtime member of the county court and Democratic legislator in the early 1830s, lived near Whig leader Edward Butts, who twice won the same seat in the mid–1830s. Their neighborhood, seven miles northwest of the courthouse, regularly recorded both Democratic and Whig votes. Similarly, Thomas J. Pretlow, a Whig, and James D. Bryant, a Democrat, future members of the county court who competed for the legislative seat in 1851, lived near each other about four miles north to northeast of Jerusalem, in a neighborhood that remained politically divided.

Throughout the antebellum South, local patterns extended widely enough to give most counties a partisan identity.[75] Southampton, however, developed closely balanced parties. Even though voters clustered by neighborhoods in an entirely typical manner, the county embraced approximately equal numbers of Whigs and Democrats. Party loyalty in Southampton, instead of simply encouraging local folk to follow the lead of influential residents, therefore institutionalized a means through which leaders could compete against each other, at least for the county's seat in the House of Delegates (Virginia had no popularly elected state or county offices until 1851). That competition forged loyalties to rival state and national organizations, each with distinctive ideologies. By 1839 and 1840 two-party politics had become a tangible reality in Old Southampton.

IN SOUTHAMPTON AND ACROSS the nation, the 1840 presidential contest brought the partisan stirrings of the previous decade to their fullest expression. Although little direct evidence survives about local manifestations of the famous "log cabin and hard cider" campaign, the results speak eloquently enough. Fully 750 voters cast ballots, twice as many as four years before and far more than in any previous presidential election. Whigs and Democrats both exerted themselves, and each party polled an impressive vote. The Whig ticket pledged to William Henry Harrison gained a slender victory, 378 to 372, over the Democratic slate supporting the incumbent president, Martin Van Buren.

The Harrison-Van Buren struggle marked a major milestone. For the first time ever, two national parties each united behind a single presidential candidate and launched aggressive campaigns in all parts of the nation. An incessant series of political events took place in metropolitan centers, and the excitement spread to the countryside. Squads of orators and visiting dignitaries fanned out to stir public interest.

Whig managers appealed to the states rights wing of the party, formidable in Virginia and the Southeast, by nominating one of their leaders for vice-president. Virginia's John Tyler, at odds with Jackson and Van Buren ever since the Nullification Crisis, also disagreed with more national Whigs on many matters of public policy. These disagreements, destined to become poisonous after the Harrison-Tyler ticket swept to victory and Tyler succeeded as president upon Harrison's untimely death, remained hidden during the campaign. Whig orators instead lambasted Van Buren for executive usurpation, asserting that "Tippecanoe" Harrison would restore the virtuous republic.[76]

Virginia provided one of the principal battlegrounds in 1840. The state supported Van Buren in 1836, but Democratic defections thereafter paralyzed the legislature, so much so that it could not fill a vacant U.S. Senate seat. Whig gains in the state elections of April 1840 added momentum and energy to the Harrison-Tyler effort. Democrats, however, battled back. Aided by a huge turnout in German-origin counties in the Shenandoah Valley and by the return to the party of John C. Calhoun's admirers in eastern Virginia, Democrats narrowly held Virginia, 43,893 to 42,501. Virginia thus resisted the national Whig trend, although its record turnout for a presidential election dovetailed perfectly with patterns elsewhere.[77]

In Southampton, no striking discontinuities separated the Whig loss in May 1839 from the razor-thin Whig victory in the presidential election a year and a half later. As in 1839, those voting in 1840 remained overwhelmingly loyal to their earlier preferences.[78] Whigs overcame a seventy-vote handicap by mobilizing a strong turnout among their upper-county supporters and by eroding the Democratic base in the lower county. Upper-county residents increased their turnout from 67 percent to 73 percent of those eligible, while maintaining a two-to-one Whig advantage. Turnout among eligibles in the lower county, where Democrats were strongest, slipped slightly from 67 percent to 66 percent. The Democratic proportion of the vote in the lower county, over 81 percent in 1839, ebbed to 75 percent in 1840.[79]

Nonslaveholders contributed greatly to the 1840 Whig victory. Known nonslaveholders and those without listed slaveholdings (most of whom probably owned no slaves) split their votes evenly in 1839, enabling Southampton slaveholders to deliver a solid Democratic victory. In 1840, however, Whigs outpolled Democrats by over fifty votes among unlisteds and nonslaveholders, an advantage just large enough that it could not be overcome by Democratic majorities among slaveholders. In both elections, nonslaveholders living in the upper county polled a big Whig vote.[80] Large slaveholders could not be blamed for the Democratic sag. In 1840 owners of ten or more slaves voted 62 percent Democratic (see app. table 4.3). Those in the lower county voted 82 percent Democratic.[81]

Most church members in Southampton voted in 1840 as they had in 1839. That is, Democrats compiled a large margin among Methodists, especially in two lower-county congregations, Barnes and Whiteheads. Baptists remained divided, although Whigs in 1840 carried the Black Creek church by a larger margin than Democrats did the South Quay church, so that Southampton Baptists overall voted Whig, 34 to 26. For the first time, local Quakers voted in tandem with their coreligionists elsewhere, delivering an 8–4 Whig margin. The greater receptivity of upper-county Quakers to 1840 Whig appeals is entirely consistent with the evidence that Whigs that year ran more strongly than in 1839 among nonslaveholders.

The measurable Whiggish trend between 1839 and 1840 also affected the legislative races. In April 1840 Democrat Robert Ridley barely held his seat in the assembly, edging James B. Urquhart by a narrower margin than the year before, 369 to 355. One year later, in April 1841, Urquhart finally gained revenge, defeating Ridley, 382 to 343.

THE SOLIDIFICATION OF DIFFERING partisan identities in upper and lower Southampton appears broadly consistent with what is already known about the socioeconomic bases of antebellum partisanship in Virginia. The Democratic party, as historian William G. Shade has noted, characteristically paired groups at opposite ends of the spectrum: an "old aristocratic leadership with a slaveless electorate." [82] In Southampton the Democratic party brought together a privileged group of traditionalist leaders and an increasing number of landless followers at the economic fringes of society. During the first stages of partisan awakening in the 1830s, Democrats ran strongest in the plantation regions of the lower county. Party managers there stirred a strong increase in voter turnout in 1839. It was not until the mid–1850s, however, after the Virginia franchise had been widened to include all adult white men, that lower-county Democratic leaders succeeded in fully mobilizing their humbler neighbors.

The Democratic base in lower Southampton had a sharply skewed concentration of landed wealth (see app. table 4.4). Almost half the adult white male household heads in the lower county owned no land, compared with less than a third in the upper county. More than six out of ten white male household heads in the upper county owned small or moderate sized parcels of property, compared with barely three out of ten in the lower county. Yet almost 22 percent of lower-county residents were among the county's largest landholders, compared with fewer than 9 percent in the upper county. Small and medium property holders predominated in the upper county, whereas the landless and the large landholders together included almost 70 percent of adult white male household heads in the lower county.

Patterns of slaveholding in the upper and lower county differed quite substantially (see app. table 4.5). Close to 71 percent of white male household heads in the upper county either owned no slaves or fewer than four. In the lower county that segment included under 59 percent. On the other hand, twice the proportion of white male household heads in the lower county owned ten or more slaves (almost 27 percent) as in the upper county (under 14 percent).

Population statistics also help to illuminate the differing characteristics of Southampton's upper- and lower-county regions (see app. table 1.1). In the late antebellum era the county overall had approximately equal numbers of slaves and whites. Because one person in eight was a free black, the county had a black majority. In the lower county slaves and free blacks together outnumbered whites almost two to one. In the upper county, however, whites substantially outnumbered slaves, and they narrowly outnumbered free blacks and slaves combined. Overall, more than 57 percent of Southampton whites lived in the upper county, whereas over 59 percent of Southampton slaves lived in the lower county.

The emerging consensus among scholars of antebellum politics depicts southern Whigs as more cosmopolitan, more oriented toward towns, trade, and manufacturing, and therefore likely to be underrepresented in outlying agricultural areas and among the lower strata of the electorate.[83] How do the Whiggish preferences of Southampton's upper-county residents square with this paradigm? The upper county did include Jerusalem, the county seat, as well as the future commercial entrepot, Franklin, where the new railroad intersected the Blackwater River. But few people lived in either town, and neither was a center of Whig strength, which clustered instead in various outlying neighborhoods.

The characteristics of Southampton's Whigs nevertheless do suggest important things, broadly consistent with the emerging paradigm, that shed a good deal of light on the makeup of party constituencies in the antebellum upper South. While Democrats tended to bring together those from the bottom and the top of the economic spectrum, Whigs ran better among those at the middle rungs, the small and medium landholders who owned either no slaves or relatively few slaves. The example of Southampton suggests that neighborhoods with sharp skews of wealth tended to be Democratic, whereas those with smallholding demographic characteristics tended to be Whig.

Almost 60 percent of the smallest landholders voted Whig in the 1840 presidential election, and Whigs outnumbered Democrats among small and medium landholders combined by a margin of over 54 percent (see app. table 4.6). Large landholders, however, voted Democratic by a margin of greater than two to one. The combined vote of nonlandowning voters and large landholders gave Democrats a margin of over 58 percent. Almost two-thirds of the Whig vote came from small and medium property holders, compared to little more than half the Democratic vote.

Residence, however, influenced voting behavior more than property holding per se (see app. table 4.7). Large property holders were more likely to live in the lower county, but those who did live in the upper county tended to vote Whig. Small property holders, conversely, were more likely to live in the upper county, but those living in the lower county voted Democratic. Differing patterns of property holding in the two regions of the county did, however, create differing partisan environments. The base of small and medium property holders in the upper county providing a setting conducive to the development of Whig loyalties.[84]

Although Whigs in Virginia and the antebellum South did attract cosmopolitian modernizers who clustered in towns and along trade routes, the party needed additional bases of support to compete effectively. In the Deep South, Whigs ran well among planters. Whigs in the upper South, however, were not a planter party. Yet in the upper South the Whig party and its successors (American, Opposition, Constitutional Union) persisted far more vigorously than in the lower South, which became overwhelmingly Democratic during the 1850s. In the upper South the Whig party plainly enjoyed a base of support that proved more durable than the planters of Georgia, Alabama, and Mississippi.[85]

Upper Southampton, with relatively few large landholdings and widespread small and medium landholdings, offers an important clue. Its emergence as a Whig stronghold had parallels elsewhere in the upper South. Similar patterns of dispersed landholding, support for economic development and transportation improvements, and a dislike of Andrew Jackson also characterized the very Whiggish parts of the North Carolina piedmont, which also shared upper Southampton's tradition of religious egalitarianism.[86]

Southampton's experience may also shed light on the perplexing question of how the slavery issue contributed to the formation of political parties in the antebellum South. Historian William J. Cooper, Jr., has insisted correctly that "slavery and slave-related issues" became a major ingredient in southern political discourse from the 1830s onward. Historian Harry L. Watson has noted, however, that southern partisans had difficulty in "putting the issue to good use." Agreeing with Cooper that "the slavery question had intense emotional power" and that each national party had a northern wing "somewhat tainted with antislavery sentiment," Watson nevertheless suggests that "swapping charges on the slavery issue" proved an ineffective way "to summon voters to the polls." Attacks on "the proslavery soundness of the opposing party" were atypical before the late 1840s, Watson concludes, because party organizers found it more productive "to emphasize the differences between the parties, not their similarities." Historian William W. Freehling likewise concludes that "outbursts over loyaltiy to slavery" were "more a periodic distraction than the constant essence of political strife" between southern Democrats and Whigs before the 1850s, especially in the upper South.[87]

No more than fragmentary evidence survives about the appeals that party organizers directed to Southampton voters. What is known, however, when combined with uniquely fine data about voter behavior, appears consistent with Watson's and Freehling's view. The most important Southampton elections during the era of party formation were the two legislative contests in 1835 and the legislative and presidential races in 1839 and 1840. These elections were watersheds in the formation of party allegiances among the electorate. The first big surge of partisan voting in Old Southampton occurred in the Butts-Goodwyn legislative races of January and April 1835. Slave-related issues do not appear to have figured in these contests at all. Both occurred before the national antiabolition panic in the summer of 1835. Moreover, voter turnout in 1835 stood well above the levels of 1836, by which time the antiabolition furor had politicized the slavery issue. The 1836 presidential election, conducted in the South amid a barrage of what Cooper has aptly called "the politics of slavery," attracted barely half as many Southampton voters to the polls as the hotly contested legislative race of April 1835.[88]

Events in Southampton in 1839 and 1840 likewise cast doubt on the idea that partisanship was fueled primarily by the politics of slavery. The Urquhart-Ridley contests for the legislative seat in 1839 and 1840, which provided the context for the 1840 presidential election race, do not appear to have involved accusations that either candidate was unsound on the slavery issue. Any such accusations would have been inherently implausible, because the candidates came from the two largest slaveholding families in the county. Although southern politicians and newspaper editors swapped charges of unsoundness on the slave issue in the 1840 presidential contest, their efforts made little impact in Southampton. Voter responses to the showdown between Van Buren and Harrison closely resembled the 1839 legislative race, with the principal difference being Whig gains in 1840 among nonslaveholders, among whom were some emancipationists. If slavery "dwarfed all other political issues" as the two-party system developed in the South, one would expect to find more corroborating evidence in Southampton, which had ample recent reason to heed such appeals.[89]

WHAT CONCLUSIONS MAY BE REACHED from this examination of party formation in Southampton? Plainly, the old stereotypes about Jacksonian politics have little applicability. One cannot depict Andrew Jackson as an egalitarian influence or the political party that supported him as a catalyst for democratization or the promotion of popular politics. In Southampton as in many other parts of eastern Virginia, Jackson's supporters had a large investment in the status quo. The Virginia version of the Jacksonian party swore fealty to traditionalistic Virginia particularism, while denouncing the nationalist heresies of John Quincy Adams and Henry Clay.

The first phase of Virginia's political awakening occurred in the 1830s, not because of any initiative by Jackson or his partisans but rather because of tensions within the Jacksonian coalition. By the mid and late 1830s, competitive two-party politics supplanted Jacksonian dominance, both in Southampton and statewide. The initiative for the transformation necessarily came from anti-Jackson elements, who formed the Whig party.

Southampton's Whig party originated as a conglomeration of political opposites. It included the previously anti-Jackson National Republicans, who favored federal support for internal improvements and economic diversification—the so-called American System associated with Clay and Adams. Disaffected Democrats, upset by Jackson's stern treatment of South Carolina, allied with the Nationals in 1833 and 1834. Southampton Whigs in 1834 elected James C. Harrison, a Nullifier, to the legislature. The coalition of Nationals and Nullifiers proved only temporary, however. Most Nullifiers gravitated back toward the Democratic party by the end of the decade.

The characteristic Whig ideology—a fear of arbitrary executive power—appealed to Virginia's particularistic traditions. Concerns about despotic and monarchical behavior resonated, and many thought Jackson and Van Buren menaced the republic. The Conservative revolt, which detached additional former Jackson loyalists from the Democratic party in the latter 1830s, gained momentum in Virginia from such fears at least as much as from the economic issues involved. Whigs thereby attracted new supporters while continuing to appeal to the Nationals. The alliance between Conservatives and Whigs stimulated two-party competition, both in Southampton and statewide. James B. Urquhart, the Whig legislator and/or candidate between 1838 and 1842, had Conservative predilections.

Virginia's Whig party could not easily position itself as an egalitarian alternative to the Democrats. Some easterners who subsequently became Whigs led the retrogressive forces at the Virginia Convention of 1829–30. As much as or more than eastern Jacksonians, they resisted efforts by westerners to democratize suffrage requirements and to modify the apportionment system that favored the slaveholding east. Prominent Virginia particularists such as Littleton Waller Tazewell and Benjamin Watkins Leigh were elevated to high office by the anti-Jackson insurgency.[90]

But the rise of the Whig party, which of necessity legitimized the phenomenon of two-party competition, posed a challenge to traditional Virginia ideology. Virginia's Republican party had long maintained a suffocating consensus, in which institutionalized partisan competition had no part. The disintegration of the Republican coalition and the rise of a fresh opposition party posed new challenges to the gentlemanly status quo. However much eastern Whigs proclaimed themselves better champions of eastern traditionalism than their Jacksonian counterparts—and many made exactly this type of appeal—their presence could not help but erode the old order.

Furthermore, the emerging Whig party in Virginia during the 1830s included the more liberal heirs of the Jeffersonian and Madisonian traditions, who remained out of step with states rights particularism. Notable examples included James Barbour, a member of John Quincy Adams's cabinet, and Charles Fenton Mercer, promoter of internal improvements and opponent of slavery. The Conservative revolt moved the prominent William Cabell Rives, a disciple of Madison's, toward the Whig party.[91]

The presence in Southampton of whites who had religious and moral objections to slavery added an unusual twist to local political alignments. However uncharacteristic in the broader spectrum of southern antebellum politics, they were connected by ties of kinship and church membership to prominent Whig leaders in the upper county. Southampton's emancipationists became an integral part of the local Whig party, making it an unusually heterogeneous coalition. Their movement into the Whig party by the late 1830s doubtless stimulated the movement of Nullifiers back toward the Democrats.

Two-party politics almost inevitably generated pressures to make government more democratic. Partisan competition drew people into the political process, thereby increasing the chance that their voices would be heard. Successful politicians necessarily became attuned to the sentiments of the electorate. Together with the expansion of the franchise in 1851, which was accompanied by making most local and state offices popularly elected rather than appointive, political parties had the potential to dilute the oligarchical qualities of state and local government in Virginia.

Yet this step toward democracy took place under paradoxical circumstances. In many parts of the country, as traditionalists often lamented, political parties opened the door to a new breed of professional politician, who gained power because of his loyalty to an organization rather than because of his intrinsic merit or stature in the community. In Southampton, however, Whigs and Democrats captured public attention by nominating men of undoubted eminence and running them against each other. The Goodwyn-Butts races of 1835–36 and the Ridley-Urquhart contests of 1839–41 had somewhat the same appeal as a horse race. The pairing of two well-known thoroughbreds, followed by rematches after the first race proved lively, must have stimulated popular interest. Withal, the first hard-fought contests between Whigs and Jacksonians in Southampton showed that "a local face-to-face politics of kith, kin, and deference" had begun to evolve into "a politics of party." [92]

Three interconnected phenomena became apparent in Southampton by 1840: turnout, loyalty to party, and linkages between local and national politics. More voters than ever before cast ballots on a regular basis. Their party allegiances, furthermore, became remarkably firm and persistent. Hardly ever did voters switch parties between one election and another. Instead, they supported the same party for Congress and the presidency that they supported for the state legislature. And their partisanship would prove durable: party choices made during the crucial six years between 1834 and 1840 persisted, often handed down from father to son.[93]

Historian Charles Sydnor's famous quip that partisanship in the antebellum South involved nothing more than "a stage duel with tin swords" applies poorly to Southampton.[94] There, with greater economic and cultural diversities than in most southern localities, the arrival of competitive two-party politics allowed two surprisingly dissimilar partisan electorates to coalesce. Smallholders who lived in the upper county, among them an increment of emancipationists, gave the local Whig party its distinctive quality. Lower-county planters and their less privileged neighbors provided the backbone for the local Democratic party. The economic and cultural differences separating upper and lower Southampton remained central to political developments during the last two decades of the antebellum era.

FIVE

Partisan Rivalry and the Expanding Electorate

THE ROOTS OF PARTISANSHIP sank deeply into Southampton's social matrix during the 1840s and 1850s. Annual elections (semi-annual in presidential years) required repeated reaffirmations of party allegiances. Close two-party competition stimulated popular interest in electoral politics. So did the removal of property qualifications for voting, as Virginia in 1851 extended the franchise to all adult white males.[1] The reform constitution of 1851 also made state and county officials popularly elected rather than appointive, creating new responsibilities for the enlarged electorate. Not surprisingly, many more people voted during the 1850s than ever before. Turnout levels also increased to new highs. From 1855 to 1860, 80 percent or more of eligible Southampton voters typically participated.

Virginia was a more Democratic state than the national average, supporting Democratic presidential candidates even in years they lost nationally. Southampton, slightly more Whiggish than the state overall, supported all three victorious presidential candidates in the 1840s (Whig in 1840 and 1848; Democratic in 1844). Local trends thus mirrored national ones: Whigs prospered at the beginning of the decade and in its last several years, but Democrats ran well in mid-decade, aided by the perceived failure of Whig economic policies and in 1844 by the Texas issue (see app. table 5.1, which summarizes Southampton election returns for 1840–61).

Whigs held the assembly seat in 1841, helping their party maintain a narrow legislative majority. When Virginia Democrats rebounded vigorously in 1842, easily recapturing the legislature, Southampton followed suit. Democrat William A. Spark defeated incumbent Whig James B. Urquhart by eleven votes, 373 to 362. Democrats lost some legislative seats in 1843 after raising taxes; one of those seats was Southampton's.[2]

A strong Democratic trend surfaced in 1844. At the spring elections Democrat Nicholas Sebrell won Southampton's assembly seat, 367 to 301, even though severe factionalism elsewhere in the state between forces for and against Van Buren prevented the party from maintaining its legislative majority. By fall, with Van Buren replaced by dark horse James K. Polk, who favored annexation of Texas, Virginia voted solidly Democratic. Southampton gave Polk a decisive margin over Henry Clay, 390 to 325. Democrats thus polled over 54 percent locally in both 1844 races. Turnout for the presidential election slightly exceeded that in the preceding legislative race, although it did not quite match the large poll in November 1840.[3]

Democrats held the Southampton legislative seat through 1847, as Whigs failed to mount strong challenges and voter turnout sagged. A new cycle began, however, in April 1848. Dr. Robert G. Griffin, a Whig, ran a spirited campaign against Democrat James Maget, who labored under the disadvantage of not wishing to speak in public. Maget counterattacked with a public letter, condemning his opponent as a "wolf in sheep's clothing" for claiming to support Democratic measures such as the recent tariff of 1846. Maget insisted that he rather than Griffin favored Jeffersonian and Jacksonian principles. Maget also made a bow toward Nullifiers, commending South Carolina for having "opened the eyes of the people to the true doctrine of states rights." When it rained on the scheduled election day, the commissioners agreed to keep the polls open for two additional days. Whig organizers fanned out through the upper county to enlist those who had not already voted. Griffin emerged victorious, 375 to 345, thanks to the strongest Whig turnout in seven years.[4]

The 1848 presidential race in Southampton followed the pattern apparent in April, although neither Whigs nor Democrats polled as full a vote. Downplaying issues and partisanship, southern Whigs attempted to exploit the popularity of presidential candidate Zachary Taylor, a war hero and Louisiana slaveholder, expecting him to have greater appeal in the South than the Democratic nominee, Lewis Cass, a political professional from Michigan. The year 1848 proved to be better than average for the Whigs in the South, or worse than average for the Democrats. Both in Southampton and across the South, the Whig campaign did a better job of diminishing Democratic strength than in building new Whig support. Locally, Taylor defeated Cass, 340 to 307.

Whigs mobilized effectively in 1849, appointing a vigilance committee in each militia district to turn out a full party vote for Dr. Griffin, who sought reelection to the legislature.[5] He secured a handsome total of 402 votes, exceeding by almost fifty a comparatively strong showing by Democrat Joseph H. Prince. The turnout of 71 percent in 1849 marked the only time between 1841 and 1850 when the participation of eligible voters exceeded the high figure of 70 percent established in the 1840 presidential race. Griffin also became the only candidate before expansion of the franchise in 1851 to poll over four hundred votes in a contested Southampton election.

The first election under the widened franchise, featuring a close race for governor, took place in December 1851. Although both parties increased their vote locally, Whigs easily surpassed Democrats. In sending Dr. Thomas J. Pretlow to the House of Delegates and supporting George W. Summers's losing bid for the governorship, Southampton Whigs won their most convincing victory ever. A few did not vote for Summers, who came from the northwestern part of Virginia and had voted in 1832 to rid the state of slavery. Most Whigs supported both of their party's candidates, however, as Pretlow defeated Democrat James D. Bryant, 501 to 410, while Summers prevailed locally over Democrat Joseph Johnson, 474 to 410.

The election of December 1851 proved to be the Whig high-water mark, although the Whig presidential candidate, Winfield Scott, received a strong vote in 1852. In Southampton as elsewhere in the South, Whigs preferred the incumbent, Millard Fillmore. Local party members resolved in April 1852 that Fillmore's support for the Compromise of 1850, "as an honorable and final adjustment of the slavery question," entitled him to the nomination. Southampton Whigs also pledged, however, to support the nominee of the Whig National Convention, so long as his "devotion to the Union shall be beyond dispute, and he shall avow his approval of the Compromise measures."[6] Some southern Whigs, interpreting the national party's refusal to nominate Fillmore as a repudiation of the Compromise, refused to back Scott. In Southampton, however, party discipline remained strong. Scott did not carry the county by quite so large a margin as Whigs had the year before, but he nevertheless polled a solid 498 votes. Democrat Franklin Pierce garnered 456, better than Democrats had done in 1851. Scott's forty-two-vote margin in Southampton exceeded that for William Henry Harrison in 1840 or Zachary Taylor in 1848. For the first time since the rise of mass parties in the 1830s, the county supported a losing presidential candidate. Scott carried only four states, two in the North and two in the South, and he lost decisively in Virginia.

The Whig party, both nationally and in Southampton, disintegrated before the next presidential election. Southampton Whigs did win the assembly seat once again in May 1853, as Democrats failed to nominate a credible candidate. (The reform constitution of 1851 lengthened terms in the assembly from one year to two, and biennial legislative elections replaced annual ones.) Democrats, however, won back the seat at spring elections in May 1855 that placed Virginia in the national spotlight. Henry A. Wise, the most flamboyant politician in the Old Dominion, captured the Democratic nomination for governor. Opposing Wise was the newly organized American party, which had shown impressive strength in many northern states the previous autumn. Most Whig leaders and voters in Virginia flocked to the American party, which nominated states rights Whig Thomas S. Flournoy for governor. Wise successfully blunted the American party thrust by mobilizing a record Democratic turnout, both in Southampton and across the state.[7] Locally, Wise polled 570 votes, soundly defeating Flournoy, whose 489 votes typified the Whig-American turnout in the sequence of elections following the elimination of suffrage restrictions. The 1855 campaign inaugurated a second phase in the new era of universal white manhood suffrage, during which Southampton Democrats convincingly overcame the initial Whig advantage in appealing to new voters.

The Democratic surge carried over into the next year's presidential contest. In 1856 Democrat James Buchanan defeated former president Millard Fillmore, the American party candidate, by an even more decisive margin, 570 to 458. At no other time between the coalescing of the two-party system in the late 1830s and the outbreak of the war in 1861 did any presidential candidate carry closely divided Southampton by a margin of over one hundred votes. Buchanan, who won an easy victory in Virginia, also captured Kentucky and Tennessee, the two historically most Whiggish states in the South. He lost only a single slave state, Maryland. Southern Democrats successfully depicted Buchanan as the only candidate who could defeat the Republican nominee, John C. Frémont.

During the latter 1850s the Opposition party, successor to the American party, scaled back Democratic gains. A similar pattern emerged statewide and across the upper South. Even though North-South partisan polarization pitted an increasingly southernized Democratic party against the antisouthern Republican party, Southampton Democrats could not convert their national party's prosouthern image into a reliable local advantage.

The election for the legislative seat in May 1857 proved quite close. Democrats squeezed out a narrow victory, 507 to 473, electing Lewis E. Mason, son of the nationally prominent John Young Mason, then ambassador to France. Lewis Mason, perhaps preoccupied by his futile efforts to stabilize the family finances, had little taste for politics and served only a single term in the House of Delegates. Traditionalist principles led him to oppose a subsidy for the Norfolk and Petersburg Railroad.[8]

Mason's 1857 challenger, Joshua Pretlow, the younger brother of Dr. Thomas J. Pretlow, ran again in 1859 and restored the assembly seat to the control of the Whiggish Opposition party. Pretlow's narrow sixteen-vote advantage over Democrat James Dillard, 542 to 526, was smaller than the Opposition margin in the concurrent election for governor. Democrat John Letcher, a westerner who won narrowly statewide, campaigned defensively in eastern Virginia because he had signed an 1847 pamphlet opposing slavery. Although Letcher vowed that he had changed his mind, several dozen Southampton Democrats cut him. His southern rights Whig-Opposition rival, William Goggin, carried the county by fifty votes, 541 to 491.

A debate in Franklin between the two candidates for governor, attended by a large crowd of perhaps fifteen hundred persons, highlighted the 1859 campaign in Southampton. Goggin led off with a speech of an hour's duration, complaining about Letcher's "abolitionist" taint. Letcher replied with a speech of equal length, defending himself and insisting that many members of Goggin's party hoped to effect a political alliance among all elements of the anti-Democratic Opposition, including the "Black Republicans." Each candidate then had half an hour for rebuttal. Observers from each party delivered diametrically opposite assessments of the event. A correspondent in the Richmond *Whig* reported that he had "never in my life seen a man so completely picked in a discussion" as Letcher. The latter "twisted his mouth in a thousand shapes" when listening to Goggin's "highly eloquent and patriotic" speech. A Democratic "looker on" described Goggin, however, as "a pleasant fellow, from whom you can draw more amusement than instruction." When Goggin opened his mouth, "the words fly like water out a pump spout, gush, gush, gush, until you stop the valve." Letcher, by contrast, was "a serious, earnest man," who was "far the superior" of Goggin as a debater, a "clearer thinker and better reasoner."⁹

Politicians from both parties did their best to carry Southampton at the fateful 1860 presidential election. The Whiggish Opposition matched its strong 1859 performance, winning 544 votes for the Constitutional Union party candidate, John Bell. But Democrats worked just as hard, polling almost exactly as many votes as Henry Wise attracted in 1855 and James Buchanan in 1856. In contrast to some other parts of Virginia, including nearby Petersburg, Southampton Democrats prevented any significant defection to national Democrat Stephen A. Douglas, who received only 9 local votes. Southern Rights Democrat John C. Breckinridge won 562 votes, giving him a narrow advantage locally. Larger Douglas totals elsewhere in Virginia allowed Bell to secure a wafer-thin plurality over Breckinridge, the only time Democrats lost a statewide election in the decade from 1851 to 1860. The total Southampton turnout, 1,115 votes, or 86 percent of those eligible, significantly exceeded any other antebellum election. Local voters plainly indicated that they wanted a voice in determining national policies, although they remained almost evenly divided between two parties.

INDIVIDUAL VOTING DATA MAKE it possible to examine closely political developments in Southampton during the 1840s and 1850s. Three elections—in 1848, 1851, and 1855—have been selected for analysis (more extensive assessment of the 1860 election and the secession crisis appears in the following chapter). The 1848 presidential election, the last before Virginia widened the franchise, serves as a baseline from which to study subsequent changes.

A comparison of the 1848 presidential returns in Southampton with those from eight years earlier shows that neither party polled as full a vote as in 1840, but that Democrats suffered larger losses. The Whig military hero, Zachary Taylor, carried the county, 340–307, over Democrat Lewis Cass. In 1848, as in 1840, residents of the two halves of the county voted dissimilarly. The upper county polled a Whig margin of almost 70 percent; in the lower county almost three out of four participants voted Democratic (see app. table 5.2).¹⁰

As in 1840, Democrats ran strongest among the largest slaveholders, whereas Whigs did best among nonslaveholders (See app. table 5.3). Thirty-one percent of Democrats came from families owning ten or more slaves; the comparable figure among Whigs was 18 percent. On the other hand, 55 percent of Whig voters came from families that owned no slaves. Among Democrats, only 41 percent could be so designated.[11]

During the 1840s the differing partisan loyalties of the upper and lower counties appear to have exerted an increasingly strong effect on the voting preferences of church members. Religiously affiliated voters in the whole county voted narrowly Whig, 59 to 55, about the same ratio as the entire electorate. In the upper county, however, Whigs won easily, 52 to 22, as the Black Creek Baptist Church (24-to-4 Whig) and the Quaker meeting (11-to-2 Whig) more than overcame the Democratic votes at South Quay Baptist and Indian Spring Methodist. In the lower county, where Democratically inclined Methodists predominated, Whigs lost badly, 34 to 7. Slaveholding among religiously affiliated Whigs and Democrats displayed even greater dissimilarities than in the larger electorate, with Democrats more likely to own slaves.[12]

Baptists divided their vote during the 1830s, and Democrats in the South Quay Baptist Church counterbalanced Whigs in the Black Creek Baptist Church. By 1840 growing Whig margins at Black Creek tipped the balance, and by 1848 no semblance of balance remained. South Quay, located in a border area of the upper county that never shared the Whig loyalties of the Black Creek region, gave Cass a narrow majority in 1848, 8 to 6, but Southampton Baptists overall voted Whig by a decisive margin, 30 to 12.

Previously apolitical Methodists first voted Democratic in large numbers during 1839 and 1840, especially members of two lower-county churches, Barnes and Whiteheads. In the county overall in 1848, Methodists preferred the Democrat, Cass, 40 to 16. Nine of sixteen upper-county Methodists voted Whig, however, among them Elliott L. Story and a majority of the congregation at Nottoway Chapel, where he maintained membership. Only at Indian Spring, where Daniel W. Cobb and several other Democrats were the most influential members of the congregation, did Whigs fail to carry an upper-county Methodist church in 1848.[13]

Because the 1850 U.S. Census listed occupations, it is possible to trace relationships between employment and party preference. Close to 80 percent of adult white males in Southampton worked as farmers. They divided their votes almost evenly in 1848, as 69 percent of farmers living in the upper county voted Whig, while 77 percent of lower-county farmers voted Democratic. Whig farmers were somewhat more likely to be nonslaveholders; Democratic farmers included proportionately more of the largest slaveholders.[14]

Residence had a greater influence on voting behavior than did farm value. In other words, upper-county residents owning more valuable farms voted Whig, even if not at quite so high a rate as those owning the least valuable farms. Lower-county farm owners displayed a Democratic tendency that cut quite uniformly across differing levels of farm value. Nevertheless, because small properties were more concentrated in the upper county, close to 59 percent of those owning farms valued at less than $400 voted Whig in 1848. Conversely, an identical percentage of those owning farms valued at more than $1,750 voted Democratic.

Southampton's agricultural economy in 1850 pivoted around the production of hogs. Smallholders who owned subsistence numbers of swine (twenty-five or fewer) voted Whig by almost a two-to-one margin. Farmers producing commercial quantities of swine (seventy-five or more) voted Democratic by nearly the same ratio. Lower-county farmers owned more swine than their counterparts in the upper county.[15] Cultivation of corn connected closely to pork production, with higher outputs per farm in the lower county. Corn was a dietary staple both for humans and hogs. The latter, although often allowed to roam free in the woods when young, were usually fattened on corn before butchering. Farmers who produced larger amounts of corn (as with pork) were more likely to be Democrats.[16]

Most Southampton farms well suited for cotton were located in the lower county. Local cotton output, hurt by weak prices, fell during the 1840s, but it rebounded briskly during the 1850s. In the 1849 census year, at a time when cotton stood somewhat out of favor, fully half the farms in the lower county produced at least some cotton, with the largest grower contributing fifty-five bales. In the upper county, by contrast, fewer than one farm out of ten produced any cotton. Because those owning larger farms in the lower county produced most of Southampton's cotton, its cultivation had a pronounced partisan skew. Approximately 73 percent of farm owners growing cotton voted Democratic in 1848. By contrast, Democrats polled only 42 percent from farm owners who did not raise cotton. Cotton agriculture and Democratic voting preferences went hand in hand in antebellum Virginia. Lower Southampton and the adjacent areas of Sussex and Greensville counties, the only part of the state with a climate and soil well suited for cotton, all voted overwhelmingly Democratic before the Civil War.

Approximately 20 percent of Southampton's adult white males had principal occupations other than farming. Over one hundred worked in the professions, broadly defined (lawyers, merchants and clerks, physicians, teachers, ministers, local government officials, and U.S. Mail personnel). More than one hundred also worked in various skilled trades (principally blacksmiths, bricklayers, carpenters, coachmakers, coopers, millers, shoemakers, tailors, and wheelwrights).

Of the ninety-six nonfarmers who voted in 1848, sixty-one voted Whig (64 percent). The total numbers, even if modest, do provide useful clues about antebellum politics. It makes sense that Whigs, generally considered more open to economic change and diversification, ran well among those with nonfarm occupations. Skilled tradesmen voted Whig by a decisive margin: twenty-six of thirty-six, or 72 percent. Although Democrats did better among skilled tradesmen during the 1850s, after the widened franchise, certain specialties such as shoemaking continued to exhibit strong Whig tendencies. Whigs in 1848 carried the professional vote by a closer margin: 57 percent (twenty-seven of forty-seven). Various groups of professionals displayed quite different preferences. All five lawyers voting in 1848 in Southampton cast Democratic ballots, as did five of the eight participating merchants and the one clerk who voted. Teachers, however, lined up as Whigs, 6 to 1. Physicians also voted Whig, 11 to 5. More than three-fourths of the skilled tradesmen and professionals who lived in the upper county voted Whig; two-thirds of their counterparts in the lower county voted Democratic.[17]

The 1848 election lacked the intensity and novelty of the log cabin and hard cider campaign, so that neither party polled as large a vote as eight years previously. The 1848 race was built on earlier foundations, however, and it elicited familiar voter responses. Whigs had a candidate whose apparent virtues made it difficult for Democrats to rouse their loyalists.

THE DECEMBER 1851 ELECTIONS brought 911 voters to the polls in Southampton, fully 264 more than for the presidential election three years before. The 41 percent increase in voter turnout was unevenly distributed, by both party and neighborhood (see app. table 5.4). Whig totals soared from 340 to 501, a 47 percent increase. Democrats collected 410 votes, up from 307, a 34 percent gain. In the upper county, voter turnout advanced from 393 to 574, 46 percent above the 1848 level. In the lower county an increase from 254 to 337 produced a more modest

33 percent gain. The upper county, which cast under 61 percent of the vote in 1848, polled 63 percent of the total in 1851.

Whigs therefore carried the first election under the widened franchise. They increased their vote totals both relatively and absolutely, securing an impressive 55 percent margin. Whigs won by effectively mobilizing the upper county. They greatly enlarged the total turnout there while maintaining a nearly 70 percent share of its votes. Democrats continued to run well in the lower county, but their percentage, compared to 1848, decreased from 74 percent to 70 percent. Slightly more than half the voters in 1851 had not voted in 1848.[18]

Liberalized qualifications enfranchised many nonslaveholders and their sons, along with some younger members of slaveholding households. The number of voters who did not head households rose from 133 in 1848 to 309 in 1851, up from 21 percent of the participating electorate in 1848 to 34 percent in 1851. Voters who headed households also increased from 514 to 602, although their proportion of the total electorate declined. Household heads who voted in 1851 were less likely to own slaves than in 1848. Then, almost 58 percent owned slaves; in 1851 the figure stood at 49 percent. Between 1848 and 1851 the proportion of all voters from slaveholding families decreased from 52 percent to 48 percent.

Voters from nonslaveholding families continued to display greater Whig affinities than voters from slaveholding families. Whigs received almost 61 percent of the nonslaveholder vote, one percentage higher than in 1848. Democrats gained 51 percent of votes cast by slaveholders, down from 54 percent in 1848 (compare app. tables 5.3 and 5.5). Whigs received 57 percent of their total vote from nonslaveholders; Democrats only 45 percent. Voters from families with ten or more slaves cast 26 percent of total Democratic votes but only 17 percent of total Whig votes.[19]

Whigs won a decisive victory in 1851 among voters with religious affiliations, 68 to 50. Although voting patterns did not deviate sharply from 1848, an accumulation of modest differences transformed a narrow Whig victory in 1848 into a solid Whig margin in 1851. James D. Bryant failed to run as well among Methodists as Democrats had earlier done, even though the candidate himself was a member of Nottoway Chapel, a small upper-county Methodist congregation. His Whig opponent, Thomas J. Pretlow, of Quaker antecedents though not himself a member of the meeting, polled an exceptionally strong vote among upper-county residents of all religious denominations. The respective slaveholdings of religiously affiliated Whigs and Democrats continued to differ widely.[20]

Occupational profiles for 1851 voters provide additional perspective on the Whig surge. Whigs gained by sharply increasing their vote among Southampton farmers, outpolling Democrats by 65 votes, 358 to 293. Three years before farmers divided their votes evenly, but in 1851 Whigs carried 55 percent of the farm vote. Whigs did especially well among persons listed as farmers in the population census but not as farm owners in the agricultural census. This large group of tenant farmers, farm laborers, and members of their households polled a Whig vote of nearly 59 percent. Whigs carried 71 percent of the farm vote in their upper-county base.[21]

A rather different picture emerges when examining Southampton's nonfarm vote in 1851. Whigs failed to benefit from the enfranchisement of additional skilled tradesmen and lesser professionals. Whigs did maintain an advantage among nonfarm occupational groups, but by a smaller margin, both absolutely and in percentage terms, than in 1848. Democrats gained more than Whigs among skilled tradesmen and lesser professionals. Predictably, the votes of skilled tradesmen and professionals split along residential lines, as Whigs ran well in the upper county.[22]

Many more skilled tradesmen voted in 1851 than in 1848: an increase from thirty-six to sixty-six total votes cast nearly doubled the earlier figure. Once again Whigs did well among skilled tradesmen, winning forty of the sixty-six votes. Compared with 1848, however, the Whig percentage shrank, from 72 percent to 61 percent. Whiggish tradesmen, either more prosperous or more politically conscious, voted in larger numbers than Democratic tradesmen before expansion of the franchise.[23]

The professional vote increased 64 percent, from forty-seven to seventy-seven. Whigs maintained a slight overall lead among voting professionals, 41 to 36, or 53 percent, down slightly from 57 percent three years before. Once again, divergent patterns emerged among professionals, as lawyers, merchants, and clerks continued to vote solidly Democratic, 18 to 7.[24] Whigs, however, enlarged their advantage among teachers (10 to 4) and physicians (14 to 5), the latter in part a vote of confidence for Dr. Pretlow from his fellow professionals. Democrats collected seven of eleven votes cast by local government officials; most deputies and constables shared the allegiance of the Democratic sheriff. On the other hand, four of five voters employed to oversee or deliver the U.S. Mail voted Whig, as would be expected at a time when Whigs controlled the federal patronage.

One element about the December 1851 election in Southampton stands out. Mobilization of first-time voters from upper-county nonslave-holding families provided the foundation for Whig gains. At a time when 48 percent of the active electorate in the county came from slaveholding families, only about one-third of new voters in the upper county did so (see app. table 5.6). Of the 191 new Whig voters in the upper county, 126 (or 66 percent) came from nonslaveholding families, providing more than the margin of Whig victory. Sixty-four percent of new Whig voters from the lower county (39 of 61) likewise came from nonslaveholding families.

Why did Whigs appeal to Southampton nonslaveholders? Even if the pattern had roots in the 1830s, the results also must have reflected the distinctive quality of the Whig ticket in 1851. George W. Summers, the candidate for governor, and Thomas J. Pretlow, the candidate for the House of Delegates, stood about as far outside the proslavery consensus as practicing southern politicians could do at that time. Summers, who lived in the trans-Allegheny and had long been identified as a critic of slavery, ran as a strong antisecession nationalist.[25] His background and views cost him a few votes in Southampton, as he ran slightly behind the ticket. Summers nevertheless polled a convincing advantage, carrying almost 54 percent of the Southampton vote. Pretlow never concealed his doubts about the slave system. Plainly, it was winning politics in upper Southampton in 1851 to reject proslavery orthodoxy; Whigs benefited there for having stayed aloof from defiant southern posturing during the 1850 crisis. The voting results point unmistakably to the existence of a bloc of upper-county nonslaveholders whose values deviated sharply from southern norms.

THE FIRST ELECTION UNDER THE widened franchise in December 1851 demonstrated that Whigs initially were more adept at taking advantage of new opportunity. Their success, however, was susceptible to imitation. Southampton's Democratic party, that alliance of privileged property holders and their economically marginal neighbors, had not yet tapped its potential. In 1855 that would change. Henry A. Wise, the only mass leader in antebellum Virginia politics, wrested the Democratic nomination for governor away from the decorous gentlemen who ran the party. Wise's flamboyant campaign roused the slumbering Democratic giant. Party leaders, temporarily shelving their anxieties about the candidate, worked hard to secure a large turnout. They were amply rewarded. Both statewide and in Southampton, Wise stimulated a record Democratic vote, sufficient to turn back the challenge of the newly formed American party, which drew almost all its support from the Whig electorate.

Wise carried his party to a stunning victory in Southampton, 570–489, the first time that a thousand votes been cast in an election. The Democratic vote soared from 410 in 1851, a 39 percent increase, while the Whig-American vote remained almost identical to its 1851 totals. How did Democrats gain their victory in 1855? They did better than Whigs in getting party loyalists to the polls. Sixty- eight percent of those who voted Democratic in 1851 repeated their vote in 1855. The comparable figure for Whigs was only 61 percent. Party switching, heretofore almost unknown and still of relatively small proportions, also aided Democrats (see app. table 5.7).[26] The mobilization of new voters produced, however, the greatest changes in Southampton voting patterns between 1851 and 1855. Democrats in 1855 brought 259 voters to the polls who had not voted in 1851. Whigs in 1855 countered with only 173 new recruits. The margin of victory for Democrats depended entirely upon the new voters, because Whigs held a narrow edge among repeaters, 306–277, and switchers alone were insufficient to tip the balance. New voters provided 45 percent of the Democratic vote in 1855, compared to 35 percent of the Whig vote. Together, new voters and switching voters contributed more than half the 1855 Democratic vote.

Democratic gains in 1855 resulted primarily from an aggressive campaign in the lower county (see app. table 5.8). Record voter turnout there combined with a sharp decrease in voting among the Whig minority hint at substantial community pressures to vote with unanimity. Democrats, who carried the lower county by 135 votes in 1851 (236 to 101), posted an unprecedented 310-vote advantage in 1855 (362 to 52). The Democratic percentage in the lower county ballooned from 70 percent to over 87 percent. In all three lower-county voting districts, Democrats scored one-sided victories. They carried Drewrysville, formerly James Tavern, 71 to 12. At the new Joyners Store district, the results were similar: 105 to 22. At Cross Keys, where Whigs never ran well, Democrats collected all but 10 of 178 votes cast.

Whigs performed quite respectably in their upper-county base, increasing their vote from 400 to 437. Democrats scored offsetting gains there, from 174 to 208. Each party added about the same number of votes in the upper county, as the Whig percentage fell slightly from 70 percent to 68 percent. Maintaining their better than two-to-one advantage in the upper county proved quite insufficient, however, to save the Whigs in 1855.

Who were the new Democrats from the lower county? Most slaveholders had become regular voters before 1855; large increases in lower-county vote totals necessarily required mobilizing nonslaveholders. In 1851 members of lower-county slaveholding families cast 143 Democratic votes, far surpassing the 93 votes from nonslaveholding families there (see app. table 5.9). In 1855 slaveholding families in the lower county produced 162 Democratic votes, a modest increase from 1851. But the Democratic vote from nonslaveholding lower-county families reached 200 in 1855, more than double the 1851 figure. Plainly the Democratic surge among lower-county nonslaveholders determined the outcome of the election.[27]

Democrats remained, as they had been since the late 1830s, more dependent than Whigs on slaveholders and members of their families. But increased support among lower-county nonslaveholders provided the crucial key to Democratic success (see app. tables 5.9 and 5.10).[28] Ninety percent of nonslaveholders there voted Democratic, exceeding the 85 percent level of Democratic support among slaveholders. Democratic managers in the lower county exerted pressures for unanimity that apparently operated with greater intensity among nonslaveholders. The pattern visible in 1855 prefigured the secession crisis. Although the turnout of lower-county nonslaveholders would then sag, those who did vote cast nearly unanimous prosecession ballots.[29]

Looking only at 1855 voters who had not participated in 1851 (see app. table 5.11), one may discover a pro-Democratic pattern in the lower county of even greater proportions than the advantage that Whigs gained among new upper-county voters in 1851. Over two-thirds of new lower-county voters in 1855 came from nonslaveholding families, and almost 90 percent of them supported the Democrat, Henry A. Wise. This decisive surge more than counterbalanced the continuing Whig appeal among new upper-county voters.[30] Democrats gained among voters of all ages (see app. table 5.12).[31]

Voting patterns in 1855 among church members remained much as before. The Quaker meeting and the Black Creek Baptist Church carried Whigs to a decisive advantage, 61 to 31, among religiously affiliated voters in the upper county. Lower-county Methodists delivered a big Democratic margin, 30 to 4, not quite enough to tip the balance as Whigs maintained a narrow margin, 68 to 61, among known church members in the entire county. Despite Democratic gains among Methodists, the votes cast by church members in 1855 deviated much less sharply from 1851 patterns than did the overall results. The relationships between religious affiliation and party preference stabilized before 1855. Changes in Southampton voting behavior between 1851 and 1855 must therefore be assigned to other factors.[32]

Voting patterns among occupational groups reveal more about the reasons for Democratic gains in 1855 than do the voting patterns of those with religious affiliations. Most notably (and entirely predictably) a majority of farmers voted Democratic, 365 to 320.[33] Democrats also scored gains among the 20 percent of Southampton voters who had a principal occupation other than farming. Skilled tradesmen, overwhelmingly Whig in 1848 and still solidly Whig in 1851, voted narrowly Democratic in 1855, 38 to 37. The difference resulted from the emphatic Democratic mobilization of the lower county.[34] Democrats, aided by a wider margin in the lower county than in 1851, also carried the county's professional vote, 33 to 30.[35]

Any analysis of Southampton's 1855 election repeatedly reveals the impact of the Democratic campaign in the lower county. Slaveholding, religious affiliation, and occupation all continued to affect voting behavior. What most differentiated the handsome Whig victory in 1851 from the severe Whig drubbing in 1855, however, was the Democratic surge in the lower county. By depressing Whig turnout while converting other lower-county Whigs and stimulating a surge of new support for their party, Southampton Democrats in 1855 made their first big breakthrough in the era of the expanded franchise.

POLITICAL PARTIES IN SOUTHAMPTON organized their campaigns by neighborhood. In March 1849, for example, "a large number of Whigs" met together in Jerusalem on court day. After renominating Dr. Robert G. Griffin for the county's seat in the House of Delegates and listening to a half-hour speech from the candidate, the meeting appointed "Committees of Vigilance" for all neighborhoods in the county. Southampton at the time included only five voting districts. Fully ten vigilance committees were appointed, however, four in the lower county and six in the upper county. The ten districts coincided with militia districts. Five men were appointed in each of the nine outlying districts, with two party leaders entrusted to handle affairs in Jerusalem "and its vicinity." [36]

A perusal of contemporary newspapers establishes that a party's vigilance committee was expected "to urge and bring out the voters to the polls on the day of election." [37] For such a system to work, vigilance committee members needed to know the partisan loyalties of individual voters. The procedure assumed that turning out a full vote among party stalwarts mattered more than attempting to convert political opponents or wooing undecided voters.

As happened during the 1830s, when party allegiances first crystallized, clusters of Whigs or Democrats often lived in close proximity to each other during the 1840s and 1850s. Prominent individuals continued to influence local partisanship. On the whole, of course, the upper county contained Whig neighborhoods; Democrats dominated the lower county. To some extent, party loyalties developed a life of their own: they could be transmitted from father to son and from neighbor to neighbor without additional stimulus from influential activists. Party leaders remained active, however, reaching out to the newly enfranchised and making sure that those with established loyalties went regularly to the polls.

Upper-county neighborhoods generally maintained the political complexion they had developed during the 1830s. For example, a nucleus of Whigs who regularly voted at Berlin lived between nine and fifteen miles north of the courthouse. Shugars Lain and Dr. A. S. H. Burges, both prominent Whig leaders, lived in the area; Sheriff Samuel Kello, elected in 1852, lived nearby. In 1851 the neighborhood produced a 34–3 margin for Dr. Pretlow, who also lived nearby. Four years later, it again voted Whig, 30–4. The Berlin voting district, which drew voters from a more substantial area of the upper county, turned out a splendid margin for Pretlow, 183 to 34. Four years later, it remained Whig, albeit by a reduced margin, 127 to 52. The erosion of Whig strength in 1855 resulted in part from the opening of new polling places at Faisons Store and Black Creek Church, each of which drew some voters from Berlin. Democrats, however, plainly polled a better vote at Berlin in 1855. The voting district included a cluster of Democrats, who lived fourteen miles northeast of the courthouse. Aged James Clayton, who carried weight in the original partisan divisions of the 1830s, remained influential. His neighborhood voted Democratic, 13 to 6, in 1851, and the margin increased to 19 to 6 in 1855.

Sixteen to twenty miles north of the courthouse lived a committed

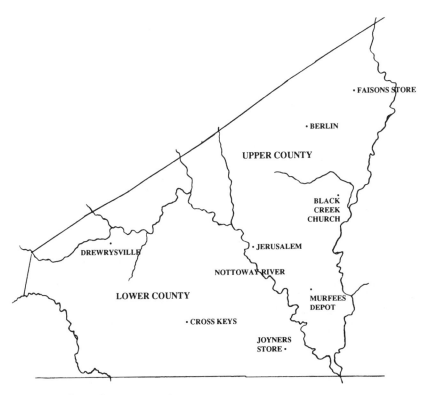

Map 7. Polling places, 1852–61

group of Whigs who had voted at Berlin or Stephensons Store through 1851 and voted thereafter at Faisons Store. Whig by a 22-to-2 margin in 1851, they polled a 26-to-1 Whig vote in 1855. This nearly unanimous Whig allegiance characterized the entire voting district, which spurned Democrat Henry A. Wise, 74 to 4. The prominent Urquhart family plainly exercised formidable influence at Faisons Store. James B. Urquhart, the former state representative, died in 1851. He was survived by several sons, notably Whitmel Hill Urquhart and James B. Urquhart, Jr., three brothers, and numerous other kin, ensuring the continuity of the Urquhart dynasty. Other prominent Whigs in the Faisons Store area included Peter J. Holmes, Patrick Doles, and John Boykin.

The neighborhood between six and eleven miles northeast of the courthouse voted Whig, 36 to 3, in 1851 and by an even larger margin, 40 to 5, in 1855. Its residents voted at three different upper-county locations until the establishment of the polling place at Black Creek Church

[157]

in 1852. The new polling place, drawing thereafter from numerous local Baptist and Quaker families, displayed a pronounced Whig tendency, voting in 1855 against Wise, 72 to 22. The Black Creek neighborhood included Beechwood, the ancestral home of the Pretlow family, where the widowed mother of Thomas J. Pretlow and his politically active brothers lived. Also residing near Black Creek were Dr. Robert G. Griffin, who represented the county in the state assembly in 1848 and 1849, and Dr. Carr Bowers and James Holmes, the patrons for Elliott L. Story's school.

By tracking the votes cast by persons sharing the same last name, one may learn how kinship networks helped to build Whig majorities in the upper county. For example, most members of the numerous Kitchen family lived in a neighborhood seven miles northeast of the courthouse. Because the Kitchens included several landless household heads and few slaveholders, they benefited from the removal of property qualifications for voting. In 1848, before the liberalized franchise, they cast five votes, including four Whig votes. In 1851 members of the Kitchen family cast eleven votes for Dr. Pretlow. Four years later, in 1855, they again delivered a solid bloc of ten Whig votes. The Kitchens, who more than doubled their turnout between 1848 and 1851, demonstrate how Whigs initially gained more than Democrats from the widened franchise. Comparably large increases of turnout among family-connected Democratic supporters in the lower county often did not take place until 1855.

Elliott Story's home neighborhood, three to seven miles east and southeast of the courthouse, above the Nottoway River, had a definite Whig orientation. Its prominent Whigs included James H. Judkins, Story's future father-in-law, several acquaintances of Story's among the Pretlow and Ricks families, which included both active and lapsed Quakers, and Benjamin F. Devany, former sheriff and member of the county court, who was also the Methodist minister at Nottoway Chapel, where Story worshiped. In 1851 the neighborhood voted Whig, 29 to 11, as a minority followed the lead of several influential local Democrats—John M. Gurley, Dr. James D. Massenburg, and Captain James D. Bryant, his party's unsuccessful challenger that year for the legislative seat. Four years later in 1855, the area again voted Whig, 30 to 12.

The new voting district established at Murfees Depot in 1852 included the emerging town of Franklin, the economic hub of the county. Within the district, in a neighborhood between nine and fifteen miles southeast of the courthouse, Democrats built their strongest local base in the generally Whiggish upper county. Democrats gained a 25-to-15 advantage in

1851, running against the strong Whig trend that year, and extended their margin to 26 to 12 in 1855. Democratic predilections among Southampton merchants and at the South Quay Baptist Church help to explain the situation. The Murfees Depot voting district, which also drew from adjacent Whig areas, voted Democratic, 79 to 72, in 1855.

Daniel Cobb lived amid a small cluster of influential Democratic neighbors. He and at least six others residing between six and ten miles northwest of the courthouse voted Democratic in 1855. William H. Nicholson and William J. Sebrell shared Cobb's partisan loyalties, as did Dr. John W. Gurley, who married Jesse Little's other daughter. Little voted only intermittently, but when he did so trouble himself, he supported Democrats. A number of people in the neighborhood, including Cobb, belonged to the small Indian Spring church, the only Methodist congregation in the upper county that shared the Democratic preferences of lower-county Methodists. Local agricultural patterns may have contributed to Democratic allegiances in Cobb's neighborhood. Most who grew cotton in Southampton took their cue from the lower-county Democratic elite. The bottomlands of the Nottoway valley near Cobb's were the one part of the upper county where cotton grew readily.

The lower county's Democratic loyalties, apparent since the 1830s, became almost monolithic in 1855, as Democrats polled a huge vote at all three lower-county voting districts—Joyners Store, Cross Keys, and Drewrysville. In each, one may identify a nucleus of prominent men who played active roles in the party. James Maget, county court member and unsuccessful candidate for the state assembly in 1848, was the most visible party spokesman at Joyners Store, which in 1855 delivered a big Democratic margin, 105 to 22. Maget lived in the very Democratic neighborhood below the Nottoway River and near the North Carolina state line, from eight to fourteen miles southeast of the courthouse. Democrats held a 19-to-1 advantage there in 1851 and a 23-to-2 margin in 1855.

Voting returns also show that partisan unity developed among persons who lived in the same lower-county neighborhood and shared the same last name. These apparent kinship networks contributed greatly to the Democratic surge in 1855. At Joyners Store that year, for example, every one of the thirteen members of the Story family who voted cast Democratic ballots, easily overwhelming the lone Whig vote cast by their cosmopolitan upper-county cousin, the diarist. Those same thirteen members of the Story family, which included only three landowners and two slaveholders, cast only two votes (both Democratic) in 1848 before the franchise was widened. In 1851, at the first election with universal white male suffrage, five of them cast Democratic ballots and two voted Whig. The Story family's big thirteen-vote Democratic bloc in 1855 may well have been engineered by young Parker D. Story, a constable and son of Miles Story. The latter's five slaves and land valued at $950 made him the wealthiest member of this far from prosperous family. Parker Story's three younger brothers added to the family's political weight.

The Vick family lined up similarly. Ten persons named Vick, among them only two landowners and one slaveholder, voted Democratic at Joyners Store in 1855. Joel Vick, Sr., a nonslaveholding landowner, appears to have influenced one of the more striking reversals in party allegiance that year, as a family-based cluster of Whig support disintegrated. Joel Vick and three sons cast Whig ballots in 1851; they and two other Vicks delivered six Whig votes that year. By 1855 all ten Vicks in the Joyners Store neighborhood voted Democratic.

Cross Keys remained the banner Democratic district in the county in 1855, even though some who had earlier voted there went to Joyners Store instead. In 1851 voters at Cross Keys gave Democrats a solid margin, 130 to 37. In 1855, however, they delivered an even more one-sided verdict, 168 to 10. The Democratic ground swell at Cross Keys in 1855 resulted from several different elements. A stratum of prominent planters—Richard Darden, Peter Edwards, Edwin Harris, Nathan Thomas, and Benjamin C. Waller—had long been loyal Democrats. Compared to Drewrysville, however, which lay farther west, Cross Keys had a smaller proportion of very wealthy men and a far larger proportion of landless farmers, carpenters, overseers, and other less privileged household heads. The key to Democratic success in 1855 at Cross Keys lay in stirring a fine turnout among ordinary white folk while reducing Whig support almost to the vanishing point.

One good way to grasp the forces at work at Cross Keys in 1855 is to focus on the Pope family, many of whom lived in the neighborhood between six and ten miles south and southwest of the courthouse, not far from the polling place. Some Popes were very well to do, notably Harrison P. Pope, a politically active member of the county court. But the family also included a number of landless and smallholding household heads. Breaking down their votes, one finds that the Popes at Cross Keys cast fourteen Democratic ballots in 1855, a sharp increase over the nine in 1851 and the eight in 1848. Here again, as with the Storys and the Vicks at Joyners Store, one may see the impact of family-connected voting, and one may see also that lower-county Democrats did not capitalize on the potential of the enlarged franchise until 1855.

At Drewrysville, the wealthiest voting district in the county, the Democratic margin increased substantially, from 57–27 in 1851 to 71–12 in 1855. Of those voting Whig there in 1851, sixteen did not vote in 1855, two switched party allegiance, and only nine repeated their earlier vote. Among the stay-at-homes were influential planters such as Joseph W. Claud and Howell Harris, both members of the county court, and William A. Jones, a former member of the county court. At the same time, Democrats gained support from twenty-nine first-time voters and five party switchers. An influx of obscure voters not listed in the 1850 census suggests that privileged party managers made a greater than usual effort to stir a large turnout.

Amid the huge Democratic tidal wave in the lower county in 1855, who still swam against the current? One finds Whigs clustered here and there. A nucleus of nine or more Whig voters lived fifteen to seventeen miles southeast of the courthouse, very near the North Carolina line. Two of them, Jonathan Britt and Orman Bryant, were members of the small New Hope church, the one Methodist congregation in the lower county with Whiggish rather than Democratic affinities. At Cross Keys, Edward Beaton, a prosperous merchant and a member of the county court, remained a Whig, as did the planter John Sykes and his two sons. Also among the few Whigs at Cross Keys was Dr. John R. Rochelle, whose family had long been prominent in the county. The identities of Whigs at Cross Keys suggest that privileged and well-connected persons could better withstand the pressures for unanimity that accompanied the partisan landslide.[38] The same possibility is suggested at Drewrysville. Conspicuous among the few Whig voters there in 1855 was John A. Persons, one of the wealthiest planters in the county but one known to have marched to a different drummer. Persons, it may be recalled, impressed his slaves as unusually kind and indulgent, thereby stirring criticism among his fellow planters.[39]

Additional evidence points to the powerful impact of neighborhoods in determining party preferences. Occasional Southampton families had branches in both parts of the county. Typically, family members in the upper and lower counties developed opposing party allegiances. A majority of the Worrell family lived in the lower county and may have taken a partisan cue from their most prominent member, Lewis Worrell, the owner of twenty-six slaves. Lower-county members of the family cast nine Democratic votes in 1855. That same year, however, all five Worrells voting in the upper county, none of them notable, cast Whig ballots. The Williams family illustrates somewhat the same process in reverse. The majority of the family lived in the upper county. They included a sprinkling of small landowners and slaveholders, though nobody of particular stature. In 1855 all fifteen members of the Williams family voting in the upper county cast Whig ballots. Yet in the lower county, eight of nine persons named Williams voting in 1855 cast Democratic ballots. The Beale family behaved similarly. Nine of eleven persons named Beale living in the upper county and participating in the 1855 election voted Whig. But all five Beales who cast ballots in the lower county that year voted Democratic.

PARTY LINES WERE TIGHTLY DRAWN in Southampton elections after the late 1830s, especially in contests for president and for the county's seat in the legislature. In circumstances where a Southampton resident faced an out-of-county candidate, however, county loyalties might supersede party, or at least trigger some kind of arrangement between the parties. In December 1851 Southampton voters selected candidates for governor, lieutenant governor, attorney general, and the House of Delegates strictly along party lines. At the same time they gave Southampton Democrat William B. Shands a bipartisan boost in his bid for the state Senate. Shands rolled up a 587-to-186 margin in the county over an out-of-county Democrat, Orris A. Brown. Every Democrat other than Shands lost decisively in Southampton that day.[40]

A well-documented example of blurred county and partisan loyalties occurred in July 1850, when Southampton and five adjacent counties chose four delegates to the state constitutional convention. Democratic strength in Greensville, Sussex, Surry, and Isle of Wight counties assured that Whigs, competitive only in Southampton and Nansemond, would lose all four seats on a party-line vote. A district Democratic convention nominated four candidates. That ticket ran into trouble, however, when a coalition of disaffected Southampton Democrats struck a bargain with Whigs. The bolting Democrats agreed to support two Whigs, Dr. A. S. H. Burges of Southampton and John R. Chambliss of Greensville, so long as Whigs would give their votes to two Southampton Democrats, Robert Ridley and John Young Mason. Friends of the latter played an instrumental role in concocting the bipartisan ticket, because the prominent Mason had been passed over at the regular party gathering on grounds that he no longer resided in the district. (Mason, who had recently served in the Tyler and Polk cabinets, spent most of his time at his home in Richmond rather than at his estate in Southampton.) The arrangement worked. Southampton voted overwhelmingly for the bipartisan slate, carrying all four of its candidates to victory in the six-county district.[41] One county thereby captured three of the four available seats, and Mason was subsequently selected to chair the state convention. Two decades earlier at the 1829–30 Convention, Mason and two other Southamptonites likewise held three of the four seats from the six-county district.

Nine years later, intraparty rivalries between Southampton Democrats and those in two adjacent counties became so severe that the party lost its normally safe seat in the Virginia Senate. Democrats in Sussex and Greensville, frustrated by Southampton's dominance of the three-county senatorial district, attempted to act independently. Announcing that they would "not allow Southampton to dictate to them," Sussex Democrats nominated their own candidate, Littlebury S. Mason, and refused to attend the officially scheduled three-county meeting. Southampton Democrats condemned "this departure from party usage, and disregard of the usual courtesy of associated counties, whereby less than one-third of the voters of the district would control the whole." Such "division and conflict in our party" gave "dangerous encouragement" to the opposing party. Brushing aside protests from the outnumbered Greensville delegation, which hoped to agree upon a candidate from Sussex or Greensville who could "command the vote" of the two less populous counties, Southampton Democrats nominated commonwealth's attorney John J. Kindred.[42]

Although heavy Democratic majorities in Sussex and Greensville meant that Democrats decisively outnumbered Whigs in the three-county district, the Whiggish Opposition had a rare opportunity to win the Senate seat in 1859. They met and nominated Dr. Thomas Hill Urquhart, a younger member of the most prominent Whig family in Southampton. The regular Democratic nominee, Kindred, attempted to repair the breach in the party by withdrawing his candidacy. The party, however, proved unable to unite. Disgruntled Southampton Democrats apparently encouraged John B. Freeman of Greensville to enter the contest. As a result, Democrats remained hopelessly divided. Most Southampton Democrats voted for Freeman, whereas most Sussex Democrats voted for Littlebury Mason. Urquhart, boosted in his home county by a series of dinners in each voting district, gained a narrow plurality victory over

Freeman, 720 to 652. Mason's 378 votes drained away enough of the normal Democratic base to determine the outcome.[43]

THE CONNECTION BETWEEN PARTISANSHIP and local government remains to be explored. Each county in Virginia was governed by the county court, which performed judicial, legislative, and executive functions. Justices of the peace, or magistrates, sat on the county court. They selected new court members, subject to the approval of the governor, which was only rarely withheld, so that the county court was effectively self-perpetuating. The county court appointed local officials, including constables, revenue commissioners, school commissioners, election supervisors, patrollers, and overseers of the poor. Of the two most powerful and patronage rich local offices, the court directly appointed the county clerk, and it submitted to the governor a list of three of its own members from which he selected the sheriff. The magistrates also appointed the commonwealth's (or prosecuting) attorney, the highest-paid local official.

The county court supervised elections by appointing officials to manage the polls and verify the results. It arranged for the upkeep of roads, bridges, and the jail. It licensed gristmills, ordinaries (or inns), and other stores that sold alcoholic beverages. It certified lawyers and ministers. It kept registries of free blacks, and it appointed whites to slave patrols. It kept records of property transactions, wills, and other legal documents. It appointed executors of estates and guardians for the estates of orphaned children. It regulated apprenticeships. It established local tax rates. It conducted trials for all but the most serious crimes committed by whites. It also selected from its own membership five or more magistrates to serve as a court of oyer and terminer empowered to try slaves even in capital cases. The county court convened once a month on court day; in Southampton, the third Monday of each month.[44]

Only with enactment of the reform constitution in 1851 did the power of the county court diminish. That instrument sharply curtailed the county court's appointment powers, requiring election of the sheriff, the clerk, the commonwealth attorney, the constables, the overseers of the poor, and the tax collectors. Also for the first time, court members themselves had to stand for election. The post-1851 county court remained, however, the significant center of local government.

Should one see the county court as a self-perpetuating oligarchy that protected the interests of a privileged elite? Or should one see it as a common-sense arrangement that channeled the energies of substantial persons into public service, thereby allowing local government to maximize its sphere of authority and preventing the growth of impersonal bureaucracies at the state and national level? The example of Southampton suggests that both characterizations have considerable validity.

The oligarchical features of the county court in the 1840s could hardly have been more pronounced (see app. table 5.13). Substantial slaveholders dominated the court. In a county where the majority of adult white male household heads owned no slaves, most court members owned ten or more. This apparent criterion for membership tipped the balance of the court decisively toward the lower-county regions where large plantations were clustered. In 1843 court members from the plantation (and Democratic) bastions in the lower county far outnumbered representatives from the small farm (and Whiggish) regions of the upper county. Only three of thirty-two members of the court in 1843 were Whigs who lived in upper-county Whig strongholds. Efforts to create a more equitable distribution of court seats in 1847 still left unmistakable imbalances. Several more Whigs did win seats on the court. Democrats, however, retained a clear advantage, and the lower county maintained disproportionate strength. Only five of thirty-eight members on the new court were Whigs who lived in the outlying upper-county neighborhoods where the party had its core constituency.

There is, however, scant evidence of popular discontent with existing arrangements. Tradition and circumstance, which assigned to men of privilege the responsibility for sitting on the county court, probably thwarted the emergence of class resentments. Perhaps too, court members exercised their authority in a manner that defused potential sources of complaint. Residents of the northernmost section of the county seem to have requested more representation in 1847, and that request was heeded.[45]

The first election of county officials, in May 1852, followed by only five months the intensely partisan statewide elections of December 1851 in which Whigs scored handsome victories in Southampton and over nine hundred total votes were cast. Almost as many voters (at least 882) reappeared in May 1852 to choose the first popularly elected county sheriff, county clerk, commonwealth's attorney, and justices of the peace to serve on the county court, the heretofore self-perpetuating mainspring of local government.

Considerable evidence suggests that Southampton elites of both parties resisted the introduction of partisanship into local government. Voters confronted a confusing muddle in May 1852. Only the contest for sheriff had reasonably clear partisan dimensions. And even there the situation was blurred, because a single Whig, Samuel Kello, faced three different Democrats, each with a distinct base of support. Because Democrats did not consolidate their strength, Kello easily won election as sheriff, even though carrying only a plurality of votes cast (392 of 878, or less than 45 percent).[46] For commonwealth's attorney, voters had a choice among candidates but not parties; Southampton lawyers all happened to be Democrats (whereas most doctors were Whigs). Because legal qualifications were a prerequisite for the commonwealth's attorney, four young Democrats from well-established families squared off against each other, and voting patterns broke along neighborhood lines. John J. Kindred, who subsequently represented Southampton at the Virginia Convention of 1861, became commonwealth's attorney with only 269 of 819 votes cast, or 33 percent.[47] Littleton R. Edwards, a nominal Democrat who was already established as county clerk (a position he would continue to hold for three more decades), won without opposition, collecting 750 votes.

The new state constitution of 1851 divided counties into magisterial districts and specified that members of the county court would be elected by district. In May 1852 each of seven magisterial districts elected four justices to serve a four-year term on the county court. The arrangement assured representation for all parts of the county. It inhibited partisan contests, however, because members of one party outnumbered members of the other in all but one district. Party affiliation would have become an important element in the selection of justices only if the candidates had run countywide.[48] In practice, however, partisanship was even more completely quarantined. Arrangements among leading Whigs and Democrats in most districts led to the selection of bipartisan slates, typically with two Whigs and two Democrats. Consequently, very Democratic Cross Keys sent two Whigs, Edward Beaton, a merchant, and Robert S. Jones, a teacher, to the county court. Likewise, Berlin's Whigs elected Democrats Milton D. Butler, a merchant, and John W. Cobb, the son of a prominent family. In five of the seven magisterial disticts, similar arrangements prevailed. Only at two districts did the apparent agreement to distribute seats to both parties break down. Democrats gained only one seat at the Courthouse–Black Creek Church district, and none at Faisons Store, the nearly unanimous Whig district in the far upper county. Whigs thereby secured 61 percent of the seats on the traditionally Democratic county court (see app. table 5.14). Upper-county Whig activists, recognizing that they had polled convincing countywide majorities in recent elections and resenting the long tradition of Democratic dominance on the court, may have decided to settle scores.[49] Voters, however, displayed little interest in the largely cut-and-dried contests for justice of the peace. The total number of votes cast in these sham elections often sagged far below the total for the sheriff's office, the one local position contested more or less along party lines. The new ground rules changed the party affiliation of magistrates more than their socioeconomic profile. Although the influx of new Whigs included William Bowers, a nonslaveholding tailor, and Stith Bishop, a farmer with only one slave, twenty of the new justices owned ten slaves or more.

Competitive grass-roots politics made little headway at the second election for local officials in May 1854. Samuel Kello won reelection as sheriff without opposition. Possibly as a quid pro quo, Democrats elected the two revenue commissioners by large margins. Voters also selected constables and surveyors in each magisterial district, often without opposition. The total turnout of around 728 voters was the lowest of the decade. As in 1852, elites appear to have discouraged the spread of partisan politics at the local level.

By 1856, however, partisanship became significant. A spirited race for sheriff pitted William W. Briggs, a Democratic revenue commissioner, against Andrew J. Kello, the twenty-five-year-old son of the incumbent, Samuel Kello. This contest produced a full turnout, with results very comparable to state and national elections in 1855 and 1856. Briggs coasted to an easy victory, approximately 560 to 474.[50] Democrats also retained the two revenue commissioners and the commonwealth's attorney.

No longer could the selection of the county court be isolated from partisanship. In every magisterial district, voters heeded party labels in choosing justices of the peace. Because all but one voting district had a top-heavy majority for one party, however, the party nomination became the equivalent of election in six of the seven districts. At strongly pro-Democratic Drewrysville and the nearly unanimous Whig district, Faisons Store, magistrates won election without opposition. At both Cross Keys and Joyners Store, a lone Whig mounted a hopeless challenge against the victorious Democratic slates. In the Courthouse–Black Creek Church district, Democrats ran a full slate which met defeat on a party-line vote, as Whigs selected Thomas J. Pretlow and Elliott L. Story, among others. Two Democrats in Berlin bled some votes from the third and fourth Whig candidates, but not enough to change the result.

Only at evenly divided Murfees Depot did both parties compete on equal terms. The result there was a horse race in which all eight candidates finished within nine votes of each other and each party elected two justices.[51] Because the other six districts voted strictly along party lines, the new county court was divided evenly between the two parties. This circumstance further inhibited it from functioning in a partisan manner.

The new arrangements did little to change the predominantly privileged makeup of the county court (see app. table 5.14). Despite a slight decrease in the number of members owning twenty or more slaves, more than three-quarters of those holding seats on the new court owned at least ten slaves. It should be noted, however, that the new court included three members of the Pretlow family: Thomas J., the former state legislator; his younger brother Joshua, who would soon occupy the same position; and their cousin John, who would have an eventful postwar career in business and politics. Elliott Story and James Holmes shared the progressive outlook of the Pretlows. The diarist Story, who had intelligence and ability but little wealth and only a minimal stake in the slave system, would never have been appointed to the pre–1851 court.

The May 1858 local elections featured a contest for sheriff between the incumbent Democrat, William W. Briggs, and former sheriff Samuel Kello, a Whig. The results paralleled preceding elections in 1855–57, as Briggs won handily, 502 to 431, gaining a larger margin in the lower county than Kello could overcome at his home base in the upper county. A respectable turnout of 933 votes, or 72 percent, fell a little below recent state and national elections.

Samuel Kello ran slightly stronger in May 1860, but he proved unable to regain the influential position he had once occupied. Democrat George W. Vick defeated Kello, 516 to 474, as 76 percent of eligibles participated. The election for sheriff had become the focal contest in local politics, quite overshadowing the election for magistrates. Many who cast a vote in the race for sheriff abstained from the district elections for justices of the peace. In six districts out of seven, of course, one party or the other had an overwhelming advantage. Fewer voters took time in 1860 to support their party nominees for magistrate than in 1856.

Democratic nominees for magistrate faced only token opposition in the three lower-county districts, while Whigs gained most upper-county seats on the court. The four Whig nominees at Faisons Store had no opposition. At Berlin, an arrangement apparently was struck to allow one of the four seats to go to Democrat Thomas J. Brister, a former magistrate, who soon afterwards sided with his district and against his party by opposing secession. The hybrid ticket overcame token Whig opposition, as many voters either acquiesced in or ignored the choice of magistrates. The Courthouse–Black Creek Church district did have a superficially contested race for magistrates. Democrats fielded a full ticket, including diarist Daniel W. Cobb, but they found themselves hopelessly outnumbered by Whigs. Three of the four victorious Whigs were incumbents: Thomas J. Pretlow, James Holmes, and diarist Elliott L. Story. Many who cast ballots in the contest for sheriff failed to vote for magistrates.

The election for magistrates at Murfees Depot, the only district with closely balanced numbers of Whig and Democratic voters, appears to have taken place in 1860 with little reference to party lines. Instead of allowing a sharply contested partisan race there as in 1856, local politicians at Murfees Depot in 1860 arranged a hybrid ticket, including incumbent Democrat Joseph E. Gillette, incumbent Whig Joshua Pretlow, and prominent merchant Alexander W. Norfleet, a Whig who soon sided with his many lower-county customers rather than his party by supporting secession. The choice of the fourth justice of the peace at Murfees Depot may have been left to chance. Most voters participating cast ballots for Gillette, Pretlow, and Norfleet, but four other candidates trailed far behind. The leader among the also-rans, and therefore the winner of the fourth seat, was a young Whig doctor, H. M. Smith.

Apparently by serendipity, Southampton once again in 1860 elected a county court with equal numbers of Whigs and Democrats. This symmetry persisted through the secession crisis, as one Democratic magistrate subsequently voted against secession and one Whig for it. The socioeconomic profile of the justices remained much as before (see app. table 5.15). Nineteen of the twenty-eight members (68 percent) owned at least ten slaves, and ten magistrates held more than twenty slaves apiece. The three Pretlows and their friends all were reelected. Much to their dismay, they soon found themselves administering local government in one part of the Confederate States of America.[52]

SIX

☙

Crisis of the Union

IN 1859, AS IF TO CELEBRATE the anniversary of the Nat Turner insurrection and to anticipate the shock that would soon be delivered by Turner's self-appointed white successor, John Brown, the sun assumed a strange appearance. Diarist Daniel W. Cobb reported that five "dimond circles" surrounded the sun before noon on August 18. Some alarmed Southamptonites said the circles were "ladys skeletons." Brilliant northern lights, rarely visible in the South, flared during the night of September 1–2. A "red streak" across the sky around 11 P.M. brightened until by 1 A.M. "it was light so as to see well." The unusual display "caused many to rise for day . . . to begin the days work." The next morning the sun again had a "singular" appearance. A week later Cobb reported "a Grate to do a bout a inserrection . . . suspected near Black Creek." Rumors suggested that black malcontents, inspired by the celestial signs and believing "white foalks the worst people in the world," plotted some kind of retribution.[1]

Little more than a month later, John Brown attacked Harpers Ferry. Cobb recorded in his diary a mixture of fact and fancy, alarm and relief. Locating Harpers Ferry somewhere upriver on the "Appermattox," Cobb reported that "15000 Negrows" led by "Browns Company" of "Abalisonest" had "expected to do much but dun little." Governor Wise had "lade the Dust with them," suffering only mimimal loss of life. But Cobb suspected worse to come: "I am perswaded this is the 1st of that sorte but only th beginning of much blood shead." In the weeks before Brown's scheduled execution, Cobb reported much talk and "excitement" about the "Harpers Ferry rebelion."[2]

Cobb's apprehensions were widely shared. "Not since the days of the

[170]

Southampton insurrection has the country been thrown into such a tremendous excitement," a nearby newspaper reported. It judged the "diabolical plot" a "direct offspring of abolitionism," defining the latter to include not only William Lloyd Garrison's *Liberator* but also mainstream Republican journals such as Horace Greeley's New York *Tribune* and the likely Republican nominee for president, William H. Seward.[3]

A meeting at the Southampton courthouse on November 21 resolved to organize a volunteer company "to repel invasion from without, or suppress insurrection from within." The "slaveholders and wealthy men" of Southampton were urged to arm and uniform the "brave young men" who were willing to fight to protect slave property. One militant warned: "You know not how soon the cloud that is rising in the North may overtake us. *We already hear the low mutterings of the distant thunder, and it is now time for us to close the shutter, and prepare for the approaching storm.*"[4]

The Harpers Ferry invasion "aroused the slumbering energies of the South," one Southampton observer reported. Local "military spirit" had been at "rather a low ebb." John Brown had, however, "fanned the dying embers into a bright flame." The local cavalry company, headed by Captain Joseph E. Gillette, "turned out like minute men" to drill. Although disappointed not to be called to Harpers Ferry for Brown's execution, the Southampton cavalry maintained a "rigid lookout" for "all suspicious characters."[5]

Surely many other white southerners saw the world much as Cobb did. Farming provided the sustaining interest of his life, and politics—especially national politics—only infrequently intruded on his consciousness. Did the South stand on the brink of disunion in 1850? Possibly, but Cobb was quite oblivious to the drama unfolding in Washington. Only twice during the entire year did he so much as refer to events there, and neither time did he suggest any awareness of efforts to hammer out a sectional compromise. Instead, Cobb noted only the deaths of John C. Calhoun and President Zachary Taylor. A similar absence of evidence marks the diary entries between 1854 and 1858, as controversies about the Kansas Territory intensified sectional rancor. Once again, Cobb simply ignored the issue.[6]

By 1857, however, Cobb had absorbed a political impression that promised nothing but future trouble. His diary shows him to have been quite credulous when Democrats tried to link their political opponents to abolitionism. "The [Know] nothing party has destroyed the Oald Whig party," Cobb observed. For the last three or four years Know-Nothings had tried all kinds of cunning "skeems" to defeat the Democrats but had failed. Why had they failed? "The nonuthingism they tell me sprang out of Avilitionism so it ought to have failed here in the South among we sotherners." [7]

In other words, Cobb was thoroughly receptive to the idea that an insidious alien force, which endangered slaveholders and southern slave society, had acquired formidable political leverage. The successor organizations to the Whig party—that is, the Know-Nothing or American party and by 1859 the Opposition party—were, in his view, tainted with abolitionism. Yet so long as the beneficiary of the supposed abolitionist influence remained local and familiar, Cobb could accept the outcome, however much he might regret the shortsightedness of Southampton voters. When Joshua Pretlow, candidate of the Opposition party, narrowly won a seat in the legislature in May 1859, Cobb responded philosophically. "I cant tell why," he confessed to his diary, "but the saying is everything for the better. I am willing to be governed by the majority." [8]

Cobb and other southerners of both parties soon had to confront a more ominous political development. The Republican party, lacking any base in the slave states whatsoever except in scattered locations along the border, became the principal Whig successor organization in the North. Cobb and others like him could not reasonably view the southern-based Opposition party as overtly dangerous. They could, however, take a very sinister view of the Republican party, which had no opportunity or incentive to defend itself to the citizens who gathered monthly in southern courthouses. Those men, with Cobb a representative specimen of the type, had ample stimulus to perceive the Republican party as an anti-southern conspiracy, especially after John Brown struck at Harpers Ferry. Would Cobb accept the results of the 1860 presidential election as readily as he did the results of the 1859 legislative elections? Would he remain willing to be governed by a constitutional majority of the electoral college?

The answers to these questions depended substantially upon the actions of local Democratic leaders. Available evidence plainly indicates that Cobb and other party loyalists received sectionally divisive cues from the party's cosmopolitian elite. John J. Kindred, commonwealth's attorney for the county, was selected as one of two delegates from the broader Norfolk region to attend the ill-fated 1860 Democratic National Convention in Charleston. There he and other Virginia delegates bolted. Southern Democrats subsequently chose their own presidential ticket, headed by John C. Breckinridge. A Democratic meeting in Southampton on July 16 endorsed Kindred's course, ratified the Breckinridge nomination, and pledged ambiguously a "sincere and loyal attachment to the union," so long as that union respected the "reserved rights of the states." Kindred thereupon stumped the district for Breckinridge.[9]

Many in Southampton reacted differently as the sectional crisis intensified. Diarist Elliott L. Story, seeing the nation as a neighborhood writ large, preferred that North and South "dwell together in unity and brotherly love forever." At no point during the period from 1846 to 1861 did Story take it upon himself to defend the South against perceived northern menace or insult. He noted the death of John Quincy Adams without any complaint about the conspicuous role the former president had played in building the political antislavery movement. Instead, Adams had "gone down to his grave in peace, 'full of years and full of honours,' and the nation mourns his loss." Northern efforts to bar slavery from the territories did not stir Story's antipathies, because he maintained a Whiggish skepticism about enlarging the national domain. He rejected President Polk's efforts to demonstrate the "justice and necessity" of the Mexican War. Story predicted, instead, that posterity would recognize "an insatiable thirst for the extension of territory" as the war's "true cause."[10]

A decade later, after John Brown's raid on Harpers Ferry, Story disdained the "great deal of talk and considerable excitement" stirred up in Southampton. Fearing that "these events will have a weighty tendency to weaken the bonds of our Union" and regretting that "our country is divided and distracted on the slavery question," he hoped the clamor would be "quelled without much further difficulty" and the crisis peacefully resolved. He had no use for southern militants who wished "to divide the Union."[11]

Story and other Southampton Whigs firmly supported John Bell, nominated for president by the Constitutional Union party. One August day in Jerusalem Story engaged a group of Breckinridge Democrats in "a rather warm political discussion." He worried, however, that efforts to avert a sectional confrontation would fail. Local southern rights promoters organized at least two chapters of the Knights of the Golden Circle, a shadowy Deep South organization that promoted Caribbean imperialism and secession. Local hotheads also forced a northerner accused of being hostile to slavery to flee the county.[12]

State elections held in Pennsylvania and other northern states in October, a month before the presidential election, showed that the Republican nominee, Abraham Lincoln, was almost certain to win. Upon hearing the news from Pennsylvania, Story feared that "the days of peace and Union in our nation are drawing to a close." He recognized that many in the South would consider Lincoln's election an intolerable affront. Soon he reported that "the probabilities of a rupture of our happy Union" had engrossed "the thoughts and much of the conversation of all reflecting men." [13]

Story's close friend and colleague on the county court, Dr. Thomas J. Pretlow, cautioned Southampton voters against overreacting. Venturing into the strongly Democratic and prosecession region of lower Southampton shortly before the presidential election, Pretlow delivered a passionate warning:

> Let me tell you my friends, if Virginia secedes from the Union your houses will be burned, your firesides will become desolate, your very hearthstones will be torn up. Virginia must sweat great drops of blood.
>
> The wailing of widows and orphans will come wafting on the breeze. The wind will sigh of the moans of the dying and the dead. From affluence you will become a poverty-stricken people. I would not snap my fingers for every slave you own. Misery and vice will stalk through the land.
>
> Pause! Pause my countrymen! There is a yawning chasm at your feet!
>
> If my voice is unheeded, I call God to witness that I discharge my duty this day to the utmost of my humble ability, that no man's blood may be on my head. [14]

Even though Story considered electioneering "a business not congenial to my feelings," he visited prospective voters in Nottoway Swamp, reminding them to turn out for Bell on election day. "Had pretty good success I think," Story judged. The numbers corroborated his impression. Bell polled 544 votes, as high a total as Whigs had ever attracted in Southampton. Such a vote could not have been achieved without strong support from the least privileged upper-county folk that Story enlisted. [15]

Unfortunately for Story, Southampton Democrats matched the zeal of local Whigs. In the weeks before the election, a Norfolk newspaper reported intense efforts for Breckinridge in "this sterling old county." [16] Local Democrats turned out a huge vote, especially in their lower-county strongholds. Moreover, they reduced to a bare 9 votes the county's support for the northern Democrat, Stephen A. Douglas, who ran well in nearby urban areas such as Petersburg and Richmond and won enough usual Democratic votes statewide to throw the state to Bell by a narrow plurality. The 562 votes polled for southern Democrat John C. Breckinridge gave him a narrow margin in the county. The 86 percent turnout of eligible voters in Southampton in November 1860 exceeded that of any other antebellum election.

But the votes cast in Southampton—indeed, the votes of the entire South—had no bearing upon the outcome of the election. Within a few days, it became clear that Abraham Lincoln had won the presidency by carrying almost every electoral vote from the free states. The impasse that Story feared had come to pass. By court day on November 19, "there was a great deal of talk about the secession movement of the southern states." Within a few days, newspapers reaching Southampton brought reports "of still greater excitement in the South in regard to the presidential election." Story feared that "the days of our happy Union are almost numbered." [17]

Story, Pretlow, and other southern Whigs understood the explosive potential of the sectional crisis better than most others, North or South. They could derive no comfort, however, from seeing their worst fears realized. During the weeks and months after Lincoln's election, Story noted that many in Southampton were "talking incessantly about secession" and that "the excitement about the state of the country was intense." His own mood, affected also by ill health and by the death of his wife only a year before, became very bleak.[18]

The example of Story offers little support for the proposition that a "great moral chasm separated the antebellum North and South on the eve of the Civil War." [19] Obviously, many other examples could be cited that better sustain the generalization. Story, however, was one of a good many southern Whigs who shared a mentality that was in many ways progressive and was certainly nonconfrontational. An emphasis on sectional polarities is likely to obscure their views and, indeed, to obscure their very presence. Sorting northerners and southerners into mutually distinct pigeonholes runs the risk of imposing an arbitrary analytical order on a messy irrational tragedy.

Before going to war, many Virginians first tried to preserve the peace. Antisecessionists, holding out hope for an eleventh-hour sectional compromise, held Virginia and the upper South in the Union during the early months of 1861.²⁰ Persistent Unionism surfaced in Southampton, puncturing the advantage that secessionists appeared to enjoy between late November and mid-January and temporarily intensifying the county's chronic political divisions.

The sequence of events in early 1861 may best be followed in Daniel W. Cobb's diary. Although his volume for 1860 has been lost, the daily record resumes in the midst of the secession crisis. Cobb found himself torn by conflicting emotions as the states of the lower South seceded and the country lurched toward the precipice of civil war. On the one hand he shared the widespread outrage about the election of an "Avalison" president. Yet at the same time, Cobb considered it ominous that he heard one hundred times more talk about war than about "piece." He hated war, thought it "awfull to think of," and feared that many lives would be lost. No fire-eater, Cobb hoped for a "frendly Compromise" on "honerable turms" to "settle matters without Blood shead." Why, Cobb wondered, couldn't an agreement be worked out to "live as here to fore," with the North and South both enjoying their "fore fathers rights"?²¹

As a good Democrat, however, Cobb was predisposed to follow the lead of Democratic secessionists. Their ranks included many men he looked up to and almost all of the other cotton growers in the county. In January 1861, when needing to select a delegate to the Virginia convention, they attempted to follow a strategy used by their counterparts in adjacent Greensville and Sussex counties. There, Democrats nominated a like-minded southern rights Whig, John R. Chambliss, so as to put the issue of secession beyond the reach of party politics. Southampton's Democrats tried to do the same thing, offering their nomination to two eminent Whigs, Dr. A. S. H. Burgess and Charles F. Urquhart. Both refused; Urquhart instead accepted an "independant" nomination to run against Democrat John J. Kindred. The latter, Cobb noted, was "a susseader" who favored "a quick go South." Urquhart, Cobb's neighbor, preferred "to stay." ²²

Antisecessionists insisted that Virginia and the upper South could arrange a peaceful Union-saving compromise. Even though Cobb had similar hopes, he conceptualized the situation in secessionist terms—"wheather Virginia will go South or not." Much to his dismay, large numbers of Southampton voters opposed the "quick go South." Instead, in balloting on February 4, 1861—a miserable day with driving rain, snow, and hail that left, Cobb reported, "more waters on the land than I ever saw at 1 time"—they divided "pretty much" as in the recent presidential election. Kindred, supported by Cobb and other Democrats, narrowly defeated Urquhart, 486 to 458. However, a scattering of Kindred voters joined almost all Urquhart's Whiggish supporters in narrowly favoring "reference," 466 to 460; that is, to submit any convention action to a statewide popular referendum. Southampton voters thereby delivered a mixed verdict, electing a secessionist while at the same time denying secessionists the free hand they wanted. To a greater extent than usual, slaveholders and nonslaveholders voted on opposite sides, the latter opposing secession. Local antisecessionists included Elliott L. Story and most of his friends.[23]

Cobb decided "we are ruin[ed]" upon learning that Virginia had elected a state convention with a large antisecessionist majority. "I shall leave V[irgini]a if the state hangs N[orth]," he insisted; "I hangs S[outh]." Secessionists fanned wild rumors, faithfully recorded in Cobb's diary. "Grate stur among us yet on politicks," he noted a week after Virginia voters had upended immediate secession. "Its thretened by whigs if the Union destroys to Rase a Reverlution a ginst the no Refference party." In other words, local hotheads suggested that those who had just won a decisive two-to-one statewide majority might revolt against the minority! The accusation, which in fact revealed much about the desperate calculations that ardent secessionists had begun to make, puzzled Cobb. If a "majority of the people" had voted for reference, he judged, they "ought to rule." But Cobb remained mystified about how his county could have supported both "Refferance" and a secessionist candidate. It appears also that Cobb found it impossible to reconcile his fear of war and his belief in majority rule with his southern and Democratic party loyalties. "I voted a Demacrat ticket threwout peace and war," he observed. "I think I am dun with politicks."[24]

All efforts to rebuild the shattered Union proved unavailing. The outbreak of war in April between the federal government and the Confederate states of the Deep South forced Virginia and the upper South to choose sides. Cobb welcomed reports that Virginia had "gone S[outh]." Blaming "Lincon" for the fateful turn of events, Cobb approved efforts to make "preperation for self defence" and to protect life and property. He remained worried, however, that the seceding states would face severe difficulties, and he found it "awfull to think of the lives that is to be lost . . . to protect self rights." War, Cobb reflected, was "something I hate."[25]

Elliott Story likewise made the same choice as almost all other white Virginians, except those in the far northwest. War left Virginia no choice but to side with the South, he reasoned. Story, however, thought the spectacle "enough to make any patriot weep." A month after the fall of Fort Sumter, he still held out hope that God might "direct the affairs of our distracted country that peace and brotherly love may speedily be restored."[26]

SOUTHAMPTON'S 1860 AND 1861 voting returns require closer analysis. The record vote cast in November 1860 closely paralleled the vote for governor in May 1855 (see app. table 6.1). Democrats won both in 1855 and 1860, but Whigs ran stronger in 1860. Democrats in 1860 almost exactly matched their 1855 vote, whereas Whigs in 1860 gained fifty-five votes, twenty-one in the upper county and thirty-four in the lower county. Members of slaveholding households voted almost identically in 1855 and 1860, giving Democrats a decisive 58 percent margin (see app. table 6.2). Whigs carried 53 percent of votes cast in 1860 by members of nonslaveholding households, 4 percent higher than in 1855. By attracting fifty additional nonslaveholders to vote for John Bell, the presidential candidate of the Constitutional Union party, Whigs made the 1860 election quite close. The relatively stable plateau of high turnout and Democratic advantage, inaugurated in 1855, clearly persisted through 1860, albeit with just enough new support for Whigs among nonslaveholders to make the 1860 election close (see app. table 6.3).[27]

Between November 1860 and February 1861, Southampton voting behavior changed more than it had during the preceding six years. In February 1861 secessionist Democrats narrowly lost the referendum, and turnout dropped significantly below the level of three months before.[28] The secession issue increased the polarization between the upper and lower county to an all-time high. Antisecessionists in the upper county polled almost as many votes as John Bell had received three months before (see app. table 6.4). The 447 pro-Union votes there totaled almost 98 percent of the 1860 Whig turnout. On the other hand, secessionists got only 125 votes in the upper county, 81 fewer than Democrats had in 1860, or 61 percent of the 1860 Democratic vote. The lower county cast 335 votes for secession, or almost 92 percent of the 1860 Democratic vote. But the number of pro-Union votes there fell to only 19, just 22 percent of the 1860 Whig vote.

All but one of the eight local voting districts in Southampton had a definite partisan identity. Only the Murfees Depot district had approximately even numbers of Democrats and Whigs. In the 1860 presidential election, these traditional patterns remained firmly in place (see app. table 6.5). Democrats swept the three voting districts in the lower county, also carrying Murfees Depot. In the four other upper-county voting districts, Whigs easily outpolled Democrats, with especially lopsided results at Black Creek Church and Faisons Store.

The February 1861 referendum produced distinctly more polarized results. Voters at the three lower-county polling places, who had in 1860 cast 82 Whig votes, close to 20 percent of the total, recorded only 9 votes against secession (ten other lower-county residents voted against secession at polling places on the other side of the Nottoway River). The pro-secession consensus in the lower county—335 to 19, almost 95 percent of those voting—allowed little room for disagreement. At Drewrysville, which had the largest concentration of planters in Southampton, every voter favored secession.

At the same time, however, residents of the upper county voted pro-Union by an even greater margin (447 to 125, over 78 percent) than they had voted Whig (69 percent). The results were especially striking in the three outlying voting districts in the upper county, which had a long history of Whig preferences and where antisecession feeling ran strongest. Democrats had gotten few votes at Black Creek Church and Faisons Store in 1860, but they had polled over 70 votes at Berlin, over a third of the total cast there. In February 1861, however, only 25 voters in the three districts favored secession, 23 of them at Berlin. Fully 300 voters, over 92 percent, opposed secession in the three outlying upper-county districts.

Voter turnout in the lower county in February 1861 fell more sharply than in the upper county. At all of the three lower-county voting districts, turnout dropped by more than 20 percent. Secessionist managers could not secure as full a vote as they had for Breckinridge. In the upper county, however, voter turnout stayed closer to 1860 levels, particularly at Black Creek Church, which had a larger percentage of nonslaveholding voters than any other voting district in the county and which opposed secession with near unanimity.

The regional polarization of the vote within Southampton in early 1861 was accompanied by a record polarization between slaveholders and nonslaveholders (see app. table 6.6). The county had long displayed a tendency for nonslaveholders to vote discernibly more Whiggish than slaveholders. The votes of slaveholders and nonslaveholders differed by 8 percent in 1855 and 11 percent in 1860. In the February 1861 referendum, however, the divergence grew to 19 percent, higher than at any other antebellum election. Almost 58 percent of voters from nonslave-holding families rejected secession, whereas more than 61 percent of voters from slaveholding families favored it. Nearly half the voters who supported secession came from slaveholding families (223 of 460, or 49 percent). Among the 466 pro-Union voters, only 141 (or 30 percent) came from slaveholding families.

Upper-county voters from nonslaveholding families overwhelmingly opposed secession, and by maintaining a higher rate of turnout than their counterparts in the lower county, they determined the overall outcome (see app. table 6.7). Over 86 percent of nonslaveholders from the upper county voted pro-Union. Although the total Southampton vote in February 1861 fell by almost 200 from November, more upper-county non-slaveholders voted against secession (318) than had voted for John Bell (310). The lower county favored secession so monolithically, however, as to keep the county almost evenly divided.[29]

The fault lines that split Southampton had parallels across the South. The upper county, like most of the upper South, had no use for secession. Upper-county nonslaveholders, who were more Whiggish and antisecession than upper-county slaveholders, in effect established the political tone for the region above the Nottoway River. The lower county, heavily Democratic and planter-dominated, shared the characteristics of other prosecession localities in both the upper and the lower South. Nonslave-holders in the lower county not only followed the lead of the elite; they did so with virtual unanimity. Democratic managers in the lower county knew how to poll lopsided margins among nonslaveholders. Even though turnout among members of nonslaveholding lower-county families fell from 247 to 193 between November 1860 and February 1861, only 7 of those who did vote in 1861 dared to challenge the secession consensus. Like the lower South, lower Southampton rejected the Union long before the first shots of the war were fired.[30]

Additional perspectives on the 1860–61 voting returns may be gained by considering continuities and discontinuities between the two elections. Whig voters in 1860 who reappeared to vote in 1861 were very likely to vote pro-Union; Democrats were equally likely to support secession (see app. table 6.8). Upper-county Whig voters from 1860 turned out at a slightly higher rate in 1861, however, than did lower-county Democats (see app. table 6.9).[31] Even though 1860 Democratic voters generally supported secession, nonslaveholding Democrats were slightly more likely than slaveholding Democrats to vote pro-Union, and considerably more likely not to vote at all in 1861 (see app. table 6.10). Nonslaveholding Whigs delivered a larger proportion of their votes against secession than slaveholding Whigs; nonslaveholding Whigs also had a slightly higher rate of turnout than slaveholding Whigs. New 1861 voters diverged sharply: 61 percent of nonslaveholders who had not voted in 1860 voted pro-Union; almost 67 percent of new voters from slaveholding families favored secession.

Religiously affiliated voters delivered a solid Democratic margin in 1860: eighty-eight for Breckinridge, sixty-two for Bell, and one for Douglas. At first glance, this figure appears a rather sharp departure from 1855, when Whigs held a narrow margin, 68 to 61, among religiously affiliated voters (see app. table 6.11). Increased numbers of Methodists (or fuller surviving Methodist records) distorted the 1860 results, however. Lower-county Methodists, by delivering all but ten of their sixty-six votes to Breckinridge (almost 85 percent), gave Democrats a majority of the overall vote among the religiously affiliated.[32] Church members in upper Southampton displayed the same Whig preferences as the larger electorate there, voting for Bell by a margin of 53 to 32 (over 62 percent). The Quaker meeting voted Whig, 11 to 4; the nearby Black Creek Baptist Church maintained its long-established Whig preference, 19 to 6; as usual, the small South Quay Baptist Church remained solidly Democratic, 8 to 2.

The 1860 outcome was replicated in early 1861, as religiously affiliated voters supported secession, 72 to 54. Voting patterns remained similar to 1860, albeit more sharply polarized. In the lower county, all but two of fifty-two voters favored secession. Four lower-county Methodist congregations voted unanimously for secession, and it carried at Whiteheads, 16 to 1. Upper-county church members, however, delivered a resounding pro-Union margin, 52 to 20, or over 72 percent. The Quaker meeting and the Black Creek Baptist Church provided the two centers of pro-Union strength: all fourteen Quaker voters rejected secession, as did twenty-two of twenty-four voters from Black Creek Baptist Church. The nearly unanimously pro-Union vote in these churches assured that the overall vote among church members from the upper county stood emphatically against secession.[33]

Church members from nonslaveholding families voted differently in 1860 than church members from slaveholding families. Fifty-nine percent of nonslaveholders favored Bell over Breckinridge, while slaveholders gave Breckinridge a 71 percent margin (see app. table 6.12).[34] In the February 1861 election regarding secession, the disparities between non-slaveholding and slaveholding church members became even more marked. Of the former, almost 70 percent opposed secession, whereas almost 77 percent of the latter favored secession.[35] One cannot help but be struck by the near unanimity among nonslaveholding church members from the upper county who opposed secession 37 to 3: five more voted against secession (37) than had voted for John Bell (32). The fifteen participating nonslaveholders from Black Creek Baptist Church all opposed secession, as did the thirteen from the Quaker meeting. Among church members even more than in the larger electorate, secession most starkly divided upper-county nonslaveholders from the slaveholding elite who set the tone for the lower county.[36]

Information in the U.S. Census for 1860 makes it possible to consider the relationship between occupation and voting behavior in 1860 and 1861. Five occupational categories may be defined: farmers, overseers, laborers, skilled tradesmen, and professionals (see app. table 6.13).[37] As in the entire electorate, farmers voted narrowly Democratic in 1860 and narrowly against secession in February 1861. Predictably too, the vote cast by farmers had a decided residential skew in 1860, as almost 70 percent of upper-county farmers voted Whig while 80 percent of lower-county farmers voted Democratic. The polarization grew even sharper in 1861 as almost 80 percent of upper-county farmers opposed secession, including 90 percent of upper-county nonslaveholding farmers. Fewer than 6 percent of lower-county farmers voted pro-Union.

Overseers and skilled tradesmen voted much as farmers: strongly Whig and antisecession in the upper county, strongly Democratic and prosecession in the lower county. Overall, overseers supported Democrats and secession at a higher rate than skilled tradesmen, reflecting the fact that a majority of overseers lived in the lower county, whereas two-thirds of skilled tradesmen lived in the upper county.

The category of laborer, used primarily by the census taker in the upper county, predictably included a preponderance of Union Whigs. Laborers apparently included a mixture of skilled tradesmen and the least privileged white Southamptonites, who lived as tenants or farm laborers. Over two-thirds of the laborers supported John Bell, and over three-quarters opposed secession. The dozen lower-county laborers voted monolithically Democratic, although half did not return to vote in 1861.[38]

Professionals living in the upper county voted narrowly for Bell and against secession, but ballots cast in the lower county assured that Southampton's professionals voted solidly Democratic, and by an even larger margin for secession. The group overall appears to have voted more on the basis of class interest than residence. Slaveholding professionals far outnumbered nonslaveholding professionals. Physicians, earlier consistently Whiggish, voted for Breckinridge, 7 to 5, and then for secession, 7 to 2. Seven of ten merchants voted for Breckinridge; nine of eleven for secession.

Contemporary observers often judged that secession had greater appeal for younger southerners. Some modern historians likewise have suggested that younger voters, especially young slaveholders and aspiring slaveholders, tended to support Breckinridge and secession.[39] How does information about voting behavior in Southampton square with such assertions? A very slight relationship between age and political outlook did exist (see app. table 6.14). The county's youngest voters, those aged twenty to twenty-nine, gave Breckinridge a margin of over 54 percent and then supported secession by over 55 percent. It should be kept in mind, however, that Democrats had successfully recruited more new voters than Whigs during the middle 1850s. One would therefore expect younger voters to include somewhat more Democrats.

At the other end of the age spectrum, Southampton voters between the ages of fifty and fifty-nine narrowly supported John Bell and delivered a margin of over 55 percent against secession. The small numbers of voters age sixty or older cast 55 percent of their vote for Bell and 58 percent against secession. These tendencies do appear to confirm the existence of a relationship between age and political behavior.

The pattern, however, is clouded by voters between the ages of thirty and forty-nine. The younger cohort, those between the ages of thirty and thirty-nine, displayed higher levels of support for Bell and against secession than voters aged forty to forty-nine. The former cast over 51 percent of their votes against secession, while the latter cast over 53 percent of their vote for it. The discrepancies are not large, but when also taking into account the relatively narrow range of percentages separating the oldest and the youngest voters, it would appear prudent not to emphasize the relationship between age and political behavior.

Additional assessments likewise suggest that age made only a slight difference. Among the voters who lived in the upper part of the county, the region where Whigs ran strongest and few voters supported secession, a modest age skew may be identified. Such support for Breckinridge and secession as did exist in that region was marginally more pronounced among younger voters (see app. table 6.15).[40] On balance, however, it would seem unwise to consider age an important variable for understanding Southampton voting behavior in 1860 and 1861. Residence, slaveholding, and religious affiliation all display far greater explanatory power.

WHAT SORT OF ORGANIZATION and leadership did Southampton's political parties employ? On court day in November 1858, a Democratic meeting appointed a roster of fifty-nine delegates to attend a state party convention to nominate a candidate for governor.[41] Of the fifty-nine, all but six may be positively identified in 1860–61 records.

Almost every one of Southampton's leading Democrats owned slaves; some owned a great many.[42] Forty of those with listed occupations were farmers; seven of the remaining nine were professionals. Leading Democrats listed in the agricultural census owned on average close to 500 improved acres apiece, with their real estate valued at more than $6,500. Their farms averaged over ten bales of cotton apiece (almost twenty for those who actually grew cotton).

The religious affiliations of prominent Democrats correspond nicely with patterns observed in the larger electorate. Fourteen of the group were church members, including eleven Methodists, or 79 percent of those with known religious ties. The other three were Baptists. All fourteen of the religiously affiliated Democrats owned slaves; nine of them, or 64 percent, qualified as members of the planter class.

The leading Democrats were dispersed around the county in relatively symmetrical fashion. Thirty-two lived in the upper county, principally in the courthouse village of Jerusalem and its environs and in or around the emerging commercial center of Franklin. Only eight lived in the outlying parts of the strongly Whiggish upper county, with all eight in the Berlin area, where Democrats regularly polled one-third of the vote. Not a single leading Democrat lived in the Faisons Store or Black Creek Church area, which voted Whig and antisecession with near unanimity. The twenty-one leading Democrats from the lower county, even if outnumbered by their upper-county colleagues, added a formidable presence within the party. Among them were two members apiece from the privileged and influential Drewry, Ridley, and Pope families, plus powerful veteran members or former members of the county court, such as James E. Peters, William E. Beale, and James Maget.

Of the fifty-nine leading Democrats, all forty-seven who voted in 1860 supported Breckinridge. Several 1860 participants did not vote in the early 1861 convention election, but those who did favored secession, 39 to 2. All but one of the Democrats who avoided voting in 1861 came from the upper county, where the party's position on secession went contrary to dominant public opinion.

A comparable list of Whig mainstays in the county may be reconstructed by identifying persons selected to the county court or as election commissioners between 1855 and 1860. A total of forty-four of these leaders voted for the Whig and Whig-successor parties. How did this group compare with the prominent Democrats?

The Whig leaders, even if notably more prosperous than the average Southampton resident, failed to equal the unusually privileged profile of the leading Democrats. Over 70 percent of the Whigs owned slaves, but twelve did not, far more than the two nonslaveholding Democrats. Whig slaveholdings were also smaller.[43] A comparably large fraction of leading Whigs were farmers: thirty of the thirty-eight listed, with the remaining eight professionally employed. Politically active Whigs typically cultivated smaller numbers of improved acres than leading Democrats, and they owned smaller amounts of personal property and real estate. Only sixteen leading Whigs (compared to twenty-seven leading Democrats) grew cotton. The Whigs who grew cotton averaged five bales apiece, less than one-third the average for leading Democrats.

The religious affiliation of leading Whigs contrasted sharply with the predominantly Methodist orientation of leading Democrats. Nine of fifteen leading Whigs with known religious affiliation (or 60 percent) were Baptists, and eight of the nine Whig Baptists belonged to Black Creek church. Of the remaining six, five were Methodists and one was a Quaker. Although nine of the fifteen leading Whigs with a religious affiliation owned slaves, six did not. The six included five members of Black Creek Baptist Church and the one Quaker. Whereas all leading Democrats with a religious affiliation owned slaves and almost two-thirds were members of the planter class, only two of the fifteen religiously affiliated leading Whigs held the requisite twenty slaves to qualify as planters.

Over 80 percent of leading Whigs resided in the upper county, almost half in the three strongly Whig outlying districts (Black Creek Church, Berlin, and Faisons Store). Another thirteen lived in the Jerusalem or

Franklin area of the upper county, while only eight lived below the Nottoway in the lower county. Not surprisingly, leading Whigs clustered in regions of the county with few leading Democrats, and vice versa.

All forty-two of the Whigs who voted in 1860 cast ballots for John Bell. Although the secession issue depressed turnout among leading Whigs even more than among leading Democrats, those who did vote in 1861 opposed secession, 29 to 4. In the strongly prosecession lower county, community pressures visibly uprooted traditional allegiances. Of the eight lower-county Whig leaders who had voted for Bell, four did not vote in 1861, and three voted for secession, leaving only one lone pro-Union vote. Upper-county Whig leaders, who cast thirty-four votes for Bell, voted 28 to 1 against secession.

WHAT DO THESE RESULTS mean? They suggest that the interconnected influences of family, neighborhood, partisanship, slaveholding, agricultural production, and religious affiliation combined to generate markedly different responses within a single county during the great crisis of 1860–61.

In lower Southampton lived a network of prominent families who owned large tracts of property and large numbers of slaves, who grew significant amounts of cotton, who not only voted Democratic but often played leading roles in the local party, and whose religious affiliation (if any) was likely to be Methodist. Members of these families had long played influential roles on the county court and had frequently represented the county in the legislature. The Ridley, Darden, Drewry, Pope, Maget, Mason, and Goodwyn families all combined wealth with political influence. Others were allied: John J. Kindred, for example, commonwealth's attorney, delegate to the 1860 Democratic National Convention, and delegate to the Virginia Convention of 1861, was the son-in-law of Samuel Drewry.[44]

Members of these lower-county families plainly spearheaded the secession movement in Southampton. Elite families clustered in Drewrysville, where secession triumphed without a single dissenting vote. Across the entire lower county, only a handful of voters dared to defy the secession consensus. Most lower-county residents who voted for John Bell in 1860 either did not vote in 1861 or voted for secession. Only nine of the eighty-six Bell voters from the lower county opposed secession.

The Democratic party in the three lower-county voting districts provided a mechanism through which elite leaders could affirm their support for popular aspirations and through which the humbler rank and file could affirm loyalty to their patrons. The full politicization of the lower county took time: not until 1855 did Democratic managers stir a full turnout there. From that point on, however, lower-county nonslaveholders not only voted in large numbers, they were even more likely than their slaveholding patrons to vote Democratic—and to vote for secession. The seemingly democratized politics of the late antebellum era thus incorporated much of the spirit of the deferential politics practiced in the eighteenth and early nineteenth centuries. Elections became repeated reenactments of an ancient ritual. Voters did not weigh the claims of rival candidates and then cast a secret ballot. Rather, voters declared in public that they had confidence in the local gentry.

There is little reason to believe that the planters of the lower county were in any way progressive or innovative. Their success in growing cotton resulted from circumstances of climate and soil rather than unusual enterprise or talent. The railroad built through the lower county during the 1830s owed nothing to local initiative. It resulted, instead, from efforts by Norfolk commercial interests. Edmund Ruffin, a friend to whatever improvement and progress he considered consistent with the slave system, blasted the farmers of the Southampton area for continuing to send crops to market in carts or wagons rather than taking advantage of the railroad or working to improve water transport.[45]

When confronted with economic stagnation, lower-county elites tended to give up on Virginia rather than take to heart Ruffin's gospel of agricultural reform. John Young Mason, the one politician from antebellum Southampton who achieved national prominence, lived so improvidently that he fell into debt, and his son undertook to sell most of his Virginia property and to relocate most of his substantial slave labor force in Mississippi. Though his slaves were grief-stricken at having to go to an unfamiliar, cholera-infested region, Mason instructed his son Lewis to supervise the new plantation and "pitch as large a crop of cotton as the hands can cultivate."[46] Similarly, James Maget, an active Democrat and prosperous lower-county member of the county court, invested in cotton lands in Arkansas and Texas and encouraged a son to take some of the family slaves west to bring the Arkansas property into cultivation. When Virginia rejected secession in February 1861, Maget's younger son, Roswald, a recent VMI graduate, wished his family would "sell out" entirely and take all the family slaves farther South—"any place just to get out of Virginia for it getting to be too much of an abolitionist state for me."[47]

If stick-in-the-mud traditionalists set the tone in lower Southampton, can a comparable case be made for the relative modernity of the upper county? Even if the average farmer in the upper county tilled a smaller plot, owned fewer slaves, and sold less to external markets, could he in some way have been more attuned to the progressive stirrings of the nineteenth century? Perhaps so. Interconnected material and cultural circumstances made upper Southampton different. Most soil there was less well suited for plantation agriculture than soil in the lower county. Furthermore, significant numbers of families in the upper county had religious scruples against the use of slave labor. Consequently, a much larger percentage of white families in upper Southampton were smallholders. Lower Southampton's white population, by contrast, included proportionately larger segments from the opposite ends of the economic spectrum: the privileged owners of ten or more slaves and those who held no property, neither slaves nor land.

Its distinctive qualities apparently made upper Southampton responsive when offered an alternative to traditional Virginia politics. Whig organizers brought two-party politics to Southampton during the mid–1830s, sharply changing the political complexion of what had been a Jacksonian stronghold. Initially supported by Nullifiers, Whigs remained competitive even after Nullifiers drifted back to the Democrats. When the new era of universal white male suffrage arrived in 1851, Southampton Whigs, who for a decade and a half had run stronger among nonslaveholders, achieved their most decisive local victories ever.

Upper-county Whigs appear to have been more aggressive politicians, sooner able to enlist and organize nonslaveholders, thereby negating the natural advantage that Democrats seem to have enjoyed among the county's upper crust. Lower-county Democrats learned to mobilize an arresting turnout of nonslaveholders in 1855 and afterwards. During the secession crisis, however, the upper county's antisecessionist nonslaveholders far outpolled prosecession nonslaveholders from the lower county, so that Southampton nonslaveholders voted markedly more pro-Union than local slaveholders.

Upper Southampton's elites appear to have been more open to change than their counterparts in the lower county. The wealthiest and most conspicuous upper-county family, the Urquharts, had more get-up-and-go than their counterparts below the Nottoway River. Descended from Scottish merchants who overcame the stigma of alleged Tory sympathies and avowed Federalist affiliations, the Urquharts appear to have welcomed innovations. Twice, in 1828 and 1836, they and other tidewater capitalists petitioned the legislature to incorporate "a cotton and woolen manufactory." They also sought ways to increase agricultural production: two of the fourteen Southampton subscribers to Edmund Ruffin's *Farmers' Register* were Urquharts. Urquharts also played a prominent and continuing role in Southampton's Whig and Whig-successor parties. James B. Urquhart ran four times for the House of Delegates, twice successfully, just as popular partisanship crystallized. In 1859 his nephew, Thomas Hill Urquhart, won a seat in the state Senate. Charles F. Urquhart, a younger brother of James B. Urquhart, was the Union candidate for the state convention in February 1861.[48]

The other most prominent upper-county family, the Pretlows, maintained social and political eminence even though some of its members were religiously heterodox. Long after their ideas had become proscribed in the South, a network of Quakers and antislavery Baptists lived in upper Southampton, prominent among them the Quaker Pretlows. The politicians in the Pretlow family during the late antebellum period were not members of the Quaker meeting, but they retained the imprint of their religious heritage. Thomas Pretlow, a magistrate on the county court, died in 1843. Three of his sons subsequently won election to the House of Delegates, most notably Dr. Thomas Jefferson Pretlow. The latter's 1851 victory demonstrated the increased political power of upper-county nonslaveowners after the new state constitution widened the franchise to include all adult white males. Subsequently a severe critic of secession and a thorn in the side of Confederate authorities, Thomas J. Pretlow attempted during Reconstruction to create a Republican party with Union Whig leadership.[49]

Two important upper-county Whig families, the Griffins and the Bowers, were associated with the Black Creek Baptist Church. State legislator Benjamin Griffin played an important role in establishing the Whig loyalties of church members during the 1830s. Dr. Robert G. Griffin, like Benjamin Griffin a member of the county court, twice represented the county in the House of Delegates in the late 1840s. The most important Baptist layman in the county, Dr. Carr Bowers, did much to promote Whig loyalties and to give the party a reformist ideology. A longtime member of the county court who served four terms in the legislature between 1815 and 1844, Bowers was considered a progressive philanthropist. During the ghastly weeks after the Nat Turner insurrection in 1831, when vengeful white mobs roamed through Southampton, Bowers was among the few willing to shelter terrified free blacks in his own home. Bowers also played the key role in establishing and sustaining Elliott L. Story's Black Water Free School. Weeks before his death in early 1861, the eighty-one-year-old Bowers voted against secession.[50]

The Kello and Burges families, interconnected by marriage with each other and also with the Urquharts, combined interests in Whig politics, medicine, and education. Samuel Kello served as sheriff during the 1850s and again during Reconstruction. Dr. Samuel B. Kello, a state legislator in the mid–1850s, held a seat on the county court during Reconstruction. Ancestors of the Kellos had served as clerks of the county court during the eighteenth and early nineteenth centuries. Dr. A. S. H. Burges, a delegate to the Virginia Convention of 1850–51, promoted education and practiced progressive agriculture. His father and grandfather had been the ministers of the county's Anglican church during the latter eighteenth century.[51]

The link between progressive agriculture and the search for alternatives to slave-based labor was personified by Matthew Harris, a "number one farmer" and a devout Quaker. Harris, who strongly supported public education, sent his children to Elliott Story's Black Water Free School. The young teacher and the "sturdy old friend" found they shared similar values and enjoyed each other's company. Harris, who served as an election commissioner at the Black Creek Church voting district, was an emphatic Whig and antisecessionist. The example of Harris suggests that agricultural reform in antebellum Virginia was not the exclusive prerogative of those such as Edmund Ruffin who sought ways to revitalize slavery and the plantation system. Harris, who owned no slaves and had religious scruples against doing so, tried to promote free-labor agriculture. His son, Edward Harris, died in Confederate captivity during the war after refusing to bear arms.[52]

The diaries of Elliott Story and Daniel Cobb provide the best evidence that Whigs in upper Southampton were more receptive to the changing world of the mid-nineteenth century than Democrats. In all kinds of revealing ways, the earnest Whig, Story, had a more modern and cosmopolitan outlook than the cotton-farming Democrat, Cobb.

The divergent political behavior of upper and lower Southampton in the late antebellum period had its roots in unmistakable economic and cultural differences. Lower Southampton, in which Democratic party politics intersected with a substantial commitment to the cultivation of cotton, had many Deep South qualities. The growing of cotton appears to have nurtured an affinity for the lower South's sectionally confrontational brand of politics. In Southampton over 70 percent of cotton growers who voted (164 of 233) went Democratic in 1860; over 80 percent of those who voted the next year supported secession (155 of 190). Throughout Virginia's miniature cotton kingdom, which also encompassed parts of adjacent Greensville and Sussex counties, support for secession in 1861 exceeded the margins that voters had traditionally given to Democratic candidates.[53]

Upper Southampton was a surprisingly unorthodox corner of the Old South. Dominated in one sense by wealthy slaveholding families, it was at the same time a setting in which those prominent families had to accommodate an egalitarian minority which included some of their blood relatives. Antislavery and emancipationist sentiments plainly persisted among some Baptists, Quakers, and others in the Black Creek area. Eager to ameliorate social injustice and to enlarge the sphere of economic well-being, Southampton's Quakers had an outlook that was fundamentally antithetical to that of lower-county traditionalists. It is, indeed, a striking oddity that two such dissimilar halves happened to be part of the same county.

Southampton's two banner voting districts stood far apart in material circumstances and ideological predilection. At Drewrysville where almost 70 percent of voters owned slaves, every single vote cast in February 1861 favored secession. At Black Creek Church where fewer than 15 percent of voters owned slaves, only 2 out of 102 voters favored secession. At Drewrysville, a majority of those who voted in 1860 and 1861 raised cotton. At Black Creek Church, hardly anybody raised cotton. The religious and cultural milieu in the Black Creek Church district differed greatly from that in the Drewrysville district. With the emancipationists at Black Creek an integral part of the Whig electorate, Southampton's Quakers and scattered other like-minded believers gained a quiet legitimacy and respectability at the very time the sectional crisis finally boiled to a head.

At least one member of Southampton's Quaker community recognized that the delicate balance could not hold. Robert S. Pretlow, a nonslaveholding cousin of the prominent Thomas J. Pretlow, decided in 1860 to move his family to Indiana. Diarist Elliott Story sadly noted that his old friend would "probably never again . . . return to the county to reside." Robert Pretlow, it appears, judged that external events would soon hopelessly disrupt the modus vivendi that enabled him to remain in Old Southampton.[54]

SEVEN

※

Civil War

THE OUTBREAK OF WAR in April appeared to erase previous disagreements about secession in Southampton. "It seems to me," Elliott Story wrote in his diary a month after the first shots of the war were exchanged at Fort Sumter, "that Virginia has done all that she could do consistent with honour and justice to settle it peaceably in the Union and there was nothing left for her but to withdraw from the old Union and cast her fortunes with the South. This she has done and I am with her." [1]

When forced to choose, most upper-county Whigs became good Confederates, as did Story. Various young Urquharts and Pretlows volunteered for combat or for the Confederate medical services. Not a single voter in the entire county dared to cast a ballot against secession when the referendum took place. The 921 votes for secession polled in Southampton on May 24 almost equaled the turnout in February, when the county had been evenly divided. "All are united to . . . defend there rights as Suthern men," Daniel Cobb noted. Such patriotic determination, he thought, might enable the South to "konker with but little blood shed." [2]

Cobb, who blamed the North for starting the war, hoped that God would favor "our side." An undercurrent of doubt continued to gnaw at him, however. Cobb never felt confident that he could fathom the wishes of an all-powerful God, and unlike many other southerners he recognized that the North would present a formidable military challenge. "I fear we are going to have a bad time of it," he decided on May 22. A "Bloody war" would have "hard and Ruinous" consequences. [3]

Cobb's diary shows that hysteria raged in Southampton during the secession crisis and the early months of the war. Cobb, always nervous about slave discontent and the prospect of internal subversion, doubtless expressed anxieties that were widely shared. The South, he believed, was "pleged and haresed [plagued and harassed]" by "Avalitonism" and "Blackrepublickism." Reports about the jailing of suspicious slaves in Norfolk and Petersburg provoked a particularly morbid assessment: "We got the Black poperlation to murder or be murdered by the Blacks and the sooner it begins the better." In late April, just after the war started, violence flared. James Williams, a "low life Carrecter" suspected of stirring mischief among slaves, was "badly beaton." Two days later a runaway slave was captured in the house of a white woman, who was discovered to have been harboring two other slaves and "selling them liquor." Self-appointed vigilantes apparently murdered all three slaves.[4]

Cobb agreed to serve in the home guard, organized in late April to prevent "all misconduct of Negrows and low life white people." Selected as captain of the guard in his neighborhood, Cobb recognized that he and his squad were little more than a glorified patrol, functioning only because the militia and men of regular military age had out-of-county obligations. "They have put on boys 14 or 16 and what good [do] they do," he asked; "I say nun." Yet Cobb initially took his home guard responsibilities seriously. After two wearisome nights of riding during the last week of May, he pronounced everything "all Right." The "servants" were "all peasable [peaceable]." Cobb had no inclination, however, to go into combat. "I am within a fiew months of 50 years of age," Cobb reflected; "they cant make me Bare arms."[5]

Cobb's eldest son Asbury, not yet eighteen, volunteered for military duty as soon as the war started. Typical of other young white southerners from privileged families, he joined the first wave of Confederate recruits. His unit, eventually to become Company A of the Thirteenth Virginia Cavalry, promptly mustered into service. Commanding Company A was Captain Joseph E. Gillette, the ardent secessionist Democrat.[6]

Cavalry volunteers needed to supply their own horses, a requirement that placed that branch of Confederate service beyond the reach of most Southamptonites. Less privileged local patriots had other options. Cobb's overseer, Nathaniel Barham, resigned to join an artillery company. Most joined the infantry. Seven Confederate companies ultimately originated in whole or in large part from Southampton: five in the infantry, one artillery battalion, and the cavalry unit. In addition to Company A of the Thirteenth Virginia Cavalry, Southampton soldiers served in Company A of the Eighteenth Virginia Artillery Battalion, Companies D (the Southampton Grays) and G of the Third Virginia Infantry (part of Kemper's Brigade), Company H of the Forty-first Virginia Infantry and Company G of the Sixty-first Virginia Infantry (both in Mahone's Brigade), and Company B of the Ninth Virginia Infantry. With not many more than one thousand white males of military age, the county plainly contributed a proportionate share of its men.[7]

In a pattern widely repeated across the South, a ceremony marked the departure of volunteer soldiers. One Southampton contingent's send-off included a speech by a local notable, General William B. Shands, followed by the presentation of a "beautiful flag," sewn by local ladies. The captain of the company responded with a speech of his own, after which all present sang "Dixie" and "hurrahed." Two more politicos spoke, after which the soldiers mustered and serenaded the ladies, who responded by throwing bouquets.[8]

Two months after the start of hostilities, the cavalry company set out for service. Although some of its members were in their teens, many were older. Cobb's younger brother-in-law, Theophilous Little, was in his thirties, as was Captain Gillette. Letters written by James Fenton Bryant and Irvin C. Wills present a firsthand perspective on the experiences of the elite unit.

Southampton's cavalry assembled at Jerusalem early on a midsummer morning, June 17. The stir of soldiers and horses only briefly disrupted the tranquillity of the small-town county seat. Leaving at perhaps 5 A.M. and riding easily, they stopped periodically for refreshments. Dr. Thomas J. Pretlow, apparently concealing his doubts about the entire Confederate undertaking, hospitably supplied some of the soldiers with "a very good Breakfast," including, for those who preferred it, a julep with ice. A midmorning break at the household of another generous patriot supplied as many more iced juleps as the men could "take care of." The dinner hour brought the recruits to Mrs. James B. Urquhart's, allowing them to dismount and avoid the early afternoon heat. The "generous and noble" widowed stepmother of Jim Urquhart, one of the volunteers, supplied the soldiers with "*everything* that our appetites could ask for," thereby upholding the reputation of one of the two wealthiest families in the county. After "partaking very freely of all the Luxuries prepared here," the cavalry company renewed their ride to Smithfield in neighboring Isle of Wight County, where they arrived before 8 P.M. in the evening.[9]

Military service initially appeared exhilarating. Colonel Roger A. Pryor, an assertive secessionist politician and journalist, commanded the regiment to which the Southampton contingent had been assigned. Welcoming "decidedly the best looking" company under his command, Pryor promised to give them "any particular and important duty in which great confidence must be reposed." The soldiers never doubted that their cause would triumph. William E. Beale explained to his sister that "no people who have risen so high in the scale of civilization, *as we the South*" would ever "submit to be governed by so base and degraded a race" as the "northern scoundrels." [10]

As the Southamptonites settled into the routine of camp life, they soon found themselves missing the conveniences and associations of home. Reporting that a number of his comrades already had personal servants, James Fenton Bryant urged his father to hire Levi, a free black man, to cook for him. When Levi apparently proved unwilling, Bryant suggested that his father send one of his slaves, Talbot. The young soldier's request competed with requisitions from the state and Confederate governments, both of which needed black laborers to build fortifications. Though apparently forced to manage without assistance, Bryant discovered other pleasures and diversions. An abundance of "intelligent and pretty young ladies" in Smithfield warmly welcomed the dashing cavalry gentlemen. [11]

Others worried that Southampton's cavalry would succumb to illicit temptations. Harrison P. Pope wrote a cautionary note to his younger brother-in-law, Roswald S. Majette, admonishing him not to be "carried astray by the influences so naturally thrown around one engaged in a soldiers life" and warning him about the danger of "disipations." Pope explained that he had been asked by one of Majette's relatives "to look after your welfare." [12]

In Southampton by midsummer 1861 the war lost much of its initial novelty, and the hysteria ebbed. Superficially, little had changed. The agricultural routine once again became the center of Daniel Cobb's life. He tried to manage his plantation as he always had. In 1861, as he had done since the late 1840s and continued to do throughout the war, Cobb celebrated the end of the cultivating season, when the crops were "laid by" in early August, by giving his slaves a holiday and a "dining" ("all they could eat or drink—lam, peas sunblins [a summer squash] potatoes bacon greens cowcombers onions and timotoes"). Disturbing news frequently jolted him, however. Yankees, he heard, were "ravishing females" and enticing slaves to run away. He commended local efforts to manufacture "Boe [Bowie] knives" that would "cut the Raskels of the North to mince." Cobb's anxieties about slaves persisted: "I fear a rebelion among us in this County," he confessed in mid-July. Unable to share the widespread elation following the Confederate victory at Manassas, he grew "down in the mouth" about the war and the absence of his son.[13]

Lurking beneath the surface were chinks in the facade of unity. The war had not yet begun to pinch, but it would before long. Nor was the Confederate consensus in the upper county more than superficial. Notwithstanding the efforts of leading families there, many ordinary folk had not followed them cheerfully out of the Union. The three upper-county districts that voted 300 to 25 against secession in February polled only 253 votes for it in May. Significant numbers of prewar Unionists obviously failed to vote. The decline in voter turnout was especially evident at Black Creek Church. There, it will be recalled, lived the smallest proportion of slaveholders in the county and the most ardent Unionists. After rejecting secession in February, 100 to 2, they recorded only 32 votes for it in May. In other words, a nucleus of seventy unreconciled Unionists lived in the Black Creek area.

At least half a dozen young Quakers and like-minded Unionists from Southampton attempted passive resistance when subsequently conscripted into the Confederate army. Some were imprisoned in a cellar at a Confederate encampment; one, Edwin W. Raiford, for more than a year. Among those who refused Confederate service was John Pretlow, a longtime acquaintance of Elliott Story's. Another Southampton Quaker, Edward Harris, the son of Story's friend Matthew Harris, died while in captivity. Persecution failed to prevent continued disaffection. Some, who judged pro-Confederate recruitment from the pulpit to be "inconsistent with Christianity," began to attend the Friends meeting near Black Creek. Soon after the war, two additional Friends meetings were established in Southampton.[14]

By the spring of 1862, the grim reality of warfare encroached on Southampton. The disastrous Confederate failure to hold Roanoke Island in early February 1862 opened the entire Albemarle Sound region to Federal naval power. The Chowan River and its tributary the Blackwater offered Federal gunboats a potential avenue of access into the heart of the Virginia tidewater. One month later, Major General George B. McClellan's Army on the Potomac arrived on the Virginia peninsula just across the James River. By early May, Confederate forces retreated back toward the Richmond defenses, abandoning Norfolk and adjacent regions south of the James. Federal forces thereupon occupied Suffolk, twenty miles east of Franklin on the Seaboard and Roanoke Railroad.

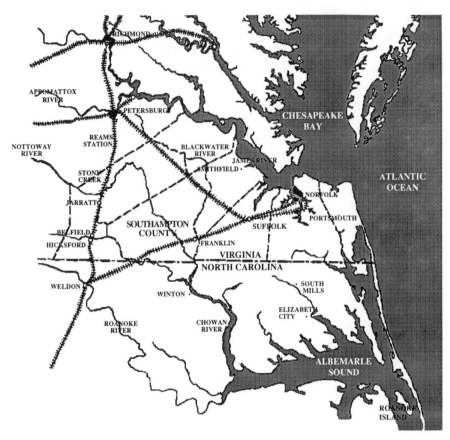

Map 8. Southampton in the Civil War. *Map adapted from Stephen B. Oates,* The Fires of Jubilee: Nat Turner's Fierce Rebellion (*New York: Harper and Row, 1975*), *72, and William Glenn Robertson,* Back Door to Richmond: The Bermuda Hundred Campaign, April–June 1864 (*Newark, Del.: Univ. of Delaware Press, 1987*), *15.*

Federal control soon extended as far as the Blackwater River, Southampton's eastern border. Jittery Confederates, hoping to stem the Federal tide, burned the railroad bridges over the Blackwater and the Nottoway. The decision to go to war, Southamptonites realized in 1862, exposed them to far greater dangers and hardships than most had expected in 1861.[15]

In March 1862 Governor John Letcher summoned all able-bodied white male adults under the age of forty-five for military service. Among those enlisted was Elliott Story, who would soon turn forty. Soon, however, Story returned home, having been "pronounced unfit for military duty by the Army surgeon." It is hard to quarrel with Story's assessment that his "physical inability" made it "imprudent" for him to serve. Only a few years earlier he had suffered such a severe bout with rheumatic fever that he could not walk for months.[16]

For Southampton's cavalry, frustration and anxiety replaced the festive mood that accompanied their original enlistment and the tedium of camp life that had followed. A majority reenlisted for the duration of the war in March 1862. But a number of the elite group, including Daniel Cobb's brother-in-law Theophilous Little, spent $1,000 each to hire substitutes.[17]

The company's first engagement turned out badly. Sent across the North Carolina line in February to shore up porous Confederate defenses in the Albemarle Sound area, it became involved in a fiasco at Winton, only a short distance south of Franklin. The Southampton cavalry and several companies of North Carolina infantry imprudently tried to decoy a small fleet of Federal gunboats in the Chowan River. A slave woman, apparently acting at the behest of her master, motioned the gunboats to approach the landing at Winton. The Federals steered toward shore, crediting a rumor that Unionists, only a few days earlier, had raised an American flag there. Instead, the ships ran into a Confederate ambush, forcing them to retreat downriver. Federal commanders decided to return to Winton the next day, February 20. As they arrived, Confederates abandoned the town. Vengeful Federals, angry about the attempted entrapment and finding more supplies than they could carry away, decided to burn Winton. The town and substantial supplies of "bacon, corn-meal, flour, sugar, powder, mess-pans, camp-kettles, knapsacks, haversacks, canteens, &c.," went up in smoke. It was "the first instance during the war on our side," a Union colonel explained, "where fire has accompanied the sword." It would not be the last.[18]

The Southampton cavalry skirmished more successfully at South Mills, North Carolina, north of Elizabeth City, on April 19, preventing the Federals from attacking the Dismal Swamp Canal. The engagement did not, however, begin auspiciously. Routed from sleep before sunrise as Yankee gunboats bombarded their camp, Southampton's finest hastily retreated amid whizzing cannonballs, powerful enough to knock down tall pine trees. Neither the men nor their horses would have "a mouthful to eat" all day. The Confederates regrouped a number of miles inland, closer to the canal. There in the afternoon, six Confederate infantry companies, supported by an artillery battalion and the Southampton cavalry, ambushed a much larger contingent of Federal infantry that had undergone a long, hot march. During four hours of fighting, the horsemen occupied an exposed position to discourage a Federal flank attack. James F. Bryant of Southampton expressed relief that Yankee soldiers "knew but little about the use of firearms." Had they "shot right," he soberly recounted, "they would have killed several of us." Confederate artillerists eventually ran out of ammunition, forcing a general retreat. But the Federals also retreated, giving the Confederates a tactical victory. Bryant judged that his company had seen more hard service "within the last week" than in "all the rest of the time together." [19]

In early May 1862, two weeks after the engagement at South Mills, the Confederates abandoned all of southeastern Virginia and northeastern North Carolina east of the Chowan-Blackwater line. With much of the tidewater "open to the incursions of the enemy," civilian morale in Southampton sagged. "A gloom seemed to rest upon the whole community and many began to think that ours was a gone cause," Elliott Story recalled. James F. Bryant took pen in hand in early May to protest defeatism. Warning that "despondency" was "little better than treason," the young soldier urged his father and family to maintain their confidence. Bryant acknowledged that the loss of nearby Norfolk and the fall of New Orleans weighed heavily. But he predicted that southerners could escape subjugation by continuing to fight. Even if Southampton fell behind enemy lines, developments elsewhere might secure Confederate independence. "Three months will decide the contest one way or the other," Bryant judged. "It can't last long as it is now." [20]

To the astonishment of Bryant and many others, the war could and did grind on indecisively. The Federal invasion of Virginia stalled in front of Richmond, and General Robert E. Lee's determined counterattack forced McClellan's army to retreat. Southampton remained precariously behind Confederate lines, even though Federal forces lurked nearby. Federal gunboats cruised up the Blackwater to Southampton in late May and again in August. A Union naval officer who landed briefly in Franklin found "no Union men there." Confederate forces, concentrated at Richmond and spread thin elsewhere in the region, offered no resistance. The Chowan-Blackwater route nevertheless remained an important Confederate conduit, supplying food to hard-pressed Richmond. [21]

For a time in the late summer and early fall, the South regained the initiative both east and west. Confederate invasions of Kentucky and

Maryland led to bloody repulses, however, exposing both Virginia and Tennessee once again to Federal pressure. Amid these absorbing events, the Southampton cavalry played only a peripheral role. Although it lost two members in a skirmish at Williamsburg in September, it escaped the earlier heavy fighting around Richmond during the Seven Days in late June, and it was not part of the force that Lee subsequently led into northern Virginia and Maryland.[22]

With the withdrawal of McClellan from the peninsula in mid-August, substantial Confederate forces returned to the Blackwater. Reports reaching Federal forces in late September indicated that fully 12,000 Confederates stood poised at Franklin, ready to strike east at Suffolk across a floating bridge that could also carry railroad cars and artillery. The Federals decided to attack first, using both infantry and gunboats. The resulting skirmish at Crumpler's Bluff, on October 3, produced the only serious fighting within the borders of the county in the entire war.[23]

Three Union ships, former ferryboats "whose shallow draft made them ideal for river operations," steamed up the Blackwater toward Franklin. Reinforced with sandbags and well armed, the small flotilla hoped to coordinate with Federal infantry marching west from Suffolk. Unfortunately for the Federals, the foot soldiers failed to appear and the three ships ended up slugging it out unassisted with sharpshooting Confederate infantry posted in ambush on both sides of the none-too-wide Blackwater. A Union naval officer reported that rebel defenders included some nonuniformed irregulars and even "some negroes." At Crumpler's Bluff, three-quarters of a mile below Franklin on the Southampton side of the river, the Union flagship, the *Perry*, ran aground under heavy fire. Confederate infantry swarmed into the water, hoping to board and capture the temporarily marooned vessel. Instead, Lieutenant William B. Cushing, "unquestionably one of the most daring and resourceful men ever to wear the uniform of the United States Navy," took charge of an exposed field howitzer and coolly fired a devastating canister charge at the massed attackers. The *Perry* and her sister ships escaped and soon retreated. Even though the two-pronged Union assault on Franklin fizzled, it may well have accomplished its objective of discouraging any immediate Confederate initiatives across the Blackwater.[24]

The impact of war fell heavily on Southampton during 1862. One Confederate soldier stationed there reported in November that the county, "once the center of civilization, refinement & wealth," had been made "poor and desolate." Confederate requisitions drained away both white and black labor, and Federal armies just across the river attracted growing numbers of runaway slaves. "Four negroes gone to the Yankies," Susan I. Berry bitterly noted; "that is six thousand dollars gone." As local agricultural production atrophied, the civilian population competed with over 10,000 Confederate soldiers for the diminishing supply of food. Conditions of life spiraled downward. Three members of Jethro Charles's family succumbed to fatal illnesses in the winter of 1862. Fissures in Confederate society, temporarily obscured during the heady early months of the war, opened widely.[25]

Confederate soldiers shared the same miseries afflicting the civilian population. An artillery battalion stationed near Black Creek Baptist Church was "half-fed, nearly naked & shoeless." Its captain, Louis H. Webb, awoke in his tent one morning early in December to find his hair and beard "heavy with ice, from my congealed breath." When he attempted to wash his face, Webb reported, "the water froze on my hair."[26]

Nor were living conditions much better for Southampton's elite cavalry unit, reorganized earlier in 1862 as Company A of the Thirteenth Virginia Cavalry in Robert E. Lee's Army of Northern Virginia. At the battle of Fredericksburg on December 13, they were "engaged as sharp shooters" on the army's right flank. The satisfaction they felt in repelling the Federal assault gave way to a miserable existence as the winter dragged on. Assigned to picket duty at several posts below the Rappahannock, they had to make do with "half rations" and often baked bread from flour "made up without a particle of salt." Lacking adequate ˀts, they were vulnerable to chill and exposure. Widespread illness ˑ the force of seventy men to only about thirty effectives in midwˑ ˑe horses shared the misery of the soldiers, suffering from insuffi ge and widely afflicted with foot disease. Under the circumstar nen celebrated a "dull" Christmas. Irvin C. Wills, who "would ᵉlished a cup of egg-nog," reported that one drink of the only avaˑ whiskey would "last a man a great while, as the man that tries it onc m ever tries it again." Helping to sustain Wills was a hope that thˑ ᵉcts for peace" were "brightening every day" because Federal soldiers, who talked to Confederate pickets across the Rappahannock, expressed themselves as "heartily tired of the war" and "willing to give us anything we ask" after suffering the terrible "thrashing" at Fredericksburg.[27]

Food shortages became a severe problem by early 1863, not just in Southampton but throughout Confederate Virginia. To feed General

Lee's hungry army, the Confederate government impressed surplus corn, bacon, and pork, claiming all farm products "except those that were actually necessary for the sustenance of life." Sugar and coffee became only a memory, the latter replaced with a beverage made from toasted corn, rye, and sweet potatoes, which made a "fairly palatable drink" when sweetened with sorghum molasses. Privileged families rationed flour for once-a-week use, making Sunday the "Biscuit Morning." Even then, Dr. W. D. Barham recalled, "we were not given a very lavish allowance." Other civilian families, reduced to a diet of sweet potatoes and peas, were "thankful for that." [28]

Some families had little or no food. As early as the summer of 1861, Cobb had given half a barrel of corn to a poor woman, Margaret Bassett, with no expectation of repayment. By 1863 many families, especially those without slaves, had no man at home to farm. "The poore must suffer for something to eat," Cobb noted in March. Southampton's 1863 crops were the shortest in memory. Rampant inflation drove corn prices to $20 a barrel in April and bacon to $1 per pound. By June corn had risen to $50 and bacon to $1.40. By December corn stood at $100. Even those who had money often "were unable to purchase corn at any price." [29]

Southampton's county court decided upon emergency action to deal with the crisis. They empowered two magistrates, one of them Elliott Story, to buy corn and bacon for "indigent soldiers families" and others in distress. The county court also appointed eight magistrates, Story again among them, to distribute the food equitably in each district. The need was acute. Story reported aiding one family that was almost entirely dependent on the labor of a son in the army. The son had not been heard from for months and was feared dead. But Story had "great difficulty" in buying "the quantity directed to be purchased by the Court." People were in no mood to sell, regardless of price. Cobb, when visited by a commissioner (probably Story), insisted that he "had none." Story faced frequent complaints, "as if I was the one that made the order" or caused the "scant supply." [30]

Southampton, although shielded from the direct fury of war, witnessed plenty of military movement. A large Confederate force—Lieutenant General James Longstreet's First Corps of the Army of Northern Virginia—gathered on the Blackwater in March, 1863, provoking anxious concern at the Federal outpost in nearby Suffolk. On April 11 four

Confederate divisions numbering at least thirty-five thousand crossed the river and besieged Suffolk for the next several weeks. The Federal commander in the Norfolk region, Major General John A. Dix, fearing the arrival of Confederate reinforcements under Major General Daniel H. Hill, judged that the enemy had come "for a campaign and not for a raid or a diversion." Dix's alarm, although understandable, proved excessive. Longstreet's "principal object" was to gather supplies of corn and bacon. So many Confederate purchasers fanned out that the price of bacon doubled. By the end of April, however, Major General Joseph Hooker moved the Army of the Potomac across the Rappahannock to Chancellorsville, and Robert E. Lee wired for Longstreet. The Confederates retreated across the Blackwater with "vast stores" of fresh provisions, ending the relatively bloodless siege of Suffolk.[31]

The stationing of a large Confederate army in the county left "everything in an unsettled condition" and added to civilian miseries. The "heavy roaring of cannon" resounded "like thunder" day and night. Jenny Camp recalled that "Longstreet's Brigade [Corps] was camped on my father's farm . . . and they were not very desirable neighbors; no hungry people are. Pig after pig disappeared until there were none left and the same with chickens, turkeys, calves, and lambs." With almost all animals butchered, tallow supplies dwindled. Southampton women learned to fashion candles from beeswax. Daniel Cobb, who had always before provided free meals for Confederate soldiers, resolved in his diary to start making the visitors pay.[32]

Southampton's Company A found itself heavily engaged far from home in 1863. Both before and during the Chancellorsville campaign, the Thirteenth Virginia tangled repeatedly with Federal cavalry. As "bullets flew like hail around us," they pursued Federal raiders under Major General George Stoneman. Just as the Confederate cavalry was preparing to screen for the invasion of Pennsylvania in early June, the Federal cavalry launched a sharp counterattack at Brandy Station. The Thirteenth fought in the midst of the subsequent action, the most extensive cavalry engagement of the entire war. During Major General J. E. B. Stuart's exhausting cavalry expedition during the Gettysburg campaign, the Thirteenth led the assault on a Federal force at Hanover, Pennsylvania, suffering four wounded and nine captured. After a great deal more riding, the Thirteenth arrived outside Gettysburg just in time to participate in heavy combat on the third day. "Never before has cavalry done such severe fighting," Lieutenant Wills reported. "We were eighteen days and nights in the saddle, which was too much for human endurance. . . . No men can stand more, and I never wish to be called on to stand as much again. I had one horse killed under me and rode three others down."[33]

The departure of Longstreet's army left civilian Southampton "without any protection." Jenny Camp recalled that "we lived in awful terror of the Federals." In June 1863, as the Pennsylvania campaign began, Cobb expected that Union armies soon would cross the Blackwater and place the county "in Yankeedom." That did not happen. The Yankees, however, remained close enough to embolden many escaping slaves. Cobb lost no runaways, but the hemorrhage elsewhere in the county became substantial. The "verry gloomy" news in July about Confederate defeats at Gettysburg and Vicksburg left Cobb pessimistic: "I fear we will be over powered by the Yankies after all the blood shed and loss of our men."[34]

By autumn the lengthening casualty list included Major Joseph E. Gillette, formerly the captain of Company A, who had been promoted to command the Thirteenth Cavalry, part of Brigadier General W. H. F. Lee's Brigade. Gillette, first wounded en route to Gettysburg, suffered a fatal wound during the Bristoe campaign in October. "One fine man," Cobb tersely memorialized the man for whom he had named his youngest son. Nightmares followed. Cobb visualized an army of men "without armes and legs" being pursued by another army. "I dream of the dead nightly and conversing with them," he reported. Cobb worried especially about his son Asbury, who remained as yet unscathed.[35]

The soldiers in Company A, who had expected a short decisive contest when they first enlisted in 1861, had to adjust to the grim reality of protracted warfare. Andrew J. Vick reminisced sadly about the "happy time" before 1861, when war was "nothing more than a good song." "What I have seen since," the young soldier observed in 1863, "I will leave you to draw your own conclusions." Lieutenant Wills, soon to be promoted to captain, resigned himself in early 1863 to a long struggle, at least as long as Lincoln remained in office. "Nothing would afford me more pleasure than to hear the war was over," he explained to his brother. Wills wished "the day would dawn that would bring peace to our distracted country, and send us all rejoicing to our homes." He doubted, however, that the war would end soon. As the romance of their undertaking disappeared, the veterans in Company A soberly reaffirmed their determination to persevere. "While my country needs [me] I am willing to battle for her rights," Wills vowed. He would "stand by her without a murmur rather than submit to Yankee rule."[36]

The Yankees had begun to adjust their own expectations. General Dix observed that originally it had been considered shrewd policy to scatter forces in the Confederate interior, hoping that "the people of the South would rally around them as a nucleus for the restoration of the Union." Experience taught him, however, that it was useless to think about "making friends of the secessionists." Having found the civilian population "bitter and implacable" in Union-occupied portions of the tidewater, Dix advised General-in-Chief Henry W. Halleck that "our only chance of success" lay in overpowering the Confederacy "by preponderance of force."[37]

As Major Gillette lay dying in October 1863, Southampton native George Henry Thomas remained busily engaged at Chattanooga, Tennessee, hundreds of miles to the southwest. A month before, Thomas's cool leadership on the battlefield had won him the sobriquet "The Rock of Chickamauga." Soon Major General Thomas commanded the assault on Missionary Ridge that sent enemy forces reeling back into Georgia. Unlike Gillette and the other white soldiers from Southampton, Thomas fought for the Union army.

In a war full of ironies, the achievements of George H. Thomas stand out. No other southerner inflicted such heavy blows on his home region. Thomas presided over the only two engagements—at Chattanooga and at Nashville—when a major Confederate army was thoroughly routed. Although he never gained the full confidence of his more renowned counterparts, Ulysses S. Grant and William Tecumseh Sherman, Thomas is now recognized as one of the ablest Union generals. He won deep respect from the soldiers he commanded, who knew that Thomas would not squander their lives impulsively.[38]

Why did Thomas choose to fight for the Union? That question has provoked unending speculation, especially among residents of his home county. At no time after Thomas enrolled at West Point in 1836 did he return home for more than brief visits. His marriage in 1852 to Frances Kellogg, from Troy, New York, must have diluted his southern allegiance. Some weight may also be given to hints that Thomas became estranged from the traditionalistic outlook and Democratic loyalties of his home neighborhood in the lower county. A lifelong student of natural science, Thomas noted with approval that Edmund Ruffin had republished Sir

Humphry Davy's *Elements of Agricultural Chemistry*. Although Thomas disavowed any political leanings, a letter that he wrote while a student at West Point revealed a sarcastic attitude toward President Van Buren. Thomas was also friends with George Butts, the son of a prominent local Whig family. In addition, there are some indications that Thomas disapproved of slavery. General Oliver O. Howard reported a black oral tradition that young Thomas had taught his black playmates to read and write, over his father's objections. It may also be pertinent that Southampton's most prominent white critic of slavery, Dr. Thomas J. Pretlow, claimed Thomas as a "friend and schoolmate." [39]

Thomas, who lived only five years after the end of the war, never returned to Southampton and never reestablished contact with his sisters and brother there. An acquaintance of the Thomas family in Southampton recalled that they regarded their famous brother not with hatred but with a feeling of mortification, disappointment, and sorrow, so much so as to prevent any reconciliation. [40]

However strange it may seem that the county's most eminent soldier fought for the Union rather than for the Confederacy, one should remember that disagreements about fundamental matters had a long history in Southampton. Patriotic Confederates, caught up in the initial wartime euphoria of 1861, might better have stopped to ponder why George H. Thomas did not join them. The defection of the Mexican War hero, to whom grateful residents of his home county had presented a handsome ceremonial sword in 1848, forewarned ominously of the ordeal that Confederate Southampton would experience.

During 1864 wartime hardships became even more acute in Southampton and across the shrinking Confederate nation. Corn reached as high as $300 per barrel locally and bacon $6.80 per pound, with little or none for sale. Many poor families apparently edged close to starvation. Elliott Story, responsible for county food distribution efforts, noted in his diary that "it is enough to excite the sympathy of the most unfeeling to learn the want and suffering that is told by some of those whom I have to furnish." [41]

Daniel Cobb assisted indigent relatives and neighbors, both with outright gifts of food and by loaning his slaves to help others plow and put in a crop; but he encountered criticism for not sharing his own apparently ample larder more liberally. A drunken man in Jerusalem pointedly insulted Cobb for hoarding corn. Local and Confederate requisitions on his corn and animals obliged Cobb to do more. At one point in 1864 a county official—in all likelihood the other diarist, Story—claimed fifteen barrels of Cobb's corn at the below-market value of $60 per barrel. Cobb paid Confederate income taxes, which in 1864 stood at 5 percent of the first $1,500, for anyone earning over $500, and 10 percent for anything in excess of $1,500. Cobb also paid Confederate taxes-in-kind and special excise assessments on his brandy operations.[42]

The shortages experienced by the Cobb family were hardly life-threatening. "The Cruel war has reduced our table to no Shugar and Coffee no flower, no flesh for brekfast and supper[,] only meats for Dinner," he reported. Forced to make do with honey and ground sorghum as sweeteners, "my wife falts and Grumbles at me heavy a bout the preshure of the war scarsity." Cobb and his wife found themselves having to entertain an influx of hungry guests, causing him to note in his diary that visitors were "not desi[r]able at [the] present crises of eating." Elliott Story made a more stoic assessment. "We ought not to complain," he wrote, because "these inconveniences are as nothing in comparison with what has been and is now being suffered by thousands and thousands of our country men."[43]

Shortages created temptations and opportunities. Story and a friend, Jordan Denson Pretlow, the younger brother of Thomas J. Pretlow, became involved in a risky and morally ambiguous scheme of trading with the enemy. They received Confederate authorization to secure "supplies for the government" by selling cotton "within the Federal lines." A successful sale would have afforded Story and Pretlow an attractive commission. Their first cotton shipment, however, was "captured by the enemy," an occurrence that convinced Story he was engaged in "a losing business." Story decided that wartime cotton trading was "not at all calculated to fit a man for sober regular business" but rather to tempt him "from the paths of virtue and religion."[44]

From May 1864 until the end of the war, Southampton stood close to the violent vortex. A Federal cavalry division of 3,000 commanded by Brigadier General August V. Kautz feinted toward Franklin and then crossed the Blackwater well upriver, cutting through adjacent Sussex County during the second week of May. The raiders seized food and supplies, ran off slaves, burned the Sussex courthouse, and wrecked a railroad bridge over the Nottoway River. People in Southampton frantically hid their property—silver, bacon, plows, harnesses, wagons, papers, and blankets. The mails stopped, "false rumers" proliferated, Yankee deserters were said to be in the woods, and new attacks were expected daily.

"The big and desiding fi[gh]t is on hand," Cobb judged. On May 28 all white Southampton men between the ages of seventeen and fifty, including the previously exempt groups under eighteen and over forty-five, were ordered to report for duty with three days' rations.[45]

Yet even as fighting moved to the county's outskirts, local politics continued unabated. An election was held in May 1864. Just as the very foundations of society were being violently sundered, Southampton attempted to maintain institutional legitimacy. Of particular interest is the sharp contest for sheriff between the Democratic incumbent and secessionist William W. Briggs and a prominent young Whig and conditional Unionist, John Pretlow.

It would appear that Pretlow attempted to capitalize on popular discontent. Daniel Cobb, who feared a "bad" result, complained that Pretlow was "lectionneering." Pretlow also threatened, or so Cobb heard, to "protest or Overthrow the E[lection]" if soldier votes were counted. Although Democrats may well have been trying to smear Pretlow, they did have reasonable basis for questioning his commitment to the Confederate cause. Pretlow, thirty-three years old when the war started, had volunteered in the elite cavalry unit. In 1862, however, he had hired a substitute. His battle-hardened former comrades took a understandably sour view of the stay-at-home Pretlow's candidacy. James F. Bryant hoped that Briggs had "given Pretlow such a whipping, that he will never again offer to run for any office in the county." Bryant thought no man younger than forty-five should be "elected to anything," because "Gen. Lee needs their important services in the military."[46]

The election of Briggs could be interpreted as an affirmation of continued popular support for the war effort, despite the severe hardships. More likely, however, voters rejected a stay-at-home, without necessarily intending to give the Confederate government in Richmond a blank check. In voting for magistrates, Southampton voters showed little inclination to honor those who supported secession before the war started (see app. table 7.1). Seventeen of the twenty-eight magistrates chosen in 1864 were Whigs; only ten were Democrats. Eleven voted against secession in February 1861; ten voted for it. Six of the seventeen who voted for John Bell in 1860 did not cast a vote in February 1861. Their ambivalence may have been widely shared. By 1864 many ordinary Southamptonites must have had second thoughts about the cause itself.

Southampton's Company A had its hands full during the heavy federal offensive launched in early May 1864. It screened for Robert E. Lee, whose army clashed repeatedly with numerically superior Federal forces under Lieutenant General Ulysses S. Grant. Other Confederate cavalry units tried to deter the Federal cavalry under Major General Philip H. Sheridan, which raced toward Richmond while Lee and Grant tangled near the Rappahannock. For over a month, the Southamptonites rode almost incessantly, often keeping their horses saddled through the night. They participated in a fierce two-day fight north of Richmond while other Confederates mauled Grant at nearby Cold Harbor. At Hanover Court House on May 31, Company A fought from an hour after sunrise until dark, and the next day at Ashland they fought again from noon until dark. In both engagements, they used carbines "dismounted as infantry," without "breastworks, or shelter to fight behind as the infantry generally have." In the opinion of James F. Bryant, the fighting on June 1 was "the hardest days work I ever did," with the men often marching "double-quick." James H. Drewry was killed, and their captain, Irvin C. Wills, suffered a severe wound. Meredith W. Holland's leg required amputation. "I did not expect to come out unhurt," Bryant confessed. At one point the men from Company A faced a Federal artillery position only forty yards away.[47]

Confederate soldiers could put their own exertions and losses in a favorable perspective because they had inflicted what appeared to be even heavier Federal losses, enough, they hoped, to "virtually close the war." Reporting to his father news of the Federal disaster at Cold Harbor, Bryant judged that "we shall exterminate them, instead of their exterminating us." Adequate rations of bacon and bread helped to sustain the morale of Company A; they also received occasional allotments of coffee, sugar, and tobacco.[48]

Heavy Union losses raised hopes that northern war-weariness might defeat Lincoln's reelection bid and enable the South to secure its independence. Daniel Cobb cited approvingly an article from a Norfolk newspaper quoting the "Yankiey bully" Grant as saying he would try Lee three or four more times and if he couldn't whip him, Lee could take his "*Dam Confederacy* and go to *hell*."[49]

Rather than retreat, however, Grant crossed the James River in mid-June, thereby endangering both Petersburg and Richmond. Lee's army arrived in the Petersburg entrenchments on June 18, just in the nick of time to stalemate a poorly coordinated Federal assault. Grant's army promptly built its own earthworks and fortifications. Siege warfare began, highlighted by daily firing and bombardments. Petersburg would remain the pivot of the eastern theater for the duration of the war.

The position of Grant's army effectively isolated Southampton. "We are now cut off from any communication with Petersburg without a great deal of hazard in getting there," Story noted. Residents no longer could ship goods to market, receive newspapers, or even maintain contact with "our friends in Gen[eral] Lee's army." Anxieties increased because the county appeared "liable to a visit from the Yankees at any time." Although Petersburg was over thirty miles from the closest part of Southampton, booming cannon fire frequently echoed in the distance. Southampton's isolation increased as fighting extended along the line of the Weldon Railroad, which ran south from Petersburg toward North Carolina.[50]

The proximity of fighting and the brutal lengthening of casualty lists weighed all the more heavily on Daniel Cobb because his son was in the midst of the struggle. Asbury Cobb suffered a slight wound in the wrist in early June. Later that month he walked home 100 miles from above the James after his horse died. Soon after returning to combat with a fresh horse, Asbury suffered a "hurte limbe." Two months later, he barely escaped being captured.[51]

The Confederate cavalry had to screen a broad front. The Thirteenth became part of an extended right flank below Petersburg, assigned to keep open the vital Petersburg and Weldon rail line. With most of its men drawn from the counties south and east of Petersburg, the Thirteenth was positioned in a familiar area near Reams Station, and the men had obvious motivation to defend their home region. Company A saw action in late June at Sappony Church, where it counterattacked against Brigadier General James H. Wilson's Federal cavalry raid southwest of Petersburg. Repositioned briefly north of the James in mid-August, the Thirteenth fought on the Charles City Road near White's Tavern, where John R. Chambliss, Jr., its brigadier general from neighboring Greensville County, was fatally wounded. Shortly thereafter, the regiment moved to Stony Creek, on the Weldon Railroad, twenty miles south of Petersburg.[52]

Cobb tried to reflect on the wrenching spectacle being enacted on Southampton's very outskirts. "The Yankees started this war for restoring . . . the Union," he noted, but the conflict had "turned out to be" about slavery. The enemy pursued the "bloody and cruel war," destroying the "bodies and soles of Southern men and women, our properties also,"

in order to free the "Negrows." To the dismay of Cobb and other Southampton slaveholders, growing numbers of local bondsmen and bonds-
women struck out for freedom, in part because so few white men remained behind in Southampton. "Four more of H[enry] Butts['s] servants
left him this morning for the Yankies which makes seven in the last
month," Cobb grimly recorded.[53]

One such escapee, Mary Pope, once owned by Amos Pope, recounted
her experiences to an interviewer in November 1864. Mary Pope, who
had lived under the control of Amos Pope's wife after he went to war,
explained that her "missus" had become increasingly harsh as the war
progressed. Although she had once been "very kind to us," the owner's
wife "could not work us hard enough" by 1864. Also embittered by the
fact that her husband had been sold in Richmond earlier in the war, Mary
Pope resolved to leave. The "missus," who had already lost one escapee
and apparently feared others would follow, pointedly warned that the
"mean Yankees" would "work me harder than she eber did, and I'd
starve at that." Mary Pope and her four children and six other slaves
nevertheless set out for freedom one night in November 1864. One child
did not survive the two-day trek that required crossing both the Nottoway and the Blackwater, but the others safely reached Union lines near
Suffolk.[54]

Among those fleeing Southampton were many men of military age.
One hundred or more Southamptonites, most of them former slaves, enlisted for military service in black regiments of the Union army during the
last year and a half of the war. "Throughout the slave states," notes historian Ira Berlin, "black enlistments and slave emancipation advanced
together and, indeed, became inseparable." The final crisis of the slave
system witnessed the transformation of bondsmen into soldiers, fighting
as part of an invading army. Nothing so well symbolized the revolutionary dynamic of the Civil War. "In smashing the manacles that bound their
people, black soldiers elevated themselves and transformed their own
consciousness. In their own eyes, in the eyes of the black community, and,
however reluctantly, in the eyes of the nation, black men gained a new
standing by donning the Union blue and participating in the nation's
great triumph."[55]

The roster of those who once owned the Southampton soldiers in the
Union army reads like a Who's Who of the local planter class. Elliott
Story's prosperous father-in-law, James Judkins, owned a slave named
Henry Judkins who ran away to Norfolk in August 1862. One year later,

in December 1863, Judkins enlisted as one of the original members of Company A of the First U.S. Colored Cavalry, a regiment that eventually enrolled over thirty Southampton soldiers. Albert Shelley, owned by the prominent Charles F. Urquhart, enlisted in the same company as Judkins, as did two other Southampton blacks. Urquhart's son, Thomas Hill Urquhart, recalled that two of his slaves, Jack Shepperd and Tom Walker, ran off to enlist in U. S. Grant's army during the siege of Petersburg. Nelson Edwards, the slave of Jordan Edwards, joined Company C of the Second U.S. Colored Cavalry in January 1864. Anthony and David Butts, probably owned by Henry Butts, escaped during the Kautz raid in May 1864 and enrolled in Company F of the Thirty-seventh U.S. Colored Infantry shortly afterwards. Henry Williams, owned by the estate of Robert Ridley, ran away to join Company B of the First U.S. Colored Cavalry in November 1864, leaving behind his young wife and child. One month later, another of Ridley's slaves, Albert Jones, enlisted in Company K of the same regiment.[56]

Unlike the typical white Civil War soldier, either Union or Confederate, Southampton blacks could not join companies drawn primarily from their own home area. Southampton remained behind Confederate lines throughout the war. Slaves typically escaped alone or in small groups. They often joined the Union army with no other apparent companions or by twos and threes. Black soldiers born in Southampton enrolled in at least two different cavalry regiments, five infantry regiments, and a light artillery battery, sometimes as the only person in the company from the county.

Nevertheless, one may discern patterns of enlistment for Southampton's black men in blue. Thirty-four joined the First U.S. Colored Cavalry, among them eight in Company I, five in Company H, and four each in Companies A, B, and C. Of the fourteen in the Second U.S.C.C., six were in Company C and three in Company D. Southampton soldiers in the infantry were most likely to join the Thirty-seventh or Thirty-eighth U.S.C.I., both of which drew soldiers from tidewater Virginia and North Carolina, with several companies in the latter from St. Marys County, Maryland. Sixteen from Southampton joined the Thirty-seventh, as did seventeen in the Thirty-eighth. Among the latter were nine men in Company G. Three Southampton soldiers found their way into the Tenth U.S.C.I., a unit drawn primarily from Virginia'a Eastern Shore. Eight Southamptonites volunteered in the Thirty-sixth U.S.C.I., a regiment raised in eastern North Carolina, as did one in the comparable Thirty-fifth. Five Southampton soldiers served in Battery B of the Second U.S. Colored Light Artillery. A total of ninety-eight Southampton soldiers appeared on the rosters of the various cavalry, infantry, and artillery units into which they would most likely have volunteered.[57]

Perhaps 20 percent of Southampton's Union volunteers had been free before the war, suggesting a rate of enlistment proportionate to the free black population in the county. Among them, for example, were four of the five Southampton soldiers listed in Company H of the First U.S.C.C.: Willis Joe, James Ricks, Samuel Ricks, and Joseph Scott. Scott was the cook for the company, and Samuel Ricks the "under cook." James Ricks was the company's chief bugler. All enlisted together in December 1863 when the company and regiment were formed.[58]

Company G of the Thirty-eighth U.S.C.I. deserves special mention, not only because its nine Southampton soldiers outnumbered those in any other company but also because its men fought together outside Petersburg at the end of September 1864, in one of the major battles involving black troops. Having enlisted in July and August 1864, the men of this company hardly had time to train sufficiently for the shock of combat. Nonetheless, the Thirty-eighth, which together with the Fifth and Thirty-Sixth U.S.C.I. constituted the Second Brigade of the Third Division of the Eighteenth Army Corps, bravely charged Confederate positions north of the James River on the morning of September 29. Taking heavy casualties (17 killed and 94 wounded in the regiment; 66 killed, 367 wounded, and 23 missing for a total of 455 casualties in the brigade), the black troops advanced under heavy fire. After an initial rebuff they regrouped and seized New Market Heights. Nine officers and enlisted men from the Second Brigade were subsequently awarded the Congressional Medal of Honor for their role on September 29.[59]

Company I of the First U.S.C.C. included eight Southampton soldiers, six of whom enlisted in November and December 1864, near the end of the war. Among these volunteers were three brothers, Henry, Harrison, and Joseph Williams, the sons of Solomon Sykes and Louisa Williams. The mother and sons were owned by Jacob Williams. Two of the brothers are listed as having been regimental carpenters before the unit was demobilized in 1866. All returned to Southampton and subsequently took their father's last name, Sykes. Joseph Sykes died before the end of the century, but Henry Sykes lived until 1912 and Harrison Sykes until 1916. Joseph Sykes and his wife became members of the Cool Spring Baptist Church, a congregation of blacks whose minister was Joseph Gregory.[60]

In 1898 one former Southampton slave, George W. Claud, wrote out his own affidavit to support the pension claim made by Margaret Sykes, the widow of Joseph Sykes. Thirty-four years had not dimmed Claud's memory of the night that his friend Joseph escaped from slavery to join the Union army: "I new hem from [?] a boy   we ware Rase Jaying [raised on adjoining] plantdations   his old master warse name Jaccobb Willams his moher war name Louisa Willams   her husban was name Salman Sykes   be for the Silvel war the Mother and Chiulderen all went By the name of willimses and After the war when the pepel be came free they clams ther one nemes   but we wre all play Children to gather   Eate plade and sleep to gather   I dew not name what Rigiment he be long to but I now the night he left hear for the nathen army." For those in Southampton of middle years or more, the enlistment of local blacks in the Union army must have brought to mind Nat Turner's prophecy—that "the great day of judgment was at hand . . . when the first should be last and the last should be first." [61]

In late May 1864, for the first time ever, Daniel Cobb suddenly began to fill his diary with biblical defenses for slaveholding. He assembled an array of citations such as chapter 6 of Ephesians, which stated that servants should be obedient to their masters. "Owning slaves is no crime," Cobb assured himself. He was "allmost perswaded" that "every man is to fill a certain station of life then die and pass away." Yet the effort proved unsatisfying. Cobb remained "much depest [depressed] in mine [mind]" and "much dejected." [62]

His confidence in the southern social order had been shaken as never before. As late as September 1863, he remained convinced that God ultimately would favor the South. A flurry of religious meetings, both in the army and in Southampton, seemed a hopeful indication. Cobb judged the "revival of religion" to be "the key of peace." By July 1864, however, he articulated a troubling new perspective. The Lord had blessed his people with "a vast quantity of worldly Good[s]." But the South had failed to thank God for his favor. God therefore willed the war, Cobb feared, in order that people be "umbled" and their wealth taken away. Although Cobb continued to pray that God would "stop this Bloody Crewell war," he began to suspect that it would be carried to a devastating conclusion. [63]

As the nightmare intensified, Cobb tried to preserve the normal routines. He considered it his duty to provide a festive holiday and "dining" for his hands when the last crop ever raised by slave labor was laid by in early August. Despite reports of Yankee cavalry raiders in the area, his slaves enjoyed two lambs, vegetables, and other delicacies, even as starvation stalked the households of many humble Southampton whites. In no way, however, did Cobb modify his views about blacks. Consistent with his morbid idea that whites would either have to kill or be killed, he purposefully jotted down examples of black treachery that had been treated summarily. He credited a rumor in 1863 that a captured regiment of 900 blacks and their white officers had all been hanged at Vicksburg. Cobb likewise thought that slaves in Petersburg, after raising a "black flag" during the initial Federal assault, had been "instantainously shot down." 64

Autumn and early winter in late 1864 failed to bring the usual respite from warfare. The cannons around Petersburg continued to "rower," more heavily than ever before. Yankees raided the Seaboard Railroad in lower Southampton, burning Murfees Depot, and some requisitioned Confederate supplies there, including Cobb's brandy. It was a cheerless time. The grim toll on local enlisted men mounted, the civilian poor struggled to find a bare subsistence, and slaves continued to escape to Federal lines. The reelection of President Lincoln in early November undermined hopes that northern war-weariness might allow a negotiation of southern independence. Most ominously for Cobb, Confederates protecting the Weldon Railroad remained embattled. 65

Assaulted at Reams Station at August and then at Stony Creek in early December, Company A retreated south to winter quarters at Belfield, close to the southwestern corner of their home county. The attenuated Confederate lifeline grew longer. Confederates had to ship supplies by wagon thirty miles from Belfield to Petersburg. Shortages of food, clothing, shoes, horses, and manpower became increasing perilous. Daniel Cobb hired a local cobbler and seamstress to make Asbury Cobb a new pair of boots and a new coat. Twice in November and December, the last months of Cobb's surviving Civil War diaries, the distracted father traveled circuitously around Federal positions to visit his son. By the time of Cobb's second visit, on December 18, bridges across the Nottoway River had been destroyed. 66

The relative stalemate lasted until late March 1865, when continued Federal flanking maneuvers threatened the South Side Railroad, forcing the Confederates to defend the one remaining rail link to Petersburg. When that rail line fell into Federal hands after the battle of Five Forks on April 1, in which soldiers from the Thirteenth were heavily engaged, Confederates had to evacuate both Petersburg and Richmond. Unable to escape to the southwest, General Lee surrendered the remnants of his army at Appomattox one week later. Asbury Cobb, who survived four years of combat, fell during the last days of the war in the Appomattox campaign.[67]

Daniel Cobb had written his most lyrical entry in thirty years of diary keeping one fine morning the previous summer, just as the principal theater of the war moved into southern Virginia. Upon walking out to see his "foalks" hoeing in a field of shoulder-high corn, Cobb remarked movingly about the panorama. "What a senery," he exclaimed. Pea plants had started to sprout up the green corn stalks, and "a small field of wheat just put on its goalden heue of harvest which still added to the senery. I was hurd to cry out grate heaven owing to the buty before my eyes and to say if a fine Crop and the [end of?] the Cruel war was to come to gather[,] how happy would the people of the south be a gain."[68] Defeat, emancipation, and the loss of his eldest son forever ended Cobb's pleasurable reverie. Nothing thereafter could make him, or the many other white southerners who saw things his way, happy again.

EIGHT

❦

The New Order of Things

SOUTHAMPTON COUNTY, PRECARIOUSLY within the perimeters
of the shrinking Confederacy until the final capitulation at Appomattox, suddenly found itself under Yankee occupation in the spring
of 1865. The exercise of federal power, limited for the first two postwar
years, became more formidable between 1867 and 1869, when federal
registrars enrolled black voters and attempted to see that elections were
conducted fairly. Military authorities appointed civilian officials for both
state and local government. The heretofore submerged freedmen of
Southampton, galvanized by unprecedented opportunity, temporarily
contested the unquestioned dominance that Southampton whites had always enjoyed. The ensuing struggle was bitter, racially polarized, and had
interlocking political and economic dimensions.

The federal presence in Southampton bequeathed a rich dividend. Numerous letters and reports, some written by Southampton citizens and a
larger number by federal officials who lived in the county or supervised
its affairs for several years after the end of the war, when combined with
newspaper articles, local records, and Daniel W. Cobb's diary, make Reconstruction the best documented period analyzed in this book.

A CONTINGENT OF THE Third New York Cavalry, commanded by Major J. H. Putnam, occupied Southampton after the end of hostilities. He
sent detachments throughout the county to take "the census of Colored
people, with names, location, and employment of each." Because many
enslaved blacks fled Confederate Southampton to the Union-controlled
region just across the Blackwater River, the demand for labor in the immediate postwar period proved brisk. "Able-bodied Negroes can very

readily find employment at fair wages," Putnam cheerfully reported. "The Provost Marshal has many applications for laborers and all that have been found without employment have been readily provided with situations." Putnam also took an upbeat view of local agricultural prospects. Spared the ravages of wartime destruction that fell heavily on many other parts of Virginia, Southampton appeared to be in "a very high state of cultivation, the farms being very generally supplied with farming implements, field laborers, horses, mules & c." [1]

Other federal observers made a differing assessment of the situation. Sounding for all the world like a disgruntled white southerner, one Freedmen's Bureau official reported that Southampton's former slaves no longer worked with proper intensity. Many chose to "leave the scene of their former bondage." Some moved from the county, but others remained: "Wherever they find a vacant house, they move in and do nothing but wander about in idleness." Under the circumstances, the freedmen were blamed for "a great deal of stealing going on." [2]

Similar reports echoed across the South in the summer and fall of 1865, confronting federal officials with a dilemma. Defeated southerners vowed that free black labor could be made productive only if directed and managed by white landowners. Convinced that a "natural disposition to self-indulgence" predisposed the freedmen to live "from day to day without plans for the future," the vanquished appealed to the victors for broad latitude in the oversight and discipline of black labor. Ex-Confederates sought to bind freedmen to a particular landowner for an entire season, with both the power of law and the threat of coercion to enforce the new arrangements. [3]

Former slaves, however, sought autonomy and independence. For the first times in their lives, they could learn to read and write, they could refuse to work for a former owner, they could travel freely, and they could seek to reunite separated families; travel often was undertaken in the hope of relocating husbands, wives, children, and other kinfolk. As individuals, as families, and as members of church congregations and other mutual benefit societies, former slaves strove to make freedom meaningful. Initially hopeful that they would be able to purchase small plots of land and establish themselves as peasant proprietors, the freedmen were disinclined to make binding arrangements with landowners, especially their former owners. Once their hopes for land ownership were dashed, the freedmen insisted upon new ground rules to govern relationships between employers and employees: the elimination of gang labor, the shortening of work hours, the right to take holidays (including half of Saturday as well as Sunday), and the exemption of black women from labor in the fields.[4]

The Freedmen's Bureau, headed by Major General O. O. Howard, faced a formidable task in attempting to reconcile the claims of former masters and slaves. As President Andrew Johnson pressured the bureau to dampen black aspirations and restore the plantation system, Howard's search for a mutually agreed-upon plan for free labor became even more difficult.[5]

For Howard, a system of contracts between landlords and laborers appeared the most promising solution to the dilemma. Contracts would spell out the rights and obligations of both parties, thereby assuring landlords a reliable, competent work force, while at the same time assuring free laborers fair wages and treatment. Starting in July 1865, Howard attempted to put theory into practice. He instructed local Freedmen's Bureau agents to arrange written contracts based on a wage rate comparable to that for "the hire of an able-bodied man when the pay went to the master." Concerned to provide laborers with "protection against avarice and extortion," Howard specified that "wages had better be secured by a lien on the crops or land." Moreover, he sternly prohibited any "substitute for slavery, like apprenticeships without proper consent, or peonage, (i.e., either holding the people by debt, or confining them, without consent, to the land by any system,)."[6]

By late autumn, as the time approached to make new labor arrangements for the coming calendar year and the prolandowner predilections of the president became unmistakable, bureau authorities in Virginia reformulated the ideas in Howard's July circular. Colonel Orlando Brown, assistant commissioner for the state of Virginia, bluntly demanded that freedmen make contracts with landowners. Downplaying Howard's expressed concerns about the potential for landlords to exploit laborers, Brown warned that the bureau would support efforts by landowners and local officials to compel the freedmen to make contracts:

> The principal function of this Bureau is not to supply a channel
> through which government aid or private charity shall be dispensed,
> but to make the Freedmen a self-supporting class of free laborers,
> who shall understand the necessity of steady employment, and the re-
> sponsibility of providing for themselves and families. Where employ-
> ment is offered on terms that will provide for the comfortable subsist-

ence of the laborers, removing them from the vices of idleness and from dependence on charity, they should be treated as vagrants if they do not accept it; and the rules of the Bureau applicable in such cases, should be rigidly enforced. While the Freedmen must and will be protected in their rights, they must be required to meet these first and most essential conditions of a state of freedmen, *a visible means of support, and fidelity to contracts.*[7]

The Freedmen's Bureau also was responsible for doing what it could to promote schooling and educational opportunity. General Howard's directive of July 12, 1865, authorized appointment of a bureau official in each state to superintend the development of schools, either in cooperation with state officials or with "the benevolent agencies which are supplying his field." The bureau would not establish schools on its own, but it would "take cognizance of all that is being done to educate refugees and freedmen, secure proper protection to schools and teachers, [and] promote method and efficiency."[8]

What did these policy guidelines actually mean in Southampton? Two bureau agents, first Captain Samuel Gilmore and then Captain Lemuel Jeffries, resided in the county in late 1865 and 1866. They certainly did arrange some contracts, though how many is unclear (the copies of contracts in a surviving bound volume may represent only a fraction of those contracts actually signed). Some freedmen were hired for annual wages, with the best male hands promised $100 or more. Freedwomen contracted for between $40 and $60. Contracts typically required landlords to provide food, clothing, and quarters. Some contracts, probably involving older or infirm freed people, called for no wages beyond food, clothing, and quarters. Other contracts provided for compensation through a division of the crop. Freedmen who required no other support from a landlord might contract to receive between one-third and one-half of specified crops such as corn, cotton, peas, and potatoes; the brandy share was reduced by some landlords to one-sixth. More typical were crop shares of between one-quarter and one-third, with landowners obligated to provide food, clothing, and quarters.[9]

Daniel W. Cobb used a variety of arrangements with the freed people. Freedmen's Bureau records suggest that three adult men he hired were to receive one-third shares of the corn and cotton crops. Two women, one with children, agreed to work for scant annual wages ($30 for one, $20 for the other). Two apparently older persons contracted for no wage or share, only subsistence and quarters. The contracts with his tenants obligated Cobb to provide food, housing (in the old slave cabins), firewood, and, for those not working on shares, clothing. Cobb also had to supply his laborers with horses and agricultural implements. The freedmen, however, would have to pay for any "provisions" beyond the basic allotment. Therein lay the key to Cobb's dominance. Additional food or liquor purchases depleted the meager black earnings. Cobb not only kept the records but also had the right to fire hands who did not please him. He bluntly described the effects of the new system: "Eating will keep Negrows poor and down." [10]

The contract between Cobb and his laborers was regulated by an agent of the Freedmen's Bureau, who visited on February 6. Cobb appeared pleasantly surprised to find that Captain Jeffries, "the Yankie [who] came to my house this evening to fix up the Negrow contract," had "acted as a gentleman." Later in the year, Cobb and one of his tenants, named Carter Harrison, got into a "fracas." The latter threatened to report Cobb to the "Yankey Officer." Cobb, confident that he had nothing to fear, "toald him to do so." The complaint "proved to no effect" as the federal official sided with Cobb. Here and elsewhere across the South in 1866, the Freedmen's Bureau often functioned in a manner that proved helpful to landowners. [11]

Altogether, thirty blacks lived at Cobb's in 1866. Many things on his farm did not change, at least not at first. Gang labor under his direct supervision appears to have been the norm. Time and again during 1866, he made diary entries that could have been written ten years before. In winter his "foalkes" cut firewood and mauled rails; in spring they plowed and planted. Day after day in the summer, there were four plows in cotton and two hoes in corn, or some such combination. That fall, the hands pulled fodder, picked cotton, and gathered corn and peas. As if to symbolize the continuity between slavery and free labor, Cobb held his annual "dining" in August. [12]

Cobb's diary makes it plain that Southampton faced major economic dislocation. All assets in slaves and in Confederate currency and bonds were wiped out. Land values stagnated or depreciated, except in favorable sites adjacent to railroads or in villages and towns. Many who owned substantial amounts of property were dragged into bankruptcy, because they had legal liability for persons who could not pay their debts or for estates that owed money. Creditors of Jesse Little, Cobb's father-in-law who died in 1863, found themselves unable to collect obligations owed them from his shrunken estate. Ripples of default dried up local sources of investment capital.[13]

High prices for agricultural products, especially cotton, afforded financially battered Southamptonites a life preserver. Thirty-one cents for a pound of cotton in 1866 meant that a 400-pound bale would bring $124, and Cobb made nine bales. His farm produced enough apples to make a profitable quantity of brandy, and it supplied ample amounts of the southern dietary staples, pork and corn. Unlike many in Southampton, Cobb also managed to stay relatively free from debt. His finances were solid enough that he could hire workmen to build an addition to his house containing a storeroom, a pantry, and an "eating room."[14]

But Cobb did not feel encouraged. Any deviation from slavery alarmed him and other Southampton landowners. "The hands I hired to tend a crop on shars looses at least 25 or 30 minutes every morning after sun rise," he complained. By sleeping half an hour longer than slaves, the freedmen might cost him only a little "per day or per week or say month," but, he insisted, "per year will count." He therefore decided to "make a charge" to offset the probable shortfall. On court day in May, his "foalks" took a holiday "as free men." Cobb was not pleased: "White men at home ploughing and Nigars frolickin," he complained. As the year continued, he repeatedly found fault with the free laborers and reported trouble with them. "Bord not urned," Cobb grumbled, after a rainy day prevented outdoor work. Nor had hands ever picked so little cotton, "say fifty pounds per day." The crop was the "sorryest" he had ever seen.[15]

From the perspective of his laborers, too, things had not gone well at Cobb's farm in 1866. Their grievances differed markedly from his, however. The successful harvest should have enabled Cobb to meet his obligations to the freedmen. Those who had contracted in shares stood to gain the most. In fact, however, Cobb made deductions that diminished or liquidated the earnings of his labor force. The morning in early December when he settled up accounts, Cobb reported "some troble with some of the hands."[16]

The example of Cobb illustrates that Southampton during 1866 was witnessing the first stages of a struggle, pitting strong forces of inertia against the freedmen's determination to improve their lives. Traditionalists plainly won the first round, as may also be seen in the second broad area of Freedmen's Bureau responsibility, education.

Captain Jeffries, the local bureau agent in early 1866, reported that a young Pennsylvania veteran, Charles Irving, had established a small freedmen's school, enrolling between eight and ten children. The school was located on property owned by another Pennsylvanian, Adrian Beans, six miles outside Jerusalem. The parents of the students paid Irving, and Beans apparently supplied a place to meet, so the school cost the government nothing. Jeffries noted that the school encountered "some opposition from the neighborhood planters," who condemned Beans for allowing "a nigger school on his farm." Jeffries promised, however, "the full protection of the Bureau against *all* evil-disposed persons." [17]

In neighboring Nansemond County, white hostility to freedmen's education was such that vigilantes burned a school in Somerton and the adjacent building that housed the Quaker meeting, which supported the school. The local bureau agent, Major J. R. Stone, reported arresting four suspects, whose "ringleader did not deny his guilt but seemed to be proud of being accused of such a crime." His principal defense consisted of "vituperation" at the Friends and "foul-mouthed slanders of the white teachers." Stone suspected that the accused arsonists had the support of "most of the disloyal crew in the neighborhood," who "although they would not commit the crime themselves, feel a secret satisfaction when 'tis done." [18]

Even had the bureau been able to overcome or suppress white hostility, the absence of any federal financial support prevented effective implementation of the bureau's educational policies in large parts of the Reconstruction South. Jeffries's successor as bureau agent, Lieutenant Morton Havens, reported in late April that no schools for freedmen remained functioning in Southampton. The school on Beans's farm had been disbanded, "for want of funds to sustain it." Havens contacted benevolent societies in Richmond, hoping to gain their assistance for an enterprise that apparently cost more than the impoverished freedmen could themselves afford. [19]

Jittery whites, unable to grasp that the end of slavery also ended the possibility of future Nat Turners, feared a black rebellion. Legislators from Southampton and neighboring Nansemond County, suspecting an imminent outbreak, demanded that Virginia governor Francis H. Pierpont confiscate arms owned by the freedmen. Major General Alfred H. Terry, military commander of the Department of Virginia, reluctantly ordered an investigation, promising to disarm blacks if there was any evidence of a planned revolt. He insisted, however, that blacks and whites should be treated alike, and he noted that blacks "were our friends when nearly every white man was our enemy." [20]

It appears that confiscation of weapons in the possession of blacks proceeded on an irregular, extralegal basis. Several months later, Havens, the local bureau agent, asked his superiors for guidance. They informed him that "no one, save proper officials, have the power to deprive colored people of arms, and this should be done by them only on just grounds," such as "careless use." Havens was authorized to restore confiscated arms "when proper guarantees are given for their careful use." Given the persistence of white anxieties, the agent could not have found it easy to enforce his instructions.[21]

Continuities linking the prewar era and the immediate postwar years were also apparent in local government. On August 3, 1865, Southampton voters elected a full complement of county officials, including a sheriff, a commonwealth's attorney, two revenue commissioners, and four members of the county court from each magisterial district, plus constables and overseers of the poor. Adult white males willing to take the amnesty oath voted without interference, except for the small number whose wealth or prewar political stature required a presidential pardon. No local whites even considered that blacks might be eligible to vote.

Samuel Kello, a prominent upper-county Whig, won the post of sheriff, which he had earlier held between 1852 and 1856. He displaced Democrat William W. Briggs. As his deputy Kello appointed the diarist Elliott Story. Voters selected Orris Moore, Story's neighbor and longtime friend, as revenue commissioner for the upper county. To this extent, Southampton's new postwar government had a distinctly more Whiggish and antisecession tone.

The membership of the county court remained, however, much as it had stood in 1864 (see app. table 7.1). Twelve members of the old court held seats on the new one. Whigs did outnumber Democrats, seventeen to nine, but because six of the Whigs had not voted in the February 1861 referendum, antisecessionists outnumbered secessionists only ten to nine. Similar to the courts elected in 1860 and 1864, the 1865 court had privileged antecedents. Fully 60 percent of its members had owned ten or more slaves.

State government, likewise, took shape in a way that minimized sharp departures. Governor Pierpont, who headed the "restored" Virginia government established during wartime, presided over its transformation into a more orthodox peacetime government. He opposed disfranchisement of former Confederates. As a consequence, conservative native whites dominated the legislature elected in October 1865. They pursued a resolutely traditionalist course during 1866, ultimately disappointing Pierpont, who hoped to develop an alliance of Whig Unionists and ex-Confederates.[22]

Several accounts of developments in Southampton appeared as letters to the Richmond *Whig* in early 1866. The anonymous correspondent took local farmers severely to task for preferring "to extend and enlarge rather than improve." Echoing complaints voiced by Edmund Ruffin over a generation before, the correspondent for the *Whig* discerned a pattern of "cultivating each parcel of land till it is prematurely exhausted, and seeking to make up the deficit in production by tilling fresh lands." He deplored the failure to use beds of marl lying just a few feet below the surface in parts of the county.[23]

The correspondent also identified other more immediate reasons for Southampton's stagnation. The county barely had produced enough corn to feed itself in 1865, and "the prospect for this year is not said to be much better." Landowners could not find adequate help in a labor market still thinned by the wartime exodus of runaway slaves because many freedmen preferred to work "only by the month or day." Officers of the Freedmen's Bureau had been unable to arrange contracts "in a majority of cases," and the freedmen had "evidently profited but little by the experience of the nine months past."[24]

The *Whig*'s correspondent mused about possible solutions for Southampton's difficulties. Unwilling to allow "the future prosperity of the South" to rest on "the precarious foundation of negro labor," he noted that "some farmers have already adopted the white labor system, and with every prospect of complete success." The "white labor system" he had in mind went beyond the hiring of landless, less privileged local folk. It contemplated instead attracting "the hardy and industrious emigrant" to the South. That required the selling of land, and therein lay the rub. However much local landowners claimed to favor "immigration," they were "loth to part with their lands." With individual "identity" bound up in landed property (and, the author might have added, at a time when identity with an even more valuable type of property had been violently sundered), any hope that the "white labor system" could transform Southampton agriculture hardly appeared cheering.[25]

The correspondent judged that the "flourishing village of Franklin," located strategically where the Seaboard and Roanoke Railroad intersected with the head of navigation on the Blackwater River, had a bright future. In the months since Lee's surrender, three stores had opened up an

extensive business with the backcountry and a steam sawmill was producing "a large amount of lumber for market." Large amounts of fish and
grain from eastern North Carolina were sold at or transshipped from
Franklin. Steamboats whisked passengers to locations in Albemarle and
Pamlico sounds, while "the iron horse, that great auxiliary to commerce,
thunders by daily, much to the convenience and gratification of the citizens." Prognostications that Franklin would emerge as a significant urban
center would prove more accurate than hopes for agricultural reform or
inauguration of the "white labor system."

The person writing for the *Whig* recognized, however, that forces of
tradition and inertia remained strong in the county. Visiting Jerusalem,
"the somewhat antiquated capital of Southampton" on court day in
March 1866, he reported that "the village, so quiet at other times, is alive
at that day." A large crowd assembled in town, and "two dozen very
respectable and intelligent looking" magistrates met, giving the court-
room "quite an imposing aspect." They displayed, however, scant tendency to innovate. Simply the task of restoring local bridges and roads to
their "*ante bellum* condition" appeared burdensome to many, and some
objected to "the increase of taxes which would be necessary." The magistrates did take steps to rebuild bridges and roads, but did not enact a
fence law requiring the enclosure of animals. Unlike large property holders in neighboring Sussex County, who stirred a hornet's nest by trying to
implement a fence law, Southampton's political leaders respected the apparent popular preference "to stick to their former customs." Domestic
animals would continue to roam freely in Southampton, and crops would
need to be enclosed against their depredations.[26]

On balance, those in Southampton who opposed change maintained
the upper hand during 1865 and 1866. As yet, however, the outcome
remained undetermined. Some local whites believed that traditionalists,
by plunging the South into a disastrous war, had forfeited their right to
dominate. Even if unsympathetic to the aspirations of the freedmen, dis-
contented whites stood ready to adopt new strategies for progress and
improvement. The question of how federal policies might tip the balance
likewise remained unresolved.

BETWEEN MAY 1866 AND January 1868, Second Lieutenant A. G.
Deacon, a native of Fond du Lac, Wisconsin, served as Freedmen's Bureau
agent in Southampton. During 1867 he held a second significant appointment, as president of the Board of Registration, responsible for enrolling

black voters while excluding whites who could not meet certain tests of wartime loyalty. Deacon's tenure in Southampton thus coincided with the time when federal Reconstruction policy moved from a passive to a more active phase. The second hat that Deacon wore by the summer of 1867 symbolized an enlarged federal effort to promote change in the South. Much may be learned by examining, in turn, his activities as bureau agent and as federal registrar.

As bureau agent, Deacon had three principal responsibilities. First, he was to promote free-labor agriculture, especially by arranging contracts between freedmen and landowners. Second, he was to encourage the development of schools. Finally, he was to function as a judicial officer, attending preliminary hearings and trials in local court cases to which blacks were a party, exercising discretionary jurisdiction over lesser cases, and recommending the transfer of major cases to military courts. The last of these three functions may well have been the bureau agent's most important public responsibility: that of an ombudsman to oversee the local judicial system.[27] These judicial duties involved him in a variety of cases that illustrate, collectively, the points where controversies most frequently occurred during the first postwar years. Freedmen sued landowners for unpaid wages, for property such as animals and clothing, and for control over black children, many of whom were bound out by apprenticeships. The agent also had to deal with episodes in which disputes turned violent or in which freedmen had been forcibly evicted.

Many obstacles impeded the development of free-labor agriculture. During the first several postwar years, freedmen frequently complained about being cheated out of wages. Occasionally they were able to bring suit successfully in freedmen's court. For example, in 1866 Lyman Parker and Richard White recovered $5 and $15, respectively. Frank Lee collected a skimpy $14 for a full seven months of work. Disputes about possessions often arose. The freedmen's court in Southampton decided against several landowners who apparently withheld promised clothing as well as wages. Other freedmen took legal action to secure animals. Mary Jones and Boling H. Ricks each recovered a cow, and Fannie Ricks regained custody of a pig.[28]

The freedmen had less success in recovering apprenticed children. A black woman who had been free before the war hoped "under the new order of things" to reclaim a son, who remained indentured to a white person until the age of twenty-one. The local agent in Southampton sent an inquiry about the case to his superiors and was told that "the woman had better stand by her contracts. It is not the policy of this Bureau to disallow contracts unless very unfavorable." Nancy Artis did recover her child from Stephen Henderson, but the prominent Thomas Ridley fended off a legal challenge from Peter Johnson, a freedman whose daughter was held by Ridley, apparently the child's former owner. The freedmen's court decided that Ridley had given "good and kind treatment" to Johnson's daughter and to his other former slaves and therefore should retain her services until she turned eighteen. In exchange, Ridley promised to pay her $15 per year, to teach her to read and write, and to give her proper food, clothing, shelter, and medical care. These cases opened the door to widespread abuse. During the next several years, the county court arbitrarily apprenticed substantial numbers of black children against the wishes of their parents. It appears unlikely that the beneficiaries honored their promises to teach the children to read and write.[29]

The bureau agent had to investigate many complaints about violence, threats of violence, and intimidation. Some of these cases came under his direct jurisdiction in freedmen's court. Many more such cases appear in the records by the summer and fall of 1867 than a year before. Had mistreatment of blacks increased over time? Perhaps so. By mid–1867 astonished whites discovered that blacks in large numbers were registering to vote, and that may have triggered increased violence and intimidation. The freedmen during 1867 may also have become emboldened to initiate action in freedmen's court.

Lieutenant Deacon resolved a number of cases. He worked out a compromise settlement between Randolph Stokes, a freedman, and James S. Harrison, whom Stokes accused of assault and battery. Deacon fined Joseph Barham $40 for assaulting freedman Ephriam Ford with intent to kill. The agent also settled the case in which Nelson Davis, a freedman, complained that he was driven away without good cause by Abner Stephenson. Davis won the right to return to his home and job, and Stephenson agreed "to have nothing more to do with Davis." In other cases, Deacon appears to have been constrained by the limited jurisdiction of the freedmen's court. When James and Albert Artis charged Chestine Magget with discharging the contents of a double-barreled shotgun at them, Deacon referred the case to the circuit court after having civil authorities impose a $400 bond on Magget to ensure his appearance.[30]

During 1867 Lieutenant Deacon conducted investigations into two incidents in which freedmen were the apparent victims of violent abuse. Because he transcribed testimony from witnesses in both cases, Deacon's reports provide significant firsthand evidence about Southampton society during the first turbulent years after the slave system ended.

Caroline Drewry, a freedwoman from lower Southampton, died under mysterious circumstances on June 27, 1867. At the behest of Joseph W. Claud, prominent local justice of the peace, twelve white jurors were empaneled the next day to view the body and to inquire about the circumstances of her death. They concluded unanimously that "the deceased came to her death from some unknown cause and not from any violence." Their conclusion relied substantially on the testimony of two doctors who reported finding no evidence of violence while conducting a post-mortem examination.[31]

The official finding did not satisfy many freedmen, who suspected that Caroline Drewry died after being beaten by Dr. L. W. Jones. Her two elder sons, George Drewry and Henry Ivey, testified that on the day before Caroline Drewry died, their younger brother and sister had come running to say that Dr. Jones was beating their mother. The older brothers, who had been visiting Henry Ivey's father on a neighboring farm about 300 yards away, ran back to confront Jones, who, they insisted, had just stopped beating their mother with a stick. George Drewry quoted Jones as admitting that he had given Caroline Drewry "a good frailing" because she had "runned me and Henry away." George Drewry reported that his mother had been bruised on her hands and head, as well as kicked. Pains in her head, neck, side, and breast prevented her from sleeping that night. Although Caroline Drewry was able to do washing and to cook dinner the next morning, she suddenly collapsed and died in the early afternoon, approximately twenty-four hours after she had been beaten.

Several significant aspects of this unhappy episode deserve mention. First, the dispute originated when Jones discovered that Caroline Drewry's sons were off visiting rather than working on a midweek day in late June, when the cotton crop needed grassing. Jones apparently blamed the mother when her sons failed to work up to his expectations. Second, it seems that some Southampton whites maintained a kind of hair-trigger touchiness about the social revolution to which they had been unwillingly subjected. The breakdown of slavelike behavior among blacks could propel former slaveowners and other whites into towering rages. Third, younger blacks especially may have tried to test the extent of their new freedom. Henry Ivey insisted that his mother "could not run me off nor make me stay." He believed himself entitled to vary the routine. Finally, however, the episode revealed the precariousness of the new freedoms that blacks were trying to enjoy. Caroline Drewry neither fled nor sought protection after the beating occurred. She stayed put and tried to carry on with her life. Nor did her sons have any redress. Indeed, the incident may have frightened them into temporary submission. After Jones had beaten their mother, the two brothers worked with him the rest of the afternoon and evening in the cotton patch.

The legal sequel to Caroline Drewry's death was predictable. Deacon arrested Jones and required that he raise a $1,000 bond as a promise of his appearance.[32] Deacon's superiors in Richmond refused, however, to reopen the case against Jones, believing that "any prosecution for murder would be useless." Acknowledging that the testimony of her sons indicated that Caroline Drewry's death resulted from "blows inflicted on her person by Dr. L. W. Jones," a judge advocate ruled that the report by the two physicians would prevent any conviction, even though they had failed to make a "proper post-mortem examination."

The other significant violent episode investigated by Deacon involved Edward ("Ned") Sykes, a freedman, and William M. Beaton, who owned a store and a cotton gin at Boykins Depot in the lower county. Sykes claimed that Beaton had assaulted him with a wooden door bar; Beaton did not deny the accusation but said that Sykes had first pulled a knife on him. Deacon subsequently gathered testimony about the incident, which occurred in December 1866.[33]

All witnesses to the case agreed that the trouble developed in Beaton's store. The two men got into an argument there after Sykes requested pay for packing cotton at Beaton's gin. Beaton gave Sykes thirty or forty cents' worth of cheese, saying he would settle for whatever else he owed at a later time. Sykes complained, whereupon Beaton ordered Sykes to leave the store. Sykes replied by saying something to the effect that "the law was as much for one man as another." Sykes's behavior apparently enraged Beaton, who chased Sykes out of the store and knocked him bloody and senseless with the door bar.

Beaton's principal witness was Thomas Archer, his store clerk. Archer testified that Sykes, who was drunk, came into the store requesting cheese and crackers. Archer, under orders not to sell to Sykes on credit, referred Sykes to Beaton, who offered him cheese and crackers in payment for whatever work he had done that day. Sykes maintained that Beaton should pay him in cash. Beaton, promising to settle fairly with Sykes after he was sober, ordered Sykes to leave the store. Sykes, however, refused to leave, and the standoff became tense. Beaton, angered, finally announced to Sykes: "I have heard enough of this and if you won't go out I'll see if I can't make you." Archer reported that Sykes thereupon retreated out of the store, while holding a knife in a "threatening attitude" and saying in substance, "I am out now. I dare you or any other man to strike me." At that point Beaton attacked Sykes with the door bar. The faithful clerk testified, however, that the bloody gash on Sykes' head was self-inflicted: Sykes tripped on the railroad track and "his head struck the rail road iron."

Beaton also gained supportive testimony from James Fuller, the superintendent of the cotton gin, and from several of the men who worked there. All testified that Sykes was "very much intoxicated" and unable to work effectively. After working desultorily for an hour, he had fallen asleep on a pile of cottonseed, thereafter waking and proceeding to Beaton's store. None of the witnesses from the cotton gin could testify, however, about the confrontation at the store.

There did seem to be general agreement that Beaton was a "peaceable man," who had been "just in all his dealings" and had never been "in a fuss before." Indeed, Sykes himself testified that he had never had any difficulty with Beaton, that his wife was working for him as a cook at the time of the incident, and that she had continued in that job despite the difficulty between her employer and her husband. Testimony also indicated that Beaton was "small and comparatively feeble."

Beaton was the most prominent member of one of the few Whig families from the lower county. He and five other Beatons voted for John Bell in 1860. The secession issue had, however, fractured the previous family solidarity: two voted against secession in February 1861, two did not vote, and two, including William M. Beaton, voted for secession. A substantial landowner and the only cotton grower in the family, he sided with the other similarly positioned men of the lower county.[34] Apparently the war caused less economic hardship for him than for many. Owning a store and a cotton gin and enjoying a favorable location directly on the railroad, Beaton was positioned to prosper.

The only witness who partially corroborated Sykes's testimony was Willis Cook, who had gone to his assistance after he was injured. Cook recounted carrying the unconscious Sykes up to Beaton's house to wash out the wound. When Sykes revived, he vowed that he would go to Jerusalem to lodge a complaint with Lieutenant Deacon "and have justice done by him." Beaton thereupon warned Sykes that if he went to the bureau officer, he should "take himself off his [Beaton's] plantation and never come there any more." Sykes nevertheless went the next day to see Deacon.

The troubles between Sykes and Beaton took place in December 1866. For some unexplained reason, Deacon did not hold a hearing on the case for seven months.[35] Finally, however, Sykes had the opportunity to testify. He was closely cross-examined by Beaton's attorney, John J. Kindred, the most prominent lawyer-politician in the county. Although Kindred did not have his client testify, he did present an array of witnesses, both white and black, who challenged Sykes's version of events. Sykes had no legal counsel.

The settlement, although apparently something of a compromise, substantially vindicated Sykes. He received $100 from Beaton to compensate for the "assault and battery" he had suffered. Sykes, in turn, promised to drop any further prosecution of the case.[36] Lieutenant Deacon left no record of the basis for his decision, but one may make inferences. Sykes may well have been inebriated. It would otherwise be difficult to picture how Beaton, a man depicted as small and feeble, could pound Sykes with a door bar. But Beaton's principal witness, Thomas Archer, did his employer little good. The shabby effort to make a case for self-defense, alleging that Sykes had pulled a knife on Beaton, contradicted other testimony that suggested Sykes was simply using a small pocketknife to eat cheese (other witnesses, unlike Archer, reported Sykes holding cheese in one hand and a pocketknife in the other). Equally farfetched was Archer's lame effort to explain Sykes's injury as the result of a fall on the railroad tracks, rather than the beating inflicted by Beaton with the door bar. The settlement in effect acknowledged that Beaton had wrongly injured Sykes.

The Sykes-Beaton case in some ways paralleled the Drewry-Jones case. In both instances, apparently upstanding white gentlemen lost their temper and violently attacked a freed person. Each episode suggests that white resentment at the new postwar order smoldered dangerously close to the surface. Both cases also suggest that blacks were animated by a new sense of their legal rights. The drunken Ned Sykes who had failed to put in an adequate day of work at the cotton gin does not arouse much sympathy. Beaton probably had reason to doubt whether Sykes in fact had packed two bales of cotton and deserved a full day's pay. But when Sykes was beaten bloody and senseless with a wooden bar, he had ample reason to complain, and his determination to "have justice done" resonates. And in this case, if not in Caroline Drewry's, the victim was able to secure mimimal legal redress and compensation. It must be noted, however, that Sykes could only make a legal challenge against Beaton because of the presence of the Freedmen's Bureau. There is no reason to believe that Southampton courts or juries would ever have convicted Beaton of anything.

Often the Freedmen's Bureau failed miserably. One case in neighboring Nansemond County quite starkly demonstrated its ineffectiveness. In June 1867 a Nansemond freedman, Nelson King, was beaten "in a shocking manner" by three brothers, John, Richard, and James Fulgum, and by their mother, Lizzie. John W. Barnes, the bureau agent, had provided King with a letter politely requesting that the Fulgums pay money they owed to King. When King presented the letter, the Fulgums injured him so badly that he was "unable to work or to do anything at all." Barnes, suspecting that there was no prospect for "justice being rendered" by civil authorities, requested that the military commissioner send troops to arrest the offending parties and take them to Norfolk. The higher-ups, however, instructed Barnes to pursue the doubtful expedient of civil action.[37]

EXPANDING BEYOND ITS ECONOMIC, educational, and legal dimensions, the struggle over Reconstruction in Southampton became increasingly political. By 1867 the Republican majority in Congress concluded that it could no longer work with the existing state governments in the South (other than Republican-controlled Tennessee). Overriding bitterend opposition from President Johnson, Congress in March 1867 adopted a mechanism to create "loyal" southern governments that would accept the terms for settlement offered in the Fourteenth Amendment. Congress empowered military authority to oversee and, if necessary, to supersede civil authority in the ten recalcitrant former Confederate states. As a first step in organizing new governments, Congress ordered elections in each state to choose delegates for constitutional conventions.

To assure that Unionists gained the upper hand over ex-rebels, Congress specified that all adult males of both races could vote except for those who failed to pass certain tests of loyalty. In other words, the freedmen could vote, but many white men could not. Moreover, federal officials took charge of registering voters and administering the elections for constitutional convention delegates. Most southern whites considered that Congress had enacted a revolutionary definition of voter eligibility and a revolutionary departure from local and state control over the electoral process.

Political calculations in Washington dovetailed with festering black grievances. Urban Virginia blacks had since 1865 repeatedly asserted their wish to vote, setting an example to freed people in outlying areas. Largely unable to secure economic opportunity, education, or legal rights, rural blacks reached out eagerly for the ballot. Their rapid politicization in 1867 "took on the character of an agrarian movement," historian Michael Fitzgerald has observed, thereby generating "rural strife almost unequaled in southern history." The enactment of Congressional Reconstruction provided the catalyst for what historian Eric Foner has called the "annus mirabilis" of the black awakening, a spectacle enacted simultaneously across the South in a thousand different localities, Southampton among them.[38]

Directives from military authorities in Richmond spelled out in close detail how the registration process should proceed and who was eligible to vote. Lieutenant Deacon, appointed president of the county Board of Registration on April 15, was authorized to choose three registers-at-large and one registering officer for each magisterial district, of which there were seven in Southampton. He was instructed to select "deserving, loyal citizens" who had "the confidence of all classes" and who could take the "ironclad oath," affirming that one had never voluntarily aided the Confederacy. The three registers-at-large would receive compensation at the quite handsome rate of $125 per month; the district officials were to receive $5 per day; reasonable travel allowances also were included.[39]

Deacon soon selected three registers-at-large and six district registrars. None of the registers-at-large had voted in Southampton in 1860–61, but all six of the district registrars were Union Whigs. Deacon organized his nine appointees into three teams, with three members each. Oswin White, the first register-at-large, worked with Orris Moore and John Pretlow, two of Elliott Story's longtime friends, in the Jerusalem district. Their jurisdiction included the Drewrysville district in the southwestern corner of the county and the Franklin district wedged between the Nottoway and the Blackwater rivers. E. E. Hedley, the second register-at-large, had responsibility for the Boykins and Joyner districts, very Democratic prosecession neighborhoods in the lower county. Assisting Hedley were two of the very few lower-county residents who voted against secession, Orman M. Bryant and Mills A. Britt. The third register-at-large, Burnham Davis, worked with Demarcus L. Doles and William C. Wrenn in the northern part of the upper county.[40]

In each magisterial district, a convenient central place was selected where all potential voters could register. Written or printed notices, advertising the location and dates for registration, were posted conspicuously in five of the "most public places" in each district. The registrars selected six additional qualified voters, "three white and three colored persons," to witness the registration process in each district. The duty of the six local persons was to challenge any prospective voter who, to their knowledge, was disqualified to vote.[41]

The military authorities in Richmond issued specific guidelines regarding eligibility. All male citizens age twenty-one or older and who had lived in Virginia for one year, "of whatever race, color, or previous condition," were eligible to take the oath and register, "except such as may be disfranchised for participation in the rebellion, or for felony." Prominent ex-Confederates who fell under the disqualification for officeholding in section three of the Fourteenth Amendment were excluded; that is, anyone who had earlier held state or federal office and then "engaged in insurrection or rebellion against the United States" could not vote. A broad definition of state officeholding was applied: it included not only members of the legislature but also the justices of county courts, the networks of influential notables who had long dominated political life in their neighborhoods.[42]

Nor could anyone vote who had held any office in the Confederate government or a Confederate state "which functions were of a nature to aid in prosecuting the war." Elliott Story and Dr. Thomas J. Pretlow, wartime justices of the peace, were automatically excluded. So was Dr. Pretlow's younger brother Jordan Denson Pretlow, who sought and won election as a justice of the peace "to prevent having to enter the Southern army."[43] Had Story's only liability been his appointment by the county court to buy food for starving civilians, would he still have been barred? Did the relief of civilian distress aid in prosecuting the war? Obviously, questions of interpretation could arise.

In addition, anyone who had voted for the ordinance of secession, who had voluntarily joined the rebel army, or who had given "aid and comfort to the enemy" could not qualify. These strictures, if strictly applied, would have excluded the great majority of white adult males in Virginia. Their potential severity was mitigated only by interpretive confusion on several key points. Who had voted for secession? Did the ban apply only to prewar secessionists who had so voted in February 1861 or to the far larger number who had so voted in May 1861? Local usage characterized as "Unionist" anyone who opposed secession before the war started. Federal officials, finding precious few who could meet more rigorous standards of loyalty, tended to give the benefit of the doubt to prewar anti-secessionists. Likewise, the condition of never having voluntarily joined the rebel army often was interpreted to exempt any professedly reluctant member of a militia company that got called for service or anyone who had enlisted after conscription began in the spring of 1862. And who had given "aid and comfort to the enemy"? Those who had given only food or clothing to a soldier could register, but anyone, including a parent, who had supplied a soldier with "a gun, horse, or other thing, to be used for hostile purposes" was supposed to remain disfranchised. It appears, however, that enforcement of these strictures could be lax. Daniel Cobb successfully registered, despite having voted for secession before the war started and having supplied his son in the Confederate cavalry with several horses.

Although the actual implementation of official orders must have varied from place to place and larger numbers of whites registered than strict interpretation would have allowed, an extraordinary process nevertheless unfolded during the summer of 1867 in Southampton and across the South. Black men, most of them former slaves, were presumptively loyal and therefore eligible to register so long as they had resided in the state for a year (any local residency requirement was superseded). Eagerly seizing the opportunity to affirm their new rights, they registered in large numbers. White men, dismayed that blacks could register, could not assume their own eligibility. Even if the standards for white eligibility were less exacting in practice than on paper, procedures existed by which ineligible registrants could be challenged.

In each voting district, the registrars had to meet for at least three full days. They had orders to keep separate lists for whites and blacks and to break each list into three categories: persons registered without challenge, persons registered despite challenge, and persons "rejected upon challenge." These lists were posted in three different places in the district. Two weeks after completion of the first registration and with ample public notice, the registrars reconvened in each district. They then could register anyone who earlier had been ill or unavoidably absent, they could entertain challenges against listed voters, and they could hear additional evidence about persons earlier rejected. At the end of the second registration, the registrars prepared and posted a final list of eligible voters in each district, with separate lists provided for "white and colored voters," and all names entered alphabetically in a book.[44]

The registrars had authorization "to summon witnesses and compel their attendance, in any case of contested registration." The registrars also had instructions to suppress any "disorder," either by enlisting local civil officials or by having "the nearest commander of troops . . . summon a special police force for the purpose." Anyone who used "violence or intimidation" to prevent a potential voter from registering was subject to "fine and imprisonment, at the discretion of a military commission."[45]

Reports from adjacent Nansemond County, fuller in some respects than the information about Southampton, provide additional insight about the voter registration process. There, as in Southampton, the Freedmen's Bureau agent, John W. Barnes, doubled as president of the county Board of Registration. In June, before registration began, one of the Nansemond registrars heard rumors that blacks who did not vote as whites instructed would be driven from any rented or leased lands. Military officials in Richmond refused to intervene on the basis of rumors, but they instructed Barnes to remain watchful and to ask for troops if necessary "to secure to the freedmen their rights of person or property."[46]

Several weeks later, the Nansemond registrars encountered a potentially dangerous situation in the town of Chuckatuck. There, William A. Butler, recently appointed a constable by General John M. Schofield, the chief military official in Virginia, behaved in an outrageous manner. During registration Butler violently threatened several freedmen and John T. Gray, who considered himself the only loyal white in town. The intoxicated Butler, who wielded a knife, vowed "to kill any G—d d—n nigger" who dared to register. Butler was disarmed and arrested, producing, Barnes reported, "a salutary effect." Butler's actions had, however, pleased "a large number of residents." Barnes strongly urged military officials to take custody of the case, because he considered local officials bitterly prejudiced against the freedmen and white loyalists. Were Butler to go unpunished, Barnes thought, "there will be no security of life or property to the Union men of this County."[47]

Between June and September the registration process continued in Southampton and across Virginia. The first round of registration in Southampton enrolled 1,353 potential black voters and 1,074 whites. As in prewar times, proportionately larger numbers of blacks lived in the

lower part of the county. After the first registration there, black registrants exceeded whites by a large margin, 766 to 450. In the upper
county, whites held a slight advantage, 624 to 587. In other words, 63
percent of registrants in the lower county were black, compared with 48
percent in the upper county.[48]

A second registration and further investigation narrowed the black advantage, so that 1,273 blacks and 1,124 whites secured eligibility. Fifty-
three percent of Southampton registrants in the final tally were black.
More whites registered, however, than had voted in the presidential election of 1860. Obviously, the registrars excluded far fewer whites than
they could have. Although one of the principal registrars, Oswin White,
complained that "there are probably twenty five names on our lists that
should be erased if we had the persons or the evidence before us," it seems
likely that white registration totals would have been cut by half or even
two-thirds had instructions from the authorities in Richmond been enforced aggressively. Plainly, a registration process that depended primarily on the judgment of local officials would not disqualify most friends,
neighbors, and kinfolk. Even if the registrars had stronger Unionist credentials than most other whites in the county, events during the summer
of 1867 probably left them no more pleased than ex-Confederates at any
further exclusion of whites from the black-majority electorate.[49]

THE ENFRANCHISEMENT OF Southampton's freedmen stands out as
the most startling single development in the county's political history. As
it took place, Union Whigs attempted to create a biracial Union Republican party, with white leadership and a primarily black electorate. When
blacks rejected that overture, white Whigs joined with white Democrats
to create the local Conservative party, and Southampton politics became
racially polarized.

Few native white Virginians were more thoroughly out of sympathy
with the Confederacy or more eager to see the state reconstructed than
Dr. Thomas Jefferson Pretlow, the scion of Southampton's most prominent Quaker family. Although Pretlow and his immediate kin no longer
were members of the meeting, and although he had owned slaves that his
wife inherited, Pretlow's ancestors had freed large numbers of bondsmen,
and the doctor himself never fit comfortably into the proslavery South.
Pretlow was, however, a man of affairs. He represented the county in the
House of Delegates between 1851 and 1853, and he held a seat on the
county court from 1856 to 1864. In 1860 he spoke out vehemently

against secession, warning that it would result only in death, destruction, and poverty. Pretlow practiced medicine, and he also managed a farm and a pork-packing business. By any standard he was influential and wealthy: the 1860 U.S. Census credited him with real estate worth $30,000 and personal property worth nearly $50,000.[50]

Taking pen in hand in December 1865, Pretlow ventured to advise Thaddeus Stevens, the leading Radical Republican in Congress. Pretlow bitterly condemned "the old rotten secession pro-slavery oligarchy" for having led the state into disaster. Congress, he insisted, should make sure that southerners who opposed the war gained political power. "Take us out of the hands of the secession tyranny," Pretlow urged. Sneering at the state government as a collection of "demoralized Union men who are in the hands of secessionists," he suggested to Stevens that Congress dissolve the existing state legislature, administer Virginia as a territory, and place it temporarily under military rule. Only in this way could power be transferred decisively from "this Secession dynasty of defunct slave-owners" to reliable Unionists.[51]

In certain ways Pretlow's perceptions were astute. Confederate supporters, albeit typically ones who had initially opposed secession, dominated the governments formed in Virginia and other southern states in 1865. Were Congress to determine that political power could not be entrusted to such persons (as it in fact did determine in early 1867), then a reorganization along the lines Pretlow suggested would indeed have become possible. His scheme, however, contained a major blind spot. Pretlow did not conceptualize any political role for blacks. To him, Reconstruction involved only a question of empowering loyal whites. What should be done, however, if disloyal whites continued to outnumber loyal ones?

The scheme finally adopted by Congress in early 1867 attempted to address these difficulties. In order to diminish the power of disloyal whites, Congress proscribed from any official duties all who held office in antebellum years and then supported the Confederacy, plus all who held office under the Confederacy. Pretlow, however, took severe exception to the congressional formulation. The ban affected him and many other Unionists who had remained behind Confederate lines. In seeking a modus vivendi to a situation not of their own making, they had found it necessary to accept the reality of Confederate power. Rather than resign from the county court, Pretlow had judged it better to remain in office, with the hope of aiding like-minded persons and mitigating some of the harsher aspects of Confederate rule. One of his younger brothers had deliberately held local office to avoid military service. Congress unwisely excluded from power "thousands of the best friends of the Union," Pretlow complained.[52] Furthermore, he balked at the means Congress adopted to increase the number of loyal southern voters. By his lights, he had long advocated just treatment for blacks, and it was well known locally that the Pretlow family had emancipated large numbers of slaves. The doctor, however, never contemplated fully equal rights. The enfranchisement of blacks dismayed him.

Nevertheless, the imposition of Congressional Reconstruction and Pretlow's well-known disagreement with many southern orthodoxies forced him to stand up and be counted. Invited to attend a mass meeting of black citizens in Jerusalem on June 21, 1867, Pretlow offered qualified support for the new order. He promised to "co-operate with the great National Union Republican Party" because it was "the only party now that can restore us to the Union." "We shall ride in the long omnibus," he continued. "It is large enough to carry all who wish to ride . . . we shall occupy the whole road and drive over all obstructions right into the Union."[53]

Daniel Cobb entered in his diary a dismayed account of Pretlow's "speach to the Negrows." Cobb quoted Pretlow as having announced "that he is a Blackrepublica[n] and has been for 30 years, And himself Brothers and ansesortus [ancestors] all ways was." An incredulous Cobb, recalling that Pretlow himself and some of his family had owned slaves, considered the outspoken doctor a hypocritical traitor who had "left the Whites and gon with the Negrows," thereby having "denied the Faith, something like Peter denied his savour."[54]

Cobb exaggerated. Pretlow and the more liberal whites in Southampton solicited black votes, but they were no more disposed than Cobb to see blacks take the political initiative themselves. Pretlow expected blacks to support his distant Quaker cousin, John Pretlow, for a seat in the state constitutional convention. John Pretlow had impeccable Unionist credentials: a mainstay of the Quaker meeting, he had been imprisoned by Confederates for refusing to bear arms. The formidable influence that Thomas J. Pretlow exercised with federal officials during Reconstruction in all likelihood gained John Pretlow appointment as a voting registrar, where he gained useful visibility with would-be voters. His candidacy for the convention was based on the expectation that he could draw support both from blacks and from white antisecessionists in the upper county.[55]

During the summer of 1867, the white Southampton Unionists supporting John Pretlow's candidacy considered themselves Republicans. On July 27 they held a meeting at Franklin and nominated seven delegates to the state Republican convention in Richmond in early August. Jordan Denson Pretlow, the younger brother of Thomas J. Pretlow, chaired the meeting. The principal speaker discoursed "at some length and with great ability on the subject of reconstruction." Every person mentioned in a newspaper report about the meeting was an upper-county Whig who had opposed secession.[56]

NINE

❦

Black Awakening and White Reaction

O N WEDNESDAY, AUGUST 7, 1867, the third annual meeting of the Colored Shiloh Regular Baptist Association of Virginia convened in Manchester, across the river from Richmond. Reflecting the rapid growth of independent black congregations during the several years after the end of the war, seventeen new churches applied for membership, among them the Cool Spring church in Southampton County. "When the Association came to vote on the letter from the Cold Spring Church," the Richmond *Dispatch* reported, "Elder Williams requested that the delegates arise, stating that this 'church was located where Nat Turner first struck for freedom.' " Amid "much shaking of hands and general felicitation," those representing the Cool Spring church "marched forward." [1]

The association, which brought together about one hundred delegates from forty-five churches in southern Virginia, then proceeded to other business. It resolved that member churches ought not use the term "African" in their titles, "as we are not Africans, but Americans." The delegates also voted to tender thanks "to the Fortieth Congress of the United States for the Reconstruction Acts passed by them, enfranchising us as citizens and giving us protection in the exercise of all our rights and privileges." [2]

Several days later, the leading white newspaper in Richmond erupted in protest. "NAT. TURNER'S massacre was the most barbarous and brutal of all the human butcheries of this century," the editor of the *Dispatch* insisted; "it was a bad-hearted act to call up such a horrid reminiscence as worthy of special commendation." Turner's alleged "first blow" for freedom was instead "the deadliest blow to kind feeling for the blacks and to the growing sentiment in favor of abolition which could have been inflicted." Reviving the old chestnut that Virginia might have abandoned slavery had not the "monomaniac" Turner and the officious Tappan brothers and William Lloyd Garrison disrupted matters, the *Dispatch* proceeded to lecture the Colored Baptists. Their "act of hostility" in commending Nat Turner worked at cross-purposes to the real interests of the freedmen. Only by inculcating "kind and conciliatory" feelings could "peaceful and prosperous relations between the blacks and the whites" be promoted.[3]

The controversy did not end there. "Equal Justice," writing in Richmond's only Radical newspaper, the *New Nation*, pointed out that Nat Turner, John Brown, and Jeff Davis had all "rebelled and failed." Turner attempted to overthrow a government which classed him and his race "with things to be bought and sold at pleasure." He and John Brown, fighting for a good cause, had inflicted violence that was "trifling and limited." Davis, on the other hand, "was moved to his greater folly and his infinitely greater crime, in order that he might establish a govenment whose 'corner stone should be slavery.'" In rebelling against a government that "limited him in expanding and perpetuating that outrage upon his fellow-men," Davis caused "hundreds of thousands of lives to be sacrificed" and "oceans of blood and tears" to be shed.[4]

The extraordinary airing of opinions triggered by the Colored Baptists took place at a pivotal moment in Virginia history. During the summer of 1867, as newly energized freedmen sought to break free from the subservient position to which they had so long been assigned, traditional boundaries of racial etiquette and public discourse were breached almost overnight. Blacks, armed for the first time with the ballot, dared to assert themselves in ways that would have been unthinkable at any time in the past.

Except for a perishingly small minority of Radicals, Virginia whites reacted to the black awakening with stupefied amazement and dread. The very phenomenon of blacks meeting independently, whether for religious or political purposes, struck many whites as quasi-insurrectionary. Those who had known only the practices of a slave society often considered themselves caught up in a social revolution that threatened all aspects of white racial advantage. An epic struggle ensued, in Southampton and across the South.

The Union League of America, often known as the Loyal League, spurred the mobilization of blacks in 1867. Thomas W. Conway, a former official of the Freedmen's Bureau, toured Virginia and other southern states between April and June to build support for the league. Large audiences, one of which was estimated at 5,000, heard Conway speak in late April in Petersburg, not far from Southampton.[5] The Union League was not a centralized organization with a well-defined hierarchy. It elicited spontaneous support at the local level. Relying on word of mouth and secrecy, league organizers in rural areas gathered freedmen in out-of-the-way places to hear the gospel of political organization. With precious little central direction, the freedmen made the organization their own in many localities, Southampton included. The creation and drilling of black militia companies often accompanied the dominance of freedmen over local leagues.[6]

League promoters such as Conway generally coupled support for equal rights with warnings against more radical measures. They deprecated discussion about confiscation that some black delegates initiated at a Republican state convention in April. Union League officials insisted that economic development required cooperation with landowners and capitalists and that the Republican party in the South needed support from whites as well as from blacks.[7]

In Virginia, however, a split developed between moderate and Radical Republicans. Moderates, led by the former Whig and unconditional Unionist John Minor Botts, attempted to broaden the party's base among white antisecessionists. Radicals, led by James W. Hunnicutt, editor of the Richmond *New Nation*, had a strong base among urban blacks, especially in Richmond and Petersburg. The Union League Club of New York held a special gathering of Republicans from each Virginia faction at Richmond in June 1867, hoping to maintain party unity. Following the gathering, both wings of the party endorsed the call for a state party convention on August 1. The two Republicans from Southampton signing the call were Dr. Thomas J. Pretlow and his brother Jordan Denson Pretlow.[8]

Between mid-June and August, black voter registration sprinted ahead, while many whites hung back. League organization both stimulated and benefited from black registration. Anti-Republican newspapers pleaded with whites to register, reassuring them that doing so was safe (it would not risk perjury prosecutions) and honorable (it would not confer recognition on an oppressive government).[9]

The state Republican convention in Richmond on August 1 and 2 marked an important watershed. Until that point, the two wings of the

Republican party remained uneasily allied, despite growing evidence that Hunnicutt held the upper hand. At the convention Hunnicutt's black followers shouldered aside the Botts contingent, refusing even to allow Botts to speak until after formal adjournment of the gathering. Although Botts himself stayed in the party, many white moderates defected. Southampton's delegation of white moderates, led by Jordan Denson Pretlow, found itself upstaged by the leader among the county's newly enfranchised blacks, Joseph Gregory, who won appointment to the state party's committee on permanent organization.[10]

Gregory, a Baptist minister, was born in North Carolina around 1834. He either was born free or became free at a young age. By the late 1850s, if not before, he lived in Southampton, where he became an "exhorter" and developed a following among fellow blacks. Gregory's Cool Spring Baptist Church grew rapidly after 1865, as black Baptists abandoned the white churches. He no doubt led his church's delegation to the meeting of Colored Baptists that produced the salute to Nat Turner. The 1870 U.S. Census identifies Gregory as a mulatto, having a wife and two children and owning $500 worth of real estate and $150 worth of personal property. A letter he wrote in 1869 shows that Gregory's command of written English paralleled that of Daniel W. Cobb's: vigorous and idiomatic, but with many rough edges.[11]

Southampton blacks totally upset the political calculations of the Pretlow family and the other white Unionists who hoped to dominate a biracial coalition. Rather than choose between white candidates, the freedmen boldly decided to put forward one of their own. The contest for convention delegate thus became a three-cornered affair, with the Quaker Unionist John Pretlow opposed not only by a white Democrat, Luther R. Edwards, but also by a black man, John Brown. Southampton's whites, already startled to find that blacks could register to vote, faced the even more astonishing prospect of being represented at the state constitutional convention by a former slave.

Who was this John Brown? The best evidence about the Southampton black leader with the memorable name comes from a letter he dictated in early 1867 hoping to reestablish contact with his daughters and his former wife in Mississippi. Lieutenant Deacon, the Freedmen's Bureau agent who soon would preside over voting registration in Southampton, wrote the letter for Brown and dispatched it through bureau channels. It eventually returned with comments made by bureau agents in Mississippi and ended up in Deacon's official correspondence. Addressed to Brown's daughters, Manerva Ann and Ann Eliza Brown, in Holly Springs, Mississippi, it reads:

My Dear Children,
I received a letter before the war from your mother, and have written in reply several times since the close of the war but received no answer. I therefore write you again, hoping that you will answer me immediately on the reception of this, informing me where you are now living, who with, how you are getting along &c &c and whether or not you desire to return to me. You will deliver my love to your mother, and all my friends[,] accepting a large portion for yourselves[.] Say to your mother that her sister Eliza desires to be remembered to her, and hopes that she will come and see her soon. I am happy to inform you that I am enjoying good health. I am still living at the place I was when you left here, and am doing well. Oblige me by writing as soon as you receive this and give me full particulars concerning yourselves and mother, what you are doing, who living with, on what terms, how you are getting along, whether you are doing well or not, and whether you need my assistance or not.

> Your affectionate father,
> *John Brown*[12]

Brown, born around 1827, had been enslaved. There is no reason to believe that he gained freedom before general emancipation in 1865. In the late 1860s he resided on lower-county property owned by Robert Ridley, Jr., whose father sat in the 1850–51 Virginia Convention. Because Brown lived at the same place he did before the war, he probably had been owned by the Ridley family. The 1870 U.S. Census lists Brown as a carpenter, forty-three years old, a mulatto, born in Virginia, and having a twenty-eight-year-old wife and three young children. Although not a landowner, he did pay taxes on a horse and several other animals. The letter that Brown dictated in 1867 suggests that he could not at that time write it himself. The 1870 Census indicates, however, that he had overcome that deficiency. It appears that Brown's prewar wife and their two daughters had been removed to Mississippi before the war, while he remained in Virginia. Brown's subsequent remarriage may explain his earlier wife's apparent disinclination to contact him. Perhaps she too remarried: forced separations often had that result. Many ex-slaves from

Southampton plainly lived near each other in Mississippi; Brown's daughters resided with an uncle having the same last name, and Brown sent greetings to all his friends there.[13]

POLITICAL DEVELOPMENTS DURING 1867 weighed heavily on the minds of Southampton traditionalists. Soon after passage of the Reconstruction Acts, Daniel Cobb complained that Congress had inflicted heavy "trobles" on "the sothern people." The prospect of a black majority governing Southampton filled him with horror: he considered "the state of our County affairs" to be "desperate." "We are in a lost condition," he mourned; "I rest badly nights on ac[coun]t of the situation of County politicks."[14]

By midsummer 1867 the flood tide of the black awakening reached Southampton. Repeatedly, his hands took off from work to hear "Negrow speaches" or to attend court day in Jerusalem. Cobb described one such occasion when at least "100 negrow men and woman passed threw my farm [in] droves of 30 or 40 to gather." He retaliated against absent laborers with harsh financial penalties, docking them between one and two dollars per day, far more than the usual daily wage.[15]

A few days after a "Negrow Union parade" in September, Cobb was "much dejected in spirits." Discussion of "lands" had become part of the campaign; he suspected that black Radicals hoped to confiscate property and break up large estates. "The events of the last few months," reported a correspondent for the Richmond *Dispatch* who visited Southampton and other counties in the lower tidewater, "have unfortunately tended very much to unsettle labor." The "delusion of confiscation" had "seized upon the minds of large number of our colored population." As the astonishing insurgency unfolded, Cobb and many other Southampton whites were gripped by traditional fears. "Rebellion among the Negrows on the W[est] side of the N[ottoway] River suspected shortly," Cobb noted tersely in his diary. "Something," he insisted, must "be dun yet" about "the colard Race." As he had at stressful moments in the past, Cobb predicted menacingly that "the negrows or whites is to die out."[16]

From Boykins Depot, in the black-majority part of the lower county near where the Nat Turner insurrection had begun in 1831, twenty-eight whites signed a petition to the military authorities protesting that "the colored people, of this neighborhood, have organized themselves into a military body, and have been drilling at three different points." Even though political rallies during this era often had quasi-military features, any such activity by blacks in Virginia had no precedent, and whites thought they saw something far more ominous. "This belligerent display," the petitioners insisted, "has caused a feeling of uneasiness to be manifested among all classes of peace-loving citizens." Hoping that the "meetings and drillings" were "unauthorized," the anxious whites earnestly solicited the military "to suppress them at once." [17]

When registration ended and lists of eligible voters had been compiled, the military authorities in Richmond issued instructions for the October 22 election. Breaking with the state's tradition of oral voting, military officials specified that voters deposit paper ballots in appropriate boxes. The president of the Board of Registration, that is, Lieutenant Deacon in Southampton, was to make sure that registration lists and ballot boxes were properly supplied at each voting district. Indeed, each district required two lists and two ballot boxes because black and white voters not only were listed separately but also voted in separate containers. [18]

Lieutenant Deacon appointed several persons to assist the registering officer in each voting district. These appointments went to a mixture of newcomers and younger men. Of the twenty-four assistants, only eight definitely had voted in Southampton during the 1860 presidential election (six for Bell and two for Breckinridge), and only five definitely had voted in the February 1861 election (four against secession and one in favor). [19]

Official instructions established procedures for receiving and counting the votes. To ensure an orderly election, the constable in each district was to remain on duty at the polls for the entire day. Any person who attempted "by force, intimidation or fraud, to prevent any qualified elector from voting freely" was to be "at once arrested and charges preferred against him by the Registering Officer, in order that he may be brought to trial before a Military Commissioner." The registrars were to count and tally the returns, indicating the support given by voters of each race for or against a state constitutional convention and for the various candidates seeking seats in the convention. [20]

The October 1867 election in Southampton must have been a fascinating spectacle. Blacks not only cast their first votes ever but did so under circumstances that made those first votes all the more resounding. Whites, few of whom had ever thought much about how their familiar social order routinely and systematically had exploited blacks, suddenly had to confront the political consequences of long years of black resentment.

**THE REGULAR
UNION REPUBLICAN TICKET!**

FOR A CONVENTION:

FOR DELEGATE TO THE CONVENTION,
John Brown.

"Thou shalt love thy neighbor as thyself."

Republican ballot, 1867. (*Courtesy of the Virginia State Library and Archives*)

Southampton's freedmen demonstrated for all time to come that they could organize a political insurgency—and that they could do so without support from local whites. Unwilling to remain subordinate, they boldly took matters into their own hands. Neatly printed Republican ballots, which included the biblical admonition to "love thy neighbor as thyself," were distributed widely. In a dramatic exhibition of group cohesion and discipline, almost 98 percent of registered blacks appeared at the polls (see app. tables 9.1 and 9.2). Every single black voter favored calling a convention and supported the black candidate, John Brown. By contrast, only 56 percent of eligible whites voted. As a result, Southampton endorsed the calling of a convention, 1,262 (1,242 blacks and 20 whites) to 612 (all whites). John Brown was elected to represent the county at the convention with even greater ease, as white voters divided between Luther R. Edwards (403) and John Pretlow (223). Brown received all 1,242 black votes and one white vote.[21]

The 1867 election was the most significant ever held in Southampton. It set the stage for a century of claustrophobic politics, in which racial solidarity became the paramount value. By rejecting the leadership of

Map 9. Polling places, 1867

white Unionists, blacks resoundingly asserted themselves. They called attention in a most unmistakable way to a long litany of black grievances and white illusions. For whites, who had grown accustomed for more than a generation to dividing their votes between competing political parties, the only way to counter the black political initiative was to build an equally inclusive political unity among whites. Before Southampton voted again, almost all whites would support the Conservative party.

That collective decision had several consequences. It foreclosed challenges against elite dominance, enabling privileged whites to consolidate their power. Even though the wrenching stresses of wartime had fueled class resentments, whites chose to subordinate their differences. So, too, the will-o'-the-wisp of racial harmony and cooperation that had hovered tantalizingly around Southampton for almost a century abruptly disappeared. The gap between blacks and well-intentioned whites became more formidable than ever. Under the pretext of countering black lawlessness, all too many whites reverted to coercion to blunt the black initiative. In Southampton and all across Virginia, a new round of evictions and generally thuggish white behavior followed the October election.

The situation became sufficiently scandalous that General Howard, head of the Freedmen's Bureau, issued a remonstrance. Vigorously worded but vague as to how it might be enforced, the directive from Howard was all too typical. Copies were distributed to local bureau agents throughout Virginia:

> It is reported officially that in some parts of Virginia, men employed are intimidated from voting by threats of discharge and that many already have been discharged for no other cause than for exercising a right conferred upon them by the Government.
>
> Take immediate and effectual measures to check and if possible prevent such infamous conduct. Have every refugee and freedman, entitled to vote, understand that he shall have the proper protection to vote just as he pleases. And if he is evidently discharged for exercising this right, see to it that he does not suffer for want of food, and take prompt measures to find him a home and employment. It matters not which party is guilty of such contemptible meanness as to make these ignoble threats the duty of the Officer of the Government.[22]

IMPLICIT IN DR. THOMAS J. PRETLOW's support for the Republican party in June and July 1867 was the assumption that black voters would support the leadership of native white Unionists and former Whigs. His confidence, of course, proved misplaced. The stunning turnout of black voters that swept John Brown to an easy victory in Southampton's October 1867 election was duplicated across the state. An alliance of white and black Radicals commanded a majority in the upcoming constitutional convention. These developments drove Pretlow to join forces with the secessionists and Democrats whom he had opposed throughout his life. In January 1868 the doctor wrote a long letter to the Richmond *Whig*. He hoped that "some good might result" if northerners could understand why a southerner with his unusual "opinions and antecedents" nevertheless opposed the Reconstruction policy implemented by Congress.[23]

Pretlow first sought to establish his antislavery credentials. "Having descended from a family, both paternally and maternally, who have been emancipationists for nearly a hundred years, and who have perhaps liberated more slaves than any other family in Virginia, it is but natural I should have fallen heir to their opinions," he noted. Moreover, he recalled reading, as a young man of eighteen, the debates about gradual emancipation in the Virginia legislature, and he then concluded that slavery "impoverished our soil, prevented the development of our material wealth, and by its rapidly increasing numbers threatened our nationality." Always thereafter favoring "a just system" of gradual, compensated emancipation, Pretlow deeply regretted that Virginia had never enacted such a policy. Instead, the national debate about slavery had become polarized, and Pretlow had disagreed with both sides, opposing "both the proslavery propagandist and the abolitionist, regarding them as equally destructive of the interests of both races."

Consistent with these views, Pretlow insisted that he had always been "a friend of the Union" and that "secession never met with a more bitter opponent than myself." He "spoke and labored against it as long as there was either hope or safety in doing so." When war erupted and Virginia did secede, Pretlow found himself in a hard position. He became "the steadfast friend of the honest Union man in distress," going in person to "Confederate camps and military commanders" and advancing thousands of dollars in gold to "procure the release of Union men from imprisonment." Yet at the same time, "nature forced me to sympathize with my kindred, neighbors and friends" who supported the Confederacy, and he "willingly and cheerfully" performed "acts of friendship, kindness, and humanity" for them as well. Ever hopeful that "some harmonious plan of adjustment" would restore "peace and good will among our people," Pretlow deplored the "prolongation of the bloody struggle."

The principal part of Pretlow's letter assessed the startling developments during the preceding year. He had made "an honest effort" to "cooperate with the Republican party for the restoration of Virginia to the Union." In particular, he and other "respectable and influential citizens," many of them wartime Unionists such as John Minor Botts, had supported the call for a statewide meeting in Richmond in early August. They had hoped, he frankly acknowledged, "to control the colored vote, and to secure the election of intelligent and reliable men to the convention" who might "procure better terms for the admission of Virginia to the Union."

Instead, however, a "motley gathering" of black and white Radicals had seized control of the meeting and had excluded its original promoters. "Their idea of Republicanism," Pretlow angrily charged, "was to degrade the white man to elevate the negro." The upshot was something Pretlow deeply opposed and dreaded—"the formation of a white man's and a black man's party." In his view, politicized blacks and their "mercenary" white advisers shared responsibility for the polarization.

"It had never occurred to me until the August assemblage at Richmond," Pretlow confessed, "that any colored man . . . would be permitted to take part in framing a fundamental law for Virginia." He continued to caution the freedmen against voting for "men of their own race," but his advice was "thrown away." Some of "the ablest men who had stood fast by the Union were defeated," going down under "the dark wave." In Southampton, Pretlow noted, "a Quaker gentleman of intelligence and respectability [his distant cousin, John Pretlow], who had made it a part of the business of his life to ameliorate as far as he could the condition of the black man, and who had been incarcerated for refusing to bear arms against the United States, received not a solitary black vote, and was beaten by his negro opponent by more than a thousand majority."

Pretlow's complaint embraced more than politics. "Up to the time of registration [that is, the summer of 1867] the conduct of our black population had been praiseworthy, but since there had been a sad change for the worse." He judged that 1867 had been "the most disastrous year of my experience in thirty years of farming." Southampton, though "in the midst of many laborers," had suffered an alarming decline of productive labor. "If we continue on the downward road to ruin at this rate much longer," he commented sardonically, "the Government will have to send a Bureau to take care of the *whites* and protect honest people against thieves, vagabonds, incendiaries, and assassins."

Pretlow provides a case study of how the Virginia Conservative party deliberately fanned white racial anxieties. Conservatives, fearing class-based Radical appeals to less privileged whites, consciously emphasized the specter of black domination.[24] The Southampton doctor's long letter to the *Whig* reveals how completely he shared those anxieties. His professed fair-mindedness toward blacks changed into undisguised outrage at the prospect of "negro government."

"I have always been the unflinching friend of justice to the black man," Pretlow insisted. He had tried as a state legislator to prevent unfair enactments against blacks. He also had been accused of being "too kind to them" because emancipated Pretlow family slaves lived on his property for thirty years without paying rent or medical fees. Although favoring "even-handed civil justice to all," Pretlow contemptuously rejected political equality. In many Virginia counties, "the blacks are numerically stronger than the whites, and under universal suffrage they would monopolize the offices" and inaugurate a "negro government."

What would a "negro government" do? It would, Pretlow insisted, impose "cruelty, folly . . . tyranny . . . bloodshed, crime, vice, and ignorance." It would "punish the innocent and reward the guilty." Worst, "the time will have arrived when the innocent maiden can no longer go forth in safety to her eventide gambols; the Goddess of virtue will have been polluted to gratify the lustful passions of the demons of vice." Pretlow's unrestrained outburst, starkly revealing the extent to which even well-intentioned whites subscribed to the prevalent racial stereotypes of the mid-nineteenth century, had both pseudoscientific and pseudohistorical underpinnings.[25]

Blacks and whites differed substantially both in anatomy and physiology, the influential doctor explained. Blacks, although part of "the human family," had a brain that "comes nearer to that of the brute creation than does that of the white man." Deficient in "reason and intellectual endowment," blacks retained some characteristics of "the baboon and orang outang." Anatomical and physiological differences thus explained why there had never been, nor could there ever be, "an intellectual negro." As evidence of limited black capabilities, Pretlow cited reports from "African travellers," who alleged that indigenous people there remained remarkably primitive. The native African "has not built a house to live in, nor has he fashioned a spoon to eat with, nor a cup out of which he may drink; indeed, is but little removed from the wild animals among which he dwells." Where, jeered Pretlow, "is his jurisprudence, his philosophy, mathematics and chemistry? Where are his doctors and divines, his mariners and military commanders?"

Pretlow's perspective led irresistibly to the conclusion that blacks could contribute to the social order only if properly supervised. "Under the guidance of the white man the negro may be useful, and is susceptible of considerable improvement," the doctor asserted, "but left to himself will sadly degenerate. When under the control of good white people he is kind and affectionate, but under the influences of bad men he displays the vilest and most brutish passions."

In other words, black political participation, except when guided by appropriate white friends, could lead only to disaster. Blacks themselves lacked "the first qualification" to participate in government. As "weak member[s] of the human family," blacks could never "exercise a political voice" among their "intellectual superiors." Even black voting was dangerous, because blacks were "pliant material for the demagogue"; they "willingly follow him who makes the most extravagant offers of profligacy."

What should be done? Any overt resistance to federal authority, Pretlow advised, would be unthinkable, likely to reopen armed conflict and stir racial warfare. But if the Radical majority in the constitutional convention at Richmond attempted to impose "unqualified negro suffrage," white voters should "cast it from us with scorn." Virginia would probably find itself placed temporarily under a provisional military government, by far the lesser of evils.

Northern whites, "the bone of our bone and the flesh of our flesh," sooner or later would recognize the unfairness of trying to impose on white southerners "the cruelty of a negro government." As soon as Virginia could "convince a majority of the Northern people" that blacks would be treated justly and enjoy all civil rights, "I believe they will be content." Pretlow, alluding to Republican losses in elections in the North in 1867, judged that "the Northern people are fast becoming convinced of it."[26]

The new circumstances of 1867–68 required that Pretlow mend fences. To slaveholders, secessionists, and Democrats, the doctor proffered an olive branch. He recognized that there had been "much bitter feeling" between supporters and opponents of secession, and he admitted to having "said and written" various "harsh and acrimonious things" that were at times "unjust." While so doing, he had received as much abuse as he had handed out. The time had come, Pretlow insisted, to "throw away our old animosities" and quit "quarreling over the past." Slaves in Virginia had been "treated well." There had been "no difference" between the "pro-slaveryist" and those who "favored emancipation" in providing magnanimous care for sick blacks. All acted from a sense of Christian duty, rather than any "mercenary motives." That same spirit ensured that "under a white government there will be safety for all races."

For the near term, however, Pretlow blended his paternalistic assertions with a warning. "It is to our interest and comfort to live on terms of friendship with the colored people. We have used our best efforts to do so. I have humiliated myself in the endeavor to benefit both races, in advising these people against their suicidal course, and in an honest effort to conciliate them for the good of all." Because his advice had gone unheeded, however, whites should stand steadfastly together to oppose the reckless course blacks had followed. "The more we have done, the worse they have become. They have clearly marked out a road for us, and the white man who refuses to follow it, is an enemy to his race and deserves to be treated as such, unless he hastens to repair the error of his ways." All respectable whites had to act together to remove "this dark cloud" from "our land."

DURING 1868, A NEW Freedmen's Bureau agent, Mortimer Moulden, took up residence in Southampton (it was to be the last year that agents remained on duty there and elsewhere in the South). A Maryland Unionist, he was among the minority of bureau appointees with civilian backgrounds. Although Moulden had not served in the military, he had been a provost marshal during the war and once had been kidnapped to Virginia by Confederate raiders. After the war he had worked as a clerk in the Quartermaster General's Office (part of the War Department), but he had lost his job when it became known that his sympathies lay with the Republican majority in Congress. General Howard, head of the Freedmen's Bureau, thereupon commissioned him for the Southampton vacancy. Moulden's reports and correspondence provide a rich source of information about Southampton for the calendar year 1868.[27]

A conscientious bureau agent led a busy life—listening to complaints, trying to resolve disputes, traveling around the district, and directing the obligatory flow of paper to his superiors. He also needed courage and self-confidence, because he inevitably faced some degree of hostility, if not danger. To compensate for its drawbacks, the job paid $100 per month. Attractive even by northern standards, an income of $1,200 per year necessarily made the agent the best-paid person in many southern localities. Few freedmen could earn in a year what the agent received in a month. Moulden also enjoyed additional allowances, totaling over $20 each month, for forage, horseshoes, and firewood. Nor did his job require disruption of family life: Moulden's wife and children resided with him in Southampton.[28]

Moulden encountered a society polarized along racial lines. Startling black political gains in 1867 had made whites almost universally hostile to the aspirations of the freedmen. Economically, Southampton also faced severe difficulties. Its faltering agricultural economy, weakened by unresolved tensions between landlords and laborers, could not provide minimal subsistence to many, especially the aged and infirm.

Moulden soon discovered that his authority to grapple with South-ampton's problems was severely limited. Several times, he and a local schoolteacher attempted to pry a few extra barrels of meal from bureau authorities, reporting that "there are people here who have not for weeks past, had enough to eat" and promising to see that it would be "judi-ciously used." Repeatedly, the pleas for assistance encountered the same response: "As no rations have heretofore been issued by the Bureau in Southampton County it is not desirable to commence the issue at this late day." Insisting that the managers of the county almshouse should take responsibility, bureau officials specified that they would provide relief only in "the most extreme cases of destitution."[29]

Moulden renewed the appeal. He insisted that "there is now much want in this County," with corn "very scarce" and selling at prices "be-yond the reach of the poor." A number of aged, crippled, and bedridden people, both white and black, lacked "the common necessaries of life." The directors of the almshouse refused to aid anyone who would not become "an inmate of said Institution," and, Moulden reported, "many will suffer rather than go there." His superior, Major J. H. Remington, remained unimpressed. "It is not the design of the Bureau to assist those who through a false pride prefer to suffer rather than become inmates of the Alms House," Remington coldly announced.[30]

Frustrated by the refusal of bureau authorities to provide relief, Moulden dispatched blunt assessments of the county's racial impasse. His monthly reports for February, March, and April, sent to General Orlando Brown, head of the Freedmen's Bureau in Virginia, offered a powerful critique of the status quo in Southampton. A reformer rather than a bu-reaucrat, Moulden wrote with unusual immediacy. He provided his su-periors with far more than the routine monthly summaries favored by many agents.[31]

Local whites were, Moulden insisted, "deeply prejudiced" and "guilty of many petty acts of injustice towards the freedmen." He especially la-mented the prevalent labor system, which did not "come up to my idea of a system": "The employer has the same cabins on his farm that he had in the days of slavery, and now occupied by the employees: He gives them from five to eight dollars a month for their labor, sells them bacon and meal &c at the highest figures, and at the end of the month the freedmen are brought in debt—: never seeing any money, or having a cent to purchase any little thing for their families. And so on for the year through—thus forcing them into a state of slavery and degredation, and depriving them of many privileges belonging to freemen." For Moulden, the distribution of food by the employer "smacks of the old system of slavery, and the freedman feels it to be so. I would rather see him have his money at the end of the month—it makes him feel his manhood." Instead, the bureau agent found himself frequently having to intercede to protect freedmen from unscrupulous whites, who would "resort to every little artifice to obtain their labor for little or nothing."

Moulden took indignant exception to the prevalent practice of apprenticeship. He described for his superiors the way that black children were "taken up by the overseers of the poor, and bound out as paupers." Typically, males worked until the age of twenty-one and females to age eighteen. Their employers paid only a pittance in wages, typically $10 to $20 per year, depending on the age of the child. In some instances, free black children who had been bound out before or during the war remained indentured. In many other cases, the binding out occurred during Reconstruction. Often children were apprenticed even though their parents were "fully able to care for and support them." Moulden charged that the system inflicted a "grievous wrong" on the children involved—reducing them to "a miserable state of bondage" and depriving them of the "privileges of home and its enjoyments." So too, it deprived their parents of needed assistance.

In addition to developing oppressive labor systems that retained many features of slavery, local whites remained bitterly opposed to any independent exercise of political rights by blacks. During March freedmen in several different parts of the county informed Moulden that whites had "commenced a system of persecution: hoping to intimidate them and thus prevent them from going to the ballot-box, or voting their sentiments." The freedmen received warnings that they would be driven from their homes and denied supplies if, as in 1867, they voted "against the whites" in the expected referendum on the new state constitution. Moulden explained to his superiors that he had waited until court day to "inquire of the more discreet and reliable freedmen from all parts of the county" about the seriousness of the threat. They vowed that the "nefarious plan" had already frightened many blacks, especially the "middle aged" and the "aged." Moulden feared that such "ignoble conduct" by whites might lead to the constitution's defeat.[32]

Moulden asked his superiors how to deal with voter intimidation. He received a pronouncement from General Brown in Richmond ordering him to tell the freedmen that "they need have no fears of injurious consequences resulting from an honest exercise of the right of suffrage" and to warn the whites that "their actions will be reported." Of course, Moulden had already reported what Southampton whites were trying to do; bureau officials effectively passed back to Moulden the difficult question of how to counter the threats.[33]

Unaided, Moulden had no effective means of protecting the freedmen. By mid-April he alerted his superiors that a secret organization "known as the 'Ku Klux Klan,'" had appeared in the county. Its supporters raised a flag at Franklin Depot, featuring a skull and crossbones emblem and the initials "K.K.K." He suspected that Klan members had also been responsible for an outbreak of "pistol firing" and an eagerness "to clean up the old 'shooting irons'." The "principal object" of the Klan, Moulden surmised, was to "indimidate the freedmen, and keep them from the polls—thus defeating the new Constitution." He reported the freedmen "much disturbed about the organization," and once again he asked his superiors what to do.[34]

By contrast, the military commander of Reconstruction in Virginia, General John M. Schofield, considered the new constiutution too Radical and feared it would win a popular referendum. Using a technicality, Schofield therefore postponed elections for state officers and for ratification of the new constitution. Local elections, however, remained scheduled to take place in late May, and a tense situation prevailed in Southampton. Black political leaders were attempting to build on their 1867 successes. Amazed reactionaries such as Daniel W. Cobb reported "grate confusion with the negrows" because of "election speaches from negrows and negrows meetings." Blaming blacks for a crime wave of "breaking in[to] dwelling houses," Cobb judged that "our prosperous County is ruin[ed]."[35]

On May 7 military authorities in Richmond bluntly directed local bureau officials such as Moulden "to take immediate steps to prevent the Colored men of your Division, from being intimidated and frightened from the polls on election day. . . . prompt action is expected of you in this matter." Southampton seems to have been a particular case in point; two days before the order was issued, Cobb made a cryptic diary notation about Klan activity in the county.[36]

It was easier to issue instructions than to enforce them at the local level. Moulden reported to General Brown that he had tried to prevent intimidation at the polls and that he had worked to reassure freedmen who faced threats of being driven from their homes and being denied access to supplies. Moulden apparently had little effect in parts of lower Southampton, however. A group of citizens from Boykins Depot complained about "outrageous treatment of Union men at that place" perpetrated by "a Band of midnight Assassins called the Ku Klux Klan."[37]

By July the situation had become so bad that the previously hopeful Moulden grimly warned his superiors to expect trouble if they did not "adopt stringent measures for this County." He reported "a terrible feeling here—which if not put down promptly will inevitably lead to bloodshed." Conservative speakers on court day had roused a large crowd with "violent language," nearly causing "a general melee." Freedmen who attended their own political meetings were being ejected from work without pay. Others had their homes attacked and searched by white vigilantes, whose ranks included "some of the richest men in the county." The invaders, who were "armed to the teeth," used "violent language" and made "terrible threats." Under the guise of "pretending to be searching for stolen property," they treated their victims in "a rude and vile manner"—threatening "to blow their brains out" or to take them to the woods and give them "one hundred lashes." Moulden deplored the introduction of tactics "successfully practiced in Mississippi."[38]

Conservative sources corroborate Moulden's impression that a vengeful hysteria gripped white Southampton. An observer writing to the Norfolk *Virginian* reported from Southampton that "we are at a white heat on politics," with whites determined "not to submit to negro domination" and with the Conservative party so "thoroughly organized" that "we have no Radical whites among us." He boasted about the abuse administered to Lucius H. Chandler, the Republican candidate for Congress and his party's featured speaker on court day in July, when both parties organized rallies.[39] Chandler, a former Whig from Norfolk who had once maintained sociable relations with many Southampton families, impressed his former acquaintances as a despicable traitor. When he attempted to get a drink at Howard's Hotel in Jerusalem, Chandler was accosted by an ugly crowd shouting insults, groans, hoots, and hisses at the "white negro" who allegedly favored "political, civil and social equality" for blacks. "The good white people of Southampton county . . . treated him with every mark of hatred, contempt and loathing they could think of, short of personal violence, and they did right. Such determined marks of the displeasure of an outraged people must and will have its effect, and force men to be white or black; for this effort to dwarf our intellect and stain our blood, if successful, will bring us down to the [level of?] the mongrel republics of Mexico and South America."[40]

The overlapping jurisdictions of the military authorities and the Freedmen's Bureau allowed a great deal of buck-passing to occur. Lieutenant G. M. Fleming, the military commissioner headquartered in nearby Suffolk, informed Moulden on July 10 that he had received reports indicating that "many Persons[,] Land holders and others[,] threaten the Freedmen with Ejection from their farms and discharge from Employ if the Freedmen vote the Radical ticket." Fleming condemned as "idle" all such threats, announced that "all Persons irrespective of color will be protected in the exercise of the rights of Suffrage," and insisted that "any attempt to threaten or prevent Persons from Voting" should be "immediately reported at this office."[41]

Shortly thereafter, Fleming received from Ned Sykes a list of thirteen freedmen from the Boykins district whose homes had been searched by white marauders "without any authority of law." Sykes, the freedman who the summer before had won compensation for being beaten with a door bar, reported that he had visited "the Beauraugh Agent" three different times but had not been able to "get any thing done." He implored Fleming: "I come to you for Protection to know what we must do as we are bound to have something done with those men in this District that dont appear to regard law." Fleming, identifying Benjamin Pope as the ringleader among the searchers, thereupon ordered Moulden to investigate "and take such action as the case may demand." The freedmen were, Fleming noted, "required in all cases to apply to the Civil Authorities." Only after "exhausting all Civil remedies" could the freedmen apply to the military commissioner having jurisdiction.[42]

Sykes and at least one other freedman, William Warren, complained to the military commissioner because Moulden had not brought the vigilantes to justice. After Fleming passed responsibility back to Moulden, the bureau agent did try to get a local grand jury to make presentments, but, not surprisingly, it "failed to do so." Nor could Moulden get his superiors to take an interest in the case. Apparently the culprits never were prosecuted.[43]

An incredulous Moulden reported in August that many Southampton whites were arming themselves to fend off a threatened "Nigger insurrection." Daniel Cobb, for example, believed that "Negrows is determined to have a war with the whites of the South." Although Moulden considered the insurrection "about as probable as water running up the side of a mountain," he recognized that the panic had become severe. Whites suspected of Radical sympathies found themselves "living in constant fear of their lives." Moulden recounted that one such person had been "taken from his home a few nights ago, and dragged all over the neighborhood by persons to him unknown." His "mysterious captors" admonished their victim that "his life hung upon his silence."[44]

The authorities exhibited similar paralysis in the face of a severe food shortage during the summer of 1868. A bad corn crop in 1867 had shortened local supplies and driven prices up. Persistent dry weather during much of the 1868 growing season kept prices high. Scarce provisions among the poor, both white and black, created "a bad state of feeling." The bureau, however, maintained its stubborn refusal to countenance any assistance. Even though it did issue rations to the poor in several southern states in 1868, the bureau ignored pleas to do so in Southampton. Late summer rains saved the corn crop and eased the food shortage, but many people remained in a precarious position.[45]

Moulden felt a particular concern about schooling. The freedmen, he reported, "take a great interest in the subject of education, and the greater portion are anxious to have schools in all parts of the County: And I trust the time is near at hand when the 'Bureau' will be enabled to accomplish so grand a mission!" He acknowledged, however, that most local whites, "especially the 'poor whites,'" opposed educating the freedmen. No landowner would sell lots on which schoolhouses could be built.[46]

For Moulden, education could do more than increase literacy. Schools would be the instruments for "improving and elevating the moral standards of the freedmen." Rather than spending "their small earnings at the whiskey shops," educated freedmen would walk "the paths of virtue." They would learn the advantages of "saving every cent for present and future wants." Moulden's enthusiasm for schools enabled him to maintain an optimistic perspective, which he tried to transmit to the freedmen. Admitting that they were "subjected to much petty and unkind treatment by white men who are void of the instincts of . . . gentlemen," Moulden advised the freedmen "to turn their steps away from such persons" rather than remonstrate or seek legal action against their persecutors. Instead, he urged the freedmen "upward and onward," expecting that "smaller obstacles" would "disappear from our pathway." Already, Moulden rejoiced, light was "streaming in" at three well-attended day schools and four Sabbath schools. The freedmen, "asking for light with their freedom" and "waking up to to the vast importance of the work in which we are all engaged," were "growing into proper manhood."

Moulden's paean to education and uplift failed to impress his superiors. General Brown rapped the knuckles of his earnest subordinate in Southampton, instructing him to write factual reports, omitting "metaphors, similies, and expressions of hope for the future." [47] Nor could the freedmen in Southampton sustain the schools that Moulden hoped to oversee. The bureau would assist those with the resources to establish a school and hire a teacher, but it would not create its own schools. Black poverty, combined with opposition from most local whites, meant that schools remained few and far between. Moulden hoped that philanthropic northerners and voluntary organizations might take responsibility for establishing schools in Southampton. In adjacent counties the New York Friends Association and the American Missionary Association supported several schools, but Southampton received no comparable outside stimulus. A Connecticut couple, Mr. and Mrs. A. W. Samson, opened a Sabbath school at Nottoway Station in November 1867. [48] By early 1868 an average of fifty students appeared each Sunday at the school, with some students coming from a distance of six or eight miles. The Samsons, attempting also to stir interest in a day school, received pledges from their students amounting to $44. Relentless white hostility discouraged the northerners, however. Having been "rudely insulted" and threatened by "whites in the neighborhood," the Samsons fled in April 1868. [49]

Southampton blacks persisted in trying to improve their educational opportunities. Levi Gillem (Gilliam?), a freedman, expressed an interest in starting a school at his home in Black Creek. The freedmen around Jerusalem, although too poor to hire a teacher, requested assistance in establishing a school. Mrs. M. A. Andrews, a white northerner who impressed Moulden as "truly a faithful servant in the Master's Vineyard," took charge of a school in Franklin. Of the seven schools operating in May, only three remained by August. "More schools might have been established," Moulden surmised, "had not the freedmen been in such a helpless condition." In some neighborhoods, they could not "raise a dollar for educational purposes." [50]

Establishing a school remained a hazardous occupation. Troubles persisted in adjacent Nansemond County, where local vigilantes had burned a Quaker-sponsored freedman's school in March 1866 and efforts to prosecute them failed. Although that school was rebuilt, another near

Franklin Depot was burned in February 1868. Lieutenant G. M. Fleming, the bureau agent in Nansemond in 1867, reported to his superiors that schools in his county "would be broken up" unless the bureau continued in operation for several years.[51]

The most outrageous attack on a freedmen's school in the Southampton area occurred in 1868 in adjacent Surry County. In July the schoolhouse and a nearby church were burned, prompting the teacher, James Taylor, to move the school into his own house. On the night of October 30, 1868, Taylor was beaten unmercifully by four vigilantes who held a pistol to his breast and told him he would be shot if he did not leave the area. Taylor then fled. Civil authorities "refused to take cognizance of the case."[52]

Moulden made few friends among Southampton's whites, with one significant exception: Dr. Thomas J. Pretlow impressed the bureau agent as "a noble man" and "one of the very few loyalists in this part of Virginia." During "the darkest days of slavery," Moulden noted, Pretlow had been "ever the kind and gentle master, and friend of the colored man." The agent made no mention of Pretlow's metamorphosis into an outspoken Conservative.[53]

Moulden's tenure in Southampton ended in December 1868, when the Freedmen's Bureau called back all its agents from across the South. Having undertaken to oversee the development of a new economic order and the establishment of a system of free schools, the bureau could hardly claim to have succeeded. Its thin veneer of agents lacked the manpower, resources, or leadership to exercise any pronounced or enduring influence. In a typically recalcitrant southern locality, the lone bureau agent was doomed to relative powerlessness and ineffectuality. Furthermore, many agents did not share Moulden's wholehearted reformist enthusiasms. By any realistic assessment, the Freedmen's Bureau failed to achieve its purposes; the decision to terminate its activities was an ignominious capitulation.

Moulden in some ways recognized as much, but his inveterate optimism obliged him to search for hopeful omens. He wanted to believe that "bitter prejudice" had diminished, that the freedmen were more "kindly treated," and that their rights were more "generally respected." Hoping that he had been "instrumental in bringing concord out of chaos," Moulden asserted that the freedmen were "now in a condition to battle successfully on the stage of life." Schools and schooling remained, in his mind, the best means to bring about progress and change. He expected that the soon-to-be-established loyal state government would adopt "a general system of education . . . for the benefit of all." In that way, "ignorant and superstitious" poor whites would overcome their fears that the freedmen would "outstrip them in the race of life." Once free schools had been established for poor whites and for poor blacks, Moulden thought, "all will be well." [54]

IN FACT, HOWEVER, the bruising political struggle that had erupted in 1867 and 1868 continued during 1869. So long as basic questions of power and authority remained unresolved, tensions could not diminish. At both local and statewide levels, 1869 inaugurated a new phase of political combat. Federal military authorities intervened more decisively in local government than ever before, replacing numerous ex-Confederates with appointed loyalists. Closer scrutiny over local government was expected to be only temporary, however, because Virginia would soon vote to ratify the new constitution and elect a civilian governor. To effect that end, military-supervised registration of voters and elections, inaugurated in 1867 for choosing convention delegates, was reestablished in 1869. All of these events reverberated in Southampton.

Virginia remained out of the Union in 1869 because of a protracted deadlock regarding the state constitution. General Schofield, the military commander of Virginia, feared that the Radical constitution's broad proscription of former Confederates would make it impossible to conduct local government in large parts of the state. He therefore decided in April 1868 against holding an election to ratify the new constitution. Schofield's successors, generals George Stoneman and Edward R. S. Canby, shared his anti-Radical predilections. A civilian government, partially appointed by military authorities, retained power. [55]

Overcoming the adamant opposition of white traditionalists in black-majority counties, a movement developed among white moderates to accept the new constitution, including black voting, in order to win readmission to the Union. Adroit Conservatives, shrewdly reaching out to moderate Republicans, maneuvered a hybrid Conservative-Republican ticket. President Ulysses S. Grant, who took office in March 1869, was sympathetic to the arrangement. He ruled in May that two features of the constitution most objectionable to Conservatives, the test oath and the disfranchisement clauses, would be submitted for separate referenda, so that voters could disapprove these two parts of the constitution while accepting the remainder. Grant scheduled the vote on the constitution and the election of a governor and a legislature for July 6, 1869.[56]

Grant did not, however, allow a separate vote to prevent the election of local government officials, a sore point among Conservatives in black-majority areas. Bitter-enders insisted that the referendum was "a mere mockery and snare to induce the white people to adopt a constitution that will inevitably subject them and their property to the control of blacks." A Southampton observer protested that Conservatives from the Shenandoah Valley, not themselves exposed to "negro rule," had "surrendered to the Republicans." County governments in the hands of blacks would "render property worthless."[57]

The Conservative-Republican candidate for governor, Gilbert C. Walker, was a carpetbagger who shared the outlook of white southern traditionalists on the key issues of Reconstruction. A native of New York, the Norfolk banker and railroad promoter carried a sharp animus against black voters, who had defeated his bid for a seat in the state constitutional convention in 1867. Having lost to a black candidate, Walker considered that election "sufficient to damn universal negro suffrage in the opinion of any sensible man." He confidentially had asked General Schofield to consider prohibiting black delegates from sitting in the convention.[58]

In early 1869 military authorities ordered all Southampton officeholders to report whether they had taken the so-called ironclad oath or whether they were disqualified from office under the terms of section three of the Fourteeeth Amendment. The ironclad oath of July 2, 1862, specified that a person had not voluntarily borne arms against the federal government nor voluntarily assisted those who did so. It also stated that a signer had neither sought nor held "any office whatever, under any authority, or pretended authority, in hostility to the United States." Section three of the Fourteenth Amendment barred from office all persons who had supported the rebellion after having held state or federal office and taken an oath to support the United States Constitution.[59]

The housecleaning of local officials established Dr. Thomas J. Pretlow, who had an apparent gift for ingratiating himself to federal officials, as an important power broker. The only native whites eligible to take the ironclad oath came from Pretlow's circle of upper-county Whig Unionists. Pretlow himself wielded principal influence over Southampton appointments. Of greatest importance was his endorsement of Demarcus L.

Doles, who was selected county sheriff in June 1869. Pretlow's reputation of "having been a staunch Union man throughout the war" persuaded the military authorities to appoint Doles. The doctor's more recent emergence as a Conservative critic of the freedmen in no way impaired his clout.[60]

Pretlow complained, as he had before, that strict enforcement of the ironclad oath disqualified many legitimate Unionists from office. He explained to General Canby that "Virginia was one great battlefield and the war came to almost every mans door, and there was scarcely a child who did not do some act of humanity for *persons* engaged in armed hostility to the United States." The general agreed that merely having furnished food or shelter to Confederate soldiers would not disqualify potential officeholders. Pretlow, however, pointed out an additional difficulty. He thought it "strange beyond comprehension" that the Fourteenth Amendment disqualified all former officeholders:

> It is a remarkable fact that while this was one of the strongest Union counties in Virginia we have not a single civil officer within its limits—for the oath is so sweeping that all fall alike under its operations. I do not see how Mr. Lincoln or Genl. Grant could have been better Union men than I was, yet because I held at the commencement of the war the local office of conservator of the peace by an oath of fidelity to the U. S. and which I never knowingly or willfully violated, I am proscribed as a rebel and traitor. . . . We have no precedent in modern history where those who were quietly engaged in the simple administration of municipal civil law for the benefit and well being of society were held to account and punished.[61]

A movement developed to place Pretlow on the state ticket as the Conservative candidate for congressman-at-large. His candidacy was considered likely to "bring voters to the polls who would not otherwise come," appealing both to Unionists and to bitter-enders in black-majority counties who still opposed ratification of the constitution.[62] At the solicitation of party leaders in Southampton, Pretlow issued a public letter indicating his availability and outlining his views on major issues. Although still deploring "the abominable Constitution," the Southampton doctor grudgingly concluded that its adoption and the election of a suitably Conservative legislature would "save us from impending ruin." Voters could immediately strike out its test oath and disfranchisement features. Nor did Pretlow consider "universal negro suffrage" to be "a fixture."

Still believing that voting rights "should only be enjoyed by the intelligent, honest and virtuous, and not by the ignorant, profligate and vicious," he predicted that unrestricted black voting would be "short lived." The Pretlow boom proved stillborn, however, because a different candidate appeared more qualified to take the oath of office.[63]

From early May through early July 1869, a swirl of political activity took place in Southampton. Military authorities commissioned growing numbers of civilian officials. In addition to the new sheriff, two revenue commissioners and numerous justices of the peace, constables, and overseers of the poor received appointments. At the same time, military officials busily reinstated the mechanisms set up in 1867 for holding a supervised election. The letter book of Captain Edward P. Pearson, Jr., the federal official immediately responsible for both processes, sheds much light on this turbulent interval in Southampton's political history.[64]

The task of finding suitable persons to hold local office and serve as voting registrars could be challenging, because federal officials showed no inclination to appoint blacks. As Dr. Pretlow suggested, many white Unionists could not take the oath and therefore were disqualified. The upper county contained enough whites who were untainted by Confederate officeholding to provide a new nucleus of officeholders and registrars. The lower county, however, which had voted almost unanimously prosecession in February 1861, contained little indigenous white Unionism. Consequently, federal officials sometimes had to appoint men who lived outside the districts in which they were to hold office. In Drewrysville, for example, three of the four persons selected to register voters and to manage the election lived elsewhere.[65]

Once again, as in 1867, federally appointed registrars compiled lists of qualified voters for each voting district, with separate registration lists drawn up for each race (see app. table 9.3). Total registration increased by several hundred voters, with blacks maintaining a 53 percent to 47 percent advantage. Overall, black eligibles outnumbered whites, 1,448 to 1,288. Only in one upper-county voting district, Berlin, did white registrants hold a solid majority. Even if whites turned out to vote at a more substantial rate than they had in 1867, blacks could expect to maintain the upper hand. That did not happen, however.

On election day, July 6, 1869, black voters only narrowly outnumbered whites, 1,257 to 1,221. All but 67 registered whites voted, a remarkable turnout rate of almost 95 percent. Black turnout fell from the level of almost 98 percent achieved in 1867 to 87 percent in 1869, as 191 registered blacks failed to vote. Unlike other adjacent counties with more black than white registrants, Southampton voted Conservative (see app. table 9.3). The Conservative candidates for governor, Congress, and House of Delegates, each received between 1,269 and 1,275 votes. Their Republicans opponents narrowly trailed, with vote totals ranging from 1,188 and 1,197. Dr. Richard U. Burges, son of the eminent Whig A. S. H. Burges, defeated Joseph Gregory, the black Baptist preacher and political leader, for the county's seat in the House of Delegates. Of the candidates on the ballot in Southampton, only a single Republican won; the candidate for Congress, James H. Platt, a Yankee carpetbagger, ran in a multicounty district with a heavy black majority.[66]

Voting patterns remained racially polarized (see app. tables 9.4 and 9.5). As in 1867, only a single white voter cast a Radical ballot. Unlike 1867, however, black voters broke ranks. Although blacks voted overwhelmingly Radical, sixty-two black defectors held the balance of power, enabling Conservatives to carry the county. The identities of the black Conservatives are not known, but existing records do indicate where they voted. Only thirteen of the sixty-two came from the lower county, where the majority of blacks lived. Of the forty-nine upper-county blacks voting the Conservative ticket, thirty-two cast ballots at Berlin, the only district in the county where whites heavily outnumbered blacks. The Berlin district included the region where Whig Unionism was strongest and Thomas J. Pretlow's political allies were numerous. Dr. Burges, the Conservative candidate for the legislature, also lived there. By some means, whites gained the support of more than one-third of the blacks voting at Berlin.[67]

Conservatives swept to a great statewide victory in the July 1869 elections. Gilbert C. Walker defeated his Republican rival, Henry H. Wells, 119,535 to 101,204. Conservatives also won large majorities in both houses of the legislature. Almost all voters favored adoption of the constitution, while a decisive majority struck out the test oath and disfranchisement clauses. Much as Thomas J. Pretlow predicted, the coalition of "Old Whigs, Democrats, Union men and Secessionists," who considered themselves "drawn together by a common bond of union for self-preservation," redeemed Virginia before a Radical government could ever be elected.[68]

Substantial evidence indicates, however, that the Conservative victory in Southampton was tainted. Two weeks before the election the shooting of a black man heightened tensions and left a group of protesting blacks in jail. According to subsequent testimony, the trouble originated with a pedestrian dispute between Jonas Barrett, a freedman, and Charles Holland, a store owner. Although the principals sharply disagreed about what had occurred, the episode illustrates that mutual suspicion and the potential for violence were pervasive as the election approached.

Barrett claimed that he tried to buy a pound of tobacco on credit from Holland, who refused the request. Holland, apparently fearing that Barrett would not repay him, angrily condemned the freedman for his "sauciness." Barrett remonstrated, telling Holland: "I am not afraid of you." As Barrett walked out into the yard, he testified, an enraged Holland picked up a pistol and shot him just above the hip. Barrett produced as evidence "the ball with which he had been hit." His testimony was corroborated by his nephew, Jacob Rawls.[69]

Holland provided a differing version of events. He testified that Barrett summarily refused to pay him $11 owed for two cart wheels. When Barrett refused to leave, Holland picked up a four-pound weight and threatened to throw it. Barrett "continued to make insulting remarks," saying that "if you throw that weight the first lick will be yours, then the second will be mine." Holland testified that "I thereupon grabbed hold of my pistol, as it was lying on the shelf," and threatened to shoot. Barrett replied, "Shoot as much as you please. I am as good a man as you are." Seeing, however, that Holland was preparing to shoot, Barrett "trotted off." But Holland, jumping over the counter, pursued Barrett out the door, and, by his own testimony, "let him have it."[70]

The shooting of Barrett took place around noon on June 22 just across the railroad bridge from Franklin, in Isle of Wight County. That night, a group of blacks gathered at Holland's to protest. That same night, a fire broke out at Neely's mill, a valuable property worth $20,000, which adjoined Holland's. Alarmed whites sent an urgent telegram to military authorities in Richmond claiming that the protesters had burned the mill and requesting troops to restore order. "We have no security for life or property," they insisted. "Night is made hideous by armed band of negroes." They telegraphed again the next night, reporting that "everything is now quiet here." They feared, however, "another disturbance tonight" because "one of the ringleaders surrounded by about forty confederates is now whispering to them an harangue near the spot of last nights disturbance."[71]

After conducting an investigation, Lieutenant John W. Whitten, the military superintendent stationed in Jerusalem, ordered Holland to appear before the next term of the county court in Isle of Wight. He remained free on $150 bond. Whitten also charged six black men—George Pretlow, Charles Webb, Harry Smallwood, George Madray, Simon Darden, and William Duncan—with unlawful assemblage at Holland's on the night of the twenty-second. A large number of other blacks stepped forward to provide $300 in security for the six accused men. Four of the six defendants lived in Southampton, as did all but one of the men providing security. Among the latter was Southampton's most prominent black politician, Joseph Gregory, the Republican candidate for the legislature. The securities—and possibly also the defendants—included the most politically active blacks in Southampton.[72]

Shortly thereafter, however, Whitten ordered the six black defendants arrested and confined to the Isle of Wight jail, pending the September convening of a grand jury. He explained to his superiors that he wanted the men in custody because they could not give bail. Whitten's action appears vindictive. His report of July 7 specified in precise detail that sufficient security had been pledged, typically in small sums of between $5 and $25, to assure the appearance of the defendants at court. It appears likely that Whitten acted at the behest of local whites.[73]

A request for the release of the prisoners, written by black Republican leader Joseph Gregory, raises severe doubts about the accusations against the six defendants and the fairness displayed by Whitten and civil officials. Unable to learn what charges had been made against the six men or why they had been jailed, Gregory explained that proper security had been pledged to secure their release. He suspected that a trumped-up arson accusation had been added to the charge of unlawful assembly. Gregory's July 24 letter, written at Franklin Depot, was addressed to Lieutenant Louis V. Caziarc, one of the military bureaucrats in Richmond:

> Dear sir the men wich they have in gail in Isle Wight Co. we cant see what they ere there for the people ask me to write to you and ask you to see the General for us unlist you can tell us what the charge is agance them Dear sir we think that if the case of these men was closley tride they wold be relest and be at home with thir familyes
>
> for they have bin turn out of dorse the roof of the house have bin knock of from over thir heades. we cant find out what the carge is. if it for going to Mr Hollon house. we unstand that to have bin tride and put of untell cort we giving baile of $3.50. dol for them untell that time. Dear sir these men did not carry thir arms to interfear Mr

Hollon they carred them to pretect them selfs as the white men was
seting on the way as they went over to his house they did not go in
his house untell he told them to do so we write this becarse we cant
find out eny thing here. it is no use to ask eny one a ward about the
case   if is is about the Mill being burnd it has bin prioved by the
wachman that it cort fire frome the ashes that was thrownout out of
the furnnish wich the watchman says it did. So we ask you to see the
General for us and ask him to exezemon [examine] them   for what
we have seen and heard abought this matter we may be rong but we
think they are clear and know nothing abought the burning of the
mill   and the only carge or evedence againce them is a boy here in
gail in this County that we put in gail for steling money and he has
bin pruved a lier before the Lieutenant Mr. Whitny   when this boy
was put in gail and before he was arrested for steling money he was
tride and exezemon abought the burning of the mill and he swoe that
he new nothing abought it. after he was put in gail Mr Neally has bin
from what we can learn has been giving him sume close and also giving other things. he has told a lie on these men   I hope this is not
rong to ask you to do this for us as we feel that we have no friend here
to help us.[74]

Gregory's account strongly suggests that the Southampton blacks had
been unjustly jailed. He insisted that the men were not guilty of arson,
the only serious crime that might have been alleged. He established that
the evidence about arson was suspect, because it was based on the testimony of a prisoner who had earlier denied knowing anything about the
burning of the mill. Would arsonists have returned en masse the next
night to the site of their crime?

Gregory's letter also appears consistent with most testimony about the
case earlier gathered by Whitten. It was by no means clear that the blacks
acted menacingly toward Charles Holland, except insofar as a group of
fifty unhappy blacks, some of whom were armed, would have appeared
dangerous to most whites. Although some witnesses remembered that
George Pretlow and other leaders of the group insisted that Holland meet
with them outside his house to explain why he had shot Jonas Barrett,
others reported that Pretlow had negotiated privately with Holland, securing his agreement "to support Barrett and his family during the time
that he was confined by his wound," and that Pretlow had not entered the
house until invited to do so by Holland and his wife. William Stancil, the

only supposed ringleader that Whitten chose not to indict, testified that Pretlow had agreed to participate with the crowd after securing a promise that "they would not do any harm to Mr. Holland." Two white witnesses, Thomas Cross and Dr. James Fenton Bryant, who crossed the railroad bridge from Franklin to meet with the crowd outside Holland's house, reported that "they listened to us very respectfully" and soon afterwards dispersed. "They said that all they wanted was justice," Bryant recalled. "We told them that that was not the way to get justice for forty or fifty of them to visit one man in that manner." [75]

George Pretlow recalled asking Holland during their discussion, "Is there any law for us?" [76] The answer, to judge from Whitten's handling of the incident, was a bleak one. The man who had done the shooting remained free on bond. But six men who, at worst, had protested the shooting faced a summer in jail, even though their friends had raised adequate security to win their release. While they festered in jail, their families were evicted from their homes. Furthermore, neither military nor civil officials would reveal why the six remained jailed or whether additional charges had been made against them.

The jailing of the Southampton blacks appears all the more suspicious because it occurred immediately before a pivotal election. Adoption of the new constitution and political control of the state both hung in the balance. Locally, a black leader, Joseph Gregory, was contesting for Southampton's seat in the legislature. By demonstrating that Gregory could not protect his followers from arbitrary arrest and imprisonment, local whites sent an unmistakably intimidating message to local blacks.

That was not all. Shortly after the election, Gregory and another Southampton black man, Braddock Johnson, filed affidavits "setting forth that [the] election in Southampton County was not fairly conducted, and especially in Franklin." They charged that "intimidation was employed against colored men, votes were changed, ballots altered, and some ballots were taken out of the boxes and destroyed by the soldiers." Gregory and Johnson also stated that "the President of the Board at Franklin and nearly all the Registrars were opposed to the Republican ticket." [77]

Military authorities asked Lieutenant Whitten to make a "thorough investigation and report" about "the alleged frauds in the election in that county." Whitten questioned Gregory, but there is no indication that he ever completed a report. Instead, military authorities soon closed down the election supervision machinery, and Whitten was assigned to other duties. In addition, Captain Pearson, who had requested the report from Whitten, suddenly was replaced as military commissioner for the Seventh Division. Pearson's removal may have been nothing more than a bureaucratic reshuffle. With other evidence suggesting that Whitten had ingratiated himself to local whites and that he had allowed Conservatives to abuse the electoral process, however, some suspicion of a cover-up must remain.[78]

A strong case can be made that Southampton officials were not acting in good faith and that Whitten, the superintendent of registration for Southampton County, did little to rectify matters. Even though all persons appointed as registrars and election officials had to take the oath, that requirement did not ensure much of a Republican presence during registration or voting. Between 1867 and 1869, only the tiniest number of Southampton whites ever voted Republican, in some elections none at all. Because Whitten appointed only whites, most of his selections necessarily must have been Conservatives. One registrar, Otho W. Hahn, unwittingly used "vulgar, obscene and profane language" that was "characterized by an intense hatred of the colored race" in the presence of James H. Platt, a prominent white Petersburg Radical who soon won a seat in Congress. Although Platt complained to higher authorities, Hahn remained a Southampton registrar.[79]

To add insult to injury, a Southampton grand jury indicted two prominent Republicans soon after the election. Frank M. Holland, the postmaster at Franklin and one of the very few white Republicans in the county, refused to close his store to help turn out the Conservative vote on election day. A committee of Conservatives visited all Franklin store owners, and Holland was the only one who rebuffed them. In retaliation, the grand jury indicted him for perjury, on grounds that he had taken the ironclad oath to qualify as postmaster after having voluntarily served in the Confederate army. Holland complained to military officials that he "could expect little mercy" if tried by a Southampton jury because all potential jurors were Conservatives. Subsequent military investigation showed that Holland had opposed secession vigorously, that he had volunteered for Confederate military service only when he was about to be drafted and knew "that it would be impossible to keep out any longer," and that he had been arrested in 1864 while in the army for uttering "disloyal language" about the Confederate government. Military officials, agreeing with Holland that his legal difficulties "originated in personal and political malice and in a spirit of revenge," quashed the indictment.[80]

Also targeted by vengeful Conservatives was Joseph Gregory, the black political leader who narrowly lost the legislative election. By protesting the treatment of the six jailed black men and alleging that the election had been conducted unfairly, Gregory further offended white sensibilities. The same Southampton grand jury that indicted Holland also delivered a perjury indictment against Gregory, charging that he gave false testimony about the election to Lieutenant Whitten. Military authorities eventually threw out Gregory's perjury indictment, as they did Holland's. An unpleasant adjunct to the Gregory indictment illustrates the estrangement between Southampton whites and blacks. Prominent Franklin resident John H. Bogart, one of the persons who brought the complaint against Gregory, had earlier been his patron. In 1867 Bogart had provided Gregory with security bond of $1,500, verifying that Gregory had been ordained by the Baptist church and enabling him "to celebrate the rites of marriage." In August 1869, however, Bogart withdrew his security, and the county court revoked Gregory's right to perform marriages.[81]

Unrelenting pressures apparently wore down Southampton's black leaders. John Brown continued to live in the county but promptly disappeared from the public arena. Joseph Gregory, who remained politically active, ultimately defected to the Conservatives. In 1875, according to the Conservative Norfolk *Virginian*, the Baptist minister abandoned the "Radical camp" and persuaded some of his followers "to renounce their wicked ways and vote for the Conservative candidate." Gregory's "apostacy" contributed to a big Conservative victory, while also provoking a hostile demonstration by black Republican loyalists at a church where he was preaching.[82]

EPILOGUE

The Reconstruction of Agricultural Labor

CONCURRENT WITH THE GREAT crisis of 1867–69 that accompanied black voting in Southampton County, a less visible, more incremental change was taking place in labor relations. The old slave system of closely supervised gang labor disintegrated, but the transition to a new system took years to effect. A contentious struggle persisted into the 1870s, as laborers tried to gain greater autonomy while landlords tried to preserve aspects of the old order. The experiences of diarist Daniel Cobb reveal how one frustrated traditionalist searched unsuccessfully for alternatives to decentralized tenant agriculture, which gradually became the standard pattern in the postwar South.[1]

Convinced that black labor on shares was a bad way to manage his land, Cobb sharply reduced his force for 1867, from ten full hands to four. In their places, he hired two white tenants, each to farm with one horse. He also assigned similar duties to his sixteen-year-old son, Jesse. The black tenants were to receive one-third shares of the crop. The two whites, who were to feed themselves, aided by small garden patches, agreed to work for half shares. Cobb supplied them, like the black tenants, with land, horses, implements, and places to live.[2]

Unfortunately for Cobb, white labor failed to live up to his expectations. One tenant quit the first week of January, and his replacement never devoted more than half his time to farm work. By midsummer only one white tenant remained. The latter, named Ferguson, worked until the spring of 1868 but never to Cobb's satisfaction. Ferguson "showed his cloven foot," Cobb complained, when it came time to settle accounts.

Probably the tenant owed more money than he had earned through his labor. Several successive white tenants proved no more competent.[3]

Other developments also upset Cobb. Disastrous weather, unwise crop choices, and black assertiveness made 1867 the worst year for agriculture that he had ever experienced. Incessant rains fell between March and June, washing out bridges, flooding fields, and requiring widespread replanting. Debt-ridden farmers planted cotton en masse, lured by the fine prices of 1866. Some who normally put ten acres in cotton sowed forty or fifty in 1867. The cotton did poorly, as did the shrunken corn crop. Black laborers refused to submit to the slavelike discipline that might have salvaged the crops after the weather finally improved at the end of June. Indeed, by that time many tenants had already quit or been fired. Before long, food supplies became tight. It was "the most difficult year ... ever seen in Virginia ... for farmers to make a crop," Cobb reported. Considering the situation "almost intolerable" and Satan "loosed," he became increasingly dejected. Should "as much turn round in this country for the next 10 years as for the last 10 I think they will be an end to Va and her Sister States," he glumly prognosticated.[4]

Nor was Cobb's household tranquil. Knowing that his wife "loves to have waitting on," he hired a house girl, a yard boy, and the "oald cook," Pheby. They did not measure up to Mary Jane Cobb's prewar standards, however. "Negrows is set at liberty," Cobb noted; they would not serve as submissively as they once had. Were they to do so, they explained to him, they could not "enjoy there freedom." Cobb certainly agreed with his wife that "it was not worth while for them to have there freedom," but he resented being "principally blamed for the negrows being fread." When she upbraided him for not finding suitable domestic help, Cobb penned a torrent of complaints in his diary: "I am fa[u]lted because I cant do with them as when slaves."[5]

Cobb's wife and his nineteen-year-old daughter, Rebecca, took matters into their own hands. Judging the house girl lazy and insolent, Beck went about "laying [the servant's] tongue" by attacking her with fire tongs. Cobb, suddenly confronted by an unruly clamor, used "threts of vilance" to restore order. That evening, the young domestic quit. Shortly afterward, the cook died. Their successors proved similarly unsuitable. One cook did not attend "to her business"; one house girl was fired "on acc[oun]t of stealing." "I cant get one but what is fa[u]lted and drivened off," Cobb complained. One senses a hint of malicious pleasure in a subsequent diary entry: "Our cook left to day[.] wife and daughter is cook."[6]

Cobb would sooner complain about his wife's inability to adjust to free labor than recognize his own shortcomings in the same area. Why did the family often have to do without a cook? It was "owing to my wifes being so hard to pleas," he noted; "I cant get one to stay with her." Relations between Cobb and hired agricultural laborers remained, however, equally turbulent. After his last cotton was picked at the end of the 1867 growing season, Cobb discharged four "disordaly" hands.[7]

Some blacks who contracted to work for Cobb in 1868 apparently demanded new housing arrangements. Abandoning the old slave quarters in the yard, the tenants built new homes in the woods. Cobb's farm thus followed a pattern observed widely across the South at this time, as freedmen sought to put greater physical distance between their residences and the "big house." In addition, some of Cobb's hired force by 1868 (quite likely the same ones who built the new cabins) made individual sharecropping contracts that relieved them from gang labor requirements and day-to-day supervision. Cobb thus noted in April that "the hands working for shears went to a negrow speach. The rest or hired hands worked."[8]

With both white and black tenants struggling to achieve a bare subsistence and larger property holders still reeling from the shocking developments of the last seven years, older paternalistic patterns of race relations withered. No longer did Cobb maintain the rituals in which he displayed his benevolence and his black laborers displayed their gratitude. Cobb's last August "dining" occurred in 1866. By 1867 and 1868, with blacks organizing politically and Cobb searching for alternatives to black labor, the old paternalist tradition had vanished. Nothing so well symbolized the new era as Cobb's response to two deaths among his work force. Roderick Barham, "a colard man," died in August 1868. He was, Cobb admitted, "about as good and as humble as any of that race among us," but Cobb docked a day's pay from the hands who missed work the next day to bury Barham. Two months later, one of Cobb's white tenants, George W. Scott, suffered the loss of an infant; Cobb provided a horse and buggy for the burial.[9]

Cobb's last three diaries run from January 1870 until shortly before he died in October 1872. The 1869 volume, now lost, might have provided information about the important election in July 1869, when white Virginians escaped further Reconstruction. One suspects that Cobb, like other traditionalists, found the new era discouraging. Only by supporting political opportunists who had a Whiggish urban orientation and gave lip service to equal rights could he oppose the dreaded Republican Radicals.

By 1870 the new system of sharecropping by individual families had become more fully developed on Cobb's farm. For the first time he noted that all tenants had "truck patches" for their own use and benefit. His regular tenants, including both white and black families, could work their own plots or go to town or to the store when they pleased. When the shared crops for which they were directly responsible were laid by in late summer, they could enjoy an interval of relaxation before the start of the harvest. Cobb extended them credit in the spring to buy manure for cotton; only after the tenants sold their crop in the fall was he reimbursed. Cobb also hired two wage laborers who remained in a more anomalous position. If they used regular work time in their truck patches, he deducted it from their wages.[10]

Unfortunately for Cobb and his tenants, cotton prices tumbled just as the 1870 crop reached market. War in Europe depressed normal demand. Cotton, worth over twenty-five cents per pound in early September, fell to just over fifteen cents when the first four bales from the Cobb farm reached Petersburg in early November. The next three bales in mid-December sold for under fourteen cents. The tenants, already "slandering and backbiting" Cobb before the discouraging sag in cotton prices, became even more sullen.[11]

The cotton harvest coincided with the highlight of the political season. Although Conservatives controlled the state government, a Radical carpetbagger from Vermont, James H. Platt, held the local seat in Congress. The day before the election in early November, Cobb reported with astonishment that "the Nigars in Town" and the "radacal whites with them" had put on "the grates[t] Beef I ever saw." They had "the Corte hous and frunt streat loomanated with long light[s]." Cobb thought not less than "2 or 3000 Negrows men women and Boys" took part, all loudly huzzahing. Platt, enjoying heavy black support, retained his seat.[12]

In 1871, for the first time in thirty years of farming, Cobb attempted to put in a crop without black labor. The initiative for this startling development did not originate with him. Instead, black laborers boycotted Cobb; "nun came up" as promised when the new year started. He appeared mystified, unable to understand why "all the negrows enjoyedment failed." Apparently Southampton experienced a temporary labor shortage. Given a choice, hands "settled with those where stors are located." Cobb found himself "more behind with labour than since Lee surrendered." In January some of the previous year's cotton and peanuts remained in the field, awaiting picking.[13]

White tenants "stuck up" with Cobb, and he soon hired two more, one for straight wages of $9 per month, the other for half shares of a one-horse crop. Things did not go well, however. At the end of June one white share tenant suddenly quit to take a better job, although he still owed Cobb $20. The exasperated diarist confessed that he was left with "nun but day hands and ½ of Saturday." Without any direct stake in the crop's success, day hands refused to work harder even if it was in danger of being lost.[14]

Matters could have been worse. On July 4 Cobb had six white day laborers at work and four plows running. Landowners dependent on black labor found themselves shorthanded. The traditional holiday had acquired political overtones; its celebration had become an occasion for Radical rallies. Thousands of blacks from the region converged on Norfolk for a four-day "picknick." Cobb thereupon dashed off the cleverest (albeit fiercely unreconstructed) line in his diary: "Well the people may pick on earth But Nick will pick them after death."[15]

Altogether, Cobb had a miserable time in 1871. Severe hail in early August, as much as three inches deep in some places, reduced his crop of cotton and corn (peanuts, safely underground, better withstood the damage). By midsummer he was able to hire some blacks, but his complaints about the irregular work habits of tenants persisted. On court day in September, Cobb's "negrow hands" took off from work and converged on Jerusalem. There they heard Congressman Platt speak, and they appointed the leading local black politician, Joseph Gregory, to represent Southampton at the upcoming "Radical Convention" in Richmond. Estimating that "from 1500 to 2000 negrows assembled in the pubblick square of the little place," Cobb distressfully noted that "Radickism is advancing."[16]

Labor relations retrogressed on Cobb's domain in 1872. The final volume of his diary contains a long litany of grievances against his laborers. Cobb chose to hire his help in 1872 for wages of $10 per month rather than for shares. This decision caused him repeated aggravation. The hands did not start work until half an hour or an hour after sunrise: Cobb vowed to deduct the time from their pay. They stopped working at noon on Saturday; "so thats whiy they are ½ clad and fed[,] [and their] families starving." In June the hands took off to attend court day in Jerusalem, and Cobb felt obliged to hire someone to plow for $1.50 per day. High labor costs made Cobb fear that the farm would not produce enough to cover expenses. "I think some times I shall have to stop farming," he mused in late July, "& would if [I] new what to begin." By late August, Cobb decided to bargain with some of his hands to work next year on halves. He apparently stood ready to accept decentralized tenant agriculture, after trying for years to maintain tighter supervision over his labor force.[17]

Cobb's homelife offered him little relief from the frustrations of managing a farm with free labor. "The head woman of the family has got the Devil in her as usual," he mourned; Mary Jane Cobb's fussing and "tantroms" were still ruining his pleasure after thirty years. In January 1871 Cobb's only daughter, Rebecca, married J. Lewis Gillette, son of the martyred Confederate cavalry officer Joseph E. Gillette. Cobb was not pleased with young Gillette, but his daughter "was determined to marry him." Behaving far more gracefully than Jesse Little had for him, Cobb provided appropriate wedding festivities. The year ended sadly as the first Cobb grandchild died a week after birth. Christmas in 1871 was "the most gloomy" Cobb had ever experienced.[18]

It also turned out to be his last. In February 1872 Cobb dreamed that he and people long since dead had brought his coffin to the "buring ground" and discussed where his grave should be located. This premonition prompted Cobb to write a will, which divided his estate equally among his surviving children and made proper provision for his wife. As executor of his estate he appointed none other than Elliott Story. Although Cobb felt "quite feeble" and at times experienced a swelling in his feet that made it difficult to wear shoes, the year proceeded uneventfully. He and his wife continued to quarrel; he continued to deplore the inadequacies of free labor; he enabled Beck and Lewis Gillette to start building a new house. In late August Cobb decided to attend a "negrow school exibition and dining," which he surprisingly pronounced "well dun." Two days later, on September 2, he suffered a chill. Cobb never wrote another word in his diary and died one month later.[19]

WHAT ABOUT THE OTHER diarist from Old Southampton? When the Civil War ended, Elliott Story still had twenty-one years to live. The concluding segments of his diary give only brief glimpses of his later life. Story greeted the end of the war with a mixture of anxiety and hope. He noted that everything "so much dreaded by the South" had actually occurred: "All the civil officers in this section are forbidden to exercise the function of their offices and we are now under military rule and the negroes are all declared to be free." Consistent with his earlier sectional moderation, however, Story wondered whether the astonishing changes might bring "blessings in disguise." Undoubtedly a loyal Confederate, he was no bitter-ender.[20]

Story served as the deputy to Samuel Kello, who was elected sheriff in August 1865. This work continued until 1869, and Story spent years afterward trying to wind up unfinished business from Kello's tenure in office. Postwar economic dislocations caused widespread nonpayment of taxes and forfeiture of property, saddling Story with responsibilities that he described as "troublesome and laborious almost beyond description." He also played a significant role in reassessing property in the upper part of Southampton in 1871. Though barred by Congress from holding the post of assessor (he had held office under the Confederacy, and such disabilities were not removed until 1872), Story kept the books and supervised the work of two persons who reported directly to him.[21]

His civil duties deprived Story of much direct experience with the initial transition to free-labor agriculture. In 1866 and 1867 he rented out almost all his land. He did, however, share the views of white Southamptonites—that the new system of labor was "deranged" because the freedmen worked "very badly." By the early 1870s Story devoted most of his time to farming. He apparently found free laborers more competent than he had originally thought. Story's health remained feeble, and he could do "but little laborious farm work," so he was dependent on hired help. In 1872 the liberal use of fertilizer enabled Story to produce "a pretty good little crop of cotton" and a patch of peanuts that "yielded very well" for the ground he planted. The next year he made five bales of cotton and 100 bushels of peanuts, enough to enable him to pay $100 to his creditors. His workers also raised enough corn, bacon, and fodder to provide subsistence for the household and food for the draft animals.[22]

The 1870 U.S. Census offers one hint that Story enjoyed a less fractious transition from slave labor to free than did Daniel Cobb. Residing next door to Story in 1870 was a black family: Samuel and Delila Story and their three children. These people must have been Story's former slave Sam and the free woman and cook Delila, whom Sam married at Story's house in 1857. By taking the same last name as their patron, Sam's former owner, the black Storys made a statement that most of Daniel

Cobb's former slaves certainly did not make. It appears probable that Samuel Story, a farm laborer, remained in Elliott Story's employ, as did his wife and sixteen-year-old son.[23]

Tragedy continued to afflict Story during the postwar years. Two sisters, Mary and Martha, had died before the war. His younger brother Frank, to whom Story had been in many ways a father, succumbed to tuberculosis in 1862. In 1867 a sudden illness felled his sister Nancy, wife of Story's close friend and neighbor George Moore, and mother of two teenaged boys and two little girls. Less than a year later tuberculosis killed Story's unmarried sister Elizabeth, who had been for several years a semi-invalid in his house. He mourned that he had "no father, mother, sisters, or brother or wife to share with me the joys and sorrows of life." One relative remained. Story's own son Jimmy, raised for several years by Nancy and George Moore, lived with Story after 1862. "Only my little boy is left," he noted anxiously after Elizabeth's death.[24]

Story's long personal travail ended in 1872 when the fifty-one-year-old widower married Margaret E. Williams, twenty-three years his junior. Her "piety and amiable heart and affectionate disposition" commended Williams to Story. Whatever the particular quality of his charm for her, it must have been reinforced by demography: war had sent a sizable proportion of men her own age to early graves. Ten months after the marriage, in August 1873, Margaret Story delivered a son, Elliott Franklin Story. Two daughters, Elizabeth and Susie Story, were born thereafter. Story returned to teaching despite intermittent bad health, and he lived an additional decade past 1876, the last year he kept a diary.[25] He appears to have been happily married, and he must have taken pleasure in watching the progress of his children, born not only to different mothers but also at very different times in the history of his native county and region.

HISTORIANS OF THE AMERICAN South have endlessly debated questions about continuity and change. Did free-labor agriculture replicate the principal features of slavery, in that white landholders continued to dominate landless black laborers? Or did emancipation effect fundamental changes that decisively separated the postwar order from its predecessor? Did the subsequent destruction of black voting rights render the new political arrangements superficial and transitory? Or did the political upheaval generated during Reconstruction have lasting effects?[26]

Marcus Sterling Hopkins, a Freedmen's Bureau agent in northern Virginia, judged that much had changed during the immediate postwar years in Prince William, Orange, and Louisa counties. Blacks, "very abject and fearful in the presence of the white master class," were often victimized during the first year after the end of the war, "scarcely ever resisting when attacked, so abject had the terrible discipline of slavery made them." They suffered from starvation wages, widespread exploitation and abuse, and a complete absence of legal and political rights. By the end of 1868, amid the political revolution that enfranchised black voters, Hopkins found that the freedmen had become markedly more assertive, insisting on better wages and gaining opportunities to buy land and homes and to build schools and churches. "Now they will generally resist when attacked," Hopkins reported, "if not with blows yet with words."[27]

In contrast to developments elsewhere in Virginia, Southampton appears retrograde, with more palpable white hostility to black advancement. Blacks continued to vote, but their economic status remained precarious. Although sharecropping and wage labor replaced gang labor, most freedmen could not escape the tyranny of extortion and indebtedness. Black farmers in Southampton relied so heavily on credits and advances that they often lost their share of the crop before it was harvested. Compared with neighboring Greensville and Sussex counties, fewer Southampton blacks in 1880 worked for shares and more worked for wages. Only an estimated 1 percent of black agricultural laborers in Southampton owned the land they farmed or the homes where they lived, comparable to Greensville and Sussex but markedly lower than in adjacent Nansemond County. The condition of Southampton's black agriculturalists in 1880 was considered poorer than that of their counterparts in the adjoining counties.[28]

Real changes, however, had taken place in Southampton. Although the county's former masters and former slaves did not agree about much, they both recognized that postwar arrangements differed fundamentally from slavery. Confronting freedmen who were determined to "enjoy there freedom" and "have justice done," Daniel Cobb concluded that continued change such as he had witnessed during the 1860s would bring "an end to Va and her Sister states."

Cobb's fears were not realized. Relations between landlords and tenants stabilized in the 1870s, and the pace of social and economic change subsided. From the perspective of the late twentieth century, "the lives of tenant farmers may seem so difficult and constricted that the differences between plantation slavery and sharecropping become indistinct, and the continuities between the two stand out more than the changes." The true

[285]

perspective, however, historian J. William Harris has noted, "is that of the 1860s, of the masters and slaves themselves. Seen from their point of view, emancipation made a profound change in everyday life and social relations." Black tenant farmers remained economically and politically disadvantaged, "but the planters' loss of coercive power changed the face and substance of southern society." For those both white and black who lived through the postwar era, "the change in the balance of power," Harris wisely observed, "could well be called revolutionary." [29]

For Cobb as for many other privileged white southerners, success in thwarting black aspirations for greater freedom provided only scant recompense for the ordeal of civil war and the loss of the slave system. "I all was [always] was able to guvern my place untwill slavery passed off," he complained. [30] White landowners such as Cobb still possessed enormous advantages. But the system of closely supervised gang labor, backed by compulsion, had collapsed. Black tenants insisted on the greater autonomy. They refused to start work at daybreak, they quit laboring on Saturday at noon, they went to Jerusalem to hear Radical speeches, and they organized their own churches.

One must also recognize that postwar social and economic change took place in a political context. Historian Michael Fitzgerald has demonstrated that the "explosive politicization of the freedmen" during 1867, immediately following the enactment of Congressional Reconstruction, led directly to the abandonment of gang labor and the rise of decentralized tenant farming in parts of the Deep South. His findings apply well to Southampton. [31]

To omit the political dimension is to omit the catalyst for most of the changes that did take place. Blacks amazed Daniel Cobb by sponsoring the most spectacular political rallies in the history of the county, with the courthouse and street in front brilliantly illuminated, with the "grates Beef" he "ever saw," with prominent Radical speakers, and with black audiences that numbered in the thousands. A month after Cobb's death blacks carried the county for President Ulysses S. Grant, 1,334 to 1,056. [32]

The political foothold black Virginians gained in 1867 created a situation "different from anything slaveholders and slaves had ever known before," historian Richard Lowe has written. The new circumstances obliged whites to treat freedmen with greater respect than slaves ever enjoyed. Even though Conservatives gained effective statewide control in 1869, blacks retained formidable leverage in the tidewater and piedmont, where they outnumbered whites in many counties and voted in large numbers for the next thirty years. In Virginia and most of the upper South, very much unlike the lower South, whites rarely attempted to tamper with black voting before the 1890s. Notwithstanding the foreclosure of black political rights engineered by turn-of-the-century whites, many of the changes that dated from the late 1860s proved irreversible.[33]

Recognizing that profound changes occurred in the late 1860s, were there nevertheless missed opportunities to enlarge the sphere of change and make the changes more durable? Lowe suggests that blacks and their Radical white allies shortsightedly spurned a political alliance with moderate whites. Virginia's Republican party might have secured an effective majority, he concludes, had it reached out to "old antebellum Whigs and conditional Unionists." Southampton, of course, provides a telling case in point. Dr. Thomas J. Pretlow and his Whig friends certainly did stand ready in the summer of 1867 to lead the local Republican party. However flagrant his shortcomings, Pretlow was as promising a white moderate as Virginia blacks could expect to find.[34] Forgetting for the moment that developments at the state level effectively precluded any such harmonious local rapprochement, one may yet ask: should John Brown and Joseph Gregory, Southampton's black leaders, have made common cause with the estimable Dr. Pretlow? Politics, after all, is the art of the possible. Had blacks more to gain by keeping Pretlow on their side rather than allowing him to defect to the Conservatives?

It would not have been a relationship among equals: Pretlow could not conceive that blacks had leadership abilities. To ally with him, Brown and Gregory would have had to subordinate themselves. In exchange, they might have become behind-the-scenes power brokers. Perhaps, as Lowe suggests, circumstances would have forced moderate whites such as Pretlow to become more attuned to their black constituents. Perhaps Pretlow's racist fulminations in 1868 should be seen as a bid for Conservative support after black Radicals spurned a biracial alliance, rather than evidence of any deep-seated antiblack animus. Doubts, however, must linger. The messianic black awakening of 1867 would have been difficult to reconcile with Dr. Pretlow's condescending white paternalism. Lowe's political arithmetic is logically compelling, but it cannot bridge the wide gap separating white moderates and former slaves during the miraculous summer of 1867.

NINETEENTH-CENTURY AMERICANS never doubted that politics were important, that parties differed, and that significant consequences hinged on the outcome of elections. Their rates of voter turnout greatly surpassed the norm today. So did the ties that bound most voters to a particular party.

The party struggles of the Jacksonian Era reflected disagreements about the emerging world of the nineteenth century and all that went with it—not just banks and paper money, but technological innovation, individual self-discipline, redefined sex roles, and differing conceptions about the socialization of children. The mass parties that took shape in the 1830s positioned themselves so that most persons who worried about change were Jacksonians and most who welcomed it were Whigs. In the upper South, party divisions were connected also to disagreements about the future of the region, with Whigs tending to favor its evolution toward something other than a plantation society and Democrats wishing to preserve the status quo.

Framed by the heritage of a generation of partisan combat, the crisis of the Union in 1860–61 ignited an intense debate in the upper South. The antisecession coalition, composed especially of nonslaveholding Whigs, not only swept the upcountry but also ran competitively in parts of the piedmont and tidewater, including Southampton. Democratic secessionists enjoyed less success in appealing to the humbler rank and file of their party.

When forced to choose sides in a war, most white Virginians (except those in the trans-Allegheny) stood shoulder to shoulder. The war, however, had exactly the opposite effect that secessionists intended. Rather than preserving the status quo, the abortive bid to secure southern independence generated social upheaval and economic misery on a scale that could hardly have been imagined in 1861. By April 1865 many thousands of Virginia soldiers had died, slavery no longer existed, and the very foundations of the social order appeared shattered. If war is politics conducted by other means, the experiment had proven ruinous.

The type of mass partisan politics that originated in the 1830s achieved unique intensity during Reconstruction. Ninety-eight percent of registered black Southamptonites flocked to the polls at the height of the black awakening in October 1867. Whites, determined to settle accounts, turned out almost 95 percent of eligibles in July 1869. Both locally and across the South, postwar political and economic insurgencies interconnected, generating an epic struggle.

Old Southampton had many distinctive qualities. The rich panorama of its history, revealed through a particularly fine array of sources, has occupied our attention here. Yet that history was part of a larger whole. Southampton's experiences, from the rise of mass-based political parties in the 1830s through to the Reconstruction era, surely were not unique. They offer, in microcosm, many suggestive insights about the world the slaveholders made and lost, about the roles played there by slaves, free blacks, and nonslaveholding whites, and about a chapter of our collective past that continues to cast a long shadow.

APPENDIX
Tables

NOTES

INDEX

APPENDIX

Table 1.1. Population, 1840-70

	White	Free black	Slave	Total
1840 total	6,143 (42.6%)	1,801 (12.5%)	6,483 (44.9%)	14,427
Upper county	3,533 (50.4)	835 (11.9)	2,642 (37.7)	7,010
Lower county	2,610 (35.2)	966 (13.0)	3,841 (51.8)	7,417
1850 total	5,971 (44.2)	1,795 (13.3)	5,755 (42.6)	13,521
Upper county	3,463 (50.8)	864 (12.7)	2,489 (36.5)	6,816
Lower county	2,508 (37.4)	931 (13.9)	3,266 (48.7)	6,705
1860 total	5,713 (44.2)	1,794 (13.9)	5,408 (41.9)	12,915
Upper county	3,441 (51.5)	886 (13.3)	2,351 (35.2)	6,678
Lower county	2,272 (36.4)	908 (14.6)	3,057 (49.0)	6,237
1870 total	5,469 (44.5)	6,817 (55.5)		12,286
Upper county	3,068 (48.7)	3,232 (51.3)		6,300
Lower county	2,401 (40.1)	3,585 (59.9)		5,986

Note: Data compiled from the manuscript U.S. Census: population for
1840, 1850, 1860, 1870; slave schedules for 1840, 1850, 1860. The
numbers in some instances vary slightly from official published
returns.

Table 1.2.   White households by region, 1850

	Upper county	Lower county	Total
Privileged	84 (12.6%)	103 (18.7%)	187 (15.3%)
Smallholding	395 (59.1)	245 (44.5)	640 (52.5)
Nonpropertied	189 (28.3)	203 (36.8)	392 (32.2)
Total	668	551	1,219

Note: Data compiled from the manuscript U.S. Census for 1850 (population, agriculture, slave schedules) and state land tax records for 1849. Privileged households owned ten or more slaves. Smallholding households included those with fewer than ten slaves, plus nonslaveholders who owned land. Nonpropertied households owned neither land nor slaves.

Table 1.3.   White households by sex, 1850

	Male heads	Female heads	Total
Privileged	152 (16.3%)	35 (12.1%)	187 (15.3%)
Smallholding	519 (55.8)	121 (41.9)	640 (52.5)
Nonpropertied	259 (27.9)	133 (46.0)	392 (32.2)
Total	930	289	1,219

Note: Same categories and sources of information as in table 1.2.

Appendix

Table 1.4. All households, 1850

	White	Free black	Slave	Total
Privileged	187 (15.3%)	0	0	187 (7.0%)
Smallholding	640 (52.5)	23 (6.6%)	0	663 (24.9)
Nonpropertied	392 (32.2)	325 (93.4)	1,096 (100%)	1,813 (68.1)
Total	1,219	348	1,096	2,663

Note: Southampton's 1850 population included 5,940 whites (43.9%);
5,755 slaves (42.6%); and 1,826 free blacks (13.5%). The 1850 U.S.
Census lists 1,219 white households, a ratio of 4.87 persons per
household, and 348 free black households, a ratio of 5.25 persons per
household. Applying the latter figure to the slave population, one
may hypothesize a total of 1,096 slave "households."

Table 1.5 White households and slave ownership, 1850

White households	Slaves owned	Per household	Percentage of total
Privileged (N = 187)	4,159	22.2	77.9%
20+ slaves (N = 65)	2,515	38.7	47.1
10-19 slaves (N = 122)	1,644	13.5	30.8
Smallholding (N = 640)	1,183	1.8	22.1
4-9 slaves (N = 152)	913	6.0	17.1
1-3 slaves (N = 163)	270	1.7	5.0
Nonslaveholding (N = 325)	0	0	0
Nonpropertied (N = 392)	0	0	0
Total (N = 1,219)	5,342	4.4	100

Note: Same categories and sources of information as in table 1.2. The
total number of slaves is less than the figure of 5,755 in the 1850
U.S. Census because of discrepancies in matching differing census
schedules and because some Southampton slaves belonged to
out-of-county owners.

Table 1.6. Wealth of households

	Mean per household	Percentage of total
County land tax valuation		
Privileged (N = 187)	$3,822	69.1%
Smallholding (N = 640)	$498	30.8
Agricultural census valuation		
Privileged	$3,085	60.2
Smallholding	$595	39.8
Real property, population census		
Privileged	$3,984	69.0
Smallholding	$524	31.0
Value of all livestock		
Privileged	$896	56.9
Smallholding	$197	42.9
Improved acres		
Privileged	469	55.8
Smallholding	108	44.0

Note: Same categories and sources of information as in table 1.2.

Appendix

Table 1.7. Output of households

	Output per farm	Percentage of total
Corn		
Privileged	1630 bushels	55.0%
Smallholding	387 bushels	44.7
Swine		
Privileged	130 animals	55.6
Smallholding	30 animals	42.9
Cotton		
Privileged	2.9 bales	65.0
Smallholding	0.5 bales	35.0
Peas		
Privileged	454 bushels	69.1
Smallholding	59 bushels	30.8

Note: Same categories and sources of information as in table 1.2.

Table 4.1. Voter turnout and party preference, 1828-42

Date and type of election	Turnout	Percentage	Whig percentage
April 1828 (Assembly; Convention)	514	48+%	
November 1828 (President)	456	43+	
April 1829 (Assembly)	377	35+	
May 1829 (Convention delegates)	231	22+	
April 1830 (Assembly; Constitution)	355	33	
October 1830 (Assembly)	441	41	
August 1831 (Assembly)	721	67	
April 1832 (Assembly)	570	53	
November 1832 (President)	285	27	
April 1833 (Assembly)	355	33	
April 1834 (Assembly)	494	46	55.9%
January 1835 (Assembly)	665	62	48.6
April 1835 (Assembly)	751	70	52.9
April 1836 (Assembly)	535	50	55.9
November 1836 (President)	377	35	49.1
April 1837 (Assembly)	287	27	38.7
April 1838 (Assembly)	441	41	59.4
May 1839 (Assembly)	718	67	46.1
April 1840 (Assembly)	724	68	49.0
November 1840 (President)	750	70	50.4
April 1841 (Assembly)	725	68	52.7
April 1842 (Assembly)	735	69	49.3

Table 4.1 (cont.)

Note: Figures in the column entitled "Percentage," which indicate the
proportion of eligible voters actually voting, are presented as whole
numbers and should be regarded as educated estimates.

The pre-1830 constitution restricted the franchise to adult white
males who owned fifty acres of unimproved land, or twenty-five acres
of improved land with a house, or a house and lot in town. A limited
number of renters and landless household heads were enfranchised by
the 1830 Constitution (Proceedings and Debates of the Virginia State
Convention of 1829-30 [Richmond: Samuel Shepherd & Co. for Ritchie &
Cook, 1830], 854).

There is no precise way to determine the actual number of
eligible voters. Figures used at the Virginia Convention of 1829-30
credited Southampton with having 1,159 eligible voters (Robert Paul
Sutton, "The Virginia Constitutional Convention of 1829-30: A Profile
Analysis of Late-Jeffersonian Virginia" [Ph.D. diss., Univ. of
Virginia, 1967], 259). That number, however, is certainly too high
for the pre-1830 era, and it appears too high for the 1830-51 period.

Information in the 1840 U.S. Census and the 1841 state land tax
lists suggests a figure of 1,069 eligible voters. The number of
eligibles in the early 1830s may have been slightly higher, because
Southampton's white population was slowly decreasing. The number of
eligibles in 1828 and 1829 must have been lower (hence the appended
plus signs), because the pre-1830 Constitution had somewhat tighter
limits on the franchise.

Poll lists suggest that approximately half the nonlandowning
adult white male household heads in Southampton voted in the
presidential election of 1840 (see tables 4.6 and 4.7 below). More
than half must therefore have been eligible to vote.

On the other hand, suffrage restrictions certainly did exclude
numerous young white male adults who did not head households. A
canvass following the April 1832 election determined that seventy-six
ineligible persons had voted, and that only 570 valid votes had been
cast.

Figures in the column entitled "Whig percentage" indicate the
proportion of those voting who favored Whig candidates. Figures are
supplied only for elections starting in 1834, once the Whig party
coalesced.

Table 4.2. 1834 assembly race: slaveholding of voters

	Parker (Dem.)	Harrison (Whig)
Slaves owned		
1 to 3	20 (40%)	30 (60%)
4 to 9	26 (50)	26 (50)
10 to 19	28 (60.9)	18 (39.1)
20 or more	27 (67.5)	13 (32.5)
All slaveholders	101 (53.7)	87 (46.3)
Nonslaveholders	34 (31.2)	75 (68.8)
Total	135 (45.5)	162 (54.5)

Note: Information about slaveholdings is drawn from the 1840 U.S. Census. Only voters listed there are included in this table. Percentages indicate each party's proportion of the total vote for each category.

Chi-square — 100% probability that the distribution was not merely random. Chi-square does not measure the strength of a relationship; it indicates only the probability that a distribution was or was not random.

Cramer's $\underline{V}$ — .274, with slaveholders divided into four categories. Cramer's $\underline{V}$, a measure of association, ranges from a value of 0 to 1. The indicated figure, .274, suggests a substantial positive relationship between owning slaves and Democratic voting.

Table 4.3. 1840 presidential race: slaveholding of voters

	Van Buren (Dem.)	Harrison (Whig)
Slaves owned		
1 to 3	54 (50.9%)	52 (49.1%)
4 to 9	60 (52.2)	55 (47.8)
10 to 19	56 (62.2)	34 (37.8)
20 or more	45 (61.6)	28 (38.4)
All slaveholders	215 (56.0)	169 (44.0)
Nonslaveholders	108 (43.5)	138 (56.5)
Total	323 (51.3)	307 (48.7)

Note: Same sources of information and percentages as in table 4.2.

Chi-square = 98.8% probability that the distribution was not merely random.

Cramer's V = .143, with slaveholders divided into four groups. This is a weaker positive relationship between owning slaves and Democratic voting than in 1834.

Table 4.4. Landholding by region, 1840

	Upper county	Lower county	Total
Value of land owned			
Under $500	206 (33.7%)	44 (9.6%)	250 (23.4%)
$500 to $1,999	165 (27.0)	94 (20.6)	259 (24.2)
$2,000 and over	52 (8.5)	99 (21.7)	151 (14.1)
Nonlandholding	189 (30.9)	220 (48.1)	409 (38.3)
Total	612	457	1,069

Note: Landholdings of adult white male household heads are drawn from the 1840 U.S. Census, supplemented by the 1841 state land tax lists. Percentages are aligned by column, to indicate the relative proportions for each category of landholding in each region.

Chi-square = 100% probability that the distribution was not merely random.

Table 4.5. Slaveholding by region, 1840

	Upper county	Lower county	Total
Slaves owned			
1 to 3	93 (17.6%)	57 (13.2%)	150 (15.6%)
4 to 9	83 (15.7)	64 (14.9)	147 (15.3)
10 to 19	41 (7.7)	65 (15.1)	106 (11.0)
20 or more	30 (5.7)	50 (11.6)	80 (8.3)
All slaveholders	247 (46.7)	236 (54.8)	483 (50.3)
Nonslaveholding	282 (53.3)	195 (45.2)	477 (49.7)
Total	529	431	960

Note: Information about slaveholdings is drawn from the 1840 U.S.
Census. Only adult white male household heads listed there are
included in this table. Percentages are aligned by column, to
indicate the relative proportions for each category of slaveholding in
each region.

The table probably understates the proportion of nonslaveholders
and small slaveholders in the upper county. Of the 109 additional
white male household heads found in the 1841 land tax lists and
tabulated in table 4.4, 83 lived in the upper county. All but 4 owned
land valued at less than $2,000; 54 owned land valued at less than
$500. One may confidently surmise that few additional upper-county
household heads owned many slaves and that a large majority owned no
slaves.

Chi-square = 100% probability that the distribution was not
merely random.

Appendix

Table 4.6. Landholding and party preference, 1840

	Democrat	Whig	Percent of eligible voters participating
Value of land owned			
under $500 (N — 174) (26.0%)	71 (20.9%)	103 (31.4%)	69.6%
$500 to $1,999 (N — 216) (32.3%)	107 (31.5)	109 (33.2)	83.4
$2,000 and over (N — 136) (20.4%)	93 (27.3)	43 (13.1)	90.1
Nonlandholding (N = 142) (21.3%)	69 (20.3)	73 (22.3)	34.7
Total (N — 668)	340	328	62.5

Note: Tabulated vote is for the 1840 presidential election. Percentages in the left margin and in the first two columns indicate the relative proportions for each category of landholding.

The participation percentages in the right column, based on table 4.4, include all adult white male household heads on the 1841 land tax lists and/or the 1840 U.S. Census. The figures for total voting percentage are between 7 and 8 percent low, because 82 of the 750 voters in 1840 cannot be matched to census or tax lists. Most of the 50 Whigs and 32 Democrats not included in the tables probably owned no land or owned only a small amount. Voter turnout among eligible nonlandowners therefore approximated 50 percent.

Chi-square — 100% probability that the distribution was not merely random.

Appendix

Table 4.7. Party preference: white male household heads who were eligible to vote, by region, 1840

	Upper county	Lower county	Total
Privileged	71 (11.6%)	115 (25.1%)	186 (17.4%)
Whig	44 (71.0)	18 (17.8)	62 (38.0)
Democrat	18 (29.0)	83 (82.2)	101 (62.0)
Total voting	62	101	163
Turnout percentage	87.3%	87.8%	87.6%
Smallholding	403 (65.9)	193 (42.2)	596 (55.8)
Whig	188 (63.5)	34 (26.8)	222 (52.5)
Democrat	108 (36.5)	93 (73.3)	201 (47.5)
Total voting	296	127	423
Turnout percentage	73.4%	65.8%	71.0%
Nonpropertied	138 (22.5)	149 (32.6)	287 (26.8)
Whig	30 (63.8)	14 (40)	44 (53.7)
Democrat	17 (36.2)	21 (60)	38 (46.3)
Total voting	47	35	82
Turnout percentage	34.0%	23.5%	28.6%
All eligibles	612 (57.3)	457 (42.7)	1,069
Whig	262 (64.7)	66 (25.1)	328 (49.1)
Democrat	143 (35.3)	197 (74.9)	340 (50.9)
Total voting	405	263	668
Turnout percentage	66.2%	57.5%	62.5%

Note: Information is based on 1840 U.S. Census (population and slave schedules) plus state land tax records for 1841. Privileged households owned ten or more slaves. Smallholding households included slaveholders with fewer than ten slaves, plus nonslaveholders who owned land. Nonpropertied households owned neither land nor slaves.

Only those voters who can be matched to census and land tax lists are included; turnout percentages, especially for nonpropertied voters, are therefore too low (see table 4.6).

Table 5.1. Voter turnout and party preference, 1840-60

Date and type of election	Turnout	Percentage	Whig percentage
November 1840 (President)	750	70%	50.4%
April 1841 (Assembly)	725	68	52.7
April 1842 (Assembly)	735	69	49.3
April 1843 (Assembly)	571	53	51.7
April 1844 (Assembly)	668	62	45.1
November 1844 (President)	715	67	45.6
April 1845 (Assembly)	498	47	32.9
April 1846 (Assembly)	635	59	45.7
April 1847 (Assembly)	588	55	47.4
April 1848 (Assembly)	720	67	52.1
November 1848 (President)	647	61	52.6
April 1849 (Assembly)	756	71	53.2
April 1850 (Assembly)	730	68	51.9
(Convention)	591	55	
August 1850 (Convention Delegates)	400	37	
October 1851 (Constitutional ratification)	378	35	
(Assembly)	324	30	59.3
December 1851 (Assembly)	911	70	55.0
December 1851 (Governor)	885	68	53.6
May 1852 (Sheriff)	878	68	44.6
November 1852 (President)	954	73	52.2
May 1853 (Assembly)	563	43	75.3
May 1854 (Local)	728	56	
May 1855 (Assembly)	1,080	83	47.1
May 1855 (Governor)	1,059	81	46.2

Table 5.1 (cont.)

May 1856 (Sheriff)	1,034	80	45.8
November 1856 (President)	1,028	79	44.6
May 1857 (Assembly)	980	75	48.2
May 1858 (Sheriff)	933	72	46.2
May 1859 (Assembly)	1,065	82	50.9
May 1859 (Governor)	1,032	79	52.4
May 1860 (Sheriff)	990	76	47.9
November 1860 (President)	1,115	86	48.8
February 1861 (Secession)	942	72	
May 1861 (Secession)	921	71	

Note: Figures in the column entitled "Percentage," which indicate the proportion of eligible voters actually voting, are presented as whole numbers and should be regarded as educated estimates. From 1840 through October 1851, they are calculated on the basis of 1,069 eligible voters, a figure derived from information in the 1840 U.S. Census and the 1841 state land tax lists (see table 4.1). In December 1851 the number of eligible voters increased, as Virginia adopted unrestricted suffrage for white males age twenty-one and older. The U.S. Censuses of 1850 and 1860 suggest that the number of white males aged twenty or older increased from 1,346 to 1,385, even though total white population declined slightly from 5,971 to 5,713. A figure of 1,300 reasonably approximates the number of eligible voters during the 1850s. Of the white males age twenty or older in Southampton at any given time during the 1850s, perhaps 3 percent would not yet have achieved their twenty-first birthday and perhaps 2 percent would not have lived in the county long enough to have established eligibility. A voter needed to have lived in the state for two years and the county for one year.

Figures in the column entitled "Whig percentage" indicate the proportion of those voting who favored Whig candidates or candidates of Whig successor parties (American, Opposition, Constitutional Union).

In April 1850 Southampton voters favored calling a convention, 567 to 24. At the subsequent election for convention delegates in August 1850 most Southampton voters favored a bipartisan slate. Voters in October 1851 opposed ratification of the new constitution, as only 125 of 378 voted in its favor. Whigs won a plurality victory for sheriff in May 1852, as Democrats divided their vote. In May 1854 a Whig sheriff was elected without opposition as Democrats won the other local contests. In February 1861 a secessionist delegate to the state convention won narrowly, 486 to 458; however, antisecessionists narrowly carried the ballot question to require a popular referendum on any convention action, 466 to 460. All 921 voters in May 1861 favored secession.

Appendix

Table 5.2. 1848 presidential race: residence of voters

	Cass (Dem.)	Taylor (Whig)
Upper county	119 (30.3%)	274 (69.7%)
Lower county	188 (74.0)	66 (26.0)
Total	307 (47.5)	340 (52.5)

Chi-square = 100% probability that the distribution was not merely random.

Phi = .428. Phi, a measure of association, ranges from a value of -1 to +1. The indicated figure, .428, suggests a significant relationship between residence and party preference.

Table 5.3. 1848 presidential race: slaveholding of voters

	Cass (Dem.)	Taylor (Whig)
Slaves owned		
1 to 3	41 (49.4%)	42 (50.6%)
4 to 9	47 (48.5)	50 (51.5)
10 to 19	60 (63.2)	35 (36.8)
20 or more	34 (55.7)	27 (44.3)
All slaveholders	182 (54.2)	154 (45.8)
Nonslaveholders	125 (40.2)	186 (59.8)
Total	307 (47.5)	340 (52.5)

Note: Slaveholdings are defined by household. Household membership is determined through the 1850 U.S. Census and 1849 state land taxes. Voters whose names appear in neither place are listed here as nonslaveholders.

Chi-square = 99.9% probability that the distribution was not merely random with slaveholders divided into four groups; 100% probability that the distribution was not merely random with slaveholders considered together.

Cramer's V = .166 with slaveholders divided into four groups.

Phi = .140 with slaveholders considered together.

Appendix

Table 5.4. 1851 legislative race: residence of voters

	Bryant (Dem.)	Pretlow (Whig)	Total
Upper county	174 (30.3%)	400 (69.7%)	574 (63.0%)
Lower County	236 (70.0)	101 (30.0)	337 (37.0)
Total	410 (45.0)	501 (55.0)	911

Chi-square — 100% probability that the distribution was not merely random.

Phi = .385.

Table 5.5. 1851 legislative race: slaveholding of voters

	Bryant (Dem.)	Pretlow (Whig)
Slaves owned		
1 to 3	53 (45.7%)	63 (54.3%)
4 to 9	64 (48.5)	68 (51.5)
10 to 19	65 (57.0)	49 (43.0)
20 or more	42 (54.5)	35 (45.5)
All slaveholders	224 (51.0)	215 (49.0)
Nonslaveholders	186 (39.4)	286 (60.6)
Total	410 (45.0)	501 (55.0)

Note: Slaveholdings are defined by household. Household membership is determined through the 1850 U.S. Census and 1849 state land taxes. Voters whose names appear in neither place are listed here as nonslaveholders.

Chi-square — 99.7% probability that the distribution was not merely random with slaveholders divided into four groups; 100% probability that the distribution was not merely random with slaveholders considered together.

Cramer's $\underline{V}$ = .133 with slaveholders divided into four groups.

Phi — .117 with slaveholders considered together.

Table 5.6. Behavior of new voters by region, 1851

	Bryant (Dem.)	Pretlow (Whig)	Total
Upper county	106 (35.7%)	191 (64.3%)	297 (62.4%)
Nonslaveholder	69 (35.4)	126 (64.6)	195 (65.7)
Slaveholder	37 (36.3)	65 (63.7)	102 (34.3)
Lower county	118 (65.9)	61 (34.1)	179 (37.6)
Nonslaveholder	59 (60.2)	39 (39.8)	98 (54.7)
Slaveholder	59 (72.8)	22 (27.2)	81 (45.3)
Total county	224 (47.1)	252 (52.9)	476
Nonslavenolder	128 (43.7)	165 (56.3)	293 (61.6)
Slaveholder	96 (52.5)	87 (47.5)	183 (38.4)

Note: Slaveholdings are defined by household. Household membership is determined through the 1850 U.S. Census and 1849 state land taxes. Voters whose names appear in neither place are listed here as nonslaveholders.

Table 5.7. Voter categories, 1851-55

	Repeat voter	Switching voter	New voter	Total
Democrat	277 (48.6%)	34 (6.0%)	259 (45.4%)	570
Whig	306 (62.6)	10 (2.0)	173 (35.4)	489
Total	583 (55.0)	44 (4.2)	432 (40.8)	1,059
Percentage Democratic	47.5%	77.3%	60.0%	53.8%

Table 5.8. 1851 gubernatorial race: residence of voters

	Wise (Dem.)	Flournoy (Amer.)	Total
Upper county	208 (32.3%)	437 (69.7%)	645 (60.9%)
Lower county	362 (87.4)	52 (12.6)	414 (39.1)
Total	570 (53.8)	489 (46.2)	1,059

Chi-square — 100% probability that the distribution was not merely random.

Phi = .540.

Table 5.9. Voting by slaveholding and region, 1851-55

| | 1851 | | 1855 | |
	Dem.	Whig	Dem.	Amer.
Members of nonslaveholding families	186 (39.4%)	286 (60.6%)	308 (50.5%)	302 (49.5%)
Upper county	93 (28.4)	234 (71.6)	108 (27.8)	280 (72.2)
Lower county	93 (64.1)	52 (35.9)	200 (90.1)	22 (9.9)
Members of slaveholding families	224 (51.0)	215 (49.0)	262 (58.5)	187 (41.6)
Upper county	81 (32.8)	166 (67.2)	100 (38.9)	157 (61.1)
Lower county	143 (74.5)	49 (25.5)	162 (84.4)	30 (15.6)
Total	410 (45.0)	501 (55.0)	570 (53.8)	489 (46.2)

Chi-square = 100% probability both in 1851 and 1855 that observed patterns of residence and party preference, when controlling for slaveholding, were not merely random.

Phi for nonslaveholders in 1851 = .337. Residence showed a strong relationship to party, with upper-county nonslaveholders more likely to vote Whig and lower-county nonslaveholders more likely to vote Democratic.

Phi for slaveholders in 1851 = .414. The voting behavior of slaveholders had an even stronger relationship to residence.

Phi for nonslaveholders in 1855 = .599. This remarkably high figure reflects the polarization of nonslaveholder voting in 1855: overwhelmingly Whig in the upper county, and even more overwhelmingly Democratic in the lower county.

Phi for slaveholders in 1855 = .456. The voting behavior of slaveholders had a strong relationship to residence, but not so strong as among nonslaveholders.

Table 5.9 (cont.)

Chi-square for the entire county in 1851 = 100% probability that the voting behavior of slaveholders and nonslaveholders was not merely random.

Phi for the entire county in 1851 = .117, that is, a significant positive relationship between slaveholding and Democratic voting.

Chi-square for the upper county in 1851 = 73.9% probability that the voting behavior of slaveholders and nonslaveholders was not merely random; in other words, upper-county slaveholders voted Whig in almost as large a proportion as upper-county nonslaveholders.

Phi for the upper county in 1851 = .047, a weaker positive relationship between slaveholding and Democratic voting than in the county overall.

Chi-square for the lower county for 1851 = 96.0% probability that the voting behavior of slaveholders and nonslaveholders was not merely random.

Phi for the lower county in 1851 = .112, a significant positive relationship between slaveholding and Democratic voting.

Chi-square for the entire county in 1855 = 98.9% probability that the voting behavior of slaveholders and nonslaveholders was not merely random.

Phi for the entire county in 1855 = .078, that is, a smaller positive relationship between slaveholding and Democratic voting than in 1851.

Chi-square for the upper county in 1855 = 99.7% probability that the voting behavior of slaveholders and nonslaveholders was not merely random.

Phi for the upper county in 1855 = .116, a more pronounced difference between the voting behavior of slaveholders and nonslaveholders than in 1851.

Chi-square for the lower county in 1855 = 92.0% probability that the voting behavior of slaveholders and nonslaveholders was not merely random.

Phi for the lower county in 1855 = -.080, a weakly negative relationship between slaveholding and Democratic voting, reversing the pattern in the upper county and the county overall. In other words, lower-county nonslaveholders in 1855 were even more likely than lower county slaveholders to vote Democratic.

Table 5.10. 1855 gubernatorial race: slaveholding of voters

	Wise (Dem.)	Flournoy (Amer.)
Slaves owned		
1 to 3	71 (54.6%)	59 (45.4%)
4 to 9	80 (59.7)	54 (40.3)
10 to 19	78 (63.4)	45 (36.6)
20 or more	33 (53.2)	29 (46.8)
All slaveholders	262 (58.4)	187 (41.6)
Nonslaveholders	308 (50.5)	302 (49.5)
Total	570 (53.8)	489 (46.2)

Note: Slaveholdings are defined by household. Household membership is determined through the 1850 U.S. Census and 1849 state land taxes. Voters whose names appear in neither place are listed here as nonslaveholders.

Chi-square = 94.3% probability that the distribution was not merely random with slaveholders divided into four groups; 98.9% probability that the distribution was not merely random with slaveholders considered together.

Cramer's V = .093 with slaveholders divided into four groups.

Phi = .078 with slaveholders considered together.

Table 5.11. Behavior of new voters by region, 1855

	Wise (Dem.)	Flournoy (Amer.)	Total
Upper county	91 (37.9%)	149 (62.1%)	240 (55.6%)
Nonslaveholder	51 (30.7)	115 (69.3)	166 (69.2)
Slaveholder	40 (54.1)	34 (45.9)	74 (30.8)
Lower county	168 (87.5)	24 (12.5)	192 (44.4)
Nonslaveholder	114 (89.8)	13 (10.2)	127 (66.1)
Slaveholder	54 (83.1)	11 (16.9)	65 (33.9)
Total county	259 (60.0)	173 (40.0)	432
Nonslaveholder	165 (56.3)	128 (43.7)	293 (67.8)
Slaveholder	94 (67.6)	45 (32.4)	139 (32.2)

Note: Slaveholdings are defined by household. Household membership is determined through the 1850 U.S. Census and 1849 state land taxes. Voters whose names appear in neither place are listed here as nonslaveholders.

Table 5.12. Voting by age, 1848-55

Age	1848		1851		1855	
	Dem.	Whig	Dem.	Whig	Dem.	Amer.
20-29	67 (45.9%)	79 (54.1%)	126 (44.2%)	159 (55.8%)	154 (53.1%)	136 (46.9%)
30-39	75 (52.4)	68 (47.6)	101 (46.8)	115 (53.2)	120 (55.0)	98 (45.0)
40-49	71 (47.0)	80 (53.0)	72 (45.0)	88 (55.0)	85 (50.9)	82 (49.1)
50-59	36 (46.1)	42 (53.9)	53 (49.5)	54 (50.5)	63 (50)	63 (50)
60+	19 (42.2)	26 (57.8)	26 (35.1)	48 (64.9)	52 (57.8)	38 (42.2)
Total	268 (47.6)	295 (52.4)	378 (44.9)	464 (55.1)	474 (53.2)	417 (46.8)

Chi-square = 71.3% probability that the 1848 results were merely random and a 74.9% probability that the 1855 results were merely random. Only the 1851 election results offer less than an even chance (38.8%) that the pattern was merely random. The message is plain: the age of the voter had little to do with party preference.

Cramer's $\underline{V}$ = .061 for 1848, .070 for 1851, and .047 for 1855, predictably low values.

Table 5.13. County court members in the 1840s

	June 1843	March 1847
Party		
Democratic	21 (66%)	23 (61%)
Whig	10 (31)	13 (34)
Unknown	1 (3)	2 (5)
Slaveholding, 1840		
1-3	0	1 (3)
4-9	6 (19)	4 (11)
10-19	11 (34)	15 (39)
20+	15 (47)	15 (39)
Nonslaveholding	0	1 (3)
Unknown	0	2 (5)
Residence		
Democratic strongholds in the lower county	14 (12 Dems, 2 Whigs)	18 (14 Dems, 4 Whigs)
Courthouse area and Murfees Depot (center county)	11 (6 Dems, 5 Whigs)	12 (7 Dems, 4 Whigs, 1?)
Whig strongholds in upper county	5 (2 Dems, 3 Whigs)	7 (2 Dems, 5 Whigs)
Unknown	2	1

Note: Those listed as Whigs, both in 1843 and 1847, include three Nullifiers and one Democrat turned Whig.

Table 5.14. County court members elected in the 1850s

	1852	1856
Party		
Democratic	11 (39%)	14 (50%)
Whig	17 (61)	13 (50)
Slaveholding, 1850		
1-3	1 (4)	1 (4)
4-9	6 (21)	3 (11)
10-19	11 (39)	15 (54)
20+	9 (32)	7 (25)
Nonslaveholding	1 (4)	2 (7)

Table 5.15. County court members elected in 1860

Party	
Democratic, 1860 (Breckinridge)	14 (50%)
Union, 1861	1
Secession, 1861	13
Whig, 1860 (Bell)	14 (50)
Union, 1861	13
Secession, 1861	1
Slaveholding, 1860	
1-3	3 (11)
4-9	5 (18)
10-19	9 (32)
20+	10 (35)
Nonslaveholder	1 (4)

Appendix

Table 6.1. Voting by region, 1855-60

	Democratic	Whig	Total
1855 total	570 (53.8%)	489 (46.2%)	1,059
Upper county	208 (32.2)	437 (67.8)	645 (60.9%)
Lower county	362 (87.4)	52 (12.6)	414 (39.1)
1860 total	571 (51.2)	544 (48.8)	1,115
Upper county	206 (31.0)	458 (69.1)	664 (59.6)
Lower county	365 (80.9)	86 (19.1)	451 (40.4)

Note: The 1860 Democratic totals include nine votes for Stephen A. Douglas. The American party vote in 1855 and the Constitutional Union party vote in 1860 are indicated as Whig.

Table 6.2. Slaveholder and nonslaveholder voting, 1855-60

	Democratic	Whig	Total
1855 total	570 (53.8%)	489 (46.2%)	1,059
Nonslaveholder	308 (50.5)	302 (49.5)	610 (57.6%)
Slaveholder	262 (58.4)	187 (41.6)	449 (42.4)
1860 total	571 (51.2)	544 (48.8)	1,115
Nonslaveholder	310 (46.8)	352 (53.2)	662 (59.4)
Slaveholder	261 (57.6)	192 (42.6)	453 (40.6)

Note: Nonslaveholders and slaveholders are defined by household. See table 6.1 for an explanation of the Democratic and Whig vote.

Table 6.3. Voting by slaveholding and region, 1855-60

	1855		1860	
	Dem.	Whig	Dem.	Whig
Members of nonslaveholding families	308 (50.5%)	302 (49.5%)	310 (46.8%)	352 (53.2%)
Upper county	108 (27.8)	280 (72.2)	105 (25.3)	310 (74.7)
Lower county	200 (90.1)	22 (9.9)	205 (83.0)	42 (17.0)
Members of slaveholding families	262 (58.5)	187 (41.6)	261 (57.6)	192 (42.4)
Upper county	100 (38.9)	157 (61.1)	101 (40.6)	148 (59.4)
Lower county	162 (84.4)	30 (15.6)	160 (78.4)	44 (21.6)
Total	570 (53.8)	489 (46.2)	571 (51.2)	544 (48.8)

Note: Nonslaveholders and slaveholders are defined by household. See table 6.1 for an explanation of the Democratic and Whig vote.

Appendix

Table 6.4. Voting by region, 1860-61

	Democratic	Whig	Total
1860 total	571 (51.2%)	544 (48.8%)	1,115
Upper county	206 (31.0)	458 (69.1)	664 (59.6%)
Lower county	365 (80.9)	86 (19.1)	451 (40.4)

	Secession	Union	Total
1861 total	460 (49.7)	466 (50.3)	926
Upper county	125 (21.8)	447 (78.2)	572 (61.8)
Lower county	335 (94.6)	19 (5.4)	354 (38.2)

Note: Nonslaveholders and slaveholders are defined by household. See table 6.1 for an explanation of the Democratic and Whig vote. All 1861 calculations are based on votes for and against "reference." Union voters favored a popular referendum to approve any convention action; secession voters opposed the referendum.

Chi-square = 100% probability that observed patterns of upper-county and lower-county voting behavior, both in 1860 and in 1861, were not merely random.

Phi = .490 for 1860; .707 for 1861. These figures indicate very strong relationships between voting behavior and residence, especially in 1861.

Table 6.5. Voting by districts, 1860-61

	1860 Dem.	1860 Whig	1861 Secession	1861 Union	Falloff percentage	Slaveholder percentage
Lower county	365 (80.9%)	86 (19.1%)	335 (94.6%)	19 (5.4%)	21.5%	43.8%
Drewrysville	62 (75.6)	20 (24.4)	62 (100)	0 (0)	24.4	69.3
Cross Keys	182 (83.9)	35 (16.1)	170 (97.7)	4 (2.3)	20.2	40.4
Joyners Store	103 (79.2)	27 (20.7)	93 (94.9)	5 (5.1)	24.6	37.3
Upper county	206 (31.0)	458 (69.0)	125 (21.9)	447 (78.1)	13.9	35.7
Murfees Depot	76 (60.3)	50 (39.7)	63 (55.3)	51 (44.7)	9.5	40.9
Black Crk. Church	9 (8.7)	94 (91.3)	2 (2.0)	100 (98.0)	1.0	14.3
Berlin	70 (35.9)	125 (64.1)	23 (14.7)	133 (85.3)	20.0	35.8
Faisons Store	3 (4.1)	71 (95.9)	0 (0)	67 (100)	9.5	50.0
Jerusalem	66 (35.1)	122 (64.9)	47 (30.9)	105 (69.1)	19.1	36.7
Total	571 (51.2)	544 (48.8)	460 (49.7)	466 (50.3)	17.0	38.9

Note: Slaveholding, partisan affiliation, and stance on secession are all defined as in table 6.4.

Falloff percentage = the percentage of reduction in voter turnout in February 1861, compared with November 1860.

Slaveholder percentage = the proportion of voters from slaveholding households who participated in one or the other of the two elections at that voting district.

The aggregate numbers for the upper and lower county do not precisely match the combined district vote, because a few upper-county residents voted at lower-county polling places, while several dozen voters from the lower county cast ballots at upper-county polling places.

Table 6.6. Slaveholdings of voters, 1860-61

	Dem.	Whig	Total
1860 total	571 (51.2%)	544 (48.8%)	1,115
Slaveholder	261 (57.6)	192 (42.6)	453 (40.6%)
1-3 slaves	87 (48.3)	93 (51.7)	180 (16.1)
4-9 slaves	78 (58.2)	56 (41.8)	134 (12.0)
1-9 slaves	165 (52.5)	149 (47.5)	314 (28.1)
10-19 slaves	58 (75.3)	19 (24.7)	77 (6.9)
20+ slaves	38 (61.3)	24 (38.7)	62 (5.6)
10+ slaves	96 (69.0)	43 (31.0)	139 (12.5)
Nonslaveholder	310 (46.8)	352 (53.2)	662 (59.4)

	Secession	Union	Total
1861 total	460 (49.7)	466 (50.3)	926
Slaveholder	223 (61.3)	141 (38.7)	364 (39.3)
1-3 slaves	81 (52.3)	74 (47.7)	155 (16.7)
4-9 slaves	63 (61.8)	39 (38.2)	102 (11.0)
1-9 slaves	144 (56.0)	113 (44.0)	257 (27.7)
10-19 slaves	46 (76.7)	14 (23.3)	60 (6.5)
20+ slaves	33 (70.2)	14 (29.8)	47 (5.1)
10+ slaves	79 (73.8)	28 (26.2)	107 (11.6)
Nonslaveholder	237 (42.2)	325 (57.8)	562 (60.7)

Note: Slaveholding, partisan affiliation, and stance on secession are all defined as in table 6.4.

Table 6.7. Voting by slaveholding and region, 1860-61

	1860		1861	
	Dem.	Whig	Secession	Union
Members of nonslaveholding families	310 (46.8%)	352 (53.2%)	237 (42.2%)	325 (57.8%)
Upper county	105 (25.3)	310 (74.7)	51 (13.8)	318 (86.2)
Lower county	205 (83.0)	42 (17.0)	186 (96.4)	7 (3.8)
Members of slaveholding families	261 (57.6)	192 (42.4)	223 (61.3)	141 (38.7)
Upper county	101 (40.6)	148 (59.4)	74 (36.5)	129 (63.5)
Lower county	160 (78.4)	44 (21.6)	149 (92.5)	12 (7.5)
Total	571 (51.2)	544 (48.8)	460 (49.7)	466 (50.3)

Note: Slaveholding, partisan affiliation, and stance on secession are all defined as in table 6.4.

Chi-square for the entire county in 1860 = 100% probability that the voting behavior of slaveholders and nonslaveholders was not merely random.

Phi for the entire county in 1860 = .106, that is, a significant positive relationship between slaveholding and Democratic voting.

Chi-square for the upper county in 1860 = 100% probability that the voting behavior of slaveholders and nonslaveholders was not merely random.

Phi for the upper county in 1860 = .160, an even more significant positive relationship between slaveholding and Democratic voting than in the county overall.

Chi-square for the lower county in 1860 = 78.1% probability that the voting behavior of slaveholders and nonslaveholders was not merely random. This is a low figure, suggesting little significant difference between the voting behavior of lower-county slaveholders and nonslaveholders.

Phi for the lower county in 1860 = -.058, a weakly negative relationship between slaveholding and Democratic voting, reversing the pattern in the upper county and the county overall.

Table 6.7 (cont.)

Chi-square for the entire county in 1861 - 100% probability that the voting behavior of slaveholders and nonslaveholders was not merely random.

Phi for the entire county in 1861 - .187, that is, a larger positive relationship between slaveholding and support for secession than between slaveholding and Democratic voting in 1860.

Chi-square for the upper county in 1861 - 100% probability that the voting behavior of slaveholders and nonslaveholders was not merely random.

Phi for the upper county in 1861 - .262, as in the county overall, a larger positive relationship between slaveholding and support for secession than between slaveholding and Democratic voting in 1860.

Chi-square for the lower county in 1861 - 88.8% probability that the voting behavior of slaveholders and nonslaveholders was not merely random.

Phi for the lower county in 1861 - -.085, once again a weakly negative relationship between slaveholding and support for secession, reversing the pattern in the upper county and the county overall.

Table 6.8. Voter transitions, 1860-61

1860	Union	1861 Secession	Nonvoter	Total
Democrat	33 (5.8%)	357 (62.5%)	181 (31.7%)	571
Whig	357 (65.6)	38 (7.0)	149 (27.4)	544
Nonvoter	76 (53.9)	65 (46.1)		141
Total	466	460	330	1,256

Note: Slaveholding, partisan affiliation, and stance on secession are all defined as in table 6.4.

Table 6.9. Voter transitions by region, 1860-61

| | | 1861 | | |
1860	Union	Secession	Nonvoter	Total
Upper county	447 (59.1%)	125 (16.5%)	184 (24.3%)	756
Democrat	27 (13.3)	98 (48.3)	81 (39.3)	206
Whig	348 (76.0)	7 (1.5)	103 (22.5)	458
Nonvoter	72 (78.3)	20 (21.7)		92
Lower county	19 (3.8)	335 (67.0)	146 (29.2)	500
Democrat	6 (1.6)	259 (71.0)	100 (27.4)	365
Whig	9 (10.5)	31 (36.0)	46 (53.5)	86
Nonvoter	4 (8.2)	45 (91.8)		49
Total	466	460	330	1,256

Note: Slaveholding, partisan affiliation, and stance on secession are all defined as in table 6.4.

Table 6.10. Voter transitions by slaveholding, 1860-61

1860	Union	Secession	1861 Nonvoter	Total
Nonslaveholders	325 (42.4%)	237 (30.9)	205 (26.7)	767
Democrat	21 (6.8)	178 (57.4)	111 (35.8)	310
Whig	240 (68.2)	18 (5.1)	94 (26.7)	352
Nonvoter	64 (61.0)	41 (39.0)		105
Slaveholders	141 (28.3)	223 (45.6)	125 (25.6)	489
Democrat	12 (4.6)	179 (68.6)	70 (26.8)	261
Whig	117 (60.9)	20 (10.4)	55 (28.7)	192
Nonvoter	12 (33.3)	24 (66.7)		36
Total	466	460	330	1,256

Note: Slaveholding, partisan affiliation, and stance on secession are all defined as in table 6.4.

Table 6.11. Voting of church members, by region and slaveholding, 1855-61

	Dem.	Whig	Total
1855 total	61 (47.3%)	68 (52.7%)	129
Upper county	28 (30.4)	64 (69.6)	92
Nonslaveholding	7 (16.3)	36 (85.7)	43
Slaveholding	21 (42.9)	28 (57.1)	49
Lower county	33 (89.2)	4 (10.8)	37
Nonslaveholding	10 (90.9)	1 (9.1)	11
Slaveholding	23 (88.5)	3 (11.5)	26
1860 total	89 (58.9)	62 (41.1)	151
Upper county	32 (37.6)	53 (62.4)	85
Nonslaveholding	9 (22.0)	32 (78.0)	41
Slaveholding	23 (52.3)	21 (47.7)	44
Lower county	57 (86.4)	9 (13.6)	66
Nonslaveholding	16 (80)	4 (20)	20
Slaveholding	41 (89.1)	5 (10.9)	46

	Secession	Union	Total
1861 total	72 (57.1)	54 (42.9)	126
Upper county	20 (27.8)	52 (72.2)	72
Nonslaveholding	3 (7.5)	37 (92.5)	40
Slaveholding	17 (53.1)	15 (46.9)	32
Lower county	52 (96.3)	2 (3.8)	54
Nonslaveholding	13 (100)		13
Slaveholding	39 (95.1)	2 (4.9)	41

Note: A few upper-county residents belonging to lower-county churches are classified by residence. Slaveholding, partisan affiliation, and stance on secession are all defined as in table 6.4.

Appendix

Table 6.12. Voting of church members, by slaveholding, 1860-61

| | 1860 | | 1861 | |
	Dem.	Whig	Secession	Union
Slaves owned				
1 to 3	20 (64.5%)	11 (35.5%)	22 (73.3%)	8 (26.7%)
4 to 9	18 (66.7)	9 (33.3)	12 (66.7)	6 (33.3)
10 to 19	11 (78.6)	3 (31.4)	12 (92.3)	1 (7.7)
20 or more	15 (83.3)	3 (16.7)	10 (83.3)	2 (16.7)
All slaveholders	64 (71.1)	26 (28.9)	56 (76.7)	17 (23.3)
Nonslaveholders	25 (41.0)	36 (59.0)	16 (30.2)	37 (69.8)
Total	89 (58.9)	62 (41.1)	72 (57.1)	54 (42.9)

Note: Slaveholding, partisan affiliation, and stance on secession are all defined as in table 6.4.

Table 6.13. Voting by occupation, 1860-61

	1860		1861	
	Dem.	Whig	Secession	Union
Farmers	268 (51.0%)	258 (49.0%)	218 (49.1%)	226 (50.9%)
Upper county	96 (30.8)	216 (69.2)	58 (21.2)	216 (78.8)
Nonslaveholding	37	114	14	126
Slaveholding	59	102	44	90
Lower county	172 (80.4)	42 (19.6)	160 (94.1)	10 (5.9)
Nonslaveholding	61	11	56	2
Slaveholding	111	31	104	8
Overseers	30 (62.5)	18 (37.5)	22 (55)	18 (45)
Upper county	5 (25)	15 (75)	2 (11.8)	15 (88.2)
Nonslaveholding	4	8	2	8
Slaveholding	1	7	0	7
Lower county	25 (89.3)	3 (10.7)	20 (87.0)	3 (13.0)
Nonslaveholding	14	1	13	1
Slaveholding	11	2	7	2
Laborers	43 (33.1)	87 (66.9)	25 (22.5)	86 (77.5)
Upper county	31 (26.3)	87 (73.7)	20 (19.1)	85 (80.9)
Nonslaveholding	25	77	13	76
Slaveholding	6	10	7	9
Lower county	12(100)	0 (0)	5 (83.3)	1 (16.7)
Nonslaveholding	11	0	4	1
Slaveholding	1	0	1	0
Skilled tradesmen	19 (50)	19 (50)	17 (47.2)	19 (52.8)
Upper county	9 (34.6)	17 (65.4)	6 (25)	18 (75)

Table 6.13 (cont.)

Nonslaveholding	5		13		4		14
Slaveholding	4		4		2		4
Lower county	10	(83.3)	2	(16.7)	11	(91.7)	1 (8.3)
Nonslaveholding	8		2		9		0
Slaveholding	2		0		2		1
Professionals	37	(58.7)	26	(41.3)	33	(64.7)	18 (35.3)
Upper county	19	(46.3)	22	(56.6)	14	(43.8)	18 (56.2)
Nonslaveholding	4		9		3		8
Slaveholding	15		13		11		10
Lower county	18	(81.8)	4	(18.2)	19(100)		0 (0)
Nonslaveholding	7		2		6		0
Slaveholding	11		2		13		0
Total	397	(49.3)	408	(50.7)	315	(46.2)	367 (53.8)
Upper county	160	(30.9)	357	(69.3)	100	(22.1)	352 (77.9)
Nonslaveholding	75	(25.3)	221	(74.7)	36	(13.4)	232 (86.6)
Slaveholding	85	(38.5)	136	(61.5)	64	(34.8)	120 (65.2)
Lower county	237	(82.3)	51	(17.7)	215	(93.5)	15 (6.5)
Nonslaveholding	101	(86.3)	16	(13.7)	88	(95.7)	4 (4.3)
Slaveholding	136	(79.5)	35	(20.5)	127	(92.0)	11 (8.0)

Note: Slaveholding, partisan affiliation, and stance on secession are all defined as in table 6.4.

Table 6.14. Voting by age, 1860-61

Age	1860		1861	
	Dem.	Whig	Secession	Union
20-29	163 (54.3%)	137 (46.7%)	138 (55.4%)	111 (44.6%)
30-39	121 (51.7)	113 (48.3)	95 (48.7)	100 (51.3)
40-49	94 (54.7)	78 (45.3)	83 (53.5)	72 (46.5)
50-59	78 (49.1)	81 (50.9)	55 (44.4)	69 (55.6)
60 or older	38 (44.7)	47 (55.3)	29 (42.0)	40 (58.0)
Total	494 (52.0)	456 (48.0)	400 (50.5)	392 (49.5)

Note: Slaveholding, partisan affiliation, and stance on secession are all defined as in table 6.4.

Chi square = 52.4% probability that the 1860 pattern was not merely random; 86.9% probability that the 1861 pattern was not merely random.

Cramer's V = .061 for 1860 and .095 for 1861, predictably low values, indicating no more than a slight relationship between age and party preference or support for secession.

Table 6.15. Voting by age, upper county, 1860-61

Age	1860		1861	
	Dem.	Whig	Secession	Union
20-49	136 (33.3%)	272 (66.7%)	89 (24.5%)	274 (75.5%)
Nonslaveholder	59 (25.6)	172 (74.4)	35 (15.8)	186 (84.2)
Slaveholder	77 (43.5)	100 (56.5)	54 (38.0)	88 (62.0)
50 or older	44 (29.3)	106 (70.7)	22 (18.2)	99 (81.8)
Nonslaveholder	24 (28.2)	61 (71.8)	5 (7.6)	61 (92.4)
Slaveholder	20 (30.8)	45 (69.2)	17 (30.9)	38 (69.1)
Total	180 (32.3)	378 (67.7)	111 (22.9)	373 (77.1)

Note: Slaveholding, partisan affiliation, and stance on secession are all defined as in table 6.4.

Appendix

Table 7.1. County court members, 1860, 1864, 1866

	1860	1864	1866
Party			
Democratic, 1860	14 (50%)	10 (35%)	9 (33%)
Union, 1861	1	1	0
Secession, 1861	13	9	8
Not voting, 1861			1
Whig, 1860	14 (50)	17 (61)	17 (63)
Union, 1861	13	10	10
Secession, 1861	1	1	1
Unknown	0 (0)	1 (4)	1 (4)
Slaveholding, 1860			
1-3	3 (11)	7 (25)	3 (11)
4-9	5 (18)	4 (14)	5 (19)
10-19	9 (32)	6 (21)	5 (19)
20+	10 (35)	9 (32)	11 (41)
Nonslaveholder	1 (4)	1 (4)	2 (7)
Unknown	0 (0)	1 (4)	1 (4)

Note: Slaveholding, partisan affiliation, and stance on secession are all defined as in table 6.4.

Appendix

Table 9.1. Voting, 1867

	White	Black	Total
Registration	1,124 (46.9%)	1,273 (53.1%)	2,397
Votes cast	632 (33.7)	1,242 (66.3)	1,874
Turnout percentage of registered voters	56.2%	97.6%	
For a convention	20	1,242	1,262
Against a convention	612	0	612
Convention delegate			
John Brown (Radical Republican)	1	1,242	1,243
Luther R. Edwards (Democrat)	403	0	403
John Pretlow (Whig Unionist)	223	0	223

Note: Voting returns are based on Election Records, Southampton County, Oct. 22, 1867, transfer box 19, Hollinger (clamshell) box, VSLA. Registration figures for 1867, together with slightly different voting returns, are found in Tally of 1867 Registration and Voting, pp. 4-5, Memorandum from Headquarters, First Military District (Virginia), May 10, 1869, VSLA.

Table 9.2. Voting by districts, 1867

	Convention		Convention delegate		
	Yes	No	Brown	Edwards	Pretlow
Lower county	713	224	710	219	7
Whites	3	224	0	219	7
Blacks	710	0	710	0	0
Drewrysville	275	63	274	61	3
Whites	1	63	0	61	3
Blacks	274	0	274	0	0
Boykins Store	298	80	296	77	4
Whites	2	80	0	77	4
Blacks	296	0	296	0	0
Joyners Store	140	81	140	81	0
Whites	0	81	0	81	0
Blacks	140	0	140	0	0
Upper county	549	388	533	184	216
Whites	17	388	1	184	216
Blacks	532	0	532	0	0
Franklin	164	83	153	51	39
Whites	12	83	1	51	39
Blacks	152	0	152	0	0
Jerusalem	179	73	179	54	25
Whites	0	73	0	54	25
Blacks	179	0	179	0	0
Berlin	79	155	79	78	70
Whites	0	155	0	78	70
Blacks	79	0	79	0	0

Table 9.2 (cont.)

Ivor	127	77	122	1	82
Whites	5	77	0	1	82
Blacks	122	0	122	0	0
Total	1,262	612	1,243	403	223
Whites	20	612	1	403	223
Blacks	1,242	0	1,242	0	0

Note: Voting returns are based on Election Records, Southampton County, Oct. 22, 1867, transfer box 19, Hollinger (clamshell) box, VSLA.

Appendix

Table 9.3. Voting, 1869

	White	Black	Total
Registration	1,288 (47.1%)	1,448 (52.9%)	2,736
Votes cast	1,221 (49.3)	1,257 (50.7)	2,478
Turnout percentage of registered voters	94.8%	86.8%	
For the constitution			2,411
Against the constitution			54
For the test oath and disfranchisement			498
Against the test oath and disfranchisement			1,449
Governor			
Gilbert C. Walker (Conservative-Republican)			1,275
Henry H. Wells (Republican)			1,196
Congress			
D. J. Godwin (Conservative)			1,269
James H. Platt (Republican)			1,197
House of Delegates			
Richard U. Burges (Conservative)			1,273
Joseph Gregory (Republican)			1,188

Note: Information based on Returns of Election of July 6, 1869, pt. 1 (pp. 6-7), pt. 2 (pp. 4-5), pt. 3 (p. 4), pt. 5 (p. 32), Memorandum from Headquarters, First Military District (Virginia), Aug. 18, 1869, VSLA. Slightly differing numbers, used here, are from Election Records, Southampton County, July 6, 1869, transfer box 11a, Hollinger (clamshell) box, VSLA.

Table 9.4. Voters by districts, 1869

	White	Black	Total
Lower county	492 (40.5%)	723 (59.5%)	1,215
Drewrysville	124 (33.0)	252 (67.0)	376
Boykins Store	135 (38.9)	212 (61.1)	347
Popes Store	68 (39.3)	105 (60.7)	173
Joyners Store	165 (51.7)	154 (48.3)	319
Upper county	729 (57.7)	534 (42.3)	1,263
Franklin	186 (53.0)	165 (47.0)	351
Jerusalem	169 (51.7)	158 (48.3)	327
Berlin	229 (71.3)	92 (28.7)	321
Ivor	145 (54.9)	119 (45.1)	264
Total	1,221 (49.3)	1,257 (50.7)	2,478

Note: Information based on Election Records, Southampton County, July 6, 1869, transfer box 11a, Hollinger (clamshell) box, VSLA.

Table 9.5. Voting by districts, 1869

	Radical	Conservative	Total
Lower county	711	503	1,214
Whites	1	490	491
Blacks	710	13	723
Drewrysville	248	128	376
Whites	0	123	123
Blacks	248	4	252
Boykins Store and Popes Store	310	210	520
Whites	1	202	203
Blacks	309	8	317
Joyners Store	153	166	319
Whites	0	165	165
Blacks	153	1	154
Upper county	485	774	1,259
Whites	0	725	725
Blacks	485	49	534
Franklin	158	193	351
Whites	0	186	186
Blacks	158	7	165
Jerusalem	152	171	323
Whites	0	165	165
Blacks	152	6	158
Berlin	60	261	321
Whites	0	229	229
Blacks	60	32	92

Table 9.5 (cont.)

Ivor	115	149	264
Whites	0	145	145
Blacks	115	4	119
Total	1,196	1,277	2,473
Whites	1	1,215	1,216
Blacks	1,195	62	1,257

Note: Information based on Election Records, Southampton County, July 6, 1869, transfer box 11a, Hollinger (clamshell) box, VSLA. The results vary slightly from totals in tables 9.3 and 9.4; four white voters from Jerusalem and one from Drewrysville apparently did not cast valid ballots.

NOTES

ॐ

Abbreviations

LC   Library of Congress
NA   National Archives
SCHS   Southampton County Historical Society, Courtland, Va.
VHS   Virginia Historical Society, Richmond
VMHB   *Virginia Magazine of History and Biography*
VSLA   Virginia State Library and Archives, Richmond

PREFACE

1. William Styron, *The Confessions of Nat Turner* (New York: Random House, 1967), "Author's Note."

2. Henry Irving Tragle, *The Southampton Slave Revolt of 1831* (Amherst: Univ. of Massachusetts Press, 1971); Stephen B. Oates, *The Fires of Jubilee: Nat Turner's Fierce Rebellion* (New York: Harper and Row, 1975), "Author's Foreword"; Thomas C. Parramore, *Southampton County, Virginia* (Charlottesville: Univ. Press of Virginia, 1978), 65–121.

3. Note, however, Philip J. Schwarz's call for a more systematic social history of the insurrection: " 'A Sense of Their Own Power': Self-Determination in Recent Writings on Black Virginians," *VMHB* 97 (1989): 296–97.

4. The case in point is William J. Cooper, Jr., *The South and the Politics of Slavery, 1828–1856* (Baton Rouge: Louisiana State Univ. Press, 1978).

5. Lacy K. Ford, Jr., "Ties That Bind?" *Reviews in American History* 17 (1989): 70–71.

6. Daniel W. Crofts, *Reluctant Confederates: Upper South Unionists in the Secession Crisis* (Chapel Hill: Univ. of North Carolina Press, 1989).

7. Richmond semiweekly *Enquirer*, Jan. 22, 1835; Norfolk *Virginian*, Sept. 27, 1872; James Maget, "The way things work down here in old Southampton," 1848[?], Majette Family Papers, sec. 3, item 118, VHS; Elliott L. Story diary, May 3, June 22, 29, 1848, Aug. 29, 1851, VHS; letters from "E.," Feb. 12, Mar. 23,

1866, in Richmond semiweekly *Whig*, Feb. 16, Mar. 30, 1866. Terms such as "Old Virginia" (see, for example, Story diary, June 29, 1848) and "Old North State" (for North Carolina) appear also to have been widely used.

PROLOGUE: SOUTHAMPTON TODAY

1. Ironies and coincidences abound. The road used by the rebels carried the same name as the Baptist minister whose critique of slavery was among the most thoroughgoing ever pronounced by a white southerner.

2. William S. Drewry, *The Southampton Insurrection* (Washington, D.C.: Neale Company, 1900), 113; Richmond *Dispatch*, Aug. 9, 12, 1867.

ONE. THE PEOPLES OF OLD SOUTHAMPTON

1. Henry W. Lewis, *Southampton Ridleys and Their Kin* (Chapel Hill: printed privately, 1961), 54–59, 120–23; Jane Turner Censer, *North Carolina Planters and Their Children, 1800–1860* (Baton Rouge: Louisiana State Univ. Press, 1984), 87; Lyndon H. Hart III, "Descendants of Thomas Pretlow and Rebecca Sebrell: An Account of the Pretlow Family of Southampton County and Some of Its Branches" (1983), 61, VSLA; William B. Shands biographical recollections, VHS.

2. Southampton County Court Minutes, June 1839, microfilm, VSLA; Harrison P. Pope to Roswald S. Majette, Apr. 12, 1862, Majette Family Papers, sec. 16, folder 4, VHS.

3. Frank L. Owsley, *The Plain Folk of the Old South* (Baton Rouge: Louisiana State Univ. Press, 1949). Owsley's statistical appendix explains how to cull information from local tax records, the federal population census, the federal agricultural census, and the slave schedules in the federal census (ibid., 150–53).

4. The Sebrell, Rochelle, Denegre, and Trezvant families were definitely Huguenot; the antecedents for the Maget family, though plainly French, are less clear (Famous Families Folder, Edgar B. Jackson Papers, SCHS, in the possession of Gilbert W. Francis, Boykins, Va.; undated draft letter from James Maget to Richard Henry Baker, Majette Family Papers, sec. 1, VHS; Louis P. Jervey, Jr., "The Remarkable Trezvants," typescript, SCHS).

5. Emerson Macaulay Babb, *History of Ivor and Its Environs* (n.p., 1965), 49–53.

6. Lucy Shelvy, legislative petition dated Dec. 15, 1812, VSLA; Elliott L. Story diary, Sept. 2, 1851, June 4, 1857, VHS.

7. R. Crawford Barrett, typed recollection, Aug. 12, 1922, SCHS.

8. Rev. Joshua Leigh, "Meherrin Circuit Steward's Book," Nottoway Chapel Membership Roster, 1859–60, item 103, SCHS; R. Crawford Barrett recollection, SCHS; Daniel W. Cobb diary, Feb. 19, 1856, VHS.

9. Bruce Montgomery Edwards, *The Cobbs of the Tidewater* (Knoxville, Tenn.: Montgomery Publishing Co., 1976), 560–62.

10. F. N. Boney, "Nathaniel Francis, Representative Antebellum Southerner," *Proceedings of the American Philosophical Society* 118 (1974): 452.

11. Hart, "Descendants of Thomas Pretlow," 27.

12. Luther Porter Jackson, *Free Negro Labor and Property Holding in Virginia, 1830–1860* (1942; rept. New York: Atheneum, 1969), 4, 6, 30–31.

13. Parramore, *Southampton County*, 114–16; Southampton County Deed Book, 7:64, Dec. 1787, VSLA.

14. Information on Steward and Taylor from U.S. Agricultural Census, 1850, Southampton County, Nottoway Parish, microfilm at VSLA; Southampton County Land Taxes, Nottoway Parish, 1849, VSLA; Daniel W. Cobb diary, May 11, June 26, 1850, VHS. Steward and Taylor were the only two free blacks in the county in 1850 to own slaves. It is possible that the five slaves owned by Steward and the one owned by Taylor were immediate family members: arrangements of this type circumvented restrictive Virginia laws that required freed slaves to leave the state.

15. U.S. Agricultural Censuses, 1850, 1860, Southampton County, St. Lukes Parish, microfilm at VSLA; Jackson, *Free Negro Labor*, 108, 130.

16. Daniel W. Cobb's slave Louisa apparently was the wife of Davy, who belonged to his father-in-law, Jesse Little. The couple, who lived at Cobb's, had at least six children, four of whom were alive in 1856. Cobb's slave Margaret, who had a child in 1858, was the wife of Charles White, apparently the slave of a neighbor, Susan Woolfram (Cobb diary, Oct. 5, 1843, Jan. 22, 1850, Aug. 24, 1855, Oct. 11, 1856, Sept. 4, 1857, Aug. 19, 1858). An inventory of slaves belonging to John Young Mason, a large slaveholder, is organized on the basis of families: "List of Negroes Belonging to J. Y. Mason," enclosed in Lewis E. Mason to John Young Mason, Jr., Feb. 1, 1855, Mason Family Papers, sec. 42, VHS.

17. Crawford interview in Charles L. Perdue, Jr., Thomas E. Barden, and Robert K. Phillips, eds., *Weevils in the Wheat: Interviews with Virginia Ex-Slaves* (Charlottesville: Univ. Press of Virginia, 1976), 74–77.

18. Ibid., 139–42.

19. Nobody named Pressman lived in Southampton during the antebellum era. In 1840 Joel Presson, who owned eighteen slaves, and Joshua Presson, who owned nineteen slaves, lived within two miles of each other in upper Southampton. They may well have been brothers. By 1850 Joshua Presson owned only three slaves, and Joel Presson had departed or died. Neither appears likely to have been the owner of Hines, who was born in 1835. All the Pressons listed in the 1860 census were smallholders. By far the most likely possibility is John A. Persons, a sixty-two-year-old resident of the lower county in 1860, who was a very large planter. He cultivated 700 improved acres, raised fifty bales of cotton, owned forty-eight slaves, and hired eight others. A probable son, twenty-seven-year-old Junius Persons, who owned seven slaves and hired four others, lived nearby. Another probable son, twenty-one-year-old Peter Persons, lived with John A. Persons. All three voted Whig in 1860. Junius Persons belonged to Clarksbury Methodist Church.

20. F. N. Boney, ed., *Slave Life in Georgia: A Narrative of the Life, Sufferings, and Escape of John Brown, a Fugitive Slave* (1855; rept. Savannah: Beehive Press,

1972), 111. A different former slave with the same name played an important role in Southampton during Reconstruction. See chapter 8 below.

21. Ibid., 5–11.

22. Ibid., 13–14, 20, 109–11, 145, 158.

23. Ibid., 139–41; C. Peter Ripley, ed., *The Black Abolitionist Papers*, vol. 1, *The British Isles, 1830–1865* (Chapel Hill: Univ. of North Carolina Press, 1985), 13–16, 19–21, 259–67.

24. *DAB*, s.v. "Mason, John Young"; Frances Leigh Williams, "The Heritage and Preparation of a Statesman, John Young Mason, 1799–1859," *VMHB* 75 (1967): 305–30.

25. John Young Mason to Lewis E. Mason, June 28, 1854, sec. 6; Mary Ann Fort Mason to Lewis E. Mason, June 1, July 10, 1859, sec. 52; Emily Ann Mason Boykin to John Young Mason, June 19, 1846, sec. 24, Mason Family Papers, VHS. Fortsville, although now considered in Sussex County, was thought to be in Southampton during Mason's lifetime; hence his Southampton-based political career.

26. Archibald Atkinson to Charles Lanman, Sept. 28, 1858, Charles Lanman Papers, VHS (on Trezvant); Majette Family Papers, esp. sec. 1, VHS; Francis T. Ridley to Lewis E. Mason, Oct. 10, 1858, Mason Family Papers, sec. 52.

27. John L. Thorp to John Young Mason, Nov. 1, 1844, Michael Wall to Mason, Nov. 18, 1844, James M. Wall to Mason, Apr. 12, 1845, George Eustis to Mason, Apr. 5, 1846, Joshua L. Martin to Mason, Sept. 26, 1847, Mason Family Papers, sec. 24.

28. Lewis E. Mason to John Young Mason, Feb. 2, 1852, sec. 6; John Jackson to John Young Mason, Sept. 15, 1846, John Towner Leigh to John Young Mason, Sept. 16, 1846, James Brown to John Young Mason, July 5, 1847, James M. Wall to John Young Mason, Apr. 12, 1845, sec. 24, ibid. For calculations on Virginia cotton output, see Daniel W. Crofts, "The Old Dominion's Cotton Belt" (paper presented at Southern Historical Association, Norfolk, Nov. 1988), 3–4.

29. John Young Mason to Lewis E. Mason, Apr. 12, 1846, sec. 24, Lewis E. Mason to Mary Anne Fort Mason, Dec. 8, 1851, sec. 40, "List of Negroes belonging to J. Y. Mason," enclosed in Lewis E. Mason to John Young Mason, Jr., Feb. 1, 1855, sec. 52, Mason Family Papers.

30. The Masons bought Bob's wife and children cheaply, because she had rheumatism. For some reason, however, the family remained separated, and several years later the injured Bob was sold. Tim's wife, though preferring Tim as a husband, was not willing to leave Virginia. The Masons allowed Tim the option of returning. It is not apparent whether he did so; an inventory of Mason slaves in 1855 does not mention his name (Lewis E. Mason to John Young Mason, Dec. 14, 1850, Jan. 20, 1852, sec. 24, John Young Mason to Lewis E. Mason, Jan. 5, 1848, sec. 6, "List of Negroes Belonging to J. Y. Mason," enclosed in Lewis E. Mason to John Young Mason, Jr., Feb. 1, 1855, sec. 52, ibid.).

31. Lewis E. Mason to John Young Mason, Oct. 15, 1847, Dec. 29, 1847, Jan. 2, 1848, Mar. 14, 1853, ibid., sec. 24.

32. Lewis E. Mason to John Young Mason, Jan. 1, Feb. 2, 1849, Pinkney C.

Sims to John Young Mason, Aug. 4, 1849, sec. 24, John Young Mason to Lewis E. Mason, Oct. 26, Dec. 22, 1849, sec. 6, ibid.

33. Pinkney C. Sims to John Young Mason, Oct. 9, 1850, Lewis E. Mason to John Young Mason, June 27, Dec. 14, 1850, Feb. 23, 1851, sec. 24, John Young Mason to Lewis E. Mason, Nov. 14, 1850, Jan. 4, 1850 [1851], Lewis E. Mason to John Young Mason, Dec. 1850, Jan. 18, 1851, sec. 6, ibid.

34. John Young Mason to Lewis E. Mason, Nov. 14, 1850, Feb. 15, 1851, Lewis E. Mason to John Young Mason, Dec. 1850, sec. 6, Lewis E. Mason to John Young Mason, Apr. 14, 20, 1851, Feb. 11, 1852, sec. 24, ibid.

35. John Young Mason to Lewis E. Mason, Feb. 15, 1851, sec. 52, Lewis E. Mason to John Young Mason, Nov. 15, 17, Dec. 3, 4, 1851, sec. 6, Lewis E. Mason to Mary Ann Fort Mason, Dec. 8, 1851, sec. 40, ibid.

36. Lewis E. Mason to John Young Mason, Dec. 4, 1851, sec. 6, Lewis E. Mason to Mary Ann Fort Mason, Dec. 8, 1851, Jan. 16, 1851 [1852], Mary Ann Fort Mason to Lewis E. Mason, Sept. 1858, sec. 40, ibid.

37. Lewis E. Mason to John Young Mason, Feb. 2, 1852, sec. 6, Lewis E. Mason to John Young Mason, July 24, 1851, sec. 24, Lewis E. Mason to Mary Ann Fort Mason, Dec. 8, 1851, sec. 40, ibid.

38. Lewis E. Mason to John Young Mason. Oct. 15–18, Nov. 2, 1852, ibid., sec. 6.

39. Lewis E. Mason to John Young Mason, Apr. 14, 1851, Mar. 14, 1852, sec. 24, Lewis E. Mason to John Young Mason, Nov. 2, 1852, sec. 6, Lewis E. Mason to Mary Ann Fort Mason, Dec. 8, 1851, sec. 40, ibid.

40. Lewis E. Mason to Mary Ann Fort Mason, Dec. 8, 1851, ibid., sec. 40.

41. Lewis E. Mason to Mary Ann Fort Mason, Dec. 8, 1851, Jan. 16, 1851 [1852], sec. 40, Lewis E. Mason to John Young Mason, Feb. 2, 1852, sec. 6, Lewis E. Mason to E. Ryland, Oct. 1, 1859, sec. 52, ibid.

42. George S. Bradford to John Young Mason, July 22, 1852, Lewis E. Mason to John Young Mason, Nov. 2, 1852, sec. 6, John F. Bradford to John Young Mason, Aug. 21, 1852, Lewis E. Mason to John Young Mason, Mar. 1, 1853, sec. 24, W. H. Dickson to Lewis E. Mason, Feb. 5, 1853, sec. 52, ibid.

43. John F. Bradford to John Young Mason, Aug. 21, 1852, sec. 24, Lewis E. Mason to John Young Mason, Nov. 22, 1852, sec. 6, ibid.

44. Charles W. Barham to Lewis E. Mason, esp. Mar. 19, 1857, Sept. 3, 1858, ibid., sec. 52.

45. Charles W. Barham to Lewis E. Mason, June 15, July 14, Sept. 8, 30, Dec. 2, 1854, July 30, Aug. 16, 1856, Mar. 19, 1857, ibid., sec. 52.

46. Lewis E. Mason to John Young Mason, Jan. 5, 1852 [1853], Mar. 14, 1853, sec. 24, Charles W. Barham to John Young Mason, Aug. 19, 1853, Sept. 19, 1853, Nov. 5, 1853, sec. 6, Lewis E. Mason, Account Book of Mississippi Farm, sec. 19, ibid.

47. Lewis E. Mason to John Young Mason, Nov. 6, 22, 1852, sec. 6, Lewis E. Mason to John Young Mason, Mar. 1, 14, 1853, sec. 24, ibid.

48. John Young Mason to Lewis E. Mason, Jan. 21, 1854, ibid., sec. 6.

49. John Young Mason, Jr., to John Young Mason, 1854 debt list, Lewis E.

Mason to John Young Mason, Mar. 1, 1854, John Young Mason to Lewis E. Mason, June 28, 1854, ibid.

50. John Young Mason to Lewis E. Mason, June 5, 28, July 25, Aug. 4, 1854, Wellington Goddin to John Young Mason, Aug. 9, 17, Sept. 29, 1854, sec. 6, James W. Cook to Lewis E. Mason, Aug. 17, 1854, sec. 52, ibid.

51. John Young Mason to Lewis E. Mason and John Young Mason, Jr., Aug. 31, Oct. 30, 1854, ibid., sec. 6.

52. John Young Mason, Jr., to Charles W. Barham, Feb. 24, Apr. 1, 8, 1855, sec. 77, F. T. Leak to Lewis E. Mason, Nov. 12, 1855, Jno. C. McLemore to Lewis E. Mason, Nov. 10, 1855, D. McNeill, Jr., to Lewis E. Mason, Nov. 28, 1855, Roscoe Briggs Heath to Lewis E. Mason, Jan. 4, 1855 [1856], Jan. 10, 1856, sec. 52, ibid.

53. James T. Moore to Lewis E. Mason, Jan. 7, 1856, John Young Mason, Jr., to Lewis E. Mason, Mar. 7, 1856, sec. 52, Lewis E. Mason to John Young Mason, Jan. 20, 1856, John Young Mason to Lewis E. Mason, Jan. 24, Mar. 15, 1856, sec. 6, Lewis E. Mason to John Young Mason, Sept. 14, 1857, sec. 24, ibid.

54. Jacob Thompson to Lewis E. Mason, Aug. 9, Sept. 1, 1856, Jan. 29, 1857, sec. 52, Lewis E. Mason to John Young Mason, Sept. 14, 1857, sec. 24, John Young Mason to Lewis E. Mason, Jan. 5, 1857, John Young Mason to Mary Ann Mason, Jan. 7, 1857, Lewis E. Mason to John Young Mason, Jan. 22, Nov. 8, 1858, sec. 6, ibid.

55. Lewis E. Mason to John Young Mason, Sept. 14, 1857, Sept. 7, 1859, sec. 24, Lewis E. Mason to John Young Mason, Apr. 26, July 18, Sept. 16, Nov. 8, 1858, sec. 6, ibid.

56. Mary Anne Mason to Lewis E. Mason, Feb. 25, 1856, John Young Mason, Jr., to Lewis E. Mason, Mar. 10, 1857, Aug. 20, 1858, sec. 52, James Buchanan to John Young Mason, Aug. 15, 1856, sec. 24, ibid.

57. John Young Mason to Lewis E. Mason, May 16, 26, 1857, sec. 6, Mary Ann Fort Mason to James Watkins Cook, May 25, 1857, sec. 40, Mary Anne Mason to Lewis E. Mason, May 25, 1857, Aug. 20, 1858, John Young Mason, Jr., to Lewis E. Mason, Jan. 9, 1859, sec. 52, ibid.

58. Lewis E. Mason to John Young Mason, May 10, June 8, 1859, ibid., sec. 24.

59. Lewis E. Mason to John Young Mason, June 21, 1859, sec. 24, John Young Mason to Lewis E. Mason, June 2, 1859, sec. 6, Mary Ann Fort Mason to Lewis E. Mason, June 1, 1859, sec. 40, ibid.

60. Cobb diary, Oct. 29, 1859.

61. David M. Potter, *The Impending Crisis, 1848–1861*, completed and edited by Don E. Fehrenbacher (New York: Harper & Row, 1976), 182–93.

62. Lewis E. Mason to Archer Anderson, Sept. 26, 1866, St. George Tucker Mason to Lewis E. Mason, Jan. 1, Mar. 31, 1866, Mason Family Papers, sec. 52.

63. Susan Harriet Barksdale Mason to Lewis E. Mason, May 8, 1869, Lewis E. Mason to Simon Fraser Blunt Mason, Mar. 9, 1874, Archer Anderson to Lewis E. Mason, Oct. 14, 1878, ibid.

64. Lewis E. Mason to Simon Fraser Blunt Mason, Mar. 9, 1874, Lewis E. Mason to Mr. Daniel, July 12, 1878, Archer Anderson to Lewis E. Mason, Feb.

1, 1873, Oct. 14, 1878, June 5, 1893, Lewis E. Mason to Sarah Olivia Mason and Susan Barksdale Mason, Jan. 6, 1878, Lewis E. Mason to Sarah Olivia Mason, Oct. 1, 1881, sec. 52, Mary Ann Fort Mason to Lewis E. Mason, 1856, sec. 40, ibid.

65. J. Ravencroft Jones to Lewis E. Mason, Feb. 12, 1861, St. George Tucker Mason to Lewis E. Mason, Apr. 21, 1861, Jan. 28, 1863, May 10, 1863, Feb. 14, 1868, Lewis E. Mason to James W. Parker, Oct. 28, 1863, sec. 52, Mary Ann Fort Mason to Lewis E. Mason, June 1, 1859, sec. 40, ibid.

66. St. George Tucker Mason to Lewis E. Mason, Feb. 14, 1868, ibid., sec. 52.

67. St. George Tucker Mason to Lewis E. Mason, Sept. 6, 1868, Dec. 11, 1874, ibid.

68. St. George Tucker Mason to Lewis E. Mason, Dec. 11, 1874, ibid.

69. Ibid.

70. St. George Tucker Mason to Lewis E. Mason, Aug. 1879, Aug. 6, 1882, ibid.; Daniel T. Balfour, *13th Virginia Cavalry* (Lynchburg, Va.: H. E. Howard, 1986), 46.

TWO. THE DIARISTS: ELLIOTT L. STORY AND DANIEL W. COBB

1. Elliott L. Story began his diary a few years earlier (1838) than Daniel W. Cobb (1842), and the last entries Story made (1876) occurred several years after Cobb's death (1872). All of Cobb's diaries and most of Story's were therefore written between the early 1840s and the early 1870s. Within the past decade, the Virginia Historical Society has acquired all extant Cobb and Story diaries. See my article, "Southampton County Diarists in the Civil War Era: Elliott L. Story and Daniel W. Cobb," *VMHB* 98 (1990): 537–612.

2. Drew Gilpin Faust, "The Peculiar South Revisited: White Society, Culture, and Politics in the Antebellum Period, 1800–1860," in John B. Boles and Evelyn Thomas Nolen, eds., *Interpreting Southern History: Historiographical Essays in Honor of Sanford W. Higginbotham* (Baton Rouge: Louisiana State Univ. Press, 1987), 99.

3. The Virginia Historical Society owns six volumes of the Story diary. The first covers from January 1838 into April 1840 and begins with a review of Story's life between 1829 and 1837. Story apparently kept a volume covering from mid-April 1840 to the end of 1841, but it has not survived. The second existing volume begins in January 1842, but most of its entries are from the 1843 calendar year. No diary survives for 1844 and 1845. The third extant volume covers a two-year interval between January 1846 and December 1847; the fourth covers only 1848. The 1846–48 diaries are the fullest and most introspective of the collection. The final two volumes cover a far longer period, from 1851 to 1876. The diary or diaries for the years 1849 and 1850 have apparently been lost, and the two remaining volumes are intermittent. Story made efforts to sketch in events for long lapses of time when he did not make daily notations, but the 187 pages devoted entirely to 1848 make much of the record that follows seem skeletal. The

fifth surviving volume consists primarily of regular notations between January 1851 and June 23, 1853, followed by a long lapse when Story attempted to go into the mercantile business. Regular entries resume on Jan. 1, 1857. The volume ends on June 30, 1857. Story's sixth and final surviving volume includes entries from July 1, 1857, until Mar. 3, 1876. Between July 1857 and July 1861, he made daily entries with some regularity. From 1862 through 1874, Story wrote brief annual summations. His final efforts to keep a daily record occurred between January and April 1875 and again between November 1875 and March 1876. Although Story lived until 1886, his journal falls entirely silent after Mar. 3, 1876.

4. Story diary, flyleaf to vol. 1, 1838.

5. Ibid., Feb. 13, 1843, Jan. 10, 1842, Mar. 25, 1848, Aug. 29, 1851.

6. Ibid., Jan. 10, 1842, Jan. 12, Apr. 11, 1848, Feb. 7, May 2, 1843.

7. Ian R. Tyrrell, "Drink and Temperance in the Antebellum South: An Overview and Interpretation," *Journal of Southern History* 48 (1982): 497–501; Samuel B. Willeford diary, Dec. 21, 1838, Feb. 17, 19, 1839, VHS; Story diary, Mar. 6, 26, Apr. 2, June 4, 5, 1843, June 1, 3, 1847, Apr. 12, 13, 1848. One Christmas holiday Story and his friends drank hard cider and eggnog and got "gentlemanly merry" (ibid., Dec. 21, 23, 26, 1846).

8. Story diary, Apr. 20, 1839, Feb. 3, 1843.

9. Ibid., Dec. 22, 30, 31, 1842, Mar. 5, Sept. 25, 26, 1843, Jan. 8, 9, 1842, May 27, June 1, 1843, Feb. 27, 28, May 29, 1846.

10. Ibid., vol. 1, initial review of his experiences, 1829–37.

11. Ibid.; Peter C. Stewart, "Railroads and Urban Rivalries in Antebellum Eastern Virginia," *VMHB* 81 (1973): 3–22; Parramore, *Southampton County*, 122–29. Story mentioned reading the Richmond *Whig*, the Petersburg *Intelligencer*, the Baltimore *Herald*, and the Philadelphia *Evening Post*, "besides others of less importance."

12. Story diary, Jan. 15, 16, 18, Feb. 5, Dec. 10, 1838, Feb. 1, 28, Mar. 22, 1839.

13. Ibid., Feb. 1, 1839, Feb. 28, Oct. 10, 11, 1843. The Literary Fund supported eighteen children in Story's school in 1843. Probably an equal number of paying students were enrolled. Daily attendance averaged well below the combined figure, with Literary Fund students more frequently absent. Story noted in his diary when as many as thirty pupils appeared (ibid., Oct. 10, 1843, Feb. 4, 13, Mar. 9, 1846).

14. Ibid., Jan. 13, 1842, Mar. 29, Apr. 4, 5, 1843, Mar. 11, 1846, July 27, 31, Aug. 2, 1848.

15. Ibid., Sept. 14, 1846, Apr. 9, 1847, Jan. 13, 14, 28, June 12, 1848.

16. Ibid., Feb. 10, Apr. 2, 1846, Mar. 31, May 2, July 27, 1848.

17. Ibid., Nov. 28, 1843, Apr. 9, 1839. See also Parramore, *Southampton County*, 58, 114.

18. Story diary, Dec. 11, 1843, Mar. 25, 27, Apr. 3, 12, May 3, 7, July 11, Sept. 18, Dec. 16, 17, 1846, Jan. 9 (quotation), July 22, 1848.

19. Ibid., May 3, 29, June 26, 1843, Feb. 1, 6, Mar. 17, July 14, Sept. 28, Oct. 7, Dec. 16, 17, 1846, Mar. 31, June 16, 25, July 9, Sept. 23, 28, 29, 1847.

20. Ibid., Jan. 26, Feb. 1, 1847, June 1, 1848.

21. Ibid., Mar. 18, 1840, June 22, 1843, Oct. 11, 1839.

22. Ibid., Mar. 4, 6, 1847, Mar. 19, June 17, 1848.

23. Ibid., Aug. 13–16, 1846; Ulysses P. Joyner, *Joyner of Southampton* (Verona, Va.: McClure Printing Co., 1975), 145.

24. Story diary, Aug. 13–16, 1846. Story made fewer criticisms about a second and similar wedding one year later, at which Elizabeth Boykin married William W. Joyner. Story was again a waiter, along with nineteen others. "Remarkably cool and pleasant" weather may have made the subsequent wedding less taxing (ibid., July 29–31, 1847; Joyner, *Joyner of Southampton*, 188).

25. Story diary, Feb. 13, 1839, Jan. 5, 1843, Mar. 1, 1846; Daniel W. Cobb diary, Feb. 21, 1842, VHS.

26. Story diary, July 10, 17, Aug. 28, Sept. 5, 11, 1846, Jan. 14, 20, 1847, Jan. 8, 12, Feb. 12, Mar. 29, July 8, Aug. 26, Oct. 19, Nov. 21, 1848.

27. Ibid., Dec. 12, 1842, Apr. 16, May 13, June 27, 1846, Mar. 26, 1847, July 13, Aug. 18, 1848, Mar. 29, 1851, Feb. 4, 1852, July 30, 1857, June 2, 1858.

28. The premier study linking economic change and partisanship is Harry L. Watson, *Jacksonian Parties and Community Conflict: The Emergence of the Second American Party System in Cumberland County, North Carolina* (Baton Rouge: Louisiana State Univ. Press, 1981). See also Watson, "Conflict and Collaboration: Yeomen, Slaveholders, and Politics in the Antebellum South," *Social History* 10 (1985): 273–98, and Watson, *Liberty and Power: The Politics of Jacksonian America* (New York: Hill & Wang, 1990).

29. Story diary, May 16, 20, 22, 1839; James B. Urquhart to John Y. Mason, May 24, 1839, Mason Family Papers, sec. 6, VHS. Election returns are available in the Southampton County Records, microfilm reels 66–72, VSLA.

30. Story diary, Jan. 29, Apr. 11, 1840. Even after Story's twenty-first birthday in 1842, he failed to meet the property qualification for adult males who did not head households; only after his father died in 1845 did Story, as a household head, cast his first vote.

31. Ibid., Sept. 23, 1839, May 24, 28, 1843.

32. Ibid., Apr. 23, 1846.

33. Major L. Wilson, *Space, Time, and Freedom: The Quest for Nationality and the Irrepressible Conflict, 1815–1861* (Westport, Conn.: Greenwood Press, 1974), 116–17; Story diary, May 24, June 22, 1848, Aug. 29, 1851.

34. Story diary, Jan. 25, Feb. 10, May 3, 24, June 29, 1848, Aug. 25, 1851. See also R. E. Devereux and Edward Shulcum, *Soil Survey of Southampton County, Virginia* (Washington, D.C.: U.S. Department of Agriculture, Bureau of Chemistry and Soils, July 1937).

35. Story diary, May 8, Sept. 9, 1847.

36. Ibid., Mar. 27, May 2, June 16, 17, Aug. 30, 31, Sept. 3, Oct. 1, 1847, May 22, June 7, 16, 17, 1851.

37. Ibid., Feb. 18, 19, Nov. 28–30, Dec. 20, 21, 1846, May 18, 19, 1847, July 30, 1851, Jan. 5, 1857; Hart, "Descendants of Thomas Pretlow," 81; Joyner, *Joyner of Southampton*, 145–46.

38. Story diary, June 14, Sept. 12, 1846, Jan. 24, 1847.

39. Ibid., Oct. 6, 11, 1847.
40. Ibid., Oct. 8, 14, 1847, Jan. 9, July 22, Sept. 12, Oct. 29, Nov. 26, 1848.
41. Ibid., June 17, July 13–16, 1852.
42. Ibid., Apr. 11, July 1, 1851, Feb. 13, 19 (18), Mar. 31, 1852.
43. Ibid., Dec. 13, 20, 24, 27, 1852, Jan. 1, Mar. 22, 24, 25, 30, Apr. 15, June 23, 1853, entry summarizing June–Dec. 1853 facing June 23, 1853.
44. Ibid., retrospective comments on 1853 and 1854; Virginia, 49:339, R. G. Dun & Co. Collection, Baker Library, Harvard Univ. Graduate School of Business Administration.
45. Story diary, retrospective comments on 1854 and 1855.
46. Ibid., Feb. 19, Nov. 29, Dec. 21, 1846, July 9, 1848, Mar. 11, May 13, July 28, Aug. 2, 1851.
47. Story diary, retrospective comments on 1856, Jan. 1, 1857; "Account of property Appraised belonging to Elizabeth Story and purchased by E. L. Story, June 14th, 1856," at end of Story diary, 1851–57 volume; U.S. Census, Population, 1850, Southampton County, Nottoway Parish, household no. 462, microfilm, NA. Story almost certainly spent more money soon after his marriage than he could have accumulated through his own efforts. The property from his mother cost $645, and he paid an unspecified amount to his brother and sister. Shortly thereafter, he hired carpenters to start construction on a new house and spent $800 on a slave. The only direct hint of financial assistance from Judkins was the latter's refinancing of a debt that Story still owed Robert Murray from the ill-fated store in Franklin (Story diary, Dec. 23, 1857). It appears improbable that Story had sufficient assets to spend as liberally as he did between 1856 and 1858 just after the fiasco of the Franklin store, which left him not only indebted to Murray but also with hundreds of dollars worth of uncollected claims. For example, Story had to settle for $50 from an estate that owed $300 (ibid., Nov. 18, 1857).
48. Story diary, Feb. 25, Mar. 18, 23, Apr. 1, May 15, June 3, 6, 8, Nov. 3, 28, Dec. 5, 1857, July 25, Aug. 8–11, 1859. Southampton was the leading county in Virginia in output of both swine and peas in 1850 and 1860 (*The Seventh Census of the United States: 1850* [Washington, D.C.: Robert Armstrong, Public Printer, 1853], 273–82; U.S. Census Office, 8th Census, 1860, *Agriculture in the United States in 1860 . . .* [Washington, D.C.: GPO, 1864], 154–65).
49. Story diary, Feb. 5–6, July 13–14, 18, Dec. 19, 1857, May 5, 15, 27, June 19, Aug. 21, Sept. 18, 1858, Oct. 17, 1859, June 4, Aug. 20, 1860; Southampton County Election Records, May 1860, VSLA.
50. Michael F. Holt, *The Political Crisis of the 1850s* (New York: Wiley, 1978), 101–38; Story diary, May 27, 1852, May 20, 1857. Story, an avid reader of newspapers as late as 1848, saw a political paper only "now and then" by 1851; thereafter his diary contains only brief detached references to political discussions (ibid., Feb. 26, Dec. 10, 1851, Aug. 19, 1852).
51. Story diary, June 25, July 1, 14, 22, Dec. 1, 12, 1857, Mar. 16, May 10, 18–19, June 17, 25, 30, July 31, 1858.
52. Ibid., July 10, 26, 29, 31, Aug. 1–4, 6, 15, 16, 31, Sept. 26, Oct. 19, 21,

31, 1857, Jan. 21, June 21, July 9, 20, Aug. 12–14, 27, 30, Sept. 6, 14, Nov. 15, 19–20, 1858, Jan. 10, Apr. 16, 1859.

53. Ibid., June 19–21, Aug. 31, 1857, June 5, 24, July 14, 19, 1858, Sept. 9–18, 1859.

54. The Virginia Historical Society owns twenty-five volumes of the Daniel W. Cobb diary, covering from 1842 to 1872. Cobb always kept a separate journal for each calendar year. The diaries for 1844, 1848, 1860, 1862, 1865, and 1869 are missing; according to the Cobb family genealogist, they were probably destroyed in a fire after having been removed by someone writing the history of a local church (Edwards, *The Cobbs of the Tidewater*, 201). The disappearance of the 1860, 1862, and 1865 diaries means that the record of Cobb's experiences and reactions during the war depends on three surviving diaries—for 1861, 1863, and 1864. Cobb's postwar diaries provide abundant information about Reconstruction; the missing volumes of 1865 and 1869 coincide, however, with emancipation and with the pivotal election that ended Reconstruction in Virginia.

55. Cobb diary, Jan. 11, 1849, Sept. 18, 1850, July 31, 1852, May 31, Sept. 12, 14, 1859, July 21, 1861; Edwards, *The Cobbs of the Tidewater*, 227–29. The federal census taker in 1870 provided a clue to pronunciation, recording the name of Cobb's eight-year-old son as "Majah" (U.S. Census, Population, 1870, Southampton County, Jerusalem Township, p. 247, microfilm, NA).

56. Cobb diary, retrospective comments after Aug. 23, 1842, Jan. 10, 1858; Edwards, *The Cobbs of the Tidewater*, 192–202.

57. Cobb diary, retrospective comments after Aug. 23, 1842, Sept. 4, 20, 1842, Mar. 11, 1843, July 27, Aug. 17, 1845, June 26, 1852, Dec. 14, 1858; Edwards, *The Cobbs of the Tidewater*, 202. Cobb regretted that he could not sing or pray in public (diary, Oct. 12, 1859).

58. Cobb diary, Oct. 6, 1842, Mar. 11, 1843, Feb. 12, 1847.

59. Ibid., Mar. 25, May 10, 24, July 3, Sept. 30, Oct. 12, 14, 1842, Jan. 1, 1843. Cobb also believed that the moon affected human physiology. Two centuries after William Harvey recognized that the heart steadily pumped blood through the circulatory system, Cobb expressed confidence that "the change of the blood" from one part of the "human sistim" to another was "entirely governed by the movements of the moon" (ibid., Mar. 25, 1842).

60. Ibid., Apr. 12, July 19, 1842, Apr. 30, 1847, Aug. 9, 1851. In 1858 a rainy Jan. 5 prompted him to note: "This day is for May so it will be a wett May if the oald mark and sines and times hoald out." In 1871, a year before his death, a "Fair Cool" New Year's Day provided a "nice day for Jan[uary] to be governed" (ibid., Jan. 5, 1858, Jan. 1, 1871).

61. Ibid., June 8, 1846, Apr. 30, 1847.

62. Ibid., July 4, 1847.

63. Ibid., Nov. 30, 1846, June 3, 1855, Jan. 7, 23, Aug. 6, 1856.

64. Ibid., Mar. 11, 1842.

65. Ibid., Feb. 21, Mar. 4, 16, Apr. 28, Aug. 24, Oct. 6, 1842. Cobb refused to vote in 1842, apparently to protest the exclusion of some militia members from

the polls. "I never intend to vote untill every man is allowed to vote that bares armes," Cobb vowed (ibid., Mar. 17, 1842). Cobb had served in the militia since his late teens, winning promotions to the rifle company and then to the cavalry (ibid., retrospective comments after Aug. 23, 1842, Oct. 11, 1842, Feb. 21, 1843). By 1846, however, Cobb decided to vote, even though Virginia did not enfranchise all adult white males until 1851 (ibid., Apr. 23, 1846). He thereafter voted regularly, invariably for Democrats.

66. Ibid., May 31, July 22, 1842, Aug. 17, 1849, Aug. 3, 1850, Oct. 31, 1853, Jan. 11, 1857, Sept. 10, 1859. See also Sept. 1842, about the jailing of a slave who had tried to purchase gun flints in Halifax County, North Carolina. Cobb, however, made no mention in his diary when one of his cousins, Selvy Cobb, was suspected of "endeavouring to stir up an insurrection" among Simon Murfee's slaves. Selvy Cobb was questioned and discharged, and his apparent accuser, Murfee, had to pay $5.87 in court costs (Story diary, Apr. 1, 1843; Southampton County Court Minutes, Apr. 5, May 15, 1843, microfilm, VSLA).

67. Cobb diary, June 8, 1842, July 12, 1843, Mar. 2 (3), 1850, June 22, 1851.

68. Ibid., June 5, Aug. 14, 1847, Aug. 28, Sept. 16, 1859.

69. Ibid., Oct. 18, 1851. In 1842, the year after Cobb's marriage and the first year he kept a diary, his wife's younger sister and a younger brother attended Cobb's school (ibid., Nov. 18, 1842). See Edwards, *The Cobbs of the Tidewater*, 202–3.

70. Cobb diary, June 22, Oct. 18, Dec. 9, 1851, Nov. 8, 1861. Within a year of her marriage, Rebecca Gurley died following childbirth (ibid., Oct. 1–2, 1852). Jesse Little also had two sons, Theophilus and Edward.

71. Ibid., Apr. 20, May 10, 21, 1845, June 22, 1851, Jan. 29, 1855.

72. Ibid., Mar. 1 (2), 1850, Feb. 29, 1852, Feb. 27, 1858, Feb. 8, 1859.

73. Ibid., July 4, 1847, Mar. 1 (2) 1850, July 26, 1859, June 25, 1863.

74. Ibid., June 22, 1851. Cobb's diary was a highly confidential document. It would probably have included some hint of extramarital liaisons, had there been any; someone with his pathological aversion to blacks would not likely have made sexual advances to black women.

75. Ibid., Apr. 15, 1852, May 15, 25, 1856; Edwards, *The Cobbs of the Tidewater*, 202, 209, 214. Only in recent years have historians recognized and begun to study North-South differentials in fertility rates that emerged in the antebellum era among native-born white women. The evidence strongly suggests that married women and their husbands in New England and the North by this time had begun to devise techniques for controlling family size. In the absence of any reliable or widely available birth control technology, they probably relied primarily on coitus interruptus. Antebellum southern white women, trapped in a more relentlessly patriarchal culture, had less success in limiting family size than their northern sisters. See Daniel Scott Smith, "Family Limitation, Sexual Control, and Domestic Feminism in Victorian America," *Feminist Studies* 1 (1973): 40–57; Anne Firor Scott, *The Southern Lady: From Pedestal to Politics, 1830–1930* (Chicago: Univ. of Chicago Press, 1970), 37–42; Catherine Clinton, *The Plantation Mistress: Woman's World in the Old South* (New York: Pantheon Books, 1982), 60–61, 152–53, 204–6; Estelle B. Freedman, "Sexuality in Nineteeenth-

Century America: Behavior, Ideology, and Politics," *Reviews in American History* 10 (Dec. 1982): 197–201; Mary P. Ryan, *Cradle of the Middle Class: The Family in Oneida County, New York, 1790–1865* (New York: Cambridge Univ. Press, 1981), 155–57; William L. Barney, *The Passage of the Republic: An Interdisciplinary History of Nineteenth-Century America* (Lexington, Mass.: D. C. Heath, 1987), 75–76; Nell Irvin Painter, Introduction to *The Secret Eye: The Journal of Ella Gertrude Clanton Thomas, 1848–1889*, ed. Virginia Ingraham Burr (Chapel Hill: Univ. of North Carolina Press, 1990), 32–33.

See, however, Jan Lewis and Kenneth A. Lockridge, "'Sally Has Been Sick': Pregnancy and Family Limitation among Virginia Gentry Women, 1780–1830," *Journal of Social History* 22 (Fall 1988): 6, which contends that "a definite trend toward lower marital fertility had commenced by the 1840s and 1850s, well before the Civil War."

76. Cobb diary, July 1, 15, Aug. 25, 1858, June 18, 21, July 26, Aug. 28, 1859; Edwards, *The Cobbs of the Tidewater*, 227. Apparently she relented no later than December 1859, because Jefferson Davis Cobb was born on Sept. 8, 1860 (ibid.).

77. Cobb diary, June 18, 21, Aug. 27, Oct. 2, 1859.

78. Ibid., May 22, July 26, Sept. 18, 1859. Three married women in Southampton, by Cobb's own account, had "gone deranged" within months of each other (ibid., Apr. 16, 1856).

79. Ibid., May 9–10, 15, 1852, Apr. 2, May 21, Nov. 17, 23, 26, 1854, Feb. 2, Mar. 13–14, 1855, July 17, Aug. 31, 1856, Mar. 23, Sept. 11, 1857, May 15, June 5, 24, 1859.

80. Ibid., June 30, 1842, Aug. 18, 1845, May 2, 1847, Sept. 29, 1850, Feb. 20, Mar. 12, 1855, Mar. 20, May 21, 1859.

81. Ibid., June 30, 1842, Apr. 15, 1846.

82. Ibid., July 24, Aug. 25, 28, 29, Dec. 5, 10, 13, 1855, Apr. 19, July 30–Sept. 18, 1856, Aug. 8, 15, 26, Sept. 19, 23, Oct. 13, Nov. 30, 1859; Story diary, Aug. 8–11, 1859. Several times Cobb noted the purchase of whiskey for his slaves (Cobb diary, Nov. 13, 1854, Feb. 10, 1855, Feb. 16, July 27, 1858). On Mar. 14, 1855, the house girl got drunk after pilfering spirits from the sideboard. Why did Cobb keep liquor available? Probably for guests.

83. Cobb diary, Aug. 26, 1850.

84. Ibid., Feb. 18, Mar. 12, 17–19, 1856. Agents for R. G. Dun and Company reported that Newsom, once "a steady and energetic man," had "become unsteady and had wasted his estate in betting on elections and other dissipation" (Virginia, 49:346, 348, R. G. Dun & Co. Collection, Baker Library, Harvard Univ. Graduate School of Business Administration).

85. Cobb diary, Apr. 11, 1842, Mar. 24, 29, Apr. 12, 17, 1845.

86. Ibid., May 5, 1850.

87. Ibid., Mar. 30, Sept. 17, 1845.

88. Ibid., Aug. 18, 1859.

89. The 1850 census and local tax records show Cobb owning no land, all of which still belonged to Jesse Little. Although the 1850 U.S. Census (Slave Schedule, Southampton County, Nottoway Parish, microfilm, NA) credited him with

ten slaves, Cobb owned only five at the time (Cobb diary, June 22, 1851). The other slaves in his employ must have been hired (ibid., Dec. 31, 1849, Jan. 2, 23, 1850). Only two of the ten slaves at Cobb's in 1850 were adults; three were in their teens and five were children under the age of eight. His own self-image in 1850 was that of a smallholder.

Ten years later, both his self-image and his property holdings placed him among the prosperous, although certainly not among the elite. The 1860 U.S. Census (Slave Schedule, Southampton County, Nottoway Parish) designated Cobb as the owner of eleven slaves. His diary validates this figure and calculates their worth as $12,000 (Cobb diary, Jan. 7, Nov. 30, 1859). Cobb also had acquired some land by 1860; he and his wife would inherit much more upon Jesse Little's death in 1863. Elliott Story's property holdings always remained in the smallholding category.

90. Faulkner's Charles Bon met his end upon returning from the war, rather than on the battlefield. The similarities between fact and fiction are, however, resonant. Cobb's chip-on-the-shoulder determination to achieve respectability is entirely Faulknerian. The experiences in tidewater Virginia that Faulkner imagined for young Thomas Sutpen closely paralleled Cobb's encounter with the Little family; see William Faulkner, *Absalom, Absalom!* (New York: Random House, 1936).

91. Cobb diary, Jan. 31, Feb. 4, Nov. 24, 1843, July 21, 22, Aug. 12, 1846, Jan. 31, 1849. Although Cobb owned no slaves above the age of twelve in 1841 or 1842, he paid taxes on three in 1843 and Little's slaveholdings dipped from twenty to seventeen between 1842 and 1843, so it appears that Cobb acquired three of Little's slaves (Personal Property Taxes, Southampton County, Nottoway Parish, 1841–43, VSLA).

92. For Cobb's ownership of five slaves, see his diary, May 14, Aug. 19, Dec. 30, 1846, June 22, 1851; also Personal Property Taxes, Southampton County, Nottoway Parish, 1854. On slave hirings, see Cobb diary, Dec. 16, 30, 1850, Dec. 18, 1854. For horse purchases, see ibid., Dec. 24, 27, 1853. The diary is full of information about rising crop prices; see Oct. 20, 1849, Oct. 7, 1850, Feb. 14, 1851, Jan. 17, Nov. 4, 1852. On increased cotton acreage, compare the entry on Apr. 30, 1849, with those of May 1–3, 1856. On financial settlements with Little, see ibid., July 27, 1849, Nov. 7, 1852. Cobb may have compensated Little for the slaves.

93. Figures in this and the next paragraph are drawn especially from two 1859 diary entries, on Jan. 7 and Nov. 30. For antebellum slaveholders as "labor lords" rather than landlords, see Gavin Wright, *Old South, New South: Revolutions in the Southern Economy since the Civil War* (New York: Basic Books, 1986).

94. Cobb diary, Sept. 7, 15, Oct. 8, 14, 1855, Aug. 29, Nov. 21, 1856, Sept. 31 (30), 1857, Mar. 14, Sept. 22, 1861. On two occasions Cobb joined Little for a trip to Petersburg, the traveling party both times including Little's son Theophilus. Cobb apparently found this brother-in-law more congenial than his father-in-law (ibid., Feb. 6–10, 1854, Sept. 1, 1858).

95. On repair of the bridge, see ibid., Oct. 29, Nov. 2, 1858. For Cobb's involvement with Barn Tavern Academy, see ibid., Jan. 29, Mar. 4, Dec. 18, 1855, Jan. 27, July 3–4, Nov. 28–29, 1856, Dec. 4, 1857. For Cobb as poll keeper, see ibid., May 24, 1855, May 22, Nov. 4, 1856. On Cobb's 1860 candidacy, see Southampton County Election Records, May 1860, VSLA.

96. Story diary, Feb. 1, 8, 1857; Cobb diary, Feb. 1, 3, 8, 1857.

97. Cooper, *The South and the Politics of Slavery*; Charles Grier Sellers, Jr., "Who Were the Southern Whigs?" *American Historical Review* 59 (1954): 335–46; John V. Mering, "The Slave-State Constitutional Unionists and the Politics of Consensus," *Journal of Southern History* 43 (1977): 395–410.

98. Story diary, May 31, 1865.

THREE. LIFE, LABOR, AND LEISURE

1. The chapter title deliberately echoes Ulrich B. Phillips, *Life and Labor in the Old South* (Boston: Little, Brown, 1929).

2. John T. Schlotterbeck, "Plantation and Farm: Social and Economic Change in Orange and Greene Counties, Virginia, 1716 to 1860" (Ph.D. diss., Johns Hopkins Univ., 1980), 8, 211–14; see also Schlotterbeck, "The 'Social Economy' of an Upper South Community: Orange and Greene Counties, Virginia, 1815–1860," in Orville Vernon Burton and Robert C. McMath, Jr., eds., *Class, Conflict, and Consensus: Antebellum Southern Community Studies* (Westport, Conn.: Greenwood Press, 1982), 3–28.

3. Emmett B. Fields, "The Agricultural Population of Virginia, 1850–1860" (Ph.D. diss., Vanderbilt Univ., 1953), 55, 68–75; Sam Bowers Hilliard, *Hog Meat and Hoecake: Food Supply in the Old South, 1840–1860* (Carbondale: Southern Illinois Univ. Press, 1972), 156; David R. Goldfield, *Urban Growth in the Age of Sectionalism: Virginia, 1847–1861* (Baton Rouge: Louisiana State Univ. Press, 1977), 238–39, 246. The *Farmers' Register*, the agricultural journal Ruffin edited between 1833 and 1842, contains far more about wheat and corn than any other crops. For a preview of work-in-progress concerning large-scale cultivation of wheat and corn by a progressive tidewater farmer, see Shearer Davis Bowman, "Conditional Unionism and Slavery in Virginia, 1860–1861: The Case of Dr. Richard Eppes," *VMHB* 96 (1988): 31–54. Bowman is preparing for publication selections from the detailed Eppes diary, VHS.

4. Story diary, Jan. 25, Feb. 10, Apr. 19, May 3, June 29, Aug. 17, Sept. 27, Oct. 28, 1848, VHS.

5. Cobb diary, VHS; Story diary, Nov. 29, 1857.

6. Lewis Cecil Gray, *History of Agriculture in the Southern United States to 1860*, 2 vols. (1932; rept. Gloucester, Mass.: Peter Smith, 1958), 2:1039.

7. *Seventh Census of the United States: 1850*, 273–82; *Agriculture in the United States in 1860*, 154–65. The figures cited are for aggregate output per county. Southampton also ranked high in output per improved acre for the crops in which it specialized. It was among the larger Virginia counties, but its total

number of improved acres (131,963 in 1860) barely placed it among the top twenty counties in the state. On postwar peanut production, see Parramore, *Southampton County*, 183–84; F. Roy Johnson, *The Peanut Story* (Murfreesboro, N.C.: Johnson Publishing Co., 1964), 85–87, 94, 139; Story diary, Nov. 29, 1857. On postwar timber production, see Parke Rouse, Jr., *The Timber Tycoons: The Camp Families of Virginia and Florida and Their Empire, 1887–1987* (Richmond: William Byrd Press for the Southampton County Historical Society, 1988). Antebellum Southamptonites cut and sold wooden staves for use as shingles, probably using durable local cypress trees; see Cobb diary, Jan. 31, Feb. 2, 3, Mar. 25, 1854, Mar. 15, 1856.

8. James Maget, "The way things work down here in old Southampton," Majette Family Papers, sec. 3, item 118, VHS; Norfolk *Southern Argus*, Apr. 21, 1860, quoted in Edgar B. Jackson, *Peanuts and Applejack* (Norfolk: privately published, 1981), 76; letter from "E.," Feb. 1, 1866, in Richmond semiweekly *Whig*, Feb. 9, 1866; W. H. T. Squires, *The Days of Yester-Year in Colony and Commonwealth: A Sketch Book of Virginia* (Portsmouth, Va.: Printcraft Press, 1928), 195–96.

9. Gray, *Southern Agriculture* 2:888–89, 1027; *Farmers' Register* 5 (1837): 5–6.

10. Joshua M. Harrell, in *Farmers' Register* 6 (1838): 574–75; Gray, *Southern Agriculture* 2:1026–27.

11. Joseph Clarke Robert, *The Story of Tobacco in America* (New York: Knopf, 1948), 58–63.

12. Gray, *Southern Agriculture* 2:888, 1027; *Seventh Census of the United States: 1850*, lxxxiv, 277–78. Errors in the 1850 U.S. agricultural census, caused by entries in pounds rather than in bales on the manuscript schedules, overstated by a factor of 400 the negligible cotton output in Chesterfield and Henrico counties. A corrected overall figure for Virginia cotton output in 1850 is therefore 3,388 bales instead of the 3,947 indicated in the published census returns; see the microfilm of the 1850 manuscript agricultural census, NA, copy at VSLA.

13. The 1860 manuscript agricultural census for Virginia (microfilm, NA, copy at VSLA) contains far more erroneous listings for 1859 cotton production, confusing pounds for bales, than in the 1850 manuscript agricultural census. Totals for the following counties were thereby inflated by a factor of 400: Buckingham, Campbell, Carroll, Dinwiddie, Essex, Isle of Wight, King William, Lee, Nicholas, Prince George, Smyth, Stafford, Warren, Wetzel, and Wythe. Virginia cotton output, instead of the 12,727 bales reported in the published agricultural census, amounted only to 5,211 bales, or 0.1 percent of the U.S. total (*Agriculture of the United States in 1860*, xciv, 154–65).

14. Gray, *Southern Agriculture* 2:1027.

15. Ibid., 2:708–9; *Farmers' Register* 2 (1834): 362.

16. Washington C. Kerr, *Report on the Cotton Production of the State of Virginia* (Washington, D.C.: U.S. Census Office, 1884), 9–10, 14–15; Devereux and Shulcum, *Soil Survey of Southampton County*, 8–14; 1860 U.S. manuscript agricultural census, microfilm, NA, copy at VSLA. The heavier clay soils in upper Southampton would be well suited for cotton, except that they do not warm up

as quickly in the spring as the lighter soils in lower Southampton; the slightly longer average growing season in lower Southampton has apparently given that area a crucial advantage in cotton agriculture (interview with Glenn H. Updike, Newsoms, Va., June 20, 1990).

17. For diary notations reflecting a definition of each season as comprising three calendar months, see the Story diary, June 1, 1846, May 31, June 1, 1848, and the Cobb diary, Sept. 1, 1842. Cobb, recalling the usage that had been supplanted almost a century before when eleven days were added to the calendar in England and the British colonies, noted on Mar. 11, 1843, that the next day, by the "oald stile count," would have been the first day of spring.

18. Story diary, Jan. 11, Dec. 4, 1848, Jan. 21, 1852; Cobb diary, Dec. 6, 1847, Jan. 11, 1849.

19. Story diary, Jan. 6–7, 1840, Jan. 8, 1848; Cobb diary, Jan. 13–14, 1851, Jan. 1–3, 1855, Jan. 5–6, 1859.

20. Story diary, Feb. 3, 7, 1846, Feb. 23, 26, 1857.

21. Ibid., Mar. 7, 1843, Apr. 25, 1846.

22. Ibid., Jan. 7, 29, 1846, Nov. 4, 1847, Nov. 3, Dec. 5, 1857; Cobb diary, Jan. 15, 24–25, Sept. 2, 19, Dec. 3, 1845, Sept. 16, 1846, Sept. 6, 1859. Most southern hogs roamed in the woods, but before butchering they were often enclosed and fattened with corn (Hilliard, *Hog Meat and Hoecake*, 95–102).

23. Cobb diary, Mar. 6–9, 13–14, 31, 1843, Mar. 11, 1846; Story diary, Mar. 22, 1838, Mar. 14, 17, 1846, Mar. 2, 1847.

24. Cobb diary, June 12, Nov. 2, 1842; Story diary, Apr. 23, 1838, Feb. 24, Dec. 18, 1848, Oct. 9, Nov. 6, 1851, Oct. 7, 23, 1853, Nov. 29, 1857, Nov. 7, 1858; Johnson, *The Peanut Story*, 75–80, 94.

25. Cobb diary, Apr. 13, 1843, Mar. 29, 31, Apr. 4, 15, 24, May 9, 20, 1845, Apr. 6, July 22, 1846, Apr. 8, 13, 1847, Apr. 23, 1857; Story diary, Apr. 5, 7, 11, 1838, Mar. 30–31, Apr. 2, 6, 15, 1846, Apr. 7, 12, 15, 1847; Nicholas P. Hardeman, *Shucks, Shocks, and Hominy Blocks: Corn as a Way of Life in Pioneer America* (Baton Rouge: Louisiana State Univ. Press, 1981), 74–78.

26. Story diary, Apr. 21, 1838, Apr. 24, 1843, Apr. 23, July 8, 1846, Apr. 27, May 4, 6, 1847, Apr. 7, 1858; Cobb diary, Apr. 20, June 11–12, 1843, Apr. 7, 1845, Apr. 14–16, 1846; Hilliard, *Hog Meat and Hoecake*, 174–76. On midsummer plantings, see Cobb diary, July 3, 1842; Story diary, June 30, 1846, July 5, 10, 1848, July 10, 16, 1857, June 16, 1858. Farmers considered plantains more likely to produce good potatoes; Story was pleased by the success of a potato crop that had used mostly draws and only a few plantains (Story diary, Oct. 29, 1857).

27. Cobb diary, Apr. 11, 1845, Apr. 3, 1847, Apr. 28–May 3, 1856, Apr. 28, 1857, Jan. 28, 1858, Apr. 22–24, 1859.

28. *Farmers' Register* 4 (1836): 52–53, 7 (1839): 668–70, 8 (1840): 168–71; Edmund Ruffin, "Communication to the Virginia State Agricultural Society," *Southern Planter* 12 (1852): 261–63; William M. Mathew, *Edmund Ruffin and the Crisis of Slavery in the Old South: The Failure of Agricultural Reform* (Athens: Univ. of Georgia Press, 1988), 112–14. After the war the use of chemical fertilizers boomed, although promoters of scientific agriculture deplored the ne-

glect of marl, which had longer-lasting benefits on the soil (Washington C. Kerr, *Report on the Cotton Production of the State of North Carolina* [Washington, D.C.: U.S. Census Office, 1884], 22–23).

29. Cobb diary, Apr. 15, 1845, May 2, Sept. 22, 24–26, 1851, Apr. 26, 30, May 2, June 19, Dec. 13, 1853; John Hebron Moore, *The Emergence of the Cotton Kingdom in the Old Southwest: Mississippi, 1770–1860* (Baton Rouge: Louisiana State Univ. Press, 1988), 13–14, 29.

30. Cobb diary, Apr. 26, 1855, May 1, 1858.

31. Ibid., Apr.–July, 1845, Apr. 14, 16, June 28, 30, 1846, June 5, 1847, June 12, 16, 1856, June 14–17, 1858. For cotton and corn cultivation in a different southern locality, see Randolph B. Campbell, *A Southern Community in Crisis: Harrison County, Texas, 1850–1880* (Austin: Texas State Historical Association, 1983), 54–61.

32. Cobb diary, June 2, 1845, June 7, 10, 1846, June 11, 1854, June 28, 1864; Story diary, June 16, 1846, June 12, 1847, June 6, 1848, June 9, 14, 1858; *Southern Planter* 14 (1854): 48–52; Moore, *Cotton Kingdom*, 34–35, 54; Hilliard, *Hog Meat and Hoecake*, 177–78; Carville Earle, "The Myth of the Southern Soil Miner: Macrohistory, Agricultural Innovation, and Environmental Change," in Donald Worster, ed., *The Ends of the Earth: Perspectives on Modern Environmental History* (New York: Cambridge Univ. Press, 1988), 201–4.

33. Story diary, May 25, June 27, July 1, Aug. 1, 1839, Nov. 27, Dec. 5, 1843, May 23, June 16, 20, Nov. 24, 1846, May 22, July 1, Nov. 27, 1847; Cobb diary, July 14, 1843, Oct. 8–9, 1845, Aug. 3–4, 1846, Aug. 21–23, 1849, Aug. 11, 13–14, 17, 1850.

34. Cobb diary, May 8, 26, 31, 1845, May 15, 17, June 16, 18, 1847, May 18, 1849, July 10–11, 17–18, 20–21, 27, 1851, June 2–5, 1858, June 12–13, 1859. The cotton plant itself was hardy enough to survive a spring frost, but cold weather slowed the young plant's growth, making it vulnerable to lice. Frostbitten cotton would probably not produce more than half its bolls (*Soil of the South* 6 [1856]: 97–98).

35. *Southern Cultivator* 2 (1844): 12–13; *Soil of the South* 6 (1856): 70–71; Cobb diary, June 22, 23, 1847, July 14, 1853, June 26, 1858.

36. Cobb diary, June 25, 1845, July 3, 12, Aug. 10, 1847, July 30, Aug. 9, 1849, July 8, Aug. 2–3, 1853, July 13, Aug. 9, 13, 1857, June 25–27, July 12, Aug. 3–4, 16, 1859.

37. Ibid., Aug. 5, 1854, Aug. 6–8, 1857, Aug. 6–7, 1858, Aug. 5–6, 1859.

38. Ibid., July 24, Aug. 25, 28, 29, 1855, July 30–Sept. 18, 1856, Aug. 8, 15, 26, Sept. 5–14, 1859.

39. Gray, *Southern Agriculture*, 2:814–15; Hardeman, *Shucks, Shocks, and Hominy Blocks*, 100–102; Cobb diary, Aug. 20–Sept. 9, Sept. 22, 24, 1845.

40. Cobb diary, June 17, 1843, June 2, Sept. 4, 10, 1845, June 7, 10, Oct. 19–20, 27–28, 1846, Oct. 7, 13, 1850; Story diary, Oct. 5, 1847, Oct. 9, Nov. 6, 1851, Oct. 23, 1852. Cobb sold forty-six bushels of black-eyed peas in 1854, for seventy cents a bushel, after planting enough more for home use and to provide seed (Cobb diary, Sept. 26, 29, Nov. 1–3, 1854). This amount was comparable to what he had grown during the 1840s, when his total farm output was much

smaller; he chose to expand corn and cotton rather than peas, perhaps because pea prices had not advanced above the relatively low levels of the depressed 1840s.

41. Cobb diary, Sept. 4, 22, 25, 1845, Sept. 9, 11, 1846, Sept. 23, 25, 1847, Sept. 11, 28, Oct. 2, 1849, Oct. 4, 1852, Dec. 5, 1853, Oct. 7, 14, Nov. 15, 1854, Nov. 10, 1856.

42. Moore, *Cotton Kingdom*, 9, 12, 85, 98, 127.

43. Cobb diary, Oct. 11–14, 25–26, 1852, Oct. 15, 19–22, Nov. 2, 6–7, 25, 30, Dec. 1, 1859. By the mid–1850s Cobb had one of his slaves make the trip to Petersburg.

44. Story diary, Nov. 2, 13, 1843, Oct. 29, 30, 1846; Cobb diary, Nov. 14, 22–24, 1843, Nov. 8–10, 16, 23–25, 1849, Nov. 13, 1854.

45. Hardeman, *Shucks, Shocks, and Hominy Blocks*, 40–45, 95–96; Owsley, *Plain Folk of the Old South*, 111–14; Jack Larkin, *The Reshaping of Everyday Life, 1790–1840* (New York: Harper and Row, 1988), 266–68, 298.

46. Cobb diary, June 22, July 14, 16, 1845; Story diary, July 12, 1852, Oct. 30, 1858; Hardeman, *Shucks, Shocks, and Hominy Blocks*, 118–37.

47. Cobb diary, Dec. 29, 1845; Story diary, Dec. 29, 1851.

48. Cobb diary, Dec. 28, 1842, Dec. 27, 1845, May 12, Aug. 14–15, Dec. 29–30, 1846, Dec. 26, 30, 1847, Dec. 28, 1853, Dec. 27, 1855; Story diary, Dec. 27, 1848, Dec. 29, 1851, Dec. 29, 1857.

49. Parramore, *Southampton County*, 31–32, 46–47; George Carrington Mason, "The Colonial Churches of Isle of Wight and Southampton Counties, Virginia," *William and Mary Quarterly*, 2d ser., 23 (1943): 41, 58–63.

50. William Wade Hinshaw and Thomas Worth Marshall, eds., *Encyclopedia of American Quaker Genealogy 6* (Ann Arbor, Mich.: Edwards Brothers, 1950): 47–49; Jay Worrall, Jr., "Black Creek Friends Meeting," typescript in posssession of author; Southampton County Deed Book, 6:91, Nov. 1782, VSLA.

51. Story diary, May 21, 1848, May 18, 1851, May 16, 1852. See Cobb diary, May 21, 1854, May 17, 1857, on poor attendance at Methodist churches because of the half-year meeting. Mary Jane Cobb and her daughter Rebecca attended the half-year meeting in 1866 (ibid., May 18–19, 1866).

52. Black Creek Baptist Church Minutes, Feb. 24, Nov. 24, 1786, June 24, Aug. 26, 1791, Nov. 22, 1793, Feb. 21, 1794, Virginia Baptist Historical Society, University of Richmond, copy at VSLA; Carlos R. Allen, Jr., "David Barrow's *Circular Letter* of 1798," *William and Mary Quarterly*, 3d ser., 20 (1963): 440–51; James David Essig, "A Very Wintry Season: Virginia Baptists and Slavery, 1785–1797," *VMHB* 88 (1980): 180–81; James D. Essig, *The Bonds of Wickedness: American Evangelicals against Slavery* (Philadelphia: Temple Univ. Press, 1982), 74–78.

53. Allen, "Barrow's *Circular Letter*," 450–51. On Barrow's continued anti-slavery efforts in Kentucky, see William Warren Sweet, *Religion on the American Frontier* (Chicago: Univ. of Chicago Press, 1931), 564–70; David T. Bailey, *Southwestern Evangelical Religion and the Issue of Slavery, 1783–1860* (Ithaca: Cornell Univ. Press, 1985), 33–38; John B. Boles, *Religion in Antebellum Kentucky* (Lexington: Univ. Press of Kentucky, 1976), 114–18.

54. Black Creek Baptist Church Minutes, Sept.–Oct. 1816, Dec. 1825, Virginia Baptist Historical Society.

55. Ibid., Dec. 1825, Mar., June, Sept., Oct., Dec. 1826, June 1827.

56. Ibid., Sept. 1827.

57. Story diary, Mar. 15, 1839, June 10, 1848.

58. Minute books for the South Quay Baptist Church, as well as those for the Black Creek Baptist Church, may be found at the Virginia Baptist Historical Society. See also Parramore, *Southampton County*, 52–53, 62–64; "A Brief Historical Sketch of the Black Creek Baptist Church" (mimeographed, 1961), item no. 58, SCHS; *Time of Small Beginnings: The History of Hebron Baptist Church, Southampton County, Virginia* (n.p, n.d.), pamphlet in the possession of Gilbert W. Francis, Boykins, Va. The Cobb diary entries of Sept. 27, 1846, and Oct. 5, 1857, show that there was a Baptist church in Jerusalem.

59. The key source for Southampton Methodists is Leigh, "Meherrin Circuit Steward's Book," SCHS. See also Kitty Bland Lassiter, *A Brief History of the Boykins United Methodist Church* (Ahoskie, N.C.: Pierce Printers, 1983), 1–2, and Dr. W. B. Barham, "Vick's Old Church," in Churches folder of Edgar B. Jackson Papers, both in the possession of Gilbert W. Francis, Boykins, Va.

60. W. E. Mac Clenny, *The Life of Rev. James O'Kelly and the Early History of the Christian Church in the South* (Raleigh, N.C.: Edwards and Broughton, 1910), 139–46, 166; P. J. Kernodle, *Lives of Christian Ministers* (Richmond: Central Publishing Co., 1909), 56–57; Donald G. Mathews, *Religion in the Old South* (Chicago: Univ. of Chicago Press, 1977), 73–74, 126; Leigh, "Meherrin Circuit Steward's Book."

61. Mathews, *Religion in the Old South*, 80.

62. Ibid., 97, 123.

63. John B. Boles, ed., "Introduction," *Masters and Slaves in the House of the Lord: Race and Religion in the American South, 1740–1870* (Lexington: Univ. Press of Kentucky, 1988), 9; Mathews, *Religion in the Old South*, 197, 226.

64. Mathews, *Religion in the Old South*, 105; Leigh, "Meherrin Circuit Steward's Book." The latter shows that white women and blacks also outnumbered white men at all other Southampton congregations for which full membership lists survive. In 1859, for example, Union (Christian and Methodist) had thirty-nine white women members, twenty-three white men, and twenty blacks (seven free and thirteen slave); Clarksbury Methodist had nineteen white women, ten white men, and nineteen blacks (mostly enslaved); Mt. Horeb Methodist had twenty-nine white women, twelve white men, and thirteen blacks; New Hope Methodist had thirty-five white women, twenty-three white men, and twenty-one blacks (sixteen free); Applewhites Methodist had twenty white women, eleven white men, and eight blacks. Proportionately smaller numbers of white men and blacks belonged to Barnes Methodist (forty-two white women, thirteen white men, six blacks).

65. John B. Boles, "Evangelical Protestantism in the Old South: From Religious Dissent to Cultural Dominance," in Charles Reagan Wilson, ed., *Religion in the Old South* (Jackson: Univ. Press of Mississippi, 1985), 26–27; Mathews, *Religion in the Old South*, 81–135. On the eighteenth century, see also Rhys

Isaac, *The Transformation of Virginia: 1740–1790* (Chapel Hill: Univ. of North Carolina Press, 1982), 161–72, 260–69, 290–92, 314–17. For the nineteenth century, see also Dickson D. Bruce, *And They All Sang Hallelujah: Plain-Folk Camp-Meeting Religion, 1800–1845* (Knoxville: Univ. of Tennessee Press, 1974), which tends to exaggerate the distance between the dominant culture and that of the plain folk. For a thoughtful assessment, see Bill Cecil-Fronsman, "The Common White: Class and Culture in Antebellum North Carolina" (Ph.D. diss., Univ. of North Carolina at Chapel Hill, 1983), chap. 6.

66. Mathews, *Religion in the Old South*, 40.

67. Cobb diary, June 10, 1843, Feb. 10, 1854.

68. Story diary, June 21, 1846, Jan. 24, 1847.

69. Ibid., Aug. 2, 1846, Sept. 29, 1852; Mathews, *Religion in the Old South*, 245.

70. Cobb diary, Aug. 6–7, 9, Sept. 4, 20, 1842.

71. Ibid., Aug. 17, 22, 24, Sept. 7, 11, 13, 15, 27, 28, 30, 1845.

72. Story diary, Aug. 27, Sept. 10–12, 23–26, 29, Oct. 6, 7, 1848.

73. Ibid., Sept. 12, 18–19, Oct. 6, 8, 10–13, 1858; Cobb diary, Sept. 11–12, 16, 19, 1858, Aug. 7, 14, 21, Sept. 4, 11, Oct. 2–7, 9, 11, 12, 16, 1859; Parramore, *Southampton County*, 153–54, quoting Petersburg *Daily Express*, Sept. 20, 24, 1859.

74. Story diary, Sept. 12, 1848; Cobb diary, Sept. 4, 1842; Ryan, *Cradle of the Middle Class*, 13. Another influential model for interpreting religious revivals and evangelicalism in the antebellum North, developed by historians Paul E. Johnson and Anthony F. C. Wallace through intensive study of specific localities in New York and Pennsylvania, sheds little light on Southampton County and the antebellum South; they suggest that the evangelical impulse in the North received key support from professional elites, who sought indirect means to preserve social order at a time when the scale of business activity in the northern free-labor economy produced rapid increases in the numbers of unsupervised wage workers (Paul E. Johnson, *A Shopkeeper's Millenium: Society and Revivals in Rochester, New York, 1815–1837* [New York: Hill and Wang, 1978]; Anthony F. C. Wallace, *Rockdale: The Growth of an American Village in the Early Industrial Revolution* [New York: Knopf, 1978]).

75. Clinton, *The Plantation Mistress*, 160–79.

76. One invited the disapproval of pious neighbors by attempting on Sunday to enlist an extra hand for Monday at the peak of the wheat harvest (Story diary, June 25, 1843).

77. Letter from "E.," Mar. 23, 1866, Richmond semiweekly *Whig*, Mar. 30, 1866.

78. Cobb diary, Mar. 20, 1843, Aug, 18, 1845; Story diary, July 20, 1846.

79. Cobb diary, May 12, Aug. 22, Oct. 11, 1842, Feb. 21, 1843, May 3, Sept. 6, Oct. 4, 1845, Apr. 4, May 2, Sept. 5, 1846; Story diary, May 6, Oct. 14, 1843, May 13, 1847, Apr. 8, May 13, Oct. 14, 1848.

80. Cobb diary, May 17, 1845; Story diary, May 9, 1846, May 13, 1847.

81. Story diary, Mar. 19, 1846, Jan. 1, Feb. 22, July 4, 1848, Apr. 22, 1859.

82. Ibid., Jan. 7, Dec. 27, 30–31, 1842, Dec. 25–31, 1848.

83. Ibid., Apr. 11, 1846, Mar. 15, Apr. 19, 1847, Apr. 8, Sept. 18, 1848, Aug. 16, 1851; Cobb diary, Apr. 24, 1859.

84. Story diary, Apr. 11, 20, 1846, Sept. 18, 1848.

85. Ibid., Dec. 11, 1843, July 17, 1848, May 12, Aug. 30, 1852.

FOUR. THE FORMATION OF POLITICAL PARTIES

1. Paul F. Bourke and Donald A. DeBats, "Identifiable Voting in Nineteenth-Century America: Toward a Comparison of Britain and the United States before the Secret Ballot," *Perspectives in American History* 11 (1977–78): 259–88; William G. Shade, "Society and Politics in Antebellum Virginia's Southside," *Journal of Southern History* 53 (1987): 163–93.

Viva voce elections, used in Virginia before 1867, resulted in poll lists, that is, records showing which voters voted for which candidates. The poll lists preserved in the Southampton County Courthouse have been deposited at the Virginia State Library and Archives, which has microfilmed most of the material (Southampton County Records, reels 66–72).

The data file for this chapter incorporates elections for the House of Delegates in 1833, 1834, 1836, and 1839, plus presidential elections in 1836 and 1840. Information from the 1840 federal census and the 1841 state land tax lists allows study of the relationships between voting behavior, landowning, slaveholdings, and residence.

Also included is information about religious affiliation from a variety of sources: minutes for the Black Creek and South Quay Baptist Churches, Virginia Baptist Historical Society, University of Richmond; Leigh's "Meherrin Circuit Steward's Book," SCHS; minutes for Barretts Christian Church, VSLA; records of the Lower Monthly Meeting (Virginia), Quaker Collection, Haverford College Library, Haverford, Pa.; Hinshaw and Marshall, *Encyclopedia of American Quaker Genealogy* 6:47–49 and ff.

All data were incorporated into a SAS file and run at the Trenton State College Computer Center.

2. Very little about the 1830s remains in the papers of John Young Mason, Southampton's most prominent politician (Mason Family Papers, VHS). One of Southampton's two diarists, Daniel W. Cobb, did not keep a journal before 1842; the other, Elliott L. Story, started his journal in 1838 and provided some interesting 1839 observations, but the volume covering April 1840–December 1841 has been lost (Cobb and Story diaries, VHS).

3. *Proceedings and Debates of the Virginia State Convention of 1829–30* (Richmond: Samuel Shepherd & Co. for Ritchie & Cook, 1830), 789–90, first called to my attention in Shade, "Society and Politics in Antebellum Virginia's Southside," 165.

4. Charles S. Sydnor, *The Development of Southern Sectionalism, 1819–1848* (Baton Rouge: Louisiana State Univ. Press, 1948), 134–202.

5. The new point of departure for understanding nineteeth-century southern

history is William W. Freehling, *The Road to Disunion*, vol. 1, *Secessionists at Bay, 1776–1854* (New York: Oxford Univ. Press, 1990).

6. Norfolk and Portsmouth *Herald*, Apr. 28, Nov. 7, 1828.

7. Those Anti-Jacksonians who were still residing in the county a decade later and about whom information is available owned the following number of slaves:

20 or more slaves	4 (7%)
10 to 19	12 (20)
4 to 9	8 (14)
1 to 3	10 (17)
0	25 (42)

The Anti-Jacksonians exhibited no discernible pattern of religious affiliation. Six belonged to churches north of the river for which membership lists survive (three were members of two different Baptist churches; two affiliated with the Quaker meeting; one belonged to the Christian Church). Seven belonged to three different Methodist churches south of the river, where most Southampton Methodists lived.

8. *Proceedings and Debates of the Virginia State Convention of 1829–30*, 369–71, 827, 892 (quotations on 369–70); Alison Goodyear Freehling, *Drift toward Dissolution: The Virginia Slavery Debate of 1831–1832* (Baton Rouge: Louisiana State Univ. Press, 1982), 45–46; Dickson D. Bruce, Jr., *The Rhetoric of Conservatism: The Virginia Convention of 1829–30 and the Conservative Tradition in the South* (San Marino, Calif.: Huntington Library, 1982), 36 and passim. An 1825 petition with many Southampton signatures protested against any disturbance of the "settled and happy order of things," insisting that "the great body of the good people of this Commonwealth" were "perfectly content with their ancient institutions, and most jealous and fearful of the spirit of innovation" (Legislative Petitions, Southampton County, Dec. 12, 1825, VSLA).

9. Freehling, *Drift toward Dissolution*, 48–81; Freehling, *Road to Disunion*, 162–77; Robert P. Sutton, *Revolution to Secession: Constitution Making in the Old Dominion* (Charlottesville: Univ. Press of Virginia, 1989), 72–106.

10. *Proceedings and Debates of the Virginia State Convention of 1829–30*, 149, 313, 316, 320–21, 858.

11. Richmond *Enquirer*, Oct. 29, 1830, Aug. 23, 1831; Norfolk *American Beacon*, Apr. 28, Oct. 29, 1830; Norfolk and Portsmouth *Herald*, Aug. 22, 1831. The total turnout of 721 in August 1831 approached the level Southampton would generate in the 1840 presidential election, when the initial surge of party rivalry reached its greatest intensity. Could the heated election campaign have in some way influenced Nat Turner's thinking? Could he have judged that whites were preoccupied or divided? For a plausible linking of earlier slave rebelliousness to white political divisions, see Douglas R. Egerton, "Gabriel's Conspiracy and the Election of 1800," *Journal of Southern History* 56 (1990): 191–214.

12. The initial returns in April 1832 gave Griffin a majority of over a hundred votes, 381 to 265. A canvass revealed, however, that 76 voters either were under-

age, had failed to pay taxes, did not own land, or had not owned land for the requisite six months. (The system of viva voce elections lent itself to after-the-fact checkups for eligibility, although only rarely did such actually take place.) The canvass had no effect on the outcome: 41 of Griffin's votes were disallowed, and 35 of Cobb's. The official tally reported 570 valid votes, with Griffin still the victor, 340 to 230.

13. Freehling, *Drift toward Dissolution*, 148–49, 158–60, 164.

14. The speech is printed verbatim in the Norfolk and Portsmouth *Herald*, Apr. 2, 4, 1832.

15. Freehling, *Drift toward Dissolution*, 129–30; Freehling, *Road to Disunion*, 178–96.

16. Norfolk and Portsmouth *Herald*, Apr. 4, 30, 1832.

17. Richard E. Ellis, *The Union at Risk: Jacksonian Democracy, States' Rights, and the Nullification Crisis* (New York: Oxford Univ. Press, 1987), 123–40.

18. Norfolk and Portsmouth *Herald*, Dec. 31, 1832, Jan. 30, 1833.

19. George Blow to John Young Mason, late Dec. 1832 or early Jan. 1833 (typed copy), Mason Family Papers, sec. 6, VHS.

20. Freehling, *Drift toward Dissolution*, 196–222.

21. Norfolk and Portsmouth *Herald*, Mar. 11, 1833.

22. Ellis, *The Union at Risk*, 129–40 (quotation on 139).

23. Lynwood M. Dent, Jr., "The Virginia Democratic Party, 1824–1847" (Ph.D. diss., Louisiana State Univ., 1974), 125–60 (quotations on 148, 159); Henry H. Simms, *The Rise of the Whigs in Virginia, 1824–1840* (Richmond: William Byrd Press, 1929), 63–87; Charles Henry Ambler, *Thomas Ritchie: A Study in Virginia Politics* (Richmond: Bell Book and Stationery Co., 1913), 155–86.

24. Simms, *Rise of the Whigs in Virginia*, 88–94; Dent, "Virginia Democratic Party," 161–70; Norma Lois Peterson, *Littleton Waller Tazewell* (Charlottesville: Univ. Press of Virginia, 1983), 232–49.

25. Simms, *Rise of the Whigs in Virginia*, 94–99; Dent, "Virginia Democratic Party," 170–77; Charles D. Lowery, *James Barbour: A Jeffersonian Republican* (University: Univ. of Alabama Press, 1984), 230–33. Leigh ignored the instructions but did not resign.

26. Of the voters known to have lived in the upper county, 150 out of 182 supported Griffin; Harrison won 58 of 84 votes cast by known residents of the lower county. To this extent the 1833 election prefigured subsequent of residence and party, because the upper county became Whiggish, while the lower county became very Democratic. But the individual votes cast in 1833 bore no relationship to earlier national allegiances (14 of the 1828 Anti-Jackson group voted for Griffin; 15 for Harrison) and only a slight relationship to subsequent ones (persisting Griffin voters in 1840 displayed a Whig tendency, 85–61; Harrison supporters still participating in 1840 then voted narrowly Democratic, 33–31).

27. Harrison, by contrast, lacked any comparable religious base. Members of the South Quay Baptist Church, nearest to his home, divided their sixteen votes evenly. Harrison did draw seven of the eleven votes cast by known Methodists,

but his pitiful turnout in lower-county Methodist strongholds doomed his candidacy. Fully fifty-three known lower-county Methodists did not vote in 1833. Information about the political behavior of church members is fragmentary and incomplete, but the surviving Southampton County church records are extensive enough to draw reasonable inferences, using the names of white male adults.

28. John Denegre to John Young Mason, Mar. 30, 1834, Mason Family Papers, sec. 24.

29. Jackson's 1828 opponents decisively supported Harrison, 36–8. Moreover, those who voted both in 1834 and in the presidential election of 1840 displayed undoubted partisan continuity, as James C. Harrison's 1834 supporters favored William Henry Harrison, 101–40, whereas Parker voters from 1834 gave Martin Van Buren a 92–30 advantage in 1840.

30. Dent, "Virginia Democratic Party," 284–87, 295–96, 300–356, 399–414; Simms, *Rise of the Whigs in Virginia*, 155–56, 163.

31. Harrison collected all twelve votes cast by members of South Quay Baptist Church, near his home, more than offsetting Parker's 13–10 margin among the still nonpoliticized lower-county Methodists. Members of several upper-county churches that had voted strongly for Griffin preferred Parker over Harrison, 10–5.

32. John Denegre to John Young Mason, Mar. 30, 1834, Mason Family Papers, sec. 24.

33. Richmond *Enquirer*, Jan. 22, 1835; "A Voter of Southampton, and Also a Native," Jan. 20, 1835, ibid., Jan. 24, 1835; "Anti-Van," Jan. 10, 1835, Richmond *Whig*, Jan. 16, 1835.

34. Richmond *Enquirer*, Jan. 3, 1835; "A Voter of Southampton, and Also a Native," ibid., Jan. 24, 1835; Richmond *Whig*, Jan. 2, 1835, quoted in Richmond *Enquirer*, Jan. 3, 1835; "Anti-Van," Richmond *Whig*, Jan. 16, 1835; ibid., Jan. 27, 1835.

35. "Anti-Van," Richmond *Whig*, Jan. 16, 1835.

36. "A Voter of Southampton, and Also a Native," Richmond *Enquirer*, Jan. 24, 1835; Richmond *Whig*, Jan. 23, 28, 1835; Norfolk and Portsmouth *Herald*, Jan. 23, 1835.

37. Richmond *Whig*, Apr. 24, 1835; Norfolk and Portsmouth *Herald*, Apr. 22, 24, 1835.

38. Richmond *Whig*, Apr. 24, 1835; "One Who Voted for Lundy," ibid., May 12, 1835.

39. The 1841 state land tax records and 1840 federal census data together suggest that 612 eligible voters lived in the upper county and 457 in the lower county. In 1836, over 47 percent of known upper-county eligibles voted; in the lower county fewer than 34 percent did so. Both percentages are between 8 and 9 percent low, because 90 of the 535 voters in 1836 cannot be identified by residence. The figures of 56 percent turnout in the upper county and 43 percent turnout for the lower county are estimates, distributing proportionately the voters who are unidentified by residence.

40. Among voters for whom there is a record of slave ownership, 61 percent of those owning no slaves preferred Butts over Goodwyn. Known nonslavehold-

ers cast over 38 percent of Whig votes and under 31 percent of Democratic votes. Larger slaveholders with more than ten slaves and planters with twenty or more slaves contributed over 30 percent of Democratic votes and around 25 percent of Whig votes. In the lower part of the county, larger slaveholders and planters contributed fully half of the Democratic vote.

41. Baptist churches, heretofore a citadel of support for Whigs and proto-Whigs, gave the Democrat, Goodwyn, a surprising 22-to-21 margin. The Black Creek Baptist Church, swept by Griffin in 1833 and carried solidly by Harrison in 1834, divided 12 to 12. The South Quay Baptist Church, unanimous for Harrison in 1834, voted for Goodwyn, 8 to 7. Nor did Butts poll a solid advantage among upper-county Christians and Quakers, carrying only nine of seventeen votes. Lower-county Methodists remained largely nonpoliticized: voters from seven congregations favored Goodwyn, 16 to 7, but nonvoting Methodists greatly outnumbered those voting.

Southampton church members during the mid-1830s did not exhibit consistent patterns of political behavior. The evidence does suggest, however, that religious communities, which by the late 1830s had acquired more definite partisan identities, played significant, if inconsistent, roles in channeling partisan stirrings.

42. Only 54 percent of voters who participated in 1833 voted in 1836, and 64 percent of those voting in 1836 had not voted three years before. An identical 54 percent of those voting in 1834 reappeared in 1836; 50 percent of 1836 voters had not voted in 1834.

43. The antiabolitionist panic in the South in the summer of 1835 is a neglected subject. Leonard L. Richards, *"Gentlemen of Property and Standing": Anti-Abolition Mobs in Jacksonian America* (New York: Oxford Univ. Press, 1970), considers only episodes in northern cities, but does call attention to the relatively sudden way in which the uproar flared. On the South, see Cooper, *The South and the Politics of Slavery*, 54–97, which offers many insights on the political consequences of the panic, as does Freehling, *Road to Disunion*, 290–307. See also William W. Freehling, *Prelude to Civil War: The Nullification Controversy in South Carolina, 1816–1836* (New York: Harper and Row, 1966), 340–48; Clement Eaton, *The Freedom-of-Thought Struggle in the Old South*, rev. and enl. ed. (New York: Harper and Row, 1964), 196–208.

44. Norfolk and Portsmouth *Herald*, July 27, 28, 1835.

45. Ibid., Aug. 14, 17, 19, 1835.

46. "For the Whig," Richmond *Whig*, Aug. 28, 1835; Norfolk and Portsmouth *Herald*, Aug. 31, 1835.

47. Richmond *Whig*, July 24, 1835. See Eaton, *Freedom-of-Thought Struggle*, 169–74.

48. Simms, *Rise of the Whigs in Virginia*, 100–105; Dent, "Virginia Democratic Party," 180–214; Cooper, *The South and the Politics of Slavery*, 85–97.

49. Simms, *Rise of the Whigs in Virginia*, 112–17; Dent, "Virginia Democratic Party," 181–214.

50. Simms, *Rise of the Whigs in Virginia*, 112, 116.

51. Southampton and thirty other Virginia counties witnessed close party competition in the three presidential elections between 1836 and 1844, with nei-

ther party gaining as much as 55 percent of the total vote cast. In eighty-seven other Virginia counties (that is, about three-quarters of the total), one party or the other collected at least 55 percent of the vote. In sixty-nine counties, considerably more than half the total, one party or the other drew at least 60 percent of the vote. Among the latter were all five Virginia counties bordering Southampton: Isle of Wight and Sussex were among the most Democratic counties in the state, Greensville and Surry both voted more than 60 percent Democratic, whereas Nansemond shared the Whig loyalties of the Norfolk region (Dent, "Virginia Democratic Party," 372–74).

52. Religious voters behaved much as they had in the spring. Baptist preferences remained identical, 22 to 21 Democratic, although Whigs ran better at Black Creek Baptist while Democrats carried South Quay Baptist. A majority of Christians and Quakers ignored the presidential election; six of the eleven who did participate supported Van Buren. Democrats carried the county with scant help from Methodists. Although several Methodist churches in the lower county would soon become bastions of Democratic strength, Van Buren collected only nine votes, while losing six, among Southampton's still-apolitical Methodists.

53. In the spring 136 nonslaveholders had participated, and of this group, 83 had voted Whig (61%). An additional 148 voters of indeterminate slaveholding had voted in the spring, and there is good reason to believe that most of them were nonslaveholders. They too voted Whig, 84 to 64, a margin of 57 percent. In the presidential election, however, only 90 nonslaveholders appeared, dividing equally between the parties. Similarly, only 84 voters whose slaveholdings cannot be determined voted in the fall, and they too divided equally between the parties. The erosion of Whig support in the upper county, where the greatest concentration of nonslaveholders lived, was especially marked. The Whig margin in the upper county shrank to a relatively narrow 57 percent.

54. Glyndon G. Van Deusen, *The Jacksonian Era, 1828–1848* (New York: Harper and Row, 1959), 105–6, 124–29. Congress repealed the Specie Circular in 1838 (ibid., 106).

55. Dent, "Virginia Democratic Party," 172, 237, 245–46 (quotation on 245).

56. Harold D. Moser, "Subtreasury Politics and the Virginia Conservative Democrats, 1835–1844" (Ph.D. diss., Univ. of Wisconsin, 1977), chaps. 3–4; Arthur C. Cole, *The Whig Party in the South* (1914; rept. Gloucester Mass.: Peter Smith, 1962), 45–53; James Roger Sharp, *The Jacksonians versus the Banks: Politics in the States after the Panic of 1837* (New York: Columbia Univ. Press, 1970), 215–38; Simms, *Rise of the Whigs in Virginia*, 118–39; Dent, "Virginia Democratic Party," 215–67, 285–87; Ambler, *Ritchie*, 187–218.

57. James Maget, "Draft of 1848 Speech for House of Delegates in Southampton County," Majette Family Papers, sec. 3, item 117, VHS; Simms, *Rise of the Whigs in Virginia*, 127–30; Dent, "Virginia Democratic Party," 218–19, 251, 258.

58. Maget, "Draft of 1848 Speech," Majette Family Papers; Dent, "Virginia Democratic Party," 258–61; Simms, *Rise of the Whigs in Virginia*, 131–34.

59. Story diary, May 16, 20, 22, 1839, VHS.

60. Samuel James Douglas to John Young Mason, May 21, 1839, James B. Urquhart to Mason, May 24, 1839, Mason to Urquhart (draft), June 1, 1839, Mason Family Papers, sec. 6.

61. Voters who had cast a Democratic ticket in the 1836 legislative elections supported Ridley, 162 to 6; their Whigs counterparts favored Urquhart, 199 to 15. A similar tally may be found when comparing relationships between the 1839 vote and the 1836 presidential election. Van Buren supporters flocked to Ridley, 130 to 12; Whigs from 1836 sided monolithically with Urquhart, 144 to 2.

62. Petition dated Mar. 5, 1839, Legislative Petitions, Southampton County, VSLA. All three representatives from Southampton to the state constitutional convention in 1829–30 had voted against allowing more than one polling place in a county (*Proceedings and Debates of the Virginia State Convention of 1829–30*, 817).

63. To elect Ridley, Democrats enlisted 210 voters (54 percent of their total) who had not voted in the 1836 legislative elections and fully 255 (66 percent of their total) who had not voted in that year's presidential contest. Whigs countered with 126 voters (38 percent of their total) who had not played a role in choosing the state legislator three years before, and 175 (53 percent of their total) who had not voted at the most recent presidential matchup.

64. Between the assembly elections of 1836 and 1839, Democrats increased their support among known residents of the upper county from 102 to 132. In the lower county, however, Democratic totals soared from 92 to 238. Whig totals in the lower county receded from 61 to 55 between 1836 and 1839. As the lower county became a Democratic bastion, Whigs would have to enlist more voters from the upper county. They did increase their upper-county turnout from 190 in 1836 to 260 in 1839, but that proved insufficient to overcome Democratic gains. Upper-county and lower-county turnout percentages used here have each been increased by 3 percent to take into account the fact that 33 of 718 voters in 1839 cannot be identified by residence.

65. The increasingly Whiggish Black Creek Baptist Church gave Urquhart a solid 21-to-9 margin, but that was offset by the increasingly Democratic preferences among members of the South Quay Baptist Church, a congregation that included numerous Nullifiers. With the addition of fragmentary information about two smaller churches, Baptists gave Urquhart a narrow 32-to-29 advantage. Nor did Urquhart gain from the votes of upper-county Christians and Quakers, who together polled eight Whig and nine Democratic votes.

The voting patterns among members of Southampton churches closely parallel what historian William G. Shade has found in Southside Prince Edward County. There, too, Baptists voted "along the same lines as the county as a whole," whereas Methodists "leaned heavily toward the Democratic party" (Shade, "Society and Politics in Antebellum Virginia's Southside," 187). In North Carolina, however, a very different relationship existed between religious affiliation and antebellum voting, with Baptists strongly Democratic and Methodists decidedly Whiggish (Gary Freeze, "The Ethnocultural Thesis Goes South: Religiocultural Dimensions of Voting in North Carolina's Second Party System," paper presented at the Southern Historical Association, Norfolk, Nov. 1988).

66. Of the 387 Democratic voters, the slaveholdings of 312 may be determined: 205 of those 312 voters (66%) owned slaves. By comparison, information about 267 of the 331 Whig voters is accessible, indicating that 149 (56%) owned slaves. In each instance, one may reasonably guess that most voters for whom information was unavailable were nonslaveholders. It may therefore be determined that at least 53 percent (205 of 387) of all Democratic voters owned slaves, and the actual percentage was probably slightly higher. For Whigs, the comparable figure is at least 45 percent (149 of 331).

67. At Cross Keys, the other new lower-county voting district, a broader cross section of voters delivered an even more thumping Democratic margin, 143 to 11. Information about 120 of these Democrats shows 61 percent owned slaves, 29 percent owned ten or more slaves, and 12 percent owned twenty or more. Taking also into account votes cast at the courthouse, information about 196 of the 238 lower county Democrats shows that 76 percent owned slaves, 40 percent owned ten or more, and 17 percent owned twenty or more.

68. The few lower county Whigs, though hardly impoverished, displayed a somewhat smaller slaveholding profile than lower-county Democrats. Data for fifty of the fifty-five Whigs shows that thirty-one (or 62 percent) owned slaves, that twelve (or 24%) owned ten or more, and that five (or 10%) owned twenty or more.

69. At the two new voting districts in the upper county, Berlin and Griffins Store, Whigs won easy victories, 88 to 37 and 77 to 31. Among the seventy-one of eighty-eight Whig voters at Berlin for whom there is a record of slaveholding, thirty-six (or 51%) owned slaves. Eleven of Berlin's Whig slaveholders (15%) owned ten or more slaves; seven (or 10%) owned twenty or more. Slaveholdings among Whigs voting at Griffins Store were slightly smaller than in Berlin. Only twenty-five of sixty-one for whom data are available (41%) owned slaves. Eight of these (13%) owned ten or more slaves; only two (or 3%) owned twenty or more. A more privileged group of upper-county Whigs voted at the courthouse. Taking into account votes cast at the two outlying districts and at the courthouse, it may be determined that 54 percent of upper-county Whigs owned slaves. This figure is 22 percent below the 76 percent of lower-county Democrats who were slaveholders.

If voters about whom no information is available are counted as nonslaveholders, as most in fact were, then the following recalculations could be made: at least 63 percent of lower-county Democrats owned slaves (149 of 238); for upper-county Whigs the comparable figure would be at least 45 percent (118 of 260).

70. Upper-county Democrats, a more numerous group than lower-county Whigs, exhibited patterns of slaveholding more like those of their Whig neighbors than those of their party allies in the lower county. Data for 118 of 132 upper-county Democrats shows that 68 (or 58%) owned slaves, with 17 (or 14%) owning ten or more, and 5 (or 4%) owning twenty or more.

71. Shade, "Society and Politics in Antebellum Virginia's Southside," 186.

72. Lewis, *Southampton Ridleys and Their Kin*, 120–23; Babb, *History of Ivor*, 24–25.

73. Lewis, *Southampton Ridleys and Their Kin*, 44, 54–55.

74. Ibid., 44, 56–60. Archaeological work on eighteenth-century remains on the Francis T. Ridley property was performed in 1986, concurrent with the widening of U.S. Highway 58; see Theodore R. Reinhart, *Material Culture, Social Relations, and Spatial Organization on a Colonial Frontier: The Pope Site (44SN180), Southampton County, Virginia* (Williamsburg, Va.: Department of Anthropology, College of William and Mary, 1987), 4–5, 104–5.

75. See Crofts, *Reluctant Confederates*, 47–48, 390 n.7.

76. Cole, *Whig Party in the South*, 53–63.

77. Simms, *Rise of the Whigs in Virginia*, 140–59; Dent, "Virginia Democratic Party," 257–90; Richard P. McCormick, *The Second American Party System: Party Formation in the Jacksonian Era* (Chapel Hill: Univ. of North Carolina Press, 1966), 341–42.

78. Van Buren received all but 12 of the 142 votes from his 1836 supporters; Whigs voted even more monolithically, as Harrison won 144 of 146 votes cast by Whigs four years before. Nor did voters who participated both in 1839 and 1840 often switch parties. Democrats from 1839 who voted in 1840 favored Van Buren, 282 to 9; all but 10 of 278 Whig supporters from 1839 participating in 1840 repeated their vote. Duplicating exactly their performance in 1839, the anti-Jackson group from 1828 voted against Old Hickory's heir, 38 to 12.

79. Turnout in the upper county increased from 392 to 434. Whigs added 27 votes to the 1839 totals, and Democrats 15, producing a comfortable Whig cushion, 287 to 147. Democrats, who had polled a 238-to-55 advantage in lower county in 1839, held a slightly narrower 218-to-73 edge in 1840. Upper-county and lower-county turnout percentages used here have each been increased by more than 2 percent, to take into account the fact that 25 of 750 voters in 1840 cannot be identified by residence.

80. In the upper county, known nonslaveholders and those without listed slaveholdings (most of whom probably owned no slaves) cast 206 of 392 total ballots in 1839 and 228 of 434 total ballots in 1840, each time between 52 percent and 53 percent. Whigs drew 142 of these votes in 1839 (69%) and 160 (70%) in 1840. Comparable figures for the 1840 election in the lower county show that Democrats had less success in attracting nonslaveholders, suffering instead a small but incrementally significant loss of support between 1839 and 1840. In 1839, 125 of 293 lower-county voters (less than 43%) either did not own slaves or cannot be found on lists of slaveholdings. In 1840 such persons provided 112 of 292 lower-county votes (38%). Democrats predictably won a large majority of the lower-county nonslaveholder vote each time, but both the total number of such votes and the Democratic share fell in 1840. Lower-county nonslaveholders cast 101 Democratic votes in 1839 (81 percent the total lower-county nonslaveholder vote), but only 82 Democratic votes in 1840 (73%).

81. Large slaveholders in the lower county contributed eighty-three Democratic votes, up from seventy-eight in 1839. They provided an imposing 43 percent of votes cast by lower-county Democrats for whom slaveholdings may be determined, up from 40 percent in 1839. Those owning twenty or more slaves

provided thirty-seven votes, or over 19 percent of the lower-county Democratic total in 1840, up from 17 percent in 1839.

Table 4.3, which analyzes the slaveholdings of 1840 voters, may be compared with table 4.2, which offers similar information on the 1834 legislative race, when party preferences first appeared. Whigs remained more dependent on the votes of nonslaveholders. As overall turnout increased and less privileged voters participated in larger numbers, the share of the Democratic votes cast by non-slaveholders grew, but it remained significantly below the comparable Whig per-centage. Slaveholders with ten or more slaves cast 20 percent of the Whig vote in 1840, almost exactly what they provided in 1834. Democrats received 31 percent of their votes in 1840 from planters and near-planters, down from 41 percent in 1834. Almost as many Democrats in 1840 owned ten slaves or more as owned none, whereas Whig nonslaveholders outnumbered large Whig slaveholders by more than two to one.

82. Shade, "Society and Politics in Antebellum Virginia's Southside," 192.

83. Ibid., 178–92; Watson, "Conflict and Collaboration," 290–93; Dent, "Virginia Democratic Party," 395–98.

84. Using data from the 1840 U.S. Census, table 4.7 delineates the broad cat-egories of privileged, smallholder, and nonpropertied first introduced in chapter 1. Table 4.7 shows the voting behavior of each group for the entire county, and also for the upper county and the lower county separately. A comparison with table 4.6 reveals many similarities. Privileged voters, who were proportionately twice as numerous in the lower county, voted Democratic by a 62 to 38 percent margin. Privileged voters displayed a turnout rate of over 87 percent. Smallhold-ers, almost 66 percent of the white male household heads in the upper county but under 43 percent in the lower county, voted narrowly Whig. Smallholders in the upper county gave Whigs an eighty-vote margin and over 63 percent of their vote. Smallholder turnout, 71 percent overall, was marginally higher in the upper county. Nonpropertied voters, who must have turned out at a somewhat higher rate than the low 29 percent indicated here—because eighty-two voters could not be matched to census and tax lists—displayed Whig majorities in the upper county and Democratic majorities in the lower county. Turnout of the non-propertied voters from the upper county exceeded that in the lower county, cre-ating a narrow Whig advantage for all nonpropertied voters.

85. Crofts, *Reluctant Confederates*, 44–45, 52–53.

86. Ibid., 41, 84, 131, 150.

87. Cooper, *The South and the Politics of Slavery*, xi–xii; Watson, *Jacksonian Politics and Community Conflict*, 292–96; Freehling, *Road to Disunion*, 298–99.

88. Cooper, *The South and the Politics of Slavery*, 74–97.

89. The two best studies of party formation in Virginia, by Lynwood M. Dent, Jr., and Henry H. Simms, do little to sustain Cooper's view that slavery served as the "center of political debate in the South," in comparison with which other issues paled into insignificance. "Sectional one-upmanship" did play a ma-jor role in southern politics, as accusations about the unsoundness of the north-

ern wing of the other party became staple partisan rhetoric. But fears of executive power and disagreements about banking policy differentiated the parties that formed in Virginia during the 1830s more effectively than did the slave issue. See Cooper, *The South and the Politics of Slavery*, xi–xii, 65, 132–48; Dent, "Virginia Democratic Party"; Simms, *Rise of the Whigs in Virginia*. Dent wrote his dissertation under Cooper's supervision.

90. Simms, *Rise of the Whigs in Virginia*, 88–94; Dent, "Virginia Democratic Party," 161–70; Peterson, *Littleton Waller Tazewell*, 232–49.

91. Lowery, *James Barbour*; Douglas R. Egerton, *Charles Fenton Mercer and the Trial of National Conservatism* (Jackson: Univ. Press of Mississippi, 1989); Drew R. McCoy, *The Last of the Fathers: James Madison and the Republican Legacy* (New York: Cambridge Univ. Press, 1989); Dent, "Virginia Democratic Party," 215–67.

92. Shade, "Society and Politics in Antebellum Virginia's Southside," 193.

93. Table 4.1 displays turnout patterns in Southampton for elections between 1828 and 1842, and Whig party percentages starting in 1834. Three of its features deserve comment. First, contrast the erratic turnout patterns between 1828 and 1838 with the high stable figures between 1839 and 1842. From time to time, notably in the legislative races of 1831, 1832, and the two in 1835, voter turnout surged. But in other elections it receded. Suddenly, in 1839, turnout stabilized at a high figure for five consecutive elections, when between 67 and 70 percent of eligible voters took time to go to the polls. Second, the presidential races between 1828 and 1836 failed to stimulate as much turnout as several other contests during the period. Only after the stable phase of high turnout and close party competition began in 1839 did the presidential contest become a standout attraction, and even then the appeal of legislative races was nearly as great. Third, note that the two parties displayed nearly equal strength in the stable phase from 1839 to 1842. In three of the five elections, the winning candidate in Southampton received 51 percent of the vote or less. It appears that closely competitive outcomes stimulated persistently high turnout.

Individual voting data are especially useful in identifying loyalty and linkages. As early as the mid-1830s, few voters would switch party allegiances. But the electorate remained volatile: each election attracted many new voters. By 1839 and 1840, however, the evidence shows that persistent voting had become the norm. More than three-quarters (76%) of those voting in the presidential election of 1840 had voted in the 1839 legislative race. Of the 372 who voted for Van Buren in 1840, 292 had voted in April 1839, when they gave overwhelming support to Democrat Robert Ridley, 283 to 9. Whigs likewise demonstrated both loyalty to party and a readiness to link local and national party preferences. Of the 278 Whig supporters in 1840 who had also voted in 1839, 268 then supported James B. Urquhart, the Whig candidate for the House of Delegates, while only 10 voted for Ridley. Whigs enjoyed slightly greater success than Democrats in attracting new voters in 1840. Democrats in 1840 drew 80 voters who had not participated in 1839, whereas Whigs drew 100, just enough to give William Henry Harrison a six-vote victory in the county.

94. Sydnor, *Development of Southern Sectionalism*, 316.

FIVE. PARTISAN RIVALRY AND THE EXPANDING ELECTORATE

1. Starting in 1851, any white male aged 21 or older who had resided in the state for two years and the county for one year could vote. The 1829–30 constitution restricted the franchise to owners of at least $25 in landed property, renters who had paid at least $20 of rent annually for five years, plus nonlandowning household heads who paid taxes (David L. Pulliam, *The Constitutional Conventions of Virginia from the Foundation of the Commonwealth to the Present Time* [Richmond: John T. West, 1901], 66, 94).

2. Dent, "Virginia Democratic Party," 266, 297–98.

3. Ibid., 334–35, 351–56. Southampton's Democratic party may have been less affected by factionalism in early 1844. Influential former legislator Robert Ridley was a Van Buren supporter (ibid., 320).

4. Story diary, Apr. 8, 17, 27–30, May 2, 1848, VHS; James Maget, "Draft of 1848 Speech for House of Delgates in Southampton County," Majette Family Papers, sec. 3, item 117, VHS.

5. Richmond semiweekly *Whig*, Mar. 30, 1849.

6. Ibid., Apr. 9, 1852.

7. Craig M. Simpson, *A Good Southerner: The Life of Henry A. Wise of Virginia* (Chapel Hill: Univ. of North Carolina Press, 1985), 106–22.

8. Former state senator William B. Shands tried to persuade Mason to take a more expedient view: "Hang it man do something for your county. It will benefit Southampton very much, and needs every vote. . . . You have been in the legislature long enough to find out that all a delegate can expect is an easy conscience not a *clear one*" (William B. Shands to Lewis E. Mason, Mar. 7, 1858, sec. 52, Lewis E. Mason to John Young Mason, Jan. 22, 1858, sec. 6, Mason Family Papers, VHS).

9. "Southampton," Apr. 25, 1859, in Richmond semiweekly *Whig*, Apr. 29, 1859; "Looker On," Apr. 21, 1859, in Richmond semiweekly *Enquirer*, May 6, 1859.

10. Whigs, who had polled 378 votes in 1840, received 340 in 1848, a decline of 38 votes (10%). Democratic totals suffered more severe erosion, falling from 372 to 307, a loss of 65 votes (over 17%). Although residence cannot be determined for a small number of 1840 voters, data for 725 of the 750 voters from 1840 may be compared with data for all 647 household heads who voted in 1848. In the upper county, Whigs in 1848 polled 274 votes, 13 fewer than in 1840, a loss of less than 5 percent. Democratic totals there sank from 147 to 119, a loss of 28 votes (19%). Democrats remained strong in the lower county, but they suffered greater proportionate losses there than did Whigs. The lower-county Whig vote declined less than 10 percent, from 73 to 66. Democratic totals there fell from 218 to 188. The loss of 30 votes amounted to almost 14 percent of the vote Democrats had recorded in the lower county in 1840.

11. Slaveholding is calculated by household and is based on the assumption that voters not listed in the U.S. Census or local land tax lists were nonslaveholders (see table 5.3). Upper-county nonslaveholders voted Whig by a margin of over 74 percent. Whigs also outnumbered Democrats among upper-county

slaveholders by a slightly smaller margin of 64 percent. Lower-county nonslaveholders voted 71 percent Democratic; slaveholders, 76 percent Democratic. Upper-county nonslaveholders cast over 57 percent of the Whig vote there; large slaveholders cast under 18 percent. Nonslaveholders cast only a handful more Democratic votes in the lower county than large slaveholders (38% and 34%, respectively).

One may also look only at household heads. Of the 307 Democrats voting, 249 were household heads with slaveholdings specified in the U.S. Census of 1850. Of these Democrats, 82, almost exactly one-third, owned ten or more slaves; 30 (or 12%) could qualify as planters for owning twenty slaves. The other Democratic voters divided symmetrically: 83 were slaveholders owning fewer than 10 slaves; 84 were nonslaveholders. Less than 20 percent of Whig voters who headed households (49 of 264) were slaveholders owning ten or more slaves. Twenty-two Whigs, or 8 percent, were planters. Eighty-four Whig voters, or just under 32 percent, were small slaveholders owning fewer than ten slaves. Nonslaveholders provided one-third of the Democratic electorate but almost one-half of the Whig electorate (131 of 264 household heads). Democrats and Whigs therefore drew equally among small slaveholders but in quite different proportions among the nonslaveholders and the large slaveholders.

12. Twenty-three of fifty-five religiously affiliated Democrats (42%) were large slaveholders, and fully thirty-seven (67%) owned at least one slave, far outnumbering the eighteen Democratic nonslaveholders (33%). Only eight of fifty-nine religiously affiliated Whigs were large slaveholders (14%); twenty-eight (47%) owned at least one slave; thirty-one (53%) owned no slaves.

13. All surviving Methodist records through 1840 pertain to the lower county. Calculations for 1848–61 include membership records for three small Methodist congregations in the upper county.

14. Data for 285 of 340 Whig voters and 262 of 307 Democratic voters reveal several interesting patterns. Listing their occupations as farmers were 226 Whigs and 227 Democrats. The definition of a farmer used in the federal population census included tenants and grown sons who remained at home. The 1850 agricultural census, which makes it possible to identify farm owners, sheds additional light on the relationship between politics and Southampton's principal occupation, farming. Census takers identified 734 farms in Southampton, 431 in the upper county and 303 in the lower county. Upper-county farm owners tended to be smallholders; those in the lower county owned, on average, larger and more valuable pieces of property. Of all farms valued at less than $400, over 70 percent were located in the upper county. By contrast, the upper county included only 42 percent of farms worth more than $1,750. Over 60 percent of all upper-county farms had a value of less than $800; over 60 percent of lower-county farms had a value of $800 or more. In 1848, 166 of 240 upper-county farm owners (69%) voted Whig; 138 of 180 lower-county farm owners (77%) voted Democratic.

15. Only 39 percent of the farms in the upper county raised more than thirty-five hogs, whereas 67 percent of those in the lower county raised that amount. Even though farm owners who raised hogs divided almost evenly in 1848, voting Democratic by the narrow margin of 211 to 206, quite pronounced dissimilarities

may be observed when hog raisers are divided into categories. Of those raising fewer than twenty-five hogs, 65 percent voted Whig, as did 54 percent of those raising between twenty-five and thirty-five hogs. But the larger hog producers voted Democratic: 55 percent of those raising between thirty-six and seventy-five hogs, and 63 percent of those raising over seventy-five hogs.

16. Only 27 percent of farms in the upper county raised as many as 500 bushels of corn, whereas close to 56 percent of lower-county farms reached that amount. Among farm owners raising corn, Democrats in 1848 narrowly outnumbered Whigs, 212 to 205. But over 63 percent of those producing fewer than 300 bushels of corn voted Whig, as did close to 56 percent of those raising between 300 and 499 bushels. The larger corn producers voted Democratic: 55 percent of those raising between 500 and 999 bushels and over 63 percent of those raising a thousand bushels or more.

17. Proportionately smaller numbers of both skilled tradesmen and professionals lived in the lower county. Of the 36 skilled tradesmen voting in 1848, only 12 lived in the lower county. Of the 12, 7 (63%) cast Democratic ballots, whereas all but 3 of the 24 votes cast by skilled trademen in the upper county in 1848 (88%) went to the Whigs. Of the 47 professionals voting in 1848, 14 resided in the lower county. They voted Democratic, 10 to 4 (71%). Upper-county professionals, in sharp contrast, voted 70 percent Whig (23 of 33).

The evidence suggests that suffrage requirements played a substantial role in depressing voter turnout. Of 53 persons in the highest-status occupations (lawyers, merchants, physicians, ministers), 33 cast ballots in 1848 (62%). Far fewer of the lesser professionals voted—barely one-third of teachers (7 of 20) and only a single one of the 20 clerks, some of whom were underage. Among the skilled tradesmen analyzed here, only 36 of 131 voted (27%). Increased voter turnout among lesser professionals and skilled tradesmen followed adoption of the reform constitution in 1851.

18. Comparisons with individual voting data from 1848 reveal that over 52 percent of the voters in 1851 had not voted three years before. Less than 48 percent of the electorate in 1851 were therefore "repeaters." Of the 340 persons who voted Whig in 1848, 243 (71%) repeated their Whig vote in 1851; Democrats drew 184 votes from their supporters of three years before, a lower persistence rate of 60 percent. Very few voters switched party loyalties between 1848 and 1851 (6 Democrats and 2 Whigs). Turnout, therefore, was the principal reason for the better Whig performance among all repeaters: only 95 Whigs from 1848 (28%) failed to reappear at the polls in 1851; 117 Democrats (38%) did not reappear.

New voters in 1851 divided up similarly to repeaters, although their voting patterns were less polarized along party lines (see table 5.5). Over 62 percent of new voters came from the upper county, and they voted Whig by a margin of over 64 percent (repeating voters there gave Whigs an even larger margin, over 75 percent). In the lower county, Democrats gained almost 66 percent of the votes cast by new voters and almost 75 percent of the vote from repeaters.

19. Of 514 household heads who voted in 1848, 296 owned slaves; in 1851, the 602 participating household heads included 294 slaveholders. Among Dem-

ocratic household heads in 1851, slaveholders outnumbered nonslaveholders, 155 to 119. Among Whigs, the figures were reversed, 139 to 189. In other words, close to 57 percent of Democratic household heads in 1851 owned slaves but only 42 percent of Whigs. Moreover, almost 25 percent of Democratic household heads owned over ten slaves, substantially more than the 14 percent of Whigs. When broken down by location, similar patterns emerge. In the upper county, 57 percent of the participating household heads (and over 59 percent of Whig house-hold heads) were nonslaveholders. In the lower county, only 42 percent of partic-ipating household heads were nonslaveholders (and only 38 percent of Demo-cratic household heads). Under 15 percent of participating upper-county household heads owned ten or more slaves. In the lower county, the comparable figure was almost 26 percent, and over 30 percent among Democrats.

Of the 911 persons voting in Southampton in 1851, 844 may be located in the 1850 federal census. Some of the others may be identified through local records. Assuming that unidentified persons were nonslaveholders, one may tabulate the slaveholdings for all voters, defining slaveholding on a family rather than an in-dividual basis. Slightly fewer than half of all voters, 439 of 911, or 48 percent, came from slaveholding families; 224 of 410 Democrats, or almost 55 percent, came from slaveholding families, as did 215 of 501 Whigs, or 43 percent. As in 1848, members of nonslaveholding families voted Whig, this time by a margin of 286 to 186. Members of larger slaveholding families remained considerably more likely to vote Democratic: they provided 107 of the 410 Democratic votes, or 26 percent, but only 84 of 501 Whig votes, or 17 percent.

An additional measurement locates the increased turnout specifically among nonpropertied voters. Between 1848 and 1851 the aggregate vote cast by privi-leged and smallholding voters remained almost constant, but the nonpropertied vote soared from 49 to 139. Whigs gained 83 of the 139 votes, or 60 percent, attracting almost 72 percent of the nonpropertied vote from the upper county and a very creditable 43 percent from the lower county.

20. James D. Bryant, a resident of the upper county, failed to mobilize lower-county Democrats, including his own coreligionists. His margin of 26 to 7 among religiously affiliated lower-county voters (in seven Methodist congregations) fell below the 34-to-7 margin recorded three years before. Among the heretofore in-tensely Democratic congregations at Barnes and Whiteheads, almost as many members failed to vote (eleven) as supported Bryant (fourteen). Whereas Meth-odists had voted Democratic, 40 to 16, in the 1848 presidential election, Bryant recorded a margin of less than two-to-one, 32 to 18.

By contrast, upper-county residents with religious ties polled a large vote. Turnout at the Black Creek Baptist Church, a Whig citadel, surged by 25 percent, as members who in 1848 had voted Whig, 24 to 4, increased the margin in 1851 to 32 to 5. This base allowed Pretlow to poll a 37-to-14 advantage among South-ampton Baptists, as South Quay Baptist gave its votes to Bryant, 9 to 4. In addi-tion to his Baptist strength, Pretlow gained the support of upper-county Meth-odists, 11 to 6, and, as would be expected, Quakers voted for him, 12 to 4. Overall, Pretlow's margin among upper-county voters with religious affiliations stood at 61 to 24, similar to but somewhat larger than the 52-to-22 advantage Zachary Taylor had enjoyed in 1848.

Democrats once again gained more votes from church members in large slave-holding families (eighteen of fifty, or 36 percent of the total) than from non-slaveholding ones (thirteen of fifty, or 26%). Whigs, supported by eighteen non-slaveholding members of Black Creek Baptist Church and eleven nonslaveholding members of the Quaker meeting, compiled thirty-seven of their sixty-eight votes (or 54%) from nonslaveholders. Only ten of the sixty-eight Whig votes, or 15 percent, were cast by large slaveholders.

21. Breaking down the farm vote by residence helps to identify the new sources of Whig strength. In 1848 farmers in the lower county gave Democrats a 101-vote margin. That figure remained nearly identical in 1851 (174 to 72, a 102-vote margin), although the Democratic percentage fell from 77 percent to 71 percent as the total lower-county farm vote increased from 189 to 246. In the upper county, however, the Whig margin increased sharply from 100 votes in 1848 to 167 votes in 1851. By outpolling Democrats 286 to 119, Whigs in 1851 carried almost 71 percent of the upper-county farm vote, up from 69 percent three years before. The total upper-county farm vote increased 53 percent; that of the lower county only 30 percent.

Plainly, Whigs effectively enlarged their traditional base by appealing to the heretofore disfranchised classes of farmers who owned no property or did not head households. In the upper county, nonlandowning farmers gave Whigs a 71 percent margin, 139 to 56. Democrats carried the lower county, 71 to 43, or about 62 percent. Overall, nonlandholding farmers polled 182 Whig votes and 127 Democratic votes (59 percent Whig). In 1848 Whigs collected a similar percentage (over 58%) but a much smaller vote (59 to 42), as suffrage restrictions kept many potential voters from the polls.

22. The number of lower-county voters employed in the skilled trades remained low: eighteen of the sixty-six in the entire county, or 27 percent, down from 33 percent in 1848. They voted Democratic 12 to 6, quite in contrast to upper-county skilled tradesmen, who voted Whig, 34 to 14. Lower-county professionals increased from 30 percent to 35 percent of the professional electorate in the county between 1848 and 1851. Their Democratic margin, 17 to 10, almost counterbalanced the Whig advantage among upper-county professionals, 31 to 19.

Liberalized suffrage requirements plainly helped to increase the percentages of voters in several skilled trades and professions. Only four of seventeen shoemakers voted 1848; that number jumped to eleven in 1851, an increase from 24 percent to 65 percent (and all voted Whig in 1851). Of the twenty teachers in the county, seven voted in 1848. That number doubled to fourteen in 1851, an increase in turnout from 35 percent to 70 percent. Even among carpenters, an apparently more marginal group of tradesmen, voter turnout rose significantly from sixteen in 1848 (30 percent of the fifty-four white male carpenters listed in the census) to twenty-six (48 percent) in 1851.

23. Among carpenters, a Democratic trend in 1851 was especially notable.

Carpenters voted Whig, 12 to 4, in 1848 but divided their vote, 13 to 13, in 1851. Shoemakers, however, displayed an emphatic Whig tendency, giving Pretlow all eleven votes cast in 1851, after having voted Whig, 3 to 1, in 1848. Coopers (four of five voting) and millers (all three voting) also cast Whig ballots in 1851.

24. Even though one tends to think of merchants as cosmopolitian modernizers who held Whiggish views about banks and transportation improvements, five of eight Southampton merchants voted Democratic in 1848, and eight of twelve in 1851. Ralph A. Wooster was likewise surprised to find that merchants serving in upper-South state legislatures during the 1850s tended to be Democrats (*Politicians, Planters, and Plain Folk: Courthouse and Statehouse in the Upper South, 1850–1860* [Knoxville: Univ. of Tennessee Press, 1975], 120). Because Southampton's dominant agricultural sector included more Democrats at the top, local Democrats had greater amounts of capital to invest than did local Whigs, and some of that capital found its way into mercantile enterprises. Wealthy Democrats from the Pope, Drewry, and Darden families owned stores in the 1840s and 1850s (Virginia, 49:341, 347, R. G. Dun & Co. Collection, Baker Library, Harvard Univ. Graduate School of Business Administration).

25. Henry T. Shanks, *The Secession Movement in Virginia, 1847–1861* (1934; rept. New York: Da Capo Press, 1970), 43–45; Crofts, *Reluctant Confederates*, 26–28, 262–63.

26. Of those who voted Whig in 1851, 306 voted Whig in 1855 while 34 voted for Wise. Of the Democratic voters from 1851, 277 voted Democratic in 1855 and only 10 cast Whig ballots. In other words, only 3 percent of Democrats deserted to the other party while 10 percent of Whigs did so.

27. A similar pattern emerges when looking only at household heads. Among the household heads from the lower county who voted Democratic in 1851 were 99 slaveholders and 61 nonslaveholders. By 1855 the proportions had become much closer: 103 slaveholders and 98 nonslaveholders.

In the least advantaged segment of the electorate—those who owned neither slaves nor land—there was also a sharp Democratic surge between 1851 and 1855 in the lower county. Of the nonpropertied household heads who lived in the lower county, thirty-three of fifty-nine (57%) voted Democratic in 1851; sixty-two of sixty-nine (90%) did so in 1855.

28. Among household heads, Whigs gained 150 votes from nonslaveholders and 113 from slaveholders. Democrats attracted 148 nonslaveholders and 157 slaveholders. The breakdown by household for all identifiable voters shows that Whigs received 302 votes from members of nonslaveholding families and 187 from members of slaveholding families. The comparable figures among Democrats were 308 votes from members of nonslaveholding families and 262 from members of slaveholding families. Nonslaveholders contributed 62 percent of the Whig vote and 54 percent of the Democratic vote.

29. Although Whigs maintained a decisive 72 percent margin among upper-county nonslaveholders between 1851 and 1855, the Democratic surge among lower-county nonslaveholders in 1855 was so great that Democrats narrowly carried the countywide vote among nonslaveholders in 1855, 308 to 302 (51%), up sharply from 39 percent in 1851. Members of slaveholding households contin-

ued, however, to display a larger Democratic margin than their nonslaveholding counterparts: the Democratic majority of 262 to 189 (58%) among all members of slaveholding families increased 7 percent between 1851 and 1855. Members of families with ten or more slaves voted 60 percent Democratic in 1855 (111 to 74). Democrats in the upper county drew 39 percent of the vote cast by slaveholders but only 28 percent of the vote cast by nonslaveholders.

30. Of the new voters from the upper county, 69 percent came from nonslaveholding families, and the same percentage of new nonslaveholders voted Whig. In the entire county new voters from slaveholding families preferred Democrats by a margin of more than two-to-one. The Democratic margin of 83 percent among new voters from slaveholding families in the lower county was less surprising than the fact that new voters from slaveholding families in the upper county produced a Democratic margin of over 54 percent. The sharp divergence of party preference among new upper-county voters in 1855, with nonslaveholders solidly Whig and slaveholders marginally Democratic, also anticipates an important aspect of voter behavior in the secession crisis.

31. Voter age bore only a slight relationship to party preference in the three elections analyzed here (see table 5.12). In 1848 over 52 percent of voters who could be identified by age cast a Whig ballot. Whigs enjoyed narrow margins among all age groups except voters in their thirties. The oldest voters displayed a slightly higher level of Whig support than any other age group. By 1851 the electorate increased substantially, and over 55 percent of the voters were Whig. But a breakdown of 1851 voters by age reveals few significant patterns. The three youngest age cohorts (voters under the age of fifty) displayed Whig percentages very close to the average. Voters in their fifties divided almost evenly, whereas the oldest voters once again displayed the strongest Whig margin, in this instance nearly 65 percent. The Democratic surge in 1855 extended rather evenly across all age groups, averaging over 53 percent. Democratic gains that resulted from mobilization of new lower-county voters included both the young and the old. Whigs maintained a nearly even split among voters in their forties and fifties.

32. Whigs remained almost exactly as strong in 1855 as in 1851 among Quakers (13 to 4) and Baptists (38 to 15). The 1855 contest stimulated a modest increase in Methodist turnout, which worked to the advantage of Democrats. They carried Methodist voters 41 to 16, an improvement on their 32-to-18 margin in 1851. Upper-county Methodists divided about evenly (a 12-to-11 Whig advantage). Religiously affiliated voters from slaveholding families delivered a Democratic margin, 40 to 29, whereas their nonslaveholding counterparts voted Whig, 39 to 21.

33. In 1851 farmers had voted Whig by an even larger margin, 358 to 293. In the upper county, Whigs in 1855 maintained a better than two-to-one majority among farmers, 287 to 125, almost identical to their 286-to-119 advantage in 1851. In the lower county, however, Whig support sagged as Democrats surged. A 174-to-72 Democratic advantage among lower Southampton farmers in 1851 grew to 240 to 33 in 1855.

34. Skilled tradesmen there, who voted 12 to 6 Democratic in 1851, produced a 24-to-2 Democratic margin in 1855. Skilled tradesmen in the upper county

voted almost identically in both years, 34 to 14 Whig in 1851 and 35 to 14 Whig in 1855. Democrats gained an overall 18-to-16 advantage among carpenters, the largest single group of skilled tradesmen. In the lower county, carpenters voted Democratic, 11 to 2. In the upper county, they voted Whig, 14 to 7. All seven participating shoemakers in the upper county cast Whig ballots, but two lower-county shoemakers voted Democratic. The pattern was pervasive.

35. Lower-county professionals voted 17 to 10 Democratic in 1851 and 17 to 5 in 1855. Poorer turnout in 1855 among upper-county professionals (31 to 19 Whig in 1851 and 25 to 16 Whig in 1855) enabled Democrats in 1855 to carry the overall professional vote. As with skilled tradesmen, voting patterns often broke sharply along residential lines. Four upper-county teachers voted Whig, but four of five in the lower county voted Democratic. Physicians, however, remained solidly Whig, 11 to 4, including a 3-to-2 margin in the lower county.

36. Richmond semiweekly *Whig*, Mar. 30, 1849.

37. Richmond semiweekly *Enquirer*, Apr. 13, 1847, with reference to appointment of a Democratic vigilance committee in Nansemond County.

38. Bourke and DeBats, "Identifiable Voting in Nineteenth-Century America," 259–88.

39. Perdue, Barden, and Phillips, *Weevils in the Wheat*, 139–42.

40. Richmond semiweekly *Whig*, Dec. 16, 1851.

41. Joseph H. Prince to John Young Mason, July 16, Aug. 20, 1850, Mason Family Papers, sec. 6, 24; Richmond semiweekly *Whig*, June 25, Sept. 3, 13, 1850; Pulliam, *Constitutional Conventions of Virginia*, 99.

42. Petersburg *Daily Express*, Mar. 18 ("Black Eagle," Mar. 16), Apr. 8, 12, 15 ("Black Eagle," Apr. 6, 12, "Ossory," Apr. 11), 1859; Richmond semiweekly *Enquirer*, Apr. 26, 1859; Cobb diary, Apr. 12, 1859, VHS.

43. Petersburg *Daily Express*, Apr. 20 ("Black Eagle," Apr. 18), May 25, 31 ("Ossory," May 23, "Black Eagle," May 30), 1859; Richmond semiweekly *Whig*, May 20, 1859; Richmond semiweekly *Enquirer*, June 7, 1859; Cobb diary, May 25, 26, 29, 1859.

44. For the most helpful and systematic study of the subject, see Tadahisa Kuroda, "The County Court System of Virginia from the Revolution to the Civil War" (Ph.D. diss., Columbia Univ., 1969). See also Wooster, *Politicians, Planters, and Plain Folk*, 97–117.

45. Complaints about the county court had little or nothing to do with the lopsided margin favoring a constitutional convention polled in Southampton in April 1850. Eastern Virginia overwhelmingly favored calling a convention after the legislature specified that its delegates would be apportioned on the "mixed" basis that gave weight to property value as well as white population, rather than on the basis of white population alone (Francis P. Gaines, Jr., "The Virginia Constitutional Convention of 1850–1851: A Study in Sectionalism" [Ph.D. diss., Univ. of Virginia, 1950], 88–106).

46. Harrison P. Pope rolled up large margins at Cross Keys and Joyners Store, the big Democratic districts near his home. Pope's chances of winning were undermined, however, because most Democrats at Drewrysville, Murfees Depot, and the Courthouse districts voted instead for William J. Sebrell. Yet another

Democrat, Richard H. Branch, collected the few regular Democratic votes at the three outlying upper-county districts, Berlin, Black Creek Church, and Faisons Store.

47. Kindred's big bloc of votes from Cross Keys and Joyners Store proved sufficient to edge out Edward W. Massenburg, who ran well at the Courthouse and Drewrysville, and William W. Cobb, who attracted considerable support from upper-county Whigs. A fourth Democrat, Joseph H. Prince, proved unable to build much beyond his base at Drewrysville.

48. Magisterial districts coincided with the eight electoral districts, except that two electoral districts, Black Creek Church and the Courthouse, shared the same magisterial district. Democrats could expect to elect justices from the three lower-county districts; Whigs would have an advantage in three of four upper-county districts, except for closely divided Murfees Depot.

49. Because Democrats controlled the state government during the 1840s, and Democratic governors occasionally connived to maintain Democratic-dominated courts in Whig-majority counties, Whigs more often than not took the lead in pushing for the popular election of magistrates. Opportunistic Democrats, not wanting to be outflanked, contributed to the reform pressures that finally succeeded at the 1850–51 Convention (Kuroda, "County Court System of Virginia," 257–73).

50. Results from one voting district are lost but can be estimated.

51. Joshua Pretlow, a Whig, led with eighty-two votes; a Whig (James W. Murfee) and a Democrat (Joseph E. Gillette) tied with eighty votes; three other candidates (two Whigs and a Democrat) collected seventy-seven votes. By some means Edwin Daughtry, a Democrat, was selected to hold the fourth seat from the district.

52. Officeholding would protect the two younger Pretlows, Joshua and John, from military service. John Pretlow initially volunteered, but he hired a substitute in May 1862 (James F. Bryant to James D. Bryant, May 7, 1862, James Fenton Bryant Papers, VSLA).

SIX. CRISIS OF THE UNION

1. Cobb diary, Aug. 25, Sept. 2, 10, 1859, VHS.

2. Ibid., Oct. 27, Nov. 3, 21, 1859.

3. Petersburg *Daily Express*, Oct. 19, 1859.

4. Ibid., Dec. 14, 1859 ("Black Eagle," Dec. 12, 1859); Petersburg *Press*, Dec. 1, 1859 ("S. W. C.," Nov. 28, 1859).

5. Petersburg *Daily Express*, Dec. 14, 1859 ("Black Eagle," Dec. 12, 1859).

6. Cobb diary, Apr. 22, July 15, 1850.

7. Ibid., entry on first page of flyleaf for 1857, probably dated May 28, 1857.

8. Ibid., May 29, 1859.

9. Norfolk *Southern Argus*, Mar. 15, July 20, Sept. 3, 14, 1860, quoted in Jackson, *Peanuts and Applejack*, 75–79.

10. Story diary, Dec. 19, 1846, Mar. 9, 1848, Feb. 8, 1860, VHS.

11. Ibid., Nov. 21, 1859, Feb. 8, Aug. 2, 1860.

12. Ibid., Aug. 2, 30, Oct. 27, 1860; Parramore, *Southampton County,* 154–55.

13. Story diary, Oct. 12, 20, 1860.

14. Thomas J. Pretlow to Thaddeus Stevens, Dec. 27, 1865, Thaddeus Stevens Papers, LC, first called to my attention by Professor Richard Lowe of the University of North Texas; Pretlow to the editor of the Richmond *Whig,* Jan. 29, 1868, in the Richmond *Whig,* Feb. 3, 1868.

15. Story diary, Nov. 3, 1860.

16. Norfolk *Southern Argus,* Oct. 20, 1860, in Jackson, *Peanuts and Applejack,* 80.

17. Story diary, Nov. 12, 19, 22, 1860.

18. Crofts, *Reluctant Confederates,* Introduction, Prologue, chaps. 1–4; Story diary, Nov. 18, 30, Dec. 13, 1860, Jan. 12, 20, 1861.

19. Bertram Wyatt-Brown, *Yankee Saints and Southern Sinners* (Baton Rouge: Louisiana State Univ. Press, 1985), 1.

20. Crofts, *Reluctant Confederates,* chap. 6.

21. Cobb diary, Jan. 19, Feb. 14, Mar. 5, 11, Apr. 20, 22, 1861.

22. Ibid., Jan. 21, Feb. 4, 1861. For a comparative analysis of secession crisis politics in Southampton, Sussex, and Greensville counties, see Crofts, "Old Dominion's Cotton Belt."

23. Cobb diary, Feb. 4, 5, 8, 1861; Story diary, Feb. 4, 5, 1861.

24. Cobb diary, Feb. 4, 11, Mar. 16, 1861. On the conspiratorial scheme to gain power developed by some Virginia secessionists, see Crofts, *Reluctant Confederates,* 281–82, 316–23.

25. Cobb diary, Apr. 18, 20, 22, 1861.

26. Story diary, May 11, 1861. See Crofts, *Reluctant Confederates,* chaps. 11–13.

27. Table 6.3, which in effect combines the results from tables 6.1 and 6.2, further pinpoints the basis for Whig gains between 1855 and 1860. Note in table 6.3 the almost glacial stability of Democratic votes in each category. Once again, the modest increment of new Whig voters from nonslaveholding families (thirty in the upper county and twenty in the lower county) commands principal attention.

28. All calculations for 1861 are based on votes for and against "reference." Union voters favored requiring a popular referendum to approve any convention action; secession voters opposed the referendum.

29. The almost unanimous prosecession voting patterns in the lower county concealed the fact that the lower-county turnout failed to equal that of the upper county. Voter turnout in the prosecession lower county declined from 451 to 354, over 21 percent. Although the upper-county turnout also declined, from 664 to 572, or 14 percent, the reduction there took place among slaveholders and prosecession nonslaveholders (see table 6.7).

In the planter-dominated lower county, the linkage between nonslaveholding, Whig voting, and opposition to secession did not exist. As had been the case since

1855, those few lower-county residents who deviated from the predominant pro-Democratic pattern in 1860 were slightly more likely to be slaveholders. By 1861, when lower-county residents with very few exceptions either voted for secession or did not vote at all, twelve of the nineteen dissenters came from slaveholding families. Although a majority of members of slaveholding families in the upper county supported Bell and voted against secession, they displayed significantly more Democratic and prosecession tendencies than their nonslaveholding neighbors.

Countywide statistics best reveal the link between slaveholding, Democratic voting in 1860, and support for secession in 1861. Slaveholding, which exhibited a significant positive relationship with Democratic voting in 1860, displayed an even stronger positive relationship with support for secession in 1861.

30. For evidence that secession tended to polarize voting behavior in the upper South, with prosecession and antisecession localities often voting in opposite ways with near unanimity, with slaveholders and nonslaveholders more divided than ever before, and with a discernible sag in turnout among nonslaveholders in prosecession localities, see Crofts, *Reluctant Confederates*, chaps. 6–7.

31. Although 78 percent of participating upper-county Democrats voted for secession, 39 percent of those who voted in 1860 did not vote in 1861. Secessionist pressures on lower-county Whigs must have been intense: over half who voted in 1860 did not vote in 1861, and most of those who did vote in 1861 supported secession.

32. In 1855 Methodists voted Democratic, 41 to 16, or 72 percent. By 1860 almost twice as many voters with Methodist affiliations could be identified; they gave Breckinridge a margin of 70 to 30, with one Douglas vote. Southampton Methodists thus continued to give Democrats 70 percent of their votes. But because Methodists increased their share of the religiously affiliated electorate from 44 percent in 1855 (57 of 129) to 67 percent in 1860 (101 of 151), the countywide results displayed a somewhat misleading Democratic surge. It should be kept in mind that most Methodists lived in the heavily Democratic lower county. Seven of ten Methodist congregations for which membership rosters are extant were located there. Among members of lower-county Methodist churches, Breckinridge outpolled Bell 59 to 11, with one for Douglas. Voters at Whiteheads Methodist delivered all 19 votes to Democrats: 18 to Breckinridge and 1 to Douglas. In the three upper-county Methodist congregations, the outcome was reversed, as Bell gathered 19 of 30 votes cast. Daniel Cobb's Indian Spring church was the one upper-county Methodist congregation to follow the lower-county pattern, delivering all 4 of its votes for Breckinridge. Elliott Story and seven other members of Nottoway Chapel voted for Bell; Breckinridge won only 2 votes at this upper-county Methodist church.

33. The three upper-county Methodist congregations voted pro-Union, albeit by a narrower margin (14 to 11) than they had supported Bell. Three members of Indian Spring church, including Daniel Cobb, voted for secession. Elliott Story was among the seven members of Nottoway Chapel who voted against secession; three others voted for it. The overall Methodist vote in the county went solidly

for secession, 64 to 18. Although all six voters from South Quay Baptist favored secession, their coreligionists at Black Creek gave Southampton Baptists a substantial pro-Union margin, 22 to 8.

34. Nonslaveholding church members cast thirty-six Whig votes in 1860, or 58 percent of the total Whig vote cast by church members. Each of the four categories of slaveholder displayed a strong Democratic preference. Church members from the planter class, that is, the owners of twenty or more slaves, voted Democratic by a six-to-one margin. Slaveholding church members cast all but twenty-five of the eighty-nine Democratic votes, about 72 percent.

35. In 1861 nonslaveholding church members provided thirty-seven of the fifty-four Union votes, or close to 69 percent. All four categories of slaveholder overwhelmingly favored secession, providing close to 78 percent of the votes for secession cast by church members.

36. In the lower county, all thirteen nonslaveholding church members voted prosecession; slaveholders voted the same way with near unanimity, 39 to 2. But whereas church members among upper-county nonslaveholding families delivered more votes against secession than for John Bell, other voters with religious affiliations displayed lower rates of turnout in 1861. In the lower county, despite the nearly unanimous prosecession vote, turnout among church members lagged. The turnout among nonslaveholding church members fell 35 percent between November 1860 and February 1861, from twenty to thirteen, and secession got four fewer votes than Breckinridge. Slaveholding lower-county church members, 41 to 5 for Breckinridge, voted 39 to 2 for secession. Upper-county church members from slaveholding families, who had supported Breckinridge, 23 to 21, displayed a 27 percent decline in turnout, from 44 to 32, as they voted for secession, 17 to 15.

37. The persons who compiled the 1860 census in Southampton did not record occupational categories in the same manner as their 1850 predecessors. Close to 80 percent of those with occupations listed in the 1850 census were farmers, but only 59 percent were listed as farmers in 1860. How may the discrepancy be explained? First, overseers were listed separately in 1860, unlike 1850. Sixty-seven overseers added 6 percent to the aggregate number of jobholders. Second, many farm laborers were listed as laborers. Ten white males were listed as farm laborers, but 199 others as laborers. Without doubt, most of the laborers were in fact farm laborers, either tenants or agricultural wage workers. The category probably included nonfarm laborers as well, because the combined percentage of farmers, overseers, and laborers substantially exceeded the percentage of farmers in 1850. Most free blacks were likewise categorized as laborers.

38. Compared with 1850, far fewer persons were listed in 1860 in such trades as carpentry and shoemaking. The decline must reflect, in large part, eccentricities in the 1860 census. Many tradesmen were listed in 1860 in the broad category of laborer. Even if factory-made shoes diminished the business of local shoemakers, no comparable economic tendency would have undercut the need for carpenters.

The overall occupational totals (see table 6.13), showing a narrow Whig margin in 1860 and a more decisive antisecession margin in 1861, suggest that census takers in the lower county performed haphazardly. Over 40 percent of the votes cast in 1860 were cast by residents of the lower county, but only 36 percent of the voters with listed occupations came from the lower county. The failure to specify lower-county occupations is particularly apparent for the category of laborer.

39. William L. Barney, *The Secessionist Impulse: Alabama and Mississippi in 1860* (Princeton, N.J.: Princeton Univ. Press, 1974), 62–66, 80–84, 90–95.

40. Upper-county slaveholders under the age of fifty were considerably more likely vote Democratic than similarly aged nonslaveholders (44% and 26%, respectively). About seven out of ten upper-county residents aged fifty or older voted Whig, whether or not they came from slaveholding households. The secession issue rather sharply divided slaveholders and nonslaveholders, both among younger and older residents of the upper county. Fewer than 16 percent of younger nonslaveholders there supported secession, and fewer than 8 percent of their older counterparts. Upper-county nonslaveholders of all ages registered unmistakable and overwhelming opposition to secession. By contrast, 38 percent of younger upper-county slaveholders supported secession, and about 31 percent of older upper-county slaveholders.

41. Petersburg *Daily Express*, Dec. 2, 1858.

42. Of the fifty-one owning slaves, forty-four owned 4 or more. Twenty-two of the fifty-three leading Democrats, or 42 percent, were members of the planter class, owning 20 or more slaves. The fifty-three leading Democrats owned 748 taxable slaves (those aged twelve or older), an average of over 15 apiece. The value of their property, reflecting especially their slaveholdings, averaged over $18,000 apiece.

43. Only fifteen of the forty-four Whigs (or 34%) owned 10 or more slaves, and only eight (or 18%) owned more than 20. By comparison, over 60 percent of leading Democrats owned 10 or more slaves, and over 40 percent owned more than 20. The forty-four leading Whigs owned 296 taxable slaves, an average of fewer than 7 apiece, less than half the average holdings of leading Democrats.

44. Story diary, Oct. 19, 1859.

45. Stewart, "Railroads and Urban Rivalries in Antebellum Eastern Virginia"; *Farmers' Register* 4 (1837): 532–33.

46. John Young Mason to Lewis E. Mason, Feb. 15, 1851, Mason Family Papers, sec. 52, VHS.

47. Roswald Sparks Majette to James Maget, Feb. 18, 1861, Majette Family Papers, sec. 1, VHS.

48. Southampton Legislative Petitions, Jan. 12, 1828, Dec. 8, 1836, VSLA; *Farmers' Register* 1 (1834): 774; Babb, *History of Ivor*, 24–25, 30–31.

49. Hart, "Descendants of Thomas Pretlow," 27, 61–64; Cobb diary, June 23, 1867; Pretlow to Thaddeus Stevens, Dec. 27, 1865, Stevens Papers; Babb, *History of Ivor*, 25.

50. Parramore, *Southampton County*, 58, 114; Babb, *History of Ivor*, 46; Cobb diary, Apr. 1, 1861.

51. Babb, *History of Ivor*, 26–29.

52. Story diary, Feb. 10, Apr. 2, 1846, May 2, July 27, 1848; Babb, *History of Ivor*, 15; Jay Worrall, Jr., to author, Mar. 22, 1990; Mathew, *Edmund Ruffin and the Crisis of Slavery in the Old South*.

53. Sussex voted 86 percent for secession; Greensville's margin was 73 percent.

54. Story diary, May 11, 21, 1860; Hinshaw and Marshall, *Encyclopedia of American Quaker Genealogy* 6:80.

SEVEN. CIVIL WAR

1. Story diary, May 11, 1861, VHS.

2. Cobb diary, Apr. 23, June 24, 1861, VHS.

3. Ibid., May 15, 22, June 24, 1861.

4. Ibid., Mar. 9, 11, Apr. 29, 1861.

5. Ibid., Feb. 11, Apr. 29, May 18, 31, 1861.

6. Balfour, *13th Virginia Cavalry.*

7. Cobb diary, Mar. 20, June 2, 1861; Civil War Records Folder, Edgar B. Jackson Papers, Southampton County Historical Society, in the custody of Gilbert W. Francis, Boykins, Va.; letters to author from Daniel T. Balfour, Aug. 29, Nov. 9, 1990.

Modern estimates suggest that the Confederacy mobilized between 850,000 and 900,000 soldiers, or around 70 percent of the approximately 1,250,000 white men between the ages of seventeen and fifty in the eleven seceding states (James M. McPherson, *Battle Cry of Freedom: The Civil War Era* [New York: Oxford Univ. Press, 1988], 306–7, n.41; William L. Barney, *Flawed Victory: A New Perspective on the Civil War* [New York: Praeger, 1975], 93).

About 25 percent of the adult white male population in Southampton was age fifty or older. Over the course of the war, around 1,100 county residents might have been liable for military service. If Southampton supplied most or all of seven companies, and perhaps scattered members of other companies, an estimate of 750 Southampton soldiers, or approximately 70 percent of those eligible, would seem reasonable. This percentage is consistent with broader patterns across the Confederacy. Elliott Story reported 400 Southampton soldiers already in service in July 1861 (Story diary, July 15, 1861).

8. Rosa Bryant to James F. Bryant, June 23, 1861, James Fenton Bryant Papers, VSLA (the entire collection of wartime letters to and from James F. Bryant has been published in Edgar Jackson, *Three Rebels Write Home* [Franklin, Va.: New Pulishing Co., 1955], 37–73).

9. James F. Bryant to James D. Bryant, June 20, 1861, Bryant Papers. Branches of the Urquhart and Ridley families owned the largest concentrations of land and slaves in Southampton.

10. Ibid.; William E. Beale to his sister, Dec. 6, 1861, Beale Family Papers, VHS.

11. James F. Bryant to James D. Bryant, July 22, 1861, Feb. 4, 1862, James F. Bryant to Cousin Mollie, June 27, Sept. 4, 1861, Bryant Papers.

12. Harrison P. Pope to Roswald S. Majette, Apr. 12, 1862, Majette Family Papers, sec. 16, folder 4, VHS.

13. Cobb diary, June 9, 13, July 15, 23, 26, 27, Aug. 3, 19, 1861.

14. Babb, *History of Ivor*, 14–17; Jay Worrall, Jr. to author, Mar. 22, 1990; Jay Worrall, Jr., "Black Creek Friends Meeting," typescript in possession of author; Francis R. Neave, *Corinth Friends Meeting: One Hundred Years* (n.p., 1982), pamphlet in the possession of Gilbert W. Francis, Boykins, Va.

15. Parramore, *Southampton County*, 158–60; *Official Records of the Union and Confederate Navies in the War of the Rebellion* (Washington, D.C.: GPO, 1894–1914), ser. 1, 7:440 (hereafter cited as *Official Records, Navies*).

16. Story diary, June 1, 1861, and retrospective comments on 1862.

17. James F. Bryant to James D. Bryant, Feb. 4, May 7, 1862, James F. Bryant to Rosa Bryant, Mar. 23, 1862, Bryant Papers.

18. *The War of the Rebellion: A Compilation of the Official Records of the Union and Confederate Armies* (Washington, D.C.: GPO, 1880–1901), ser. 1, 9:110, 193–96 (hereafter cited as *Official Records, Armies*); Thomas C. Parramore, "The Burning of Winton in 1862," *North Carolina Historical Review* 39 (1962): 18–31.

19. *Official Records, Armies*, ser. 1, 9:304–32; *Official Records, Navies*, ser. 1, 7:250–51, 255–56; James F. Bryant to James D. Bryant, Apr. 16, 1862, May 3, 1862, James F. Bryant to Cousin Mollie, Apr. 12, 29, 1862, Bryant Papers; Balfour, *13th Virginia Cavalry*, 4; Parramore, *Southampton County*, 158–59.

20. Story diary, retrospective comments on 1862; James F. Bryant to James D. Bryant, May 7, 1862, Bryant Papers.

21. *Official Records, Navies*, ser. 1, 7:440 (quotation), 632–33; Parramore, *Southampton County*, 160–62.

22. Balfour, *13th Virginia Cavalry*, 4–5.

23. *Official Records, Navies*, ser. 1, 8:104–7; Maria S. Dashiell to James W. Wills, Sept. 19, 1862, James W. Wills Papers, VHS (the Wills letters, like the Bryant letters, are printed in Jackson, *Three Rebels Write Home*, 75–91); Parramore, *Southampton County*, 162.

24. *Official Records, Navies*, ser. 1, 8:107–13 (quotation on p. 113); Parramore, *Southampton County*, 162–65; R. J. Roske and Carl Van Doren, *Lincoln's Commando: The Biography of Commander W. B. Cushing, U.S.N.* (New York: Harper and Row, 1957).

25. Excerpts from the diary of Louis H. Webb, Nov. 20, 21, 1862, in an undated clipping from the *Tidewater News* (Franklin, Va.) in the Edgar B. Jackson Papers, quoted in Parramore, *Southampton County*, 166; Susan I. Berry to James W. Wills, Dec. 4, 1862, Jethro Charles to James W. Wills, Jan. 10, 1863, Wills Papers. On the Confederate buildup along the Blackwater in the winter of 1862–63, see *Official Records, Armies*, ser. 1, 18:458–60, 474, 485, 509–13, 535–36, 539; *Official Records, Navies*, ser. 1, 8:269–72.

26. Webb diary, Dec. 7, 1862, quoted in Parramore, *Southampton County*, 166.

27. Irvin C. Wills to James W. Wills, Dec. 10, 1862, Jan. 1, 23, 1863, Wills Papers; James F. Bryant to James D. Bryant, Dec. 9, 1862, Bryant Papers; Balfour, *13th Virginia Cavalry*, 9–11.

28. W. D. Barham, in the *Tidewater News* (Franklin, Va.), Mar. 25, 1932, quoted in Parramore, *Southampton County,* 168–69; "Jenny Camp Norfleet's Memoirs," in Rouse, *Timber Tycoons,* 237.

29. Cobb diary, Aug 23, 1861, Mar. 31, Apr. 9, June 5, Dec. 14, 1863; Story diary, retrospective comments on 1863, July 8, 1864; Parramore, *Southampton County,* 165–68, 174.

30. Story diary, July 8, 25, Aug. 31, 1864; Cobb diary, Nov. 25, 1863; Southampton County Court Minutes, Dec. 21, 1863, Apr. 18, July 18, Oct. 17, Dec. 19, 1864, Feb. 20, 1865, microfilm, VSLA.

31. *Official Records, Armies,* ser. 1, 18:550–63, 590–91, 600–601, 605–702, 958–1045 (quotations on pp. 632 and 996–97); *Official Records, Navies,* ser. 1, 8:713–800; Douglas Southall Freeman, *Lee's Lieutenants: A Study in Command,* 3 vols. (New York: Charles Scribner's Sons, 1942–44), 2:467–94; Susan Leigh Blackford, *Memoirs of Life in and out of the Army in Virginia during the War Between the States,* 2 vols. (Lynchburg, Va.: J. P. Bell Co., 1896), 2:40–45; Parramore, *Southampton County,* 167–68.

32. "Jenny Camp Norfleet's Memoirs," 237–38; Cobb diary, Mar. 11, 17, 26, Apr. 11, 14, 20, 21, 1863. It is not apparent whether Cobb acted on his rather unpatriotic impulse to start asking visiting soldiers to pay for meals; he probably did not.

33. Irvin C. Wills to James W. Wills, May 18, 1863, July 29, 1863, Wills Papers; Balfour, *13th Virginia Cavalry,* 12–28.

34. "Jenny Camp Norfleet's Memoirs," 237; Cobb diary, June 5, 15, July 12, 20, 23, 1863.

35. Cobb diary, Nov. 1–2, 1863; *Official Records, Armies,* ser. 1, 29:pt.1, pp. 474–76; Daniel T. Balfour, "A Sketch of the Life of Major Joseph E. Gillette," *Southampton County Historical Society Bulletin,* no. 6 (Mar. 1989): 22–27; Balfour, *13th Virginia Cavalry,* 12–28.

36. A. J. Vick to Roswald S. Majette, Sept. 5, 1863, Majette Family Papers, sec. 16, folder 5; Irvin C. Wills to James W. Wills, Feb. 6, Apr. 17, May 18, 1863, Wills Papers. St. George Tucker Mason, in Company H of the Thirteenth Virginia, likewise explained to his brother Lewis E. Mason in early 1863 that "I do pray peace may soon be made but I have no hope of it" (St. George Tucker Mason to Lewis E. Mason, Jan. 28, 1863, Mason Family Papers, sec. 52, VHS).

37. *Official Records, Armies,* ser. 1, 18:649, 711.

38. See Francis McKinney, *Education in Violence: The Life of General George H. Thomas and the History of the Army of the Cumberland* (Detroit: Wayne State Univ. Press, 1961); Wilbur Thomas, *General George H. Thomas: The Indomitable Warrior* (New York: Exposition Press, 1964); Frank A. Palumbo, *General George Henry Thomas, Major General U.S.A.: The Dependable General, Supreme in Tactics of Strategy and Command* (Dayton, Ohio: Morningside House, 1983); Richard O'Connor, *Thomas: Rock of Chickamauga* (New York: Prentice-Hall, 1948); and especially Freeman Cleaves, *Rock of Chickamauga: The Life of General George H. Thomas* (Norman: Univ. of Oklahoma Press, 1948). For brief assessments, see Daniel T. Balfour, "A Sketch of the Life of

General George H. Thomas," *Southampton County Historical Society Bulletin*, no. 5 (Mar. 1983): 12–22; Herman Hattaway and Michael L. Gillespie, "Soldier of Conscience: George H. Thomas; A Virginian Fights for the Union," *Virginia Cavalcade* 34 (Autumn 1984): 64–75; Peter Andrews, "The Rock of Chicka-mauga," *American Heritage* 41 (March 1990): 81–91.

39. George H. Thomas to John W. Thomas, Feb. 16, 1839, Sept. 27, Oct. 19, 1840, Oct. 25, 1848, copies in the Thomas and Mahone folder of the Edgar B. Jackson Papers; Squires, *Days of Yester-Year in Colony and Commonwealth*, 189; O. O. Howard, *Personal Recollections of the Rebellion* (New York: Military Order of the Loyal Legion, 1890), 287, cited in Thomas, *General George H. Thomas*, 53–54; O'Connor, *Thomas*, 55–56; Thomas J. Pretlow to Thaddeus Stevens, Dec. 27, 1865, Thaddeus Stevens Papers, LC.

40. W. B. Barham, "Recollections of the Thomas Family of Southampton County," *Virginia Historical Magazine* 45 (1932): 328–34.

41. Story diary, July 13, 1864; Cobb diary, May 5, 1864.

42. Cobb diary, Apr. 4, 15, 18, 23, 26, May 26, 27, Sept. 13, 23, Dec. 23, 30, 1864; Joseph H. Prince to Lewis E. Mason, Mar. 25, 1864, Mason Family Papers, sec. 52.

43. Story diary, July 8, 13, 1864; Cobb diary, June 5, 10, Sept. 10, 29, Oct. 1, 1864.

44. Story diary, retrospective comments on late 1864 and 1865; Ludwell H. Johnson III, "Blockade or Trade Monopoly? John A. Dix and the Union Occu-pation of Norfolk," *VMHB* 93 (1985): 54–78; Parramore, *Southampton County*, 174–76.

45. Cobb diary, May 7, 9, 13, 22–23, 28–30, 1864; *Official Records, Armies*, ser. 1, 36:pt.2, pp. 171–91.

46. James F. Bryant to James D. Bryant, May 7, 1862, June 5, 1864, Bryant Papers; Cobb diary, May 21, 26, June 1, 1864. No evidence has come to hand to indicate the vote totals or to suggest whether soldiers voted.

47. James F. Bryant to James D. Bryant, June 5, 1864, Bryant Papers; Balfour, *13th Virginia Cavalry*, 29–34.

48. James F. Bryant to James D. Bryant, June 5, 1864, Bryant Papers.

49. Cobb diary, June 17, 1864.

50. Story diary, July 13, 22, 1864; Cobb diary, June 18, 19, 22, 24, 25, Aug. 18, Oct. 10, 11, 1864.

51. Cobb diary, June 8, 28, July 20, Aug. 14–16, Oct. 8, 1864; James F. Bryant to James D. Bryant, June 5, 1864, Bryant Papers.

52. See Douglas Southall Freeman, *R. E. Lee: A Biography*, 4 vols. (New York: Charles Scribner's Sons, 1934–35), 3:479–91, 521; Shelby Foote, *The Civil War: A Narrative*, vol. 3, *Red River to Appomattox* (New York: Random House, 1974), 441–46, 545–48; Steven Z. Starr, *The Union Cavalry in the Civil War*, vol. 2, *The War in the East: From Gettysburg to Appomattox, 1863–1865* (Baton Rouge: Louisiana State Univ. Press, 1981), 176–207, 386–420; Balfour, *13th Virginia Cavalry*, 34–41; Noah Andre Trudeau, *The Last Citadel: Peters-burg, Virginia, June 1864–April 1865* (Boston: Little, Brown, 1991), 158–89.

53. Cobb diary, June 15, Sept. 2, 1864.

54. *Freedman's Journal* (Boston), Jan. 1865, quoted in Parramore, *Southampton County,* 169.

55. Ira Berlin, ed., *Freedom: A Documentary History of Emancipation, 1861–1867,* ser. 2, *The Black Military Experience* (New York: Cambridge Univ. Press, 1982), 1, 27.

56. Civil War pension files for Henry Judkins, Albert Shelley, Jackson Shepherd, Henry Williams, and Nelson Edwards, RG 15, Records of the Veterans Administration, NA; Company and Regimental Descriptive Books for First U.S.C.C., Second U.S.C.C., Thirty-seventh U.S.C.I., RG 94, NA; Adjutant General's Office, Civil War (Union) Compiled Military Service Records, First U.S.C.C., ibid.

57. Information in this paragraph is drawn primarily from the various Company and Regimental Descriptive Books in RG 94, NA.

58. Information in this paragraph is based on the Company and Regimental Descriptive Books, the Compiled Military and Service Records (all in RG 94, NA), and the Civil War pension files for Scott and the two Ricks, who may well have been brothers (RG 15, NA). The figure of 20 percent is an educated guess. Intensive examination of all pertinent records for the thirty-four members of the First U.S.C.C. produced the names of seven certain or probable free blacks. Family names such as Ricks and Artis in other units suggest a comparable frequency of free blacks.

59. *Official Records, Armies,* ser. 1, 42:pt.1, pp. 126, 819–20; Richard J. Sommers, *Richmond Redeemed: The Siege at Petersburg* (Garden City, N.Y.: Doubleday, 1981), 36–38, 461, 485. Although critical of what he considers subsequent exaggeration of the Second Brigade's achievement—on grounds that the Confederate defenders of New Market Heights withdrew to blunt a Union attack elsewhere—Sommers acknowledges "the valor of Draper's men who resumed the advance after suffering so severely" (ibid., 38). Colonel Alonzo G. Draper commanded the Second Brigade.

60. Civil War pension files for Harrison Sykes (alias Harrison Williams), Henry Sykes (alias Henry Williams), and Joseph Sykes (alias Joseph Williams), RG 15, NA.

61. Civil War pension file for Joseph Sykes (alias Joseph Williams), RG 15, NA (the editorial method of using spaces at likely sentence breaks follows the procedure recommended in Berlin, *Freedom: A Documentary History of Emancipation*); *The Confessions of Nat Turner . . . ,* in Eric Foner, ed., *Nat Turner* (Englewood Cliffs, N.J.: Prentice-Hall, 1971), 44–45.

62. Cobb diary, May 22, 28, June 1, 3, 6, 20, 29, July 5, 12, 21–23, 1864.

63. Ibid., Sept. 12, 1863, July 5, 1864.

64. Ibid., June 13, 1863, June 26, Aug. 5–6, 1864.

65. Ibid., Aug. 29, Oct. 11, 16, 20, 28, 1864.

66. Ibid., Nov. 2–6, 21, 28, 30, Dec. 1–3, 11, 18, 1864; Trudeau, *The Last Citadel,* 266–85.

67. Edwards, *The Cobbs of the Tidewater,* 208–12; Balfour, *13th Virginia Cavalry,* 42–45.

68. Cobb diary, June 28, 1864.

EIGHT. THE NEW ORDER OF THINGS

1. Maj. J. H. Putnam to Lt. W. L. Ogden, June 12, 1865, enclosing Capt. John M. Post to Lt. Col. T. H. Harris, June 10, 1865, Unregistered Letters and Telegrams Received, Office of Assistant Commissioner, Virginia Records, box 1, ser. 3799, Records of the Bureau of Refugees, Freedmen, and Abandoned Lands (hereafter cited as BRFAL), RG 105, NA, item A–7481 consulted in the office of the Freedmen and Southern Society Project, History Department, University of Maryland.

2. Joel Cranford to Lt. Jno. K. Keatley, July 12, 1865, Letters and Orders Received, Norfolk, Va., Virginia Records, box 44, ser. 4180, RG 105, NA, item A–7942 consulted in the office of the Freedmen and Southern Society Project.

3. Joseph Daniel Pope to Maj. Gen. Q. A. Gillmore, June 29, 1865, Miscellaneous Records, ser. 4171, Department of the South, Records of U.S. Army Continental Commands, 1821–1920, RG 393 (pt. 1), NA, quoted in Ira Berlin et al., "The Terrain of Freedom: The Struggle over the Meaning of Free Labor in the U.S. South," *History Workshop* 22 (Autumn 1986): 114.

4. This paragraph summarizes a rich and sprawling new literature; for a fine overview, see Eric Foner, *Reconstruction: America's Unfinished Revolution, 1863–1877* (New York: Harper and Row, 1988), chap. 3.

5. William S. McFeely, *Yankee Stepfather: General O. O. Howard and the Freedmen* (New Haven: Yale Univ. Press, 1968).

6. Maj. Gen. O. O. Howard to Capt. A. S. Flagg, July 12, 1865, Circular No. 11, Circulars Received, Jerusalem, Va., Virginia Records, box 31, ser. 4026, RG 105, NA.

7. Col. Orlando Brown, Circular to Virginia Agents, Nov. 4, 1865, ibid.

8. Maj. Gen. O. O. Howard to Capt. A. S. Flagg, July 12, 1865, ibid.

9. Contract Register for Southampton (mostly for 1866; a few 1867), Jerusalem, Va., bound vol. no. 254, ser. 4024, ibid.

10. Ibid.; Cobb diary, Jan. 1, Oct. 6, Dec. 7, 1866, VHS. Cobb's diary, which cannot be fully reconciled with the bureau records, reports that he hired ten hands in January 1866 for the first full year of free-labor agriculture; it appears that Cobb's calculation of "hands" included the wives of the three adult men specified in bureau records.

11. Cobb diary, Feb. 6–7, July 23–24, 1866; Foner, *Reconstruction*, 153–70.

12. Cobb diary, Jan. 1, Aug. 17, 1866, and passim. On continuities linking slavery and the first years of free-labor agriculture, see Foner, *Reconstruction*, 171–72; Gregg L. Michel, "From Slavery to Freedom: Hickory Hill, 1850–1880," in Edward L. Ayers and John C. Willis, eds., *The Edge of the South: Life in Nineteenth-Century Virginia* (Charlottesville: Univ. Press of Virginia, 1991), 118–20. Cobb's records show that his crops in 1866 were raised by gang labor rather than on individual plots (Cobb diary, Dec. 7, 1866).

13. Cobb diary, Mar. 1, Apr. 18, July 4, 1868, Mar. 11, Apr. 7, 1870.

14. Ibid., Jan. 22–23, May 23, July 21, 30–31, Aug. 16, Nov. 12–16, Dec. 7, 1866, Feb. 20, May 20, Nov. 16, 23, Dec. 3, 6, 18, 1867, Jan. 23, Oct. 19, 1871. Severe wartime inflation had approximately doubled prewar prices; Cobb's earnings had only around half the purchasing value of the same prewar dollar figures. Even if discounted 50 percent, however, thirty-one cents was a fine price for a pound of cotton.

15. Ibid., Mar. 1, May 13, 21, July 26, 29, Sept. 30, Oct. 5, 11, 18, 1866. An able slave had been expected to pick 100 pounds of Virginia cotton daily.

16. Ibid., Dec. 7, 1866.

17. Capt. Lemuel Jeffries to Capt. A. S. Flagg, Mar. 12, 1866, Letters Received, Subassistant Commissioner, First District, Virginia Records, box 40, ser. 4153, RG 105, NA, item A–7925 consulted in the office of the Freedmen and Southern Society Project.

18. Maj. J. R. Stone to Capt. A. J. Bates, Mar. 31, 1866, microfilm ser. M1048, reel 44, frames 414–18, Records of the Assistant Commissioner for the State of Virginia, BRFAL, 1865–69, RG 105, NA.

19. Lt. Morton Havens to Capt. A. S. Flagg, Apr. 30, 1866, Virginia Records, box 40, ser. 4153, RG 105, NA, item A–7925 consulted in the office of the Freedmen and Southern Society Project.

20. Nathaniel Riddick, "Notes of Meetings with Francis Pierpont and Alfred H. Terry," Dec. 1865, Riddick Family Papers, VSLA.

21. Capt. A. S. Flagg to Lt. Morton Havens, Apr. 19, 1866, Virginia Records, box 44, ser. 4180, RG 105, NA, item A–7950A consulted in the office of the Freedmen and Southern Society Project.

22. See Richard Lowe, *Republicans and Reconstruction in Virginia, 1856–1870* (Charlottesville: Univ. Press of Virginia, 1991), chaps. 2–4; Lowe, "Another Look at Reconstruction in Virginia," *Civil War History* 32 (1986): 58–63; Jack P. Maddex, Jr., *The Virginia Conservatives, 1867–1879: A Study in Reconstruction Politics* (Chapel Hill: Univ. of North Carolina Press, 1970), 38–41; Dan T. Carter, *When the War Was Over: The Failure of Self-Reconstruction in the South, 1865–1867* (Baton Rouge: Louisiana State Univ. Press, 1985).

23. "Letter from Southampton County" (written by "E."), Feb. 12, 1866, in Richmond semiweekly *Whig*, Feb. 16, 1866.

24. Ibid., Feb. 1, 12, 1866, in Richmond semiweekly *Whig*, Feb 9, 16, 1866.

25. Ibid.

26. Ibid., Mar. 23, 1866, in Richmond semiweekly *Whig*, Mar. 30, 1866.

27. Virginia BRFAL, circulars of Feb. 7 and Mar. 12, 1866, Letters and Orders Received, Jerusalem, Va., Virginia Records, box 31, ser. 4025, RG 105, NA.

28. Records of Freedmen's Court, Southampton, Feb. 17, Mar. 9, 16, Apr. 14, 21, 1866, vol. 255, ser. 4024, ibid.

29. Ibid., Apr. 14, 1866; Lt. Morton Havens to Capt. A. S. Flagg, May 3, 1866, Virginia Records, box 31, ser. 4025, ibid. See Lynda Jane Morgan, "Emancipation in the Virginia Tobacco Belt, 1850–1870" (Ph.D. diss., Univ. of Virginia, 1986), 190–94, on unfair apprenticeships elsewhere in eastern Virginia in 1865–66.

30. Records of Freedmen's Court, Southampton, 1867 (most cases apparently Sept. 27, 1867), vol. 256, ser. 4024, RG 105, NA.

31. Lt. A. G. Deacon to Asst. Adj. Gen. S. F. Chalfin, July 25, 1867, Jerusalem, Va., First Military District, Letters Received, 1867, box 6, item D255, ser. 5068, RG 393, NA. Information about this case in the next several paragraphs is drawn from the testimony compiled by Deacon, unless otherwise indicated.

32. Lt. A. G. Deacon to Asst. Adj. Gen. S. F. Chalfin, Sept. 12, 1867, item D324, filed with D255, ibid.

33. Lt. A. G. Deacon, Report of Testimony in the case of Edward Sykes versus William M. Beaton, July 24, 1867, Virginia Records, box 31, ser. 4025, RG 105, NA. Information about this case in the next several paragraphs is drawn from the testimony compiled by Deacon, unless otherwise indicated.

34. Data drawn from 1860 U.S. population and agricultural censuses, 1860 county tax lists, and 1860–61 records of individual voting.

35. By July 1867 the political situation in Southampton had changed radically. Federally supervised voter registration was by then enlisting more black registrants than whites. It may be conjectured that leading blacks urged Deacon to reopen the Sykes-Beaton case.

36. Records of Freedmen's Court, Southampton, July 24, 1867, vol. 255, ser. 4024, RG 105, NA.

37. John W. Barnes to Bvt. Maj. J. H. Remington, June 18, 1867, Barnes to William D. McClenny, June 22, 1867, Third Division Letters Received (actually, copies of letters sent), first of two bound volumes, ser. 5267, RG 393, NA.

38. Lowe, *Republicans and Reconstruction in Virginia*, 112–20; Michael W. Fitzgerald, *The Union League Movement in the Deep South: Politics and Agricultural Change during Reconstruction* (Baton Rouge: Louisiana State Univ. Press, 1989) 176; Foner, *Reconstruction*, 282. Much still needs to be learned about Reconstruction at the local level in Virginia. Developments at the state level are expertly analyzed in Lowe, *Republicans and Reconstruction in Virginia*; Lowe, "Another Look at Reconstruction in Virginia"; and Maddex, *Virginia Conservatives*.

39. Circular from Asst. Adj. Gen. S. F. Chalfin to Lt. A. G. Deacon, Apr. 15, 1867, First Military District (Virginia), General Orders No. 28, May 13, 1867, copy received by Lt. A. G. Deacon, Virginia Records, box 31, ser. 4025, RG 105, NA.

40. Lt. A. G. Deacon to Brig. and Bvt. Maj. Gen. John M. Schofield, July 27, 1867, box 6, item D252, ser. 5068, RG 393, NA. Subsequently, however, Deacon had Davis dismissed: "When he is not sick he is drunk" (Deacon to Asst. Adj. Gen. S. F. Chalfin, Sept. 30, 1867, Jerusalem, Va., Register of Letters Received, First Military District, item D338, ser. 5067, ibid.).

41. General Orders No. 28, May 13, 1867, copy received by Lt. A. G. Deacon, Virginia Records, box 31, ser. 4025, RG 105, NA.

42. General Orders No. 34, June 3, 1867, copy received by Lt. A. G. Deacon, ibid. Quotations in the next several paragraphs come from the same source unless otherwise indicated.

43. J. D. Pretlow to Bruce M. Rogers, Feb. 22, 1869, Miscellaneous Letters, 3d Military Division, ser. 5268, RG 393, NA.

44. General Orders No. 28, May 13, 1867, copy received by Lt. A. G. Deacon, Virginia Records, box 31, ser. 4025, RG 105, NA.

45. Ibid.

46. John W. Barnes to Brig. and Bvt. Maj. Gen. John M. Schofield, June 7, 1867, Suffolk, Va., Letters Received (actually copies of letters sent), first of two bound volumes, Third Division, Virginia, ser. 5264, Asst. Adj. Gen. S. F. Chalfin to John W. Barnes, June 10, 1867, Miscellaneous Letters, ser. 5268, RG 393, NA.

47. John W. Barnes to Asst. Adj. Gen. S. F. Chalfin, July 13, 15, 31, 1867, ser. 5264, Frederick S. Burr to Barnes, July 4, 1867, ser. 5268, Barnes to Edward Murphy, July 29, 1867, vol. 1, ser. 5267, statement by W. A. Butler concerning his actions on July 1, 1867, vol. 2, ser. 5267, ibid.; Barnes to Chalfin, July 4, 1867, box 2, ser. 5068, ibid., item SS–1015 consulted in the office of the Freedmen and Southern Society Project.

48. Record of Persons Registering and Voting in Virginia, 1867–69 (actually only 1867), p. 48 of bound volume, ser. 5253, RG 393, NA.

49. Oswin White to Brig. and Bvt. Maj. Gen. J. M. Schofield, Sept. 3, 1867, Virginia Records, box 31, ser. 4025, RG 105, NA; Tally of 1867 Registration and Voting in Virginia, pp. 4–5 of Memorandum from Headquarters, First Military District (Virginia), May 10, 1869, VSLA.

50. U.S. Census, Population, Slave Schedules, 1860, Southampton County, Nottoway Parish, household no. 482, microfilm, NA.

51. Thomas J. Pretlow to Thaddeus Stevens, Dec. 27, 1865, Thaddeus Stevens Papers, LC.

52. Norfolk *Virginian*, July 1, 1867.

53. Ibid.

54. Cobb diary, June 23, 1867.

55. None of the more immediate members of Thomas J. Pretlow's family were qualified to run: congressional strictures barred the doctor himself, his brothers, Jordan Denson Pretlow (a former magistrate) and Joshua Pretlow (a former state legislator), and his son-in-law John Pretlow, the former magistrate and candidate for sheriff in 1864.

That two persons were named John Pretlow invites confusion. The candidate for the convention, John Pretlow (1825–1901), sometimes designated John Pretlow, Sr., was a birthright Quaker who never owned slaves. His father, Joseph Pretlow, was one of Elliott Story's teachers; John Pretlow, Sr., was Story's student and longtime friend. In 1870 he owned $4,000 of real estate and $1,100 of personal property.

John Pretlow (1827–1899), sometimes designated John Pretlow, Jr., the son of a prosperous slaveholder, Robert Pretlow, was Thomas J. Pretlow's first cousin and his son-in-law, having married his eldest daughter, Eva Pretlow (1838–1880). John Pretlow, Jr., owned $17,000 worth of real estate and $10,000 worth of personal property in 1870. Both John Pretlow, Sr., and John Pretlow, Jr., were farmers in 1870 (Hart, "Descendants of Thomas Pretlow," 1, 7, 10, 17, 32, 46,

46a, 61, 69, 81; U.S. Census, Population, 1870, Southampton County, Franklin Depot Township, pp. 205, 217, microfilm, NA).

56. Richmond semiweekly *Whig*, July 31, 1867.

NINE. BLACK AWAKENING AND WHITE REACTION

1. Richmond *Dispatch*, Aug. 9, 12, 1867. I thank Professor John O'Brien of Dalhousie University for calling this episode to my attention.

2. Ibid., Aug. 9, 1867.

3. Ibid., Aug. 12, 1867.

4. Richmond weekly *New Nation*, Aug. 22, 1867.

5. New York *Tribune*, April 20, 1867; Richmond *Enquirer*, Apr. 23, 25, 1867. Earlier studies of the Union League are badly dated. Susie Lee Owens, "The Union League of America: Political Activities in Tennessee, the Carolinas, and Virginia, 1865–1870" (Ph.D. diss., New York Univ., 1943), depicts the league as a sinister organization. A somewhat more balanced overview may be found in Clement Mario Silvestro's "None but Patriots: The Union Leagues in Civil War and Reconstruction" (Ph.D. diss., Univ. of Wisconsin, 1959), which includes a segment on Virginia (pp. 274–79). The only high-quality modern study of the league is Michael W. Fitzgerald's *Union League Movement in the Deep South*, which focuses on Alabama and Mississippi.

6. On the pattern of black dominance over local leagues, see Fitzgerald, *Union League Movement in the Deep South*, 58–71. Evidence of league activity in Southampton comes primarily from antileague newspapers, notably the Norfolk *Virginian*, July 27, 1868, in which a "letter from Southampton," July 22, 1868, noted: "The loyal leagues had circulated the notices [of a Republican meeting] at every cross road and by-way in the county."

7. Richmond *Enquirer*, Apr. 23, 1867.

8. Union League Club of New York, *Report of the Proceedings of the Conference at Richmond, June 11th and 12th, 1867* (New York, 1867); Richmond *Dispatch*, June 14, 1867; Lowe, *Republicans and Reconstruction in Virginia*, 72–90; Richard H. Abbott, *The Republican Party and the South, 1855–1877: The First Southern Strategy* (Chapel Hill: Univ. of North Carolina Press, 1986), 122–25.

9. Norfolk *Virginian*, June 20, 26, 27, 1867; Petersburg *Index*, June 29, 1867.

10. Lowe, *Republicans and Reconstruction in Virginia*, 90–96; Lowe, "Another Look at Reconstruction in Virginia," 64–67; Abbott, *Republican Party and the South*, 126–27; Richmond semiweekly *Whig*, July 31, 1867; Richmond weekly *New Nation*, Aug. 8, 1867.

11. U.S. Census, Population, 1870, Southampton County, Franklin Depot Township, p. 218, microfilm, NA; Joseph Gregory to Lt. Louis V. Caziarc, July 24, 1869, item G404, First Military District, Letters Received, 1869, ser. 5068, RG 393, NA; Civil War pension file for Abram Barrett, RG 15, NA. The coinciding political and religious gatherings in Richmond during the first week of August almost certainly placed Gregory there.

12. Sent from Jerusalem, Va., on Apr. 24, 1867, the letter was lost or delayed for almost a year. On Mar. 25, 1868, however, bureau agent John Power, in Holly Springs, Miss., noted that Manerva Ann and Ann Eliza were "living with their Uncle Jessee Brown . . . 8 Miles North of Holly Springs Miss. They are doing well; and any remittance from their Father will be forwarded to them by me." The original document, with Power's endorsement, was thereupon routed back to Southampton (Letters and Orders Received, Jerusalem, Va., Virginia Records, box 31, ser. 4025, RG 105, NA).

13. General John M. Schofield, who commanded the First Military District (Virginia), made a sour assessment: "*John Brown*. Colored. Farmer. Slave until emancipated by the war. Illiterate. Esteemed honest, but is ignorant, and has no force of character. *Radical*" (Richard G. Lowe, "Virginia's Reconstruction Convention: General Schofield Rates the Delegates," *VMHB* 80 [1972]: 354). The Richmond daily *Whig*, Oct. 28, 30, 1867, identified Brown as a mulatto.

John Brown is listed in 1868, 1869, and 1870 among persons living with Robert Ridley, Jr. (Personal Property Taxes, Southampton County, St. Lukes Parish, VSLA). The 1870 U.S. Census lists Brown and his wife, Chloe Brown, a black farm laborer, with three children: Robert Brown, age eight, black; James Brown, age five, mulatto; and Lizzie Brown, age three, mulatto. A commonsense reading of the census would suggest that John Brown was not Robert Brown's father and that James and Lizzie Brown were his biological offspring. If so, John Brown had remarried during the war. The 1870 census also indicates that Brown's wife, like her husband but unlike most adult blacks in Southampton, had learned to read and write (U.S. Census, Population, 1870, Southampton County, Drewrysville Township, household no. 220, microfilm, NA). In 1880 the family included two additional young children (U.S. Census, Population, 1880, Southampton County, Drewrysville Township, microfilm, NA).

14. Cobb diary, Mar. 6, 9–10, 1867, VHS.

15. Ibid., June 8, 10, 23, July 15, Aug. 19, 1867.

16. Ibid., Aug. 10, Sept. 7, 11–12, Oct. 22, 1867; "Letter from Petersburg," Aug. 6, 1867, in Richmond *Dispatch*, Aug. 8, 1867.

17. Carr Holland et al. to "Genl." [J. M. Schofield?], Sept. 10, 1867, Virginia Records, box 31, ser. 4025, RG 105, NA.

18. First Military District, General Orders No. 68, Oct. 4, 1867, copy received by Lt. A. G. Deacon, ibid. Election officials in each district were instructed to record the names of persons who voted. These poll lists no longer showed how individuals voted, simply that they voted. Yet because black and white voters were tallied separately, and because voting patterns often polarized nearly completely along racial lines, records indicating who voted often show with a high degree of probability how individuals voted. Many of the ballots from the 1867 Southampton election survive; some include the name of the person who cast the ballot (Election Records, Southampton County, Oct. 22, 1867, transfer box 19, Hollinger [clamshell] box, VSLA). Brent Tarter of the Virginia State Library and Archives took special pains to help me locate Southampton's 1867 and 1869 election records.

19. Lt. A. G. Deacon to Brig. and Bvt. Maj. Gen. J. M. Schofield, Oct. 9, 1867, ser. 5068, 1867, box 6, item D344, RG 393, NA.

20. General Orders No. 68, Oct. 4, 1867, copy received by Lt. A. G. Deacon, Virginia Records, box 31, ser. 4025, RG 105, NA.

21. Record of Persons Registering and Voting in Virginia, ser. 5253, RG 393, NA; Tally of 1867 Registration and Voting in Virginia, pp. 4–5 of Memorandum from Headquarters, First Military District (Virginia), May 10, 1869, VSLA; Election Records, Southampton County, Oct. 22, 1867, transfer box 19, Hollinger [clamshell] box, VSLA. Brown's greatest margins (710 of 936 votes cast) were in the lower county, where blacks outnumbered whites. He also won easily in the upper county (533 of 933 votes cast). Pretlow's support was confined primarily to former Whigs in the upper county, where he received all but 7 of his 223 votes. Edwards, who ran best among former Democrats, collected 219 votes in the lower county and 186 in the upper county (see table 9.4). Pretlow's vote may provide some indication of the number of Union Whigs in the county who were genuinely out of sympathy with the Confederacy, although some of his more prominent supporters were disfranchised in this election.

22. Maj. Gen. O. O. Howard to Bvt. Brig. Gen. Orlando Brown, Dec. 2, 1867, copy in Virginia Records, box 31, ser. 4025, RG 105, NA.

23. Lowe, *Republicans and Reconstruction in Virginia*, 121–29; Richard H. Hume, "Negro Delegates to the State Constitutional Conventions of 1867–69," in Howard N. Rabinowitz, ed., *Southern Black Leaders of the Reconstruction Era* (Urbana: Univ. of Illinois Press, 1982), 135–36; Hume, "The Membership of the Virginia Constitutional Convention of 1867–1868: A Study of the Beginnings of Congressional Reconstruction in the Upper South," *VMHB* 86 (1978): 477–78; Thomas J. Pretlow to the editor, Jan. 29, 1868, in Richmond *Whig*, Feb. 3. 1868. Information and quotations in subsequent paragraphs are drawn from Pretlow's letter, unless otherwise indicated.

24. Maddex, *Virginia Conservatives*, 62–63; Alrutheus Ambush Taylor, *The Negro in the Reconstruction of Virginia* (Washington, D.C.: Association for the Study of Negro Life and History, 1926), 224–26.

25. See George M. Fredrickson, *The Black Image in the White Mind: The Debate on Afro-American Character and Destiny, 1817–1914* (New York: Harper & Row, 1971), 71–96, 187–91.

26. See Michael Les Benedict, "The Rout of Radicalism: Republicans and the Election of 1867," *Civil War History* 18 (1972): 334–44.

27. There is an autobiographical sketch in Mortimer Moulden to Bvt. Maj. J. H. Remington, July 31, 1868, Jerusalem, Va., letter book vol. 253, ser. 4024, RG 105, NA.

28. Bvt. Maj. J. H. Remington to Mortimer Moulden, Jan. 29, 1868, Virginia Records, box 31, ser. 4025, Moulden to Remington, Apr. 18, 1868, letter book vol. 253, ser. 4024, ibid.

29. Mortimer Moulden to Bvt. Maj. J. H. Remington, Feb. 4, 1868, [Mrs.] M. A. Andrews to Remington, June 12, 1868, Remington to Moulden, June 18, 1868, Virginia Records, box 31, ser. 4025, ibid.

30. Mortimer Moulden to Bvt. Maj. J. H. Remington, June 23, 1868, Remington to Moulden, July 3, 1868, ibid.

31. Mortimer Moulden to Bvt. Brig. Genl. Orlando Brown, Feb. 28, Mar. 25, Apr. 25, 1868, ibid. Quotations in the next several paragraphs are extracted from Moulden's reports.

32. Mortimer Moulden to Bvt. Maj. J. H. Remington, Mar. 17, 1868, letter book vol. 253, ser. 4024, Moulden to Bvt. Brig Gen. Orlando Brown, Mar. 25, 1868, Virginia Records, box 31, ser. 4025, ibid.

33. Mortimer Moulden to Bvt. Maj. J. H. Remington, Mar. 17, 1868, Jerusalem, Va., letter book vol. 253, ser. 4024, Bvt. Brig. Gen. Orlando Brown to Remington, Mar. 27, 1868, Virginia Records, box 31, ser. 4025, ibid.

34. Mortimer Moulden to Bvt. Maj. J. H. Remington, Apr. 16, 1868, Jerusalem, letter book vol. 253, ser. 4024, Moulden to Bvt. Brig. Gen. Orlando Brown, Apr. 25, 1868, Virginia Records, box 31, ser. 4025, ibid.

35. James L. McDonough, "John Schofield as Military Director of Reconstruction in Virginia," *Civil War History* 15 (1969): 251–55; Lowe, *Republicans and Reconstruction in Virginia*, 148–55; Cobb diary, May 10, 14, 16, 18, 1868.

36. Bvt. Capt. Will. A. Coulter to Mortimer Moulden, May 7, 1868, Virginia Records, box 31, ser. 4025, RG 105, NA; Cobb diary, May 5, 1868.

37. Mortimer Moulden to Bvt. Brig. Gen. Orlando Brown, May 25, 1868, Virginia Records, box 31, ser. 4025, RG 105, NA; petition forwarded by George Teamoh, June 5, 1868, Letters Received, Third Division of the First Military District (Virginia), ser. 5267, RG 393, NA.

38. Mortimer Moulden to Bvt. Brig. Gen. Orlando Brown, Moulden to Bvt. Maj. J. H. Remington, both July 31, 1868, Virginia Records, box 31, ser. 4025, RG 105, NA.

39. Lucius H. Chandler, the U.S. district attorney from Norfolk, had been an unconditional Unionist. He allied with the moderate wing of the Republican party led by John Minor Botts. Radical Republicans tried to prevent his nomination (Norfolk *Virginian*, Apr. 29, May 2, 9, 13, 22, 24, June 1, 1868; Lowe, *Republicans and Reconstruction in Virginia*, 42–44, 92, 149, 154).

40. "Letter from Southampton," July 22, 1868, in Norfolk *Virginian*, July 27, 1868.

41. Lt. G. M. Fleming, circular, July 10, 1868, Virginia Records, box 31, ser. 4025, RG 105, NA.

42. Ned Sykes statement, July 23, 1868, in Lt. G. M. Fleming to Mortimer Moulden, July 24, 1868, ibid. Benjamin Pope was either one of the wealthiest planters in Southampton, Benjamin E. Pope, or his son, Benjamin J. Pope. In 1860 Benjamin E. Pope owned sixty-eight slaves (U.S. Census, Population, Slave Schedules, 1860, Southampton County, St. Lukes Parish, households nos. 205, 207, microfilm, NA).

43. Mortimer Moulden to Bvt. Brig. Gen. Orlando Brown, July 31, Aug. 31, 1868, Virginia Records, box 31, ser. 4025, RG 105, NA.

44. Ibid., Aug. 31, 1868; Cobb diary, Aug. 22, 1868.

45. Mortimer Moulden to Bvt. Brig. Gen. Orlando Brown, July 31, Aug. 31, Sept. 30, Oct. 31, 1868, F. D. Sewall to Brown, Sept. 30, 1868, M. A. Andrews

to Bvt. Maj. J. H. Remington, June 12, 1868, Virginia Records, box 31, ser. 4025, RG 105, NA.

46. Mortimer Moulden to Bvt. Brig. Gen. Orlando Brown, Feb. 28, Mar. 25, Apr. 25, 1868, ibid. Quotations in the following paragraph are also extracted from Moulden's reports, especially the ones written in March and April.

47. Bvt. Brig. Gen. Orlando Brown to Mortimer Moulden, May 6, 1868, ibid.

48. A Sabbath school would not necessarily have featured any more religious indoctrination than a day school; for adult freedmen who had to work six days a week, only the Sabbath school offered an opportunity to gain literacy.

49. Mortimer Moulden to Bvt. Maj. J. H. Remington, Mar. 31, 1868, Mrs. A. W. Samson to Moulden, Mar. 27, 1868, enclosed in Moulden to Remington, Apr. 4, 1868, ibid.

50. Mortimer Moulden to Bvt. Maj. J. H. Remington, Mar. 31, Apr. 25, May 27, Aug. 31, 1868, A. B. Corliss to Moulden, Apr. 17, 1868, M. A. Andrews to Remington, June 12, 1868, ibid.; Moulden to Remington, Apr. 4, 1868, Moulden to Corliss, Apr. 23, 1868, letter book vol. 253, ser. 4024, ibid.; Monthly Southampton County School Report (submitted by Moulden), May 1868, microfilm series M1053, reel 13, ibid.

51. Extract from the *American Missionary*, May 1867, in Letters and Orders Received, Suffolk, Va., vol. 437, ser. 4277, Lt. G. M. Fleming to Bvt. Brig. Gen. Orlando Brown, Dec. 25, 1867, vol. 439, ibid., Monthly Nansemond County School Reports, February 1868, ser. 4279, George W. Black to Bvt. Maj. J. H. Remington, school report for Feb. 1868, Suffolk, Va., Virginia Records, box 57, ser. 4280, ibid.

52. P. H. McLaughlin to Maj. J. R. Stone, Nov. 23, 1868, box 27, ser. 5068, RG 393, NA, item SS–1134 consulted in the office of the Freedmen and Southern Society Project, History Department, University of Maryland.

53. Mortimer Moulden to Bvt. Maj. J. H. Remington, Aug. 15, 1868, letter book vol. 253, ser. 4024, RG 105, NA.

54. Mortimer Moulden to Bvt. Maj. J. H. Remington, Nov. 30, Dec. 31, 1868, Moulden to Bvt. Brig. Gen. Orlando Brown, Nov. 30, Dec. 31, 1868, Virginia Records, box 31, ser. 4025, ibid.

55. Maddex, *Virginia Conservatives*, 60–66; Lowe, *Republicans and Reconstruction in Virginia*, 158, 169.

56. Maddex, *Virginia Conservatives.*, 67–82; Lowe, *Republicans and Reconstruction in Virginia*, 159–72.

57. Norfolk *Virginian*, May 21, 1869, "Letter from Southampton," May 22, 1869, ibid., May 26, 1869; Lowe, *Republicans and Reconstruction in Virginia*, 139, 145, 172.

58. Gilbert C. Walker to Brig and Bvt. Maj. Gen. John M. Schofield, Oct. 24, 1867, John M. Schofield Papers, box 9, LC.

59. Numerous copies of the ironclad oath may be found in First Military District (Virginia), Letters Received, 1869, ser. 5068, RG 393, NA. Congress specified in July 1867 that all persons elected or appointed to office in any of the reconstructed states should sign copies of the oath.

60. Capt. Edward P. Pearson, Jr., to Col. C. A. Hartwell, May 19, 1869, Pear-

son to Lt. Louis V. Caziarc, May 19, 1869, Pearson to Demarcus L. Doles, June 1, 1869, Hicksford, Va., second of four letter books, Letters Sent, Seventh and Ninth Divisions, ser. 5278, RG 393, NA (hereafter cited as Pearson letter book).

61. Dr. Thomas J. Pretlow to Gen. Edward R. S. Canby, Apr. 30, 1869, item P196, box 94, 1869, ser. 5068, ibid.

62. *Daily Richmond Whig*, June 4, 9, 19, 1869.

63. T. J. Pretlow to William B. Shands, June 14, 1869, ibid., June 19, 1869; Norfolk *Virginian*, June 29, 1869.

64. Pearson letter book.

65. Capt. Edward P. Pearson, Jr., to Lt. Louis V. Caziarc, May 26, 1869, ibid.

66. *Returns of Election of July 6, 1869*, pt. 1 (pp. 6–7), pt. 2 (pp. 4–5), pt. 3 (p. 4), pt. 5 (p. 32), Memorandum from Headquarters, First Military District (Virginia), Aug. 18, 1869, VSLA; Election Records, Southampton County, July 6, 1869, transfer box 11a, Hollinger (clamshell) box, ibid.; Richmond semi-weekly *Whig and Advertiser*, July 16, 31, 1869.

67. Election Records, Southampton County, July 6, 1869, transfer box 11a, Hollinger (clamshell) box, VSLA. Most of the ballots are in box 11a, wrapped in packets organized by district and race.

68. *Daily Richmond Whig*, June 19, 22, 23, 29, 1869; Maddex, *Virginia Conservatives*, 82–85; Lowe, *Republicans and Reconstruction in Virginia*, 170–79.

69. Jonas Barrett and Jacob Rawls, sworn testimony before Lt. John W. Whitten, June 29, 1869, item P408, box 95, ser. 5068, RG 393, NA.

70. Charles Holland testimony, ibid.

71. E. F. Murfee et al. to Maj. Gen. Edward R. S. Canby, June 23, 1869 (telegram), Jno. H. Bogart to Canby, June 23, 1869 (telegram), items S554 and S559 enclosed in Capt. Edward P. Pearson, Jr., to Lt. Louis V. Caziarc, July 4, 1869, item P433, Pearson to Caziarc, June 29, 1869, item P394, box 94, ibid.; Norfolk *Virginian*, June 24, 25, 1869.

72. Lt. John W. Whitten to Lt. Louis V. Caziarc, July 2, 7, 1869, items P433 and P448, box 95, 1869, ser. 5068, RG 393, NA.

73. Lt. John W. Whitten to Lt. Louis V. Caziarc, July 20, 1869, item P501, ibid.

74. Joseph Gregory to Lt. Louis V. Caziarc, July 24, 1869, item G404, ibid. The editorial method, transcribing the letter verbatim with extra space added at likely sentence breaks, follows the procedure recommended in Berlin, *Freedom: A Documentary History of Emancipation*.

75. Lt. John W. Whitten to Lt. Louis V. Caziarc, July 7, 1869, enclosing testimony taken on July 5, 1869, and security agreements reached on June 26, 1869, item P448, box 95, 1869, ser. 5068, RG 393, NA.

76. Ibid.

77. The original affidavits apparently no longer exist. This summation of their contents appears in Capt. Edward P. Pearson, Jr., to Lt. John W. Whitten, July 14, 1869, Pearson letter book. The voting patterns and totals in Franklin, polarized by race with only seven blacks casting Conservative ballots, appear consistent with returns from other parts of the county (see tables 9.4 and 9.5). On the other hand, it would not have required extensive fraud or intimidation, in Franklin or

elsewhere, to affect the countywide result. Although the one known white Republican in the county, Frank M. Holland, voted at Franklin, the ballots officially cast there by whites included no Republican tickets (Election Records, Southampton County, July 6, 1869, transfer box 11a, Hollinger [clamshell] box, VSLA).

Racial frictions also flared violently in Brunswick County, another part of Pearson's command. Three days before the election, a riot broke out in Lawrenceville between whites and blacks, in which two blacks were wounded by gunfire, one white was struck on the head, and one white was kicked and beaten (Pearson to Lt. Louis V. Caziarc, July 21, 1869, enclosing Lt. Jno. R. Mullikin to Pearson, July 9, 1869, Pearson letter book).

It appears wise to qualify Joseph Patrick Harahan's conclusion that black voters in Virginia hardly ever encountered violence, intimidation, or fraud before 1890. Harahan's Ph.D. dissertation, "Politics, Political Parties, and Voter Participation in Tidewater Virginia during Reconstruction, 1865–1900" (Michigan State Univ., 1973), based on shrewd assessments of voter turnout and careful scrutiny of newspaper sources, is surely correct for most localities and most elections. Southampton County, however, should be considered an exception, at least in 1868 and 1869.

78. Capt. Edward P. Pearson, Jr., to Lt. John W. Whitten, July 14, 1869, Pearson to Lt. Louis V. Caziarc, July 14, 1869, Pearson to Bvt. Col. Thomas R. Shea, July 30, 1869, Pearson letter book; Southampton County Court Minutes, Aug. 16, 1869, microfilm, VSLA.

79. Capt. Edward P. Pearson, Jr., to Lt. John W. Whitten, June 16, 1869, Pearson letter book; Election Records, Southampton County, July 6, 1869, Hollinger (clamshell) box, VSLA.

80. Frank M. Holland to Maj. Gen. Edward R. S. Canby, Sept. 10, 1869, item H1085, enclosed in Bvt. Col. Thomas Shea to Lt. Louis V. Caziarc, Dec. 27, 1869, item S1216, Inventory (pt. 1), Letters Received Book, Headquarters of First Military District, 1869, vol. 5 (actually vol. 15), ser. 5067, RG 393, NA; Shea to the Clerk of the Southampton County Court, Sept. 17, 1869, Dec. 16, 1869, Shea to Caziarc, Dec. 27, 1869, Letters Sent, Seventh and Ninth Division, the third of four letter books, ser. 5278, RG 393, NA (hereafter cited as Shea letter book); Southampton County Court Minutes, Aug. 16, 1869, Jan. 15, 1870, microfilm, VSLA. The 1860 U.S. Census (Population, Southampton County, Nottoway Parish, household no. 807, microfilm, NA) shows F. M. Holland to have been a twenty-one-year-old clerk who did not own land. He did not vote in 1860 or in 1861. He did, however, pay local taxes in 1860 on $235 worth of property (Personal Property Taxes, Southampton County, Nottoway Parish, VSLA). Frank Holland is identified in the 1870 U.S. Census as a thirty-one-year-old merchant, owning $1,500 of real estate and $2,000 of personal property (U.S. Census, Population, Southampton County, Franklin Depot Township, p. 204, microfilm, NA).

81. Southampton County Court Minutes, Dec. 16, 1867, Aug. 16, 1869, Nov. 27, 1869, microfilm, VSLA; Bvt. Col. Thomas R. Shea to the Clerk of the Southampton County Court, Dec. 16, 1869, Shea letter book.

82. Norfolk *Virginian*, Nov. 3, 4, 1875, "Letter from Suffolk," Dec. 6, 1875, ibid., Dec. 7, 1875.

EPILOGUE. THE RECONSTRUCTION OF AGRICULTURAL LABOR

1. On the rise of decentralized tenant agriculture, see Foner, *Reconstruction*, 170–75, 401–8; J. William Harris, "Plantations and Power: Emancipation on the David Barrow Plantations," in Orville Vernon Burton and Robert C. Mc-Math, Jr., eds., *Towards a New South? Studies in Post-Civil War Southern Communities* (Westport, Conn.: Greenwood Press, 1982), 246–64; Morgan, "Emancipation in the Virginia Tobacco Belt," 250–59, 351–55.

2. Cobb diary, Oct. 2–3, 1866, Jan. 1, Feb. 4, 1867, VHS.

3. Ibid., Jan. 5, Feb. 4, June 30, July 20, 1867, May 4, 1868.

4. Ibid., Mar. 20, 25, 30, June 3–5, 15, 24–27, 30, 1867, Oct. 6, Nov. 21, 1868.

5. Ibid., June 14, Aug. 23, 1867.

6. Ibid., July 27, Aug. 23, Sept. 15, 1867, Dec. 29, 1868, Apr. 18, June 8, Dec. 7, 1870.

7. Ibid., Dec. 2, 1867, Jan. 18, Feb. 4, May 15, 29, Aug. 21, 1872.

8. Ibid., Feb. 8, 13, 19, Apr. 25, 1868. Some hands stayed in the yard in 1868; see ibid., Aug. 13, 1868. On sharecropping and the abandonment of communal slave quarters, see Foner, *Reconstruction*, 170–75, 405, 407.

9. Cobb diary, Aug. 10–11, Oct. 24–25, 1868. On the disappearance of paternalistic race relations during Reconstruction, a time when elites were frightened and "racial hegemony itself appeared to be in jeopardy," see C. Vann Woodward, *American Counterpoint: Slavery and Racism in the North-South Dialogue* (Boston: Little, Brown, 1971), 242–59 (quotation on 252).

10. Cobb diary, Mar. 9–13, 26, Apr. 6, 16–18, June 1, July 5, 26, Aug. 8, 23, 27, 1870.

11. Ibid., Aug. 25, Sept. 7, Nov. 2–4, Dec 14, 1870.

12. Ibid., May 3, 19, 22, 25, 29, Nov. 7–8, 1870.

13. Ibid., Jan. 1, 5–6, Oct. 13, 1871.

14. Ibid., Jan. 1, 14, 15, May 14, June 30, July 1, 1871.

15. Ibid., July 4, 1871.

16. Ibid., July 7, 23–24, Aug. 3, 9, 22, Sept. 18, Oct. 13, 1871.

17. Ibid., Feb. 23, Apr. 13, May 23, June 16, 28, July 27, Aug. 20, 24, 1872.

18. Ibid., Jan. 24–25, Apr. 19, 21, May 17, Aug. 13, Oct. 24, Dec. 1, 8, 25, 1871, Jan. 28, 1872.

19. Ibid., Feb. 8, Apr. 9, June 4, 6, 16, July 5, 27, Aug. 9, 29, 31, Sept. 2, 1872; Edwards, *The Cobbs of the Tidewater*, 206–7. Story's reputation for probity most likely led Cobb to make him his executor. Cobb and Story were superficially acquainted but certainly not friends; neither apparently knew that the other kept a diary.

20. Story diary, May 31, 1865, VHS.

21. Story diary, 1865–76, esp. retrospective comments on 1868 and 1871 and Dec. 7, 1875.

22. Story diary, retrospective comments on 1866, 1867, 1872, 1873. Fertilizers stimulated postwar cotton production in Virginia. Fertilized cotton matured slightly faster, allowing its cultivation in areas such as upper Southampton where it had not previously flourished. Peanuts, however, became the principal crop in the area, except at times of high cotton prices (Kerr, *Report on the Cotton Production of the State of Virginia*, 3, 10; Crofts, "The Old Dominion's Cotton Belt").

23. U.S. Census, Population, 1870, Southampton County, Jerusalem Township, p. 249, microfilm, NA. The slender postwar Story diary does not mention Samuel and Delila Story. Story hired a white tenant in 1876, apparently having relied earlier on black labor (Story diary, Jan. 4, 1876).

24. Story diary, retrospective comments on 1862, 1867, 1868; Cobb diary, Oct. 11, 1868.

25. Story diary, retrospective comments, 1872, 1873, 1874, Nov. 1875; see also Story diary, Jan. 4, 6, 8, 21, 26, Mar. 26, Apr. 7, 14, 29, 1875, Jan. 7, 14, 18, 1876; Edwards, *The Cobbs of the Tidewater*, 539. I enjoyed meeting F. Story Cutchin of Franklin, Va., during a visit to Southampton in June 1990. Cutchin, a great-grandson of Elliott L. Story, donated the Story diary to the Virginia Historical Society.

26. C. Vann Woodward, *Thinking Back: The Perils of Writing History* (Baton Rouge: Louisiana State Univ. Press, 1986), 62–79; Woodward, *American Counterpoint*, 275–83; Foner, *Reconstruction*, 410–11; Foner, "Reconstruction Revisited," *Reviews in American History* 10 (Dec. 1982): 82–100.

27. William F. Mugleston, ed., "The Freedmen's Bureau and Reconstruction in Virginia: The Diary of Marcus Sterling Hopkins, a Union Officer," *VMHB* 86 (1978): 99–101.

28. Kerr, *Report on the Cotton Production of the State of Virginia*, 21. Lynda Morgan contends that sharecropping became characteristic in tobacco regions and led to a definite improvement in living conditions for freedmen ("Emancipation in the Virginia Tobacco Belt," 250–59, 351–55).

29. Harris, "Plantations and Power," 249, 256–57.

30. Cobb diary, July 1, 1871.

31. Fitzgerald, *Union League Movement in the Deep South*, 4–7, 248–52.

32. Norfolk *Virginian*, Nov. 7, 1872.

33. Lowe, *Republicans and Reconstruction in Virginia*, 188; Harahan, "Politics, Political Parties, and Voter Participation in Tidewater Virginia during Reconstruction."

34. Lowe, *Republicans and Reconstruction in Virginia*, 96, 193.

Index